Political Secularism, Religion, and the State
A Time Series Analysis of Worldwide Data

This book examines 111 types of state religion policy in 177 countries between 1990 and 2008. Jonathan Fox argues that policy is largely a result of the competition between political secular actors and religious actors, both of which try to influence state religion policy. While there are other factors that influence state religion policy and both the secular and religious camps are divided, Fox offers that the secular-religious competition perspective provides critical insight into the nature of religious politics across the globe. Many states have either increased or decreased their involvement in religion; Fox demonstrates, however, that states that have become more involved in religion are far more common.

Jonathan Fox is a professor of political science in the Department of Political Studies at Bar-Ilan University in Ramat Gan, Israel. He also serves as a director of the Religion and State project (www.religionandstate.org) and as a senior research Fellow at the Begin-Sadat Center for Strategic Studies. He is the author or editor of nine books, including the most widely used textbook on religion and world politics. He currently serves on the editorial or advisory boards of four journals and was the recipient of the 2009 Distinguished Article Award from the Society for the Scientific Study of Religion.

Cambridge Studies in Social Theory, Religion, and Politics

Editors
David C. Leege, *University of Notre Dame*
Kenneth D. Wald, *University of Florida, Gainesville*
Richard L. Wood, *University of New Mexico*

The most enduring and illuminating bodies of late nineteenth-century social theory – by Marx, Weber, Durkheim, and others – emphasized the integration of religion, polity, and economy through time and place. Once a staple of classic social theory, however, religion gradually lost the interest of many social scientists during the twentieth century. The recent emergence of phenomena such as Solidarity in Poland; the dissolution of the Soviet empire; various South American, Southern African, and South Asian liberation movements; the Christian Right in the United States; and Al Qaeda have reawakened scholarly interest in religiously based political conflict. At the same time, fundamental questions are once again being asked about the role of religion in stable political regimes, public policies, and constitutional orders. The Cambridge Studies in Social Theory, Religion, and Politics series produces volumes that study religion and politics by drawing on classic social theory and more recent social scientific research traditions. Books in the series offer theoretically grounded, comparative, empirical studies that raise "big" questions about a timely subject that has long engaged the best minds in social science.

Titles in the Series:
Luke Bretherton, *Faith, Citizenship, and the Politics of a Common Life: Resurrecting Democracy*
David E. Campbell, John C. Green, and J. Quin Monson, *Seeking the Promised Land: Mormons and American Politics*
Paul A. Djupe and Christopher P. Gilbert, *The Political Influence of Churches*
Joel S. Fetzer and J. Christopher Soper, *Muslims and the State in Britain, France, and Germany*
François Foret, *Religion and Politics in the European Union: The Secular Canopy*
Jonathan Fox, *Political Secularism, Religion, and the State: A Time Series Analysis of Worldwide Data*
Jonathan Fox, *A World Survey of Religion and the State*
Anthony Gill, *The Political Origins of Religious Liberty*
Brian J. Grim and Roger Finke, *The Price of Freedom Denied: Religious Persecution and Conflict in the 21st Century*
Kees van Kersbergen and Philip Manow, editors, *Religion, Class Coalitions, and Welfare States*
Karrie J. Koesel, *Religion and Authoritarianism: Cooperation, Conflict, and the Consequences*
Ahmet T. Kuru, *Secularism and State Policies toward Religion: The United States, France, and Turkey*
Pippa Norris and Ronald Inglehart, *Sacred and Secular: Religion and Politics Worldwide*, second edition
Amy Reynolds, *Free Trade and Faithful Globalization: Saving the Market*
Peter Stamatov, *The Origins of Global Humanitarianism: Religion, Empires, and Advocacy*

Political Secularism, Religion, and the State
A Time Series Analysis of Worldwide Data

JONATHAN FOX
Bar-Ilan University

CAMBRIDGE
UNIVERSITY PRESS

32 Avenue of the Americas, New York, NY 10013-2473, USA

Cambridge University Press is part of the University of Cambridge.

It furthers the University's mission by disseminating knowledge in the pursuit of education, learning, and research at the highest international levels of excellence.

www.cambridge.org
Information on this title: www.cambridge.org/9781107433915

© Jonathan Fox 2015

This publication is in copyright. Subject to statutory exception and to the provisions of relevant collective licensing agreements, no reproduction of any part may take place without the written permission of Cambridge University Press.

First published 2015

A catalog record for this publication is available from the British Library.

Library of Congress Cataloging in Publication Data
Fox, Jonathan, 1968–
Political secularism, religion, and the state : a time series analysis of worldwide data / Jonathan Fox.
　pages cm. – (Cambridge studies in social theory, religion, and politics)
Includes bibliographical references and index.
ISBN 978-1-107-07674-7 (hardback) – ISBN 978-1-107-43391-5 (paperback)
1. Religion and state – Cross-cultural studies.   2. Religion and politics – Cross-cultural studies.   3. Secularism – Political aspects – Cross-cultural studies.   I. Title.
BL65.S8F688   2015
322'.1–dc23   2014037190

ISBN 978-1-107-07674-7 Hardback
ISBN 978-1-107-43391-5 Paperback

Cambridge University Press has no responsibility for the persistence or accuracy of URLs for external or third-party Internet Web sites referred to in this publication and does not guarantee that any content on such Web sites is, or will remain, accurate or appropriate.

Contents

Acknowledgments		*page* ix
1	Introduction	1
2	Secularism or Secularization? The Secular-Religious Competition Perspective and Beyond	16
3	Establishment, Support, Neutrality, or Hostility: The Varieties of Official Religion Policy	39
4	State Support for Religion	64
5	Regulation, Restriction, and Control of the Majority Religion or All Religions	105
6	Religious Discrimination	136
7	Education, Abortion, and Proselytizing	168
8	Religion in Constitutions	201
9	Conclusions	231
Appendix: Data Collection and Reliability		251
Bibliography		269
Index		281

Acknowledgments

I thank Roger Finke whose support and advice made this book possible. I thank Yasemin Akbaba, Chris Bader, Jeff Haynes, Patrick James, Ted Jelen, Daniel Philpott, Nukhet Sandal, Shmuel Sandler, Ani Sarkissian, Shlomo Shpiro, and Baruch Susser for their advice and help at various points in the project, as well as the series editors and anonymous reviewers for their insightful comments, which significantly improved this book. I thank Ted R. Gurr for giving me the skills to design, manage, and complete a project like this one. Also, thanks to all of the research assistants who worked on Round 2 of the Religion and State project, including Jeremy Brown, Ariela Di Castro, Sherrie Figelson, Rebecca Finesilver, Mollie Gerver, Benjamin Graffer, Batsheva Waltuch Gross, Laerira Kahn, Talia Katz, Ayal Kellman, Nava Posey, Yuri Teper, Nirit Topol, and Efrat Ya'ari. Finally, I thank the John Templeton Foundation for supporting this research. The opinions expressed in this study are solely my own and do not necessarily reflect those of the John Templeton Foundation.

1

Introduction

The rules of etiquette declare that religion and politics are topics that should be avoided in polite conversation. Perhaps this is because both engender strong, uncompromising opinions and can result in heated disagreements. This is certainly the case for opinions regarding the proper role of religion in government. Contemporary politics in countries across the world include spirited and often high-stakes debates over government religion policy ranging from debates over specific policies such as religious education in public schools to the larger issue of whether a state should in general support, restrict, or be neutral toward religion. These debates are complicated by the fact that there are differing opinions on what exactly is meant by neutrality toward religion, not to mention the proper religion for a state to support.

In this study, I take no position on any of these normative debates over the role religion *ought* to play on government. Rather, I focus on the question of what role religion *does* play in government. Specifically, I focus on 111 types of government religion policies in 177 countries between 1990 and 2008.

Nonetheless, these normative debates overshadow this study. This clash of opinions is fought not only within intellectual circles and debate clubs.[1] The question of how a government should relate to religion is a critical political issue that has been the object politics at all levels of government. This debate has involved the full range of legitimate political activity, including elections, lobbying campaigns, organized protests, and wrangling over policy within legislatures and governments. It has also involved most forms of politically motivated violence, including riots, terrorism, and civil wars. The government religion policies that are the object of this study are essentially the outcomes of these political struggles.

---

[1] For a discussion of the role religion ought to play in government see, among others, Fradkin (2000), Mazie (2004), Morgenstern (2012), and Stepan (2000).

In fact, I posit that each country is potentially an arena for this conflict. In particular, political secularism – which I discuss in more detail in Chapter 2 and define as an ideology or set of beliefs advocating that religion ought to be separate from all or some aspects of politics or public life (or both) – is competing with religion over this aspect of the public agenda. Each country has both people who think the state is not sufficiently religious and those who think it is not secular enough. Many of them take their opinions to the political arena to change government policy in the direction they desire. As a result, it is certainly difficult and arguably impossible for a national government to avoid the issue of religion. I call this view of state religion policy the *secular-religious competition perspective* (or, for short, the *competition perspective*), which I discuss in detail in Chapter 2.

The relevance of this debate is demonstrated by my finding that only 16.4% of the countries in this study had the same religion policy at the end of the study period as they had at the beginning. In most cases, these changes resulted in greater government involvement in religion. That is, the majority of countries were more involved in religion in 2008 than they were in 1990. Also, the overwhelming majority of the 111 types of state religion policy were more common in 2008 than they were in 1990. This is not to say that this increased ubiquity of government involvement in religion was monolithic. Some countries became less involved in religion, and some types of policy became less common, but these decreases are greatly outnumbered by the increases.

Put differently, state religion policy is an active policy area in most of the world, one that people care enough about to effect change in the overwhelming majority of the world's countries. I discuss these findings in detail in Chapters 3 through 6. As I discuss in more detail in Chapter 2, this finding also has significant theoretical relevance to the ongoing academic debate over the role religion plays in the public sphere.

This struggle between political secularism and religion is complex. One aspect of this complexity is the overlapping issues of support and control. Most countries that support religion also seek to control it. In fact, as I discuss in more detail in Chapters 3 and 4, support for religion often includes an element of control. Financial support, for example, usually comes with explicit or implied strings. This can result in religious institutions becoming dependent on or otherwise beholden to the government. Governments that support religion often draw the line between support and allowing religious institutions and actors to encroach on the prerogatives and power of the political elites. Conversely, as I demonstrate in Chapter 5, efforts to control religion are always combined with supporting it to at least some small extent. Perhaps this is because supporting religion is among the most effective strategies to make religious institutions dependent on the government, and thereby more subject to its control. Although this significantly complicates our ability to comprehend the contest between religious and secular political forces, accounting for this factor provides a better understanding of the nature of state religion policy.

As broad as a discussion of 111 types of religion policies across 177 states may be, the topic of this study nevertheless focuses on one aspect of religion and politics. Religion interacts with the political on multiple levels. The religious beliefs of individuals influence their political behavior. This is true of both policy makers and ordinary citizens who can influence politics through a range of avenues including voting and participation in political activities and organizations. Religious institutions and clergy can act as interest groups and lobbyists. In many cases, formal interest groups are formed around religious ideals. Many countries have religious political parties. All of these and other potentially religiously motivated or influenced actors are not the focus of this study. However, they nevertheless enter into this discussion because all of these actors can potentially influence government religion policy.

Furthermore, religion's many interactions with politics are only one aspect of the larger religious economy. Stark and Finke (2000: 193) define the religious economy as "all of the religious activity going on in any society: a 'market' of current and potential adherents, a set of one or more organizations seeking to attract and retain adherents, and the religious culture offered by the organizations(s)." Others, particularly Gill (2008), have explicitly expanded this concept to include the interactions between religion and politics. Thus, religion has a broad range of intersections with topics of interest to social scientists.

Why this focus on government religion policy? First and foremost, it is likely impractical, if not impossible, to include all aspects the religious economy into a single study of 177 countries. Such a study would need to include all interactions by all religiously motivated individuals as well as all religious organizations with all aspects of society and politics in all states in the world. This is not to mention that many individuals and organizations operate in an international context (Fox & Sandler, 2004; Sandal & Fox, 2013; Thomas, 2005). Nevertheless, this study is at least as broad as any other cross-country data collection of which I am aware, the broadest of which include Norris and Inglehart (2004) and Grim and Finke (2011).

Second, when limiting the scope of a study to the realm of politics, national governments are perhaps the most classic and important units of analysis. States remain the most powerful actors in both domestic and international politics. Their qualities of sovereignty and a monopoly of force give them a critical influence over the national religious landscape, which essentially allows them to set the rules of the game. Governments regularly declare official religions; choose one or some religions over others; regulate, control, and restrict religious organizations and practices within their domain; and single out certain religions for restrictions that are not placed on all religions within their territory. The outcomes of these policies have profound influences on the well-being and success of religions. Because of this, all other religious political actors tend to seek to influence state religion policy. This makes it a central aspect of religion and politics.

Third, the state as the unit of analysis is particularly useful given current political science methodology. Excluding surveys, it is the most common unit of analysis in quantitative research that allows any study using it to combine its results with other studies to produce significant results. In this study, I take advantage of this to examine interactions between state religion policy with factors such as economic development, religious demography, and levels of democracy.

Fourth, among all aspects of religion's interaction with politics, state policy is likely among the most straightforward to measure. States are easily identified, and, as discussed in more detail in the Appendix, there is no shortage of sources to identify state policy on religious issues. Also, despite each state's religion policy being unique, they are also comparable across states.

Finally, over the past decade, research on religion and politics has increased exponentially. However, cross-national data remain scarce. Grim and Finke (2006: 1) lament that "the study of religion is severely handicapped by a lack of adequate cross-national data. Despite the prominence of religion in international events and recent theoretical models pointing to the consequences of regulating religion, cross-national research on religion has been lacking." Since Grim and Finke introduced a new cross-national dataset on religious freedom in the article I quote, there have been no new major cross-national data collections on religion and politics of which I am aware that were not an update of an existing dataset. Thus, a contribution that focuses on this basic element of politics and religion – which, as I discuss in detail later, is itself an expansion of an existing data collection – is not only justified; it significantly increases the available cross-national data.

Goals and Objectives

This book has four central goals and objectives: presenting and categorizing state religion policy, identifying important trends in state religion policy, evolving a new perspective for understanding state religion policy, and identifying the correlates of state religion policy. I discuss each of these in more detail in the following subsections.

Presenting and Categorizing State Religion Policy
The first objective is to present Round 2 of the Religion and State (RAS2) project's data collection and in doing so provide a complete lexicon and taxonomy of state religion policy. I discuss the technical details of the project in the following section and focus here on how I present the data and findings in this study.

The Religion and State (RAS) project has identified 111 types of state religion policy, which can be divided into four categories. Three of these categories have several subcategories.

Official religion policy is a single 14-category variable intended to measure the broad parameters of a state's religion policy. The categories range from those states most hostile to religion to those that most strongly support a single religion. I discuss this variable in Chapter 3.

Religious support includes 51 types of state support for religion, which can be placed in seven subcategories: laws on relationships, sex, and reproduction; laws restricting women; legislation related to other religious precepts; the enforcement of religion; funding of religion; entanglement between government and religious institutions; and other types of support. I discuss these variables in Chapter 4.

Religious restrictions includes 29 ways in which the government restricts, regulates, or controls religion in general in a country. This means that these policies apply to all religions, especially the majority religion. These policies can be divided into four subcategories: restrictions on religion's political role; restrictions on religious institutions; restrictions on religious practices; and other forms of regulation, control, and restrictions. I discuss these variables in Chapter 5.

Religious discrimination includes 30 types of restrictions placed on the religious institutions and practices of religious minorities that are not placed on the majority group. This final aspect of the definition means that governments are singling out some or all religious minorities for treatment that does not apply to the majority religion. This makes it distinct from the previous category. These policies can be divided into four categories: restrictions on religious practices, restrictions on religious institutions and clergy, restrictions on conversion and proselytizing, and other restrictions. I discuss these variables in Chapter 6.

Although this study is intended to accomplish more than providing a simple listing and taxonomy of all the types of government religion policies that exist in the world, this, in my estimation, is of value in and of itself. To my knowledge, while some – such as Chaves and Cann (1992), Chaves et al. (1994), Gill (1999), Grim and Finke (2011), and Norris and Inglehart (2004) – have provided lists of some aspects of state religion policy, this is the first listing that is arguably complete. These previous studies all are based on what the authors considered to be important aspects of state religion policy.

In contrast, the 111 types of policy included in this study constitute all types of identifiable religion policies that exist in today's states. They are based on a comprehensive country-by-country evaluation of all 177 countries included in the study, which was used to build a list of all polices that were found.[2] Such a list has several advantages and uses. If applied to all states, it can help yield information on all aspects of government religion policy without advertently or inadvertently leaving any out. This allows one to draw conclusions regarding trends in state religion policy based on what is as close to complete information

---

[2] I describe the full methodology for building this list in Appendix.

as possible. It also provides a map for future scholars studying the topic, whether they are using comparative or quantitative methodology. With a list of all extant policies in at least a few states, someone studying state religion policy in any context, be it a single state, a region, or globally, will likely produce a more comprehensive and accurate result. Knowing what to ask and where to look is of significant value.

In the context of this study, I posit that no previous study, including the previous round of the RAS project, has produced a comprehensive listing of state religion policy. Thus, simply listing and discussing this information can provide insights into state religion policy that have not previously been possible. The categorization element of this taxonomy provides further insight into which elements of state religion policy are common and becoming more common, as well as in which types of states this is true. For all of these reasons, I devote a large portion of this study to listing and discussing in some detail each of these 111 types of policies.

In addition, I examine a sampling of religion policies in depth. In Chapter 7, I examine state policies on religious education in public schools, restrictions on abortion,[3] and limitations on proselytizing and missionaries. All three of these types of policy are among the most common and complicated of the 111 types of policy examined here. This requires a more detailed examination than a simple accounting of whether such policies are present or not in a state. These policies are also the subject of intense contention, which makes them particularly poignant in examining tensions between political secularism and religious political actors.

When examining these 111 policies, I highlight the difference between official religion policy and actual religion policy. As discussed in Chapters 3 and 8, states set parameters for their religion policies in central documents such as constitutions and religion laws. While these parameters are correlated with religion policy in practice, the link between the two is less determinative than one might think. I show in Chapter 8 that only a minority of states with official separation of religion and state (SRAS) or secular policies actually follow them. Similarly, declaring an official religion, as demonstrated in Chapter 4, does not always lead to high levels of actual support for that religion. For example, Argentina, Bolivia, and Costa Rica all have official religions. However, by the RAS2 religious support measure, many countries without official religions, including Germany, Hungary, Lithuania, and Nigeria, support religion more strongly than these three countries. Another form of policy that is rarely followed thoroughly is policies of religious freedom. As demonstrated in Chapter 8, the majority of states that declare religious freedom in their constitutions still engage in religious discrimination, a clear violation of the principle of religious freedom.

---

[3] Chapter 7 also includes a discussion of why I consider abortion an issue that is strongly identified with religion.

Again, this does not mean these declared policies have no impact. States that declare policies of SRAS or secularism, on average, engage in less support for religion. States with official religions, on average, support religion more strongly. States with religious freedom clauses in their constitutions, on average, discriminate less against religious minorities. The key term in these findings is "on average." There are numerous exceptions, and in the case of religious support, all states in the world with the exception of South Africa (since 2003) engage in at least some religious support, even if they have clear secularist or SRAS policies. This means any evaluation of state religion policy that relies only on official or declared policies will miss the significant variation in the actual policies of states within these broader categories.

Identifying Trends
The second goal is to take the 111 types of religion policy just discussed and use them to identify important trends. In Chapters 3 through 6, I include a discussion of each of the 111 policies, including how they have been shifting over time. Perhaps the most important trend I identify is that, as noted earlier, states are becoming more involved in religion. Specifically, between 1990 and 2008, most types of state religion policies have become more common, and this trend is common to the majority of the world's countries. Of course, this rise is not monolithic, and some states have discontinued some of their religion policies. Nevertheless, new policies and states increasing their involvement in religion greatly outnumber discontinued policies and states becoming less involved in religion. This examination of trends is not limited to questions of a general rise or fall in government involvement in religion. I also examine each policy and each category of policies to determine whether they have their own unique trends.

A related trend is the pervasiveness of state intervention in religion. As I argue in Chapter 2, there was a time when the majority of serious scholars believed that religion as a public influence would shortly be a thing of the past. This time has passed, and now, other than a few holdouts, most accept that religion is and will for the foreseeable future remain a significant public and political influence. However, there is no agreement on the extent of this influence. The findings presented here demonstrate that government involvement in religion is so common that countries avoiding such involvement are the exception rather than the rule, even among states that officially espouse secular ideologies.

In addition, I provide an analysis in Chapter 8 that examines how many states in practice meet the definition of being secular or having SRAS. I find that even among states that declare the state's secularity or SRAS in their constitutions, in 2008, depending on one's definition of SRAS and secularism, between none and 42.9% actually meet these standards. Thus, the evidence that states are regularly involved in supporting and regulating religion is strong.

Evolving a New Perspective for Understanding State Religion Policy

The third goal is to elucidate the secular-religious competition perspective (or competition perspective) and analyze its validity. Chapter 2 contains the main theoretical argument for why I posit that this perspective is essential to understanding the role of religion in today's politics. In brief, a significant element of contemporary religious politics is the struggle between political secularism and religious political actors. Although this is certainly not the only significant component of religion and politics, it is one that is essential to understand.

I evolve the competition perspective from secularization theory – the prediction that religion will inevitably decline or disappear in modern times. I argue that this prediction has proven to be false, which requires that the theory itself be discarded. However, much of the secularization literature that focuses on the modern challenges to religion is accurate. These challenges exist and are mostly either consequences or causes of the rise of secularism as an ideology. Secularism has been challenging religion in both the private and public spheres for centuries. These aspects of the secularization literature can be recycled into a new perspective on religion, politics, and society that uses them as a description of the causes, nature, and, to a limited extent, the results of this challenge.

In politics, secularism manifests as political secularism. Proponents of this ideology struggle to remove religion from the public sphere and, in extreme cases, also the private sphere. At the same time, religiously motivated political actors seek to accomplish the opposite. This competition exists to some extent in every state in the world, and although victories are possible, total and final victory is unlikely in the foreseeable future. I posit that the analysis in Chapters 3 through 8 of this study lends support to the argument that this secular-religious competition exists. It also demonstrates that, at least during the 1990 to 2008 study period, religion has been gaining more ground than political secularism in the arena of government religion policy.

Finding the Correlates of State Religion Policy

Finally, I seek to examine the correlates of government religion policy. Which types of states are more or less likely to engage in all the types of religion policies I discuss here? In Chapters 3 through 6, I examine the impact of a state's majority religion and world region. In Chapter 8, I add the impact of regime type, economic development, and demography to this analysis.

A Note on the "Arab Spring"

The "Arab Spring" is likely one of the most important events with regard to government religion policy in the past decade. It has the potential to be a turning point of similar importance as events such as the Iranian revolution and the fall of the Soviet Union. The Arab Spring consists of a number of active opposition movements in the Middle East, which began on December 18, 2010,

Introduction

in Tunisia. At the time of this writing, these movements are or were recently active, in particular in Bahrain, Egypt, Libya, Syria, Tunisia, and Yemen. Although these movements have the potential to change many aspects of the regimes in these countries, I do not deal with these uprisings in this book because the analysis here is centered around the RAS2 dataset, which is current only through 2008. Also, even at the time of this writing, the influence of these movements on state religion policy is still unclear and perhaps waning. Libya and Syria are essentially in states of civil war, the outcomes of which are likely to be significantly different from the democratic goals of the Arab Spring movement. In both of these countries, it is likely that the new governments that emerge from these civil wars will either include or be dominated by fundamentalist elements that seek more extensive implementation of Sharia (Islamic) law.

Bahrain's government remains in power. In countries where the situation seems to be resolving itself, it appears that state support for religion in these countries will remain stable or increase. Egypt elected a new government that was dominated by the Islamic Brotherhood and Salafi parties, both of which advocate the imposition of Sharia law beyond its current status, in which elements of it, but not all of it, are enforced by the state. This government has been overturned, and its supporters are being suppressed at the time of this writing by a government that is similar to the one from before the events of the Arab Spring. The Islamist Ennahda party won the largest number of seats, but not a majority, in Tunisia's 2011 elections. As of September 2013, it had stepped down from power but still signals an increased role for Islam in Tunisia. The opposition movement in Syria is dominated by Islamists. Libya's civil war is primarily tribal, but Islamist forces will most likely play a significant role in any government that emerges.

It will likely be years before the Arab Spring's long-term results become apparent. However, in cases in which the status quo does not remain intact, all the potential changes in government involve placing Islamic religious parties in a position of greater power than they had in the past or perhaps governments that likely will increasingly seek to regulate Islam for fear of its potential political power. All of these Islamic parties support increased state support for Islam and enforcement of Islamic law. Thus, in the long run, the Arab Spring is likely to create changes in government religion policy consistent with the current trend of increasing government involvement in religion.

The Religion and State Round 2 Dataset

The RAS2 dataset is designed to code government religion policy. By *code*, I mean to convert actions taken by governments into variables suitable for quantitative analysis. It includes yearly data for 1990 to 2008 for 177 countries. This includes all countries with a population of 250,000 and a sampling of less populous countries.

The Religion and State Project

To fully understand the RAS2 dataset, a brief history of the RAS project is in order. The RAS project began in 2000 with the idea of developing and collecting cross-country state-level measures of state religion policy. Through a series of papers and grant proposals, I developed a list of government religion policies that resulted in a dataset consisting of 62 variables, using basically the same categories as described earlier, which covered 1990 to 2002. These indexes were expanded in Round 2, which was completed in 2011.

The data collection methodology, described in detail in Appendix, was similar for both rounds, but the construction of the list of variables included in the indexes was different. Round 1 of the data collection (RAS1) used a list of variables on the religion policies that the project staff, in consultation with numerous colleagues,[4] expected to find. In the early stages of the data collection for RAS1, variables were added as research assistants uncovered religion policies that had not been anticipated. However, approximately one-third of the way into the data collection process, the list was closed to changes because of the logistical difficulties of adding new variables. Adding new variables required going over all of the cases previously covered, which became untenable within the framework of the resources available to the project. Nevertheless, as new religion policies were discovered, they were incorporated into a working variable list for RAS2. Thus, as RAS1 was completed, a list of variables had already been developed for RAS2 that included all relevant government policies found to exist in practice. The data collection process for RAS2 revealed no additional policies that were present in a sufficient number of states to justify adding any new variables. Each index also includes at least one "other" variable for behaviors that are sufficiently important and relevant to be recognized but also sufficiently rare or unique that they do not warrant a separate variable.

This means that the variables included in the RAS2 indexes are based on a ground-up comparative project that uncovered all relevant extant government religion policies. All previous data collections of which I am aware, including RAS1 were, in contrast, based on what the researchers expected to find based on various theories and the experience of the researchers. This makes RAS2 uniquely capable of providing a comprehensive, detailed, and accurate picture of state religion policy across the world.

---

[4] Although I did not keep precise records, I estimate that at least 25 colleagues were consulted. This includes 14 who commented on the grant proposals for the research, another 5 who commented on articles submitted to journals describing the proposed format for the research, and at least 6 who were consulted on a less formal basis and were specifically asked whether they could think of any variables that should be included that were not on the list. This pool expanded considerably after the completion of Round 1 to include referees for publications based on RAS1, audiences at presentations based on the data, and colleagues who showed an interest in the data collection.

What Makes a Religion Policy?

Stating that the RAS project covers state religion policy seems simple, but the question of what constitutes a policy is less straightforward than it may appear at first. A straightforward approach would be to focus on laws, but what about laws that are on the books yet never enforced? What about policies that are consistently followed but have never been enacted into law? To deal with these issues, the variables used here were coded according to the following rules.

First, "if there was a relevant national law. In cases where this law was on the books but rarely enforced (a relatively rare occurrence) this was taken into account in the scaling of the variable when possible but always coded unless there is clear and positive information that the law has not been enforced at all for at least several decades."[5] Second, "if there was a relevant national policy. For example if there was no law against proselytizing, yet by official or unofficial policy those who proselytize were arrested or otherwise harassed this would have been coded."[6]

This means that the project coded policies, laws, and actions equally because they are all elements of state religion policy. This approach recognizes that policy can be made in multiple ways. For example, a state can limit proselytizing through a law. However, if only laws influenced the variables in a case in which a state had such a law on the books but rarely enforced it, this state would be coded as having such a policy, while a state with no such law that regularly arrested and harassed proselytizers under various pretexts would not be coded. I posit that including policies that are created both formally and informally presents the most accurate representation of state religion policy.

Similarly, it can be argued that laws that are on the books but not enforced should not be coded. In contrast, it is also arguable that laws that have not been repealed still have import if only because the difficulty of repealing them demonstrates that they are still potentially relevant. In practice, the coding rules are clear that when there is positive and reliable information that a law has not been enforced for decades, it is not coded. The project's research uncovered few laws that meet this criterion for lack of enforcement. I speculate that there might be more long-unenforced laws on the books, but this lack of enforcement resulted in their not being recorded in any of the sources uncovered by the project's researchers.

Third, "if there is no national policy or law but a significant plurality of local or regional governments had such policies or laws, the relevant variable was coded. In such cases the proportion of the country's population which was under the rule of these regional or local governments was taken into account both with regard to whether the variable was coded and, when relevant, how high a coding on the scale was assigned."[7] The reasoning behind this rule is

---

[5] RAS2 codebook, www.religionandstate.org.
[6] RAS2 codebook, www.religionandstate.org.
[7] RAS2 codebook, www.religionandstate.org.

that when a plurality of local and regional governments engage in a policy, this creates a result that is similar to a policy created at the national level that is enforced at least sporadically. It also remains a government action that, at the very least, the national government does not successfully prevent.

Fourth, "the project codes only actions taken by governments and their representatives. Societal actions are not coded. This is not because societal attitudes and actions are unworthy of study. It is simply not within the purview of the RAS project. As a result the [researchers] are not searching for information on religion on society in the reports which means that any codings based on the RAS reports that focus on religion in society may be based on incomplete information."[8]

Fifth, courts with the power of judicial review are part of the legislation and policy-making process. Policies, laws, or activities that the courts overturned or banned were not coded from the point of the court action unless, despite the court's ruling, the government continued engaging in the codable action or policy. In cases in which the policy, law, or activity was overturned shortly after the action was taken or the law or policy came into force and the government heeded the ruling, it was not coded at all. Court rulings that effectively declare or change government religion policy are also coded.

The Study Period

This study covers the 1990 to 2008 period. This means each variable is coded for each year during this 19-year period. However, not all countries are coded for each of these 19 years. Countries were not coded for a year if one of two circumstances applied. First, the country did not exist in the year in question. This applies primarily but not exclusively to a number of former Soviet bloc states, which were not independent until after 1990. Armenia, Azerbaijan, Belarus, Croatia, Estonia, Georgia, Kazakhstan, Kyrgyzstan, Latvia, Macedonia, Moldova, Slovenia, Tajikistan, Turkmenistan, Ukraine, and Uzbekistan all became independent in 1991. Eritrea and Slovakia became independent in 1993. Timor became independent in 2002, as did Montenegro in 2006.

Second, countries were not coded if there was a year in which there was no government to code. This is because a working government is necessary for there to be a government religion policy. These cases include Afghanistan until 1992, Bosnia until 1995, and Iraq in 2002, when there was effectively no government.[9]

---

[8] RAS2 codebook, www.religionandstate.org.
[9] I used a broad definition for the presence of a government, so even in war-torn states such as Somalia, for much of this period, the presence of even a nominal government that had control over some territory was deemed sufficient to code that government's policy. This allows researchers who wish to use these cases to do so and allows those who feel that using them is unwarranted to drop them from the study. The analyses presented here use all coded cases.

Thus, throughout this book I use terms such as "1990 (or the earliest available date)" and "from the beginning of the study period." This is meant to refer to the time period for all states from the first year of available data from each state until 2008.

Other Similar Data Collections
There are relatively few datasets that collect data on state religion policy and cover the entire world. None have all of the features of the RAS2 data collection. For example, the World Christian Encyclopedia includes a state-level variable for whether the state has a religious "philosophy" and one measuring the treatment of Christians (Barret et al., 2001). However, the former variable does not fully coincide with whether a state has an official religion and only has two possible values, as opposed to the multivalue variable to measure the same issue, which I discuss in Chapter 3, and the detailed variable on religious support that I discuss in Chapter 4. The second variable looks only at treatment of Christians and not any other religious minorities, whereas the religious discrimination variable I describe in Chapter 6 covers all religious minorities. The encyclopedia's variables do not address the regulation of the majority religion at all, as I do with the variables described in Chapter 5.

Grim and Finke (2011) provide a more sophisticated data collection, which focuses on religious freedom, essentially a subset of what RAS2 contains. It combines the treatment of religious minorities and the regulation of the majority religion into a single measure, which makes it difficult to distinguish between the two. Grim and Finke (2011) do not systematically address the presence of an official religion or support for religion in their work. In addition, their work covers a much shorter time span than the 1990–2008 period covered by RAS2.

On this basis I posit that the RAS2 is the most detailed and comprehensive dataset on the topic of state religion policy currently available.

The Evolution of Goals and Objectives
Earlier this chapter I discuss the goals and objectives for this book. While many aspects of these goals and objectives have been consistent throughout the RAS project, some of them have evolved. When I began the project in 2000, the academic landscape was very different. Little attention was paid to religion, and many still held the belief that religion was not of any significance in politics. This belief was supported by a body of theory known as secularization theory. I discuss the reasons behind this and how thinking has evolved on this issue since then in Chapter 2.

Accordingly one of my primary goals was to disprove secularization theory. Much of the research based on RAS1 was designed to accomplish this. The results from RAS1 demonstrated, among other things, a significant and rising presence of government involvement in religion and that most countries, including liberal democracies, did not have SRAS. Although I addressed the issue of secularism in this context, it was of secondary importance.

The primary presentation of the project's results, *A World Survey of Religion and the State* (Fox, 2008), was designed to accomplish this task. Rather than placing the primary emphasis on every type of religion policy, it focused on a region-by-region, country-by-country discussion of each state's religion policy. This approach successfully demonstrated the overwhelmingly common presence of religion in government policy but at the expense of understanding in depth how each type of government religion policy worked. Because at that point the list of policies was not fully complete, this strategy was likely the best under the circumstances.

In the past several years, both the academic landscape and the RAS project have evolved. Secularization theory is of waning popularity as growing numbers of social scientists are focusing their efforts on studying religion. This is reflected in increased publications on the issue in academic journals (Kettell, 2012) as well as the founding of several new journals focusing on the topic of religion and politics. At the same time, RAS2 now includes a complete list of all government religion policies present in the world.

These circumstances combine to encourage a new focus for the RAS project. It is time to move beyond secularization theory. As I discuss in detail in Chapter 2, there is still something to be learned from the theory, although it is not exactly what its creators intended. Political secularism as an ideology is a significant influence on politics, and proponents of this ideology compete and often clash with religious political actors over state religion policy, an insight that is the central theoretical focus of this book. This analysis of RAS2 is still grounded in much of the same literature as the previous round of research, but it sees this literature from a new perspective that, as noted, I call the secular-religious competition perspective.

This new focus on the competition between two sets of ideologies has implications for the questions asked as well as how they are best answered. A focus on the 111 religion policies identified by RAS2 best meets these needs for at least two reasons. First, while most states changed their religion policies, most of these individual changes were not earthshattering, although as I discuss in Chapter 9, there are certainly exceptions. Thus, a country-by-county focus is not the most useful framework to address this issue. Rather, a policy-by-policy approach allows a view of the collective changes across the world that can highlight which types of policies are becoming more or less common and to what extent. Put differently, the most significant changes are not the small number of states that dramatically changed their religion policies. Rather, the large number of states that made more modest changes collectively demonstrate a significant and widespread shift that is occurring worldwide.

Second, while the widespread presence of government involvement of religion is important, the dissipation of the imperative to counter secularization theory makes it more essential to focus on the nature of government religion policy itself. In the past when secularization theory was still prominent in the social sciences, a major priority among those who saw religion as a significant social and political force was to oppose the arguments of secularization theory. Essentially, the influence of secularization theory caused all research to gravitate toward it like a black hole. Even the theory's opponents could not escape its pull and had no choice but to design research that was primarily intended to counter it. This deterrence of research on religion and the diversion of existing research toward combatting secularization theory will likely be its most lasting impact on the study of religion. Today this seems less important, and it is time to focus on creating a better understanding of how religion interacts with politics. Thus, we need to go beyond simply demonstrating the widespread presence of religion and focus more on examining the nature and dynamics of government religion policy. I posit that a policy-by-policy focus is an efficient, productive, and useful way to contribute to this process.

In sum, I believe that this book is part of a new generation of research on religion and politics. It is part of a growing literature that has left secularization theory behind and has begun to focus more exclusively on understanding the relationship between religion and politics. However, this must be tempered by the understanding that while we have left secularization theory behind, secularism as a political ideology remains a central element of the landscape of religion and politics. As I argue in the secular-religious competition perspective, the contest between supporters of secularism and supporters of religion is a central element, although certainly not the only element, of modern religious politics.

2

Secularism or Secularization? The Secular-Religious Competition Perspective and Beyond

Although I argue that it is time to leave secularization theory behind, it nevertheless remains a useful starting point in any discussion of the role of religion in government. Secularization theory, in its various manifestations, predicts either the decline or demise of religion in modern times. While it was never unchallenged, secularization theory was clearly the dominant theory on religion in the social sciences until at least the 1980s and perhaps through the new millennium. Even today it remains influential (Appleby, 2000: 3; Berger, 1997; Casanova, 1994: 17; Gill, 2001; Gorski & Altinordu, 2008; Philpott, 2009; Pollack, 2008; Toft et al., 2011; Warner, 1993).

Recently this theory has been characterized by two trends. First, the theory's supporters now make weaker claims and rarely predict religion's demise. Rather, they predict that it will decline but remain relevant. Second, and more important, these supporters are increasingly in the minority. Yet even as secularization theory has been losing its popularity, a large portion of research on religion has centered around or at least been heavily influenced by the debate over the theory's validity.

This "for or against" debate has, I argue, blinded us to a third option – asking whether it is possible to use elements of secularization theory to understand religion's role in politics and society without accepting all aspects of the theory, especially the prediction of religion's decline. As I discuss in detail in this chapter, arguments that religion remains a significant and vibrant political force are nothing new. However, most previous versions of this argument require that secularization theory be discarded in its entirety. That is, because they discredit the theory, they jettison all of it, yet to discard all of its elements is to ignore many aspects that can still help us understand religion's role in politics and society. Many of secularization theory's insights remain relevant, but not as a description of an inevitable process. Rather, they can help us to understand the genesis and influence of a family of ideologies that can be placed under the label of secularism.

Accordingly, in this chapter I use secularization theory as a starting point in a process intended to build a new perspective on religion's role in politics and society, which I call the *secular-religious competition perspective* or, for short, the *competition perspective*. This perspective modifies secularization theory in two ways. First, I posit that, on inspection, most of the insights of secularization theory do not require religion's demise to be *inevitable*. This allows us to reconcile two contradictory facts. The first is that all of the forces that secularization theorists believe are a challenge to religion in the modern era in fact exist and challenge religion. The second is that, despite these challenges, religion has not disappeared and remains a potent and vibrant political and social force in the world.

The second modification is a focus on *secularism* as an ideology rather than *secularization*. That is, the forces and processes described by secularization theory resulted in the rise of a group of secular ideologies that challenged and continue to challenge religion. Many social scientists mistook this challenge for an unstoppable, historically deterministic, social, and political process in which religion was doomed to become an epiphenomenon. However, from the competition perspective, this social and political dynamic represents a contest between two families of ideologies for dominance in society and politics. Advocates of the religious and secular ideologies compete in social and political settings to fill the same social and political space. However, it is unlikely that either side will claim total victory any time in the near future.

In sum, I argue that although secularization theory should be left behind, it remains a useful starting point for building a new theory. Removing the prediction of religion's inevitable demise or decline essentially amputates secularization theory's heart and soul. What remains can no longer be called secularization theory. Yet much of what remains can provide the building blocks for a new understanding of religion's role in society and politics, which is embodied in the secular-religious competition perspective. This perspective focuses on secularism as an ideological challenge to religion in the political and social arenas. For this reason, I begin this chapter with a discussion of the rise of secularization theory and its evolution over time. From this discussion, I draw out the elements of secularization theory that are retained in the competition perspective.

I also want to emphasize that secularization theory, and potentially the competition perspective, encompass the role of religion in multiple aspects of politics and society. However, the emphasis here is on its role in politics and government. I include other parts of the religious economy, such as personal religiosity, in the discussion when relevant, but the goal of this chapter is to discuss religion's political manifestations. Also, I focus here on the competition between secularism and religion, but there are clearly divisions and competition within and the secular and religious camps. That is, neither religion nor secularist ideologies are monolithic. While I account for this in the discussion in this chapter, for the sake of simplicity, I often refer to them as simply secularism and religion.

Classic Secularization Theory

In the 1960s, predictions of religion's demise were common. One of the more dramatic versions of this argument include prominent sociologist Peter Berger's prediction in 1968 that by "the twenty-first century, religious believers are likely to be found only in small sects, huddled together to resist a worldwide secular culture."[1] Similarly, in 1966, Anthony F. Wallace confidently predicted that the "evolutionary future of religion is extinction.... Belief in supernatural powers is doomed to die out, all over the world" (Wallace, 1966: 266–267). While this expectation of religion's disappearance is extreme, these two quotes are not isolated examples. The sentiment that religion was at the very least in significant decline was the dominant stream of thought on the topic in the 1960s and well thereafter (Casanova, 1994: 17; Gorski & Altinordu, 2008; Thomas, 2005; Toft et al., 2011).

Secularization theory is a diverse body of theory, even more so because the nature of the claims that were made evolved over time. The one commonality between all secularization theorists is the minimum claim of religion's decline as a political or social force. The roots of this body of theory can be traced back to prominent 18th- and 19th-century thinkers including August Comate, Emile Durkheim, Sigmund Freud, Karl Marx, Friedrich Nietzsche, Ferdinand Toennies, Voltaire, and Max Weber. The ideas that began with these thinkers coalesced into secularization theory in the 20th century and manifested in the absolutist form that dominated much of modern social thought on the topic in the post–World War II era (Appleby, 1994; Shupe, 1990; Turner, 1991).

However, even in its heyday, it was never monolithic. Its supporters differed as to exactly what social and political forces would cause secularization, how this secularization would manifest, and to what extent it would manifest. For the purposes of this discussion, these nuances are not of critical importance. What is critical is to identify the factors that support secularism and how it manifests in politics and society. The issue of the extent to which secularism has encroached on the political and social territory of religion is precisely one of the questions this book sets out to answer. I address the issue later in this and subsequent chapters, although not in the light of the estimations of the supporters of secularization theory but rather in the light of empirical evidence.

The Classic Causes of Secularization
Most individual expositions of secularization theory do not include all of the following social and political causes of secularization, but the body of theory as a whole attributes secularization to several distinct causes.

---

[1] "A Bleak Outlook on Religion," *New York Times*, February 25, 1968.

Urbanization undermined the social structure that supported religion. Religion thrived in small rural communities. In this setting where everyone knows everyone else's business, the maintenance and enforcement of social norms including religion was simple. Ironically, however, the larger the city, the easier it is for someone to maintain anonymity. Cities also often have multiple subcultures, which allow people to seek out the one that fits their point of view. In essence, an urban setting gives everyone the choice of choosing religion or joining a social group that rejects it (Sahliyeh, 1990: 3; Voicu, 2009; Wilson, 1982).

In premodern times the clergy maintained a near monopoly on knowledge. A number of modern processes have undermined this monopoly. Before modernization, few people other than the clergy could read. *Mass literacy and education* broke this monopoly and facilitated knowledge acquisition by the masses. A population that was once dependent on the clergy for all knowledge, including knowledge of what was written in holy texts, had direct access to these texts as well as writings that challenged those texts. Mass literacy also increased the pool of individuals able to write texts that challenged religious texts (Lambert, 1999; Swatos & Christiano, 1999; Wilson, 1982).

Science and technology challenged religion's monopoly on explaining existence, another significant element of religion's monopoly on knowledge. Before science, in the Christian world, the book of Genesis contained the only explanation for the world's existence. Science provided alternative explanations such as the Big Bang and evolution for the larger questions and many additional explanations for more specific phenomena (Gill, 2001: 121; Wilson, 1982).

Rationalism constitutes an additional challenge to religion's monopoly on knowledge. Rationalism undermines religion's monopoly over how to seek knowledge by asserting that reason and empirical experience can be a source of knowledge and understanding. This challenges divine revelation as a source of knowledge, and to many rationalists, religion is not even a legitimate or useful source (Bruce, 2009; Dobbelaere, 1999: 232; Gellner, 1992: 2; Gill, 2008: 34–37; Lambert, 1999; Luttwak, 1994: 8–10; Martin, 1978: 8–9).

Before the Enlightenment, religion was the dominant political ideology. It was so central to legitimizing the state that kings derived their right to rule from God. This system of political legitimacy was essentially a pyramid with God on the top and the people on the bottom. The masses had no choice but to accept God's decisions as they manifested through the king. Modern political thinkers like Hobbes, Locke, Marx, and Rousseau, among others, reversed this relationship, putting the people on top and removing God from the equation. The concept that the government derives its right to rule from the people is a basic tenet common to diverse modern political ideologies including liberalism socialism, communism, and fascism, although this manifests differently in each ideology (Turner, 1991; Wilson, 1982: 54).

Political ideologies aside, the power of the modern state has increased relative to religion. Toft et al. (2011) argue that this process dates back to around 1450. It was catalyzed by the 1648 treaty of Westphalia, which ended the Thirty Years War and established that issues of religion were to be determined solely within the state. Over time the state became disproportionally strong relative to religion and began to support the majority religion financially as well as enforce its rules. This process transformed religion from an independent force with its own sources of revenue and enforcement to an institution dependent on the state. Eventually, this led to the point where the state no longer needed religion and could reject it.[2] In addition, the modern state began to provide services formerly under the sole purview of religion such as welfare, medicine, and education. This reduced the state's reliance on religion for services as well as the social influence of religion (Bruce, 2009; Gill, 2001: 121; 2008: 33; Gorski & Altinordu, 2008: 62; Kaspersen & Lindvall, 2008: 122; Wilson, 1982: 149).

Modernity has transformed politics from the sole purview of the elites to one that includes the masses. Modern political ideologies have led to the *mass participation in politics*. This undermines the ability of elites of any sort, including religious elites, to dominate individuals (Lambert, 1999).

Capitalism and economic modernization increased levels of *wealth and prosperity*. This increased satisfaction and security in this world leads to less of a reliance on an afterlife. Economic success is strongly linked with lower levels of individual religiosity (Norris & Inglehart, 2004).

Finally, both people and ideas have increasing *mobility*. The mobility of information and ideas has increased access to knowledge and ideas. With the rise of the Internet, anyone with an Internet connection has instant access to nearly any idea that has ever been raised. This has further undermined the former religious monopoly on knowledge and represents a "super-urbanization" in that individuals can seek like-minded people anywhere in the world. Similarly, migration is fashioning increasingly diverse societies and undermining the ability of a single religion to maintain demographic dominance (Bruce, 2009; Spohn, 2009: 365).

The Classic Manifestations of Secularization
All of these causes of secularization are, according to the theory, transforming society. Essentially, religion, which once served important functions in society, is being replaced by secular modern social and political institutions that serve these functions.

Two of these manifestations are congruent with the causes addressed in the foregoing paragraphs. First, religion is no longer necessary for *legitimacy*. Modern political ideologies now fulfill this function. Second, religion is no

---

[2] See also Bryan (1995), Goldewijk (2007: 29–30), Haynes (2009: 293), Juergensmeyer (2012), Philpott (2002; 2009: 187–188), and Thomas (2005: 54–55).

longer the primary source of *knowledge* (Dobbelaere, 1999: 233; Turner, 1991: 109–133; Wilson, 1982). The other manifestations are consequences of the causes just discussed.

Third, religion is being replaced as the primary form of *social control and order*. In the past, people obeyed social rules and norms because they believed in an omniscient, omnipotent God who punishes transgressions. Today social control is enforced primarily through the fear of getting caught by humans. Science and technology, including surveillance and forensic technology, generates this fear. Similarly, science and rationalism are replacing religion as the source of social order. In the past, laws and morals were based on religion. In modern times, rules are made by a bureaucratic process involving scientifically trained experts. For example, banking laws are influenced by economists and financial experts rather than religious laws, many of which ban interest. Similarly, secular regimes of morals, such as the international human rights regime, are becoming more influential (Dobbelaere, 1999: 233; Turner, 1991: 109–133; Wilson, 1982).

Fourth, religion is moving from the *public sphere* to the *private sphere*. That is, religion's influence on public life and institutions is declining and, to the extent that it remains present, it does so in the private sphere. Public religious institutions are becoming less prominent and control declining resources. Secular institutions are becoming more independent from religion (Chaves, 1994; Wilson, 1982: 149). As I discuss in more detail subsequently, this aspect of secularization is arguably a more recent addition to the theory.

Fifth, secular *institutions* are fulfilling functions formerly provided by religious ones. Both the government and private secular institutions now provide services that were once the almost exclusively provided by religious institutions including welfare, education, and medicine. To the extent that religious institutions still fill these functions, they are heavily regulated by the government. For example, in the past, spiritual health was the exclusive purview of the clergy. Today, the focus on spiritual health has been to a great extent replaced with mental health, which is in the purview of mental health professionals guided by rationalist and scientific knowledge. Many clergy are required by their religious organizations to gain training is secular psychological and mediation techniques. Even so, the combination of the competition from secular institutions and government regulation has removed religion and the primary provider of many of these services.

Sixth, *relative truth* is replacing absolute truth. Religion holds to an absolute truth. Today, many consider truth relative. This means that there is no one truth. Everyone's competing truth or narrative is legitimate (Almond et al., 2003: 94; Bruce, 2009: 152; Gellner, 1992: 2, 22, 72–73; Lambert, 1999: 323; Swatos & Christiano, 1999: 221–222).

For our purposes, the extent to which secularism has encroached on religion is less important than the fact that it has. Essentially, these processes describe why secularism was able to gain strength and how it competes with religion.

The Evolution of Secularization Theory

While the foregoing description of secularization theory is sufficient to understand how secularism became influential in mainstream intellectual circles, the evolution of secularization theory is important in demonstrating that, other than a few holdouts, few supporters of secularization theory argue today that religion will disappear. The absolutist version that assumes religion's future irrelevance has a dwindling number of supporters, and most current supporters of the theory have revised the absolutist version or are among those who never supported it. The current versions are diverse, but all of them have one thing in common: they agree that religion continues to have some form of relevance. I divide them into five categories.

The first category of contemporary secularization theory posits that religion will weaken but not disappear. This includes arguments that religion is of declining influence in the public sphere but remains strong in the private sphere and acknowledges that many individuals remain religious (Chaves, 1994; Dobbelaere, 1999). Some sociologists have gone as far as to redefine secularization as "differentiation" – a process in which religion has changed from being a dominant social institution that influenced all aspects of society to one that influences a more narrow range of society and competes with other institutions (Achterberg et al., 2009; Bruce, 2009; Dobbelaere, 1985; 1999; Kaspersen & Lindval, 2008; Lambert, 1999: 319–320). Put differently, although religion was once an integral part of all elements of society, it has become nothing more than a category (Casanova, 2012: 70–72).

Others posit that religion has shifted from being a public choice to an individual choice. The declining authority and dominance of religion has freed individuals to choose their religion, including the right to choose no religion at all (Bruce, 2009: 147–148; Dobbelaere, 1999: 236–241; Lambert, 1999: 315, 322; Pollack & Pickel, 2007; Thomas, 2001: 521–522). "Individual religiosity has emancipated itself from the custody of the large religious institutions; religious preferences are increasingly subject to the individual's autonomous choices. Churches no longer define comprehensive belief parameters; individuals instead decide on their own worldviews and spiritual orientations" (Pollack, 2008: 171). Some manifestations of this category are less nuanced and make the same arguments as described earlier but are careful to note that religion is declining rather than disappearing (Beyer, 1999; Bruce, 2009; Chaves, 1994; Davie, 2000; Hallward, 2008; Lechner, 1991; Presser & Chaves, 2007; van der Brug et al., 2009; Voye, 1999; Yamane, 1997).

In a second prominent revision of secularization theory, Norris and Inglehart (2004) argue that those who have existential security – "the feeling that survival is secure enough that it can be taken for granted" (Norris & Inglehart, 2004: 4) – have less of a need for religion. Thus, people living in developed and peaceful states will be less religious. A survey of 76 countries shows that people in wealthier countries, and more wealthy people no matter where they live, are less religious. However, other studies demonstrate that even if this is true, by 2005, 90%, of the world's population lived in zones without existential security, so this form of secularization influences a limited population (Thomas, 2007).

Third, Charles Taylor (2007) argues that the decline in religion, which is occurring but not to the extent that religion will disappear, is not the key element of secularization. Rather, secularism itself – the idea that one can understand the world without reference to religion – is a form of secularization. It represents "a move from a society where belief in God is unchallenged... to one in which it is understood to be one option among others" (Taylor, 2007: 3). This is a shift from religion being the only option to one in which many consider not believing the only plausible option. Thus, it is similar to differentiation theory but applies to ideologies rather than societal institutions.

Taylor's argument assumes that before secularism, there was no option other than to accept religion. This is an example of what Rodney Stark (1999) calls the "myth of past piety." "Most prominent historians of medieval religion now agree that there never was an 'Age of Faith'" (Stark, 1999: 255). Swatos and Christiano (1999: 200) similarly note that the medieval world was considered religious because of its many monasteries, but "if the medieval world was so full of the sacred, why did people want to withdraw from it in such numbers?" There were always people who were not religious. Taylor argues that the presence of secularism transforms this lack of belief into secularization. As I discuss in more detail later in the chapter, I concur that the secular option is a significant game changer but disagree with Taylor's characterization of this phenomenon as secularization.

A fourth category of contemporary secularization theory is the argument that the theory remains accurate but only for Europe, the West, or some subsection of the West. For example, Berger (1996/1997; 1999; 2009) argues secularization is still occurring in Western and Central Europe and certain intellectual circles. Marquand and Nettler (2000: 2) similarly argue that "Western Europe appears to be an exception.... Organized religion almost certainly plays a smaller role in politics in 2000 over most of the territory of the European Union than it did in 1950."[3]

Haynes (1997; 1998; 2009) postulates that this Western secularization is a result of government policy including equality policies and the co-optation and subordination of religious institutions. Crouch (2000) argues that that increased individualism has caused Europeans to reduce ties to their churches' more restrictive collective identities. He argues that church attendance and political influence are declining and that the post–World War II atmosphere of liberalism has forced European churches to focus more on tolerance, which has undermined their authority in society.

---

[3] See also Emerson and Hartman (2006: 140) and Jelen (2007: 29).

This type of argument is also often made as a passing reference in studies of Islam's influence on politics (e.g., Hefner, 2001: 492–493; Tezcur et al., 2006: 218; Tibi, 2000). Studies that categorize different forms of secularity likewise focus on the West and sometimes also Turkey (e.g., Hurd, 2004a; 2006; Madeley & Enyadi, 2003; Kuru, 2009). Although not always discussed explicitly, these secularist ideologies are assumed to have originated in the West, and that is where they are primarily to be found. Finally, this type of argument overlaps with two of the categories previously noted. Taylor (2007) explicitly limits his arguments to the West, and Norris and Inglehart's (2004) arguments essentially posit secularization primarily in the West. Because secularization theory originally posited that the Western experience would eventually become global, this retreat to arguing that it still applies to the West is essentially the secularization argument returning to its roots.

A fifth type is what Toft et al. (2011: 8) call "neo-atheists." Writers in this genre, including Richard Dawkins (*The God Delusion*, 2008) and Christopher Hitchens (*God Is Not Great: How Religion Poisons Everything*, 2009), accept that religion remains present in society but wish it would disappear. They see religion as irrational, primitive, violent, intolerant, and repressive. Even some nonatheists make similar arguments. For example, Charles Kimball (2002; *When Religion Becomes Evil*) argues that "true" religion supports peace and tolerance but "corrupted" religion creates violence and intolerance. This body of literature is arguably more of a postsecularization argument than a revision of secularization theory. It does not necessarily predict religion's demise, or even its decline. Rather, it takes a moral stand that either all religion or some religion is bad and the world would be better off without it. While this is not fully compatible with secularization theory, it is compatible with secularism as an ideology.

Primarily, although not exclusively, with regard to the first category, there is some debate over whether these revisions of secularization theory are actually revisions. Many current supporters of the theory posit that secularization never meant that religion would disappear, only that it would decline. Stark (1999) disagrees, attesting that the argument positing that religion will move from the public to the private sphere and that public religion will weaken but not disappear is clearly a revision of secularization theory. The quotes from Berger and Wallace earlier in this chapter certainly support Stark's contention. Stark (1999: 251) goes further and accuses many of these theorists of shifting "definitions as needed in order to escape inconvenient facts" (Stark, 1999: 251) and provides numerous quotes from prominent secularization theorists to support his claim. He agrees that some aspects of religion have declined, but "the prophets of secularization theory were not and are not writing about something so obvious and limited" (Stark, 1999: 252). Personal piety and religious institutions are linked. If one fades, so will the other.

Be that as it may, the extent to which these modern versions of secularization theory are new or were always part of secularization theory are not important to my central argument. What is critical is that today's supporters of secularization theory agree that religion is neither dying nor dead. It remains present and influential in society. The extent and exact nature of this presence and influence is a matter of debate, but the fact of it is not. Thus, even today's secularization theorists, with perhaps the exception of an increasingly rare breed of holdouts, are making arguments that are not incompatible with the argument that there is a competition between the secular and the religious in society. They simply believe that secularism is winning the competition.

The Impact of Secularization Theory on the Social Science Study of Religion

The dominance of secularization theory in the social science literature, and especially the political science literature, until the 1990s and perhaps a bit later has had a significant influence on the social science study of religion. Specifically, it had two effects. First, it arguably deterred research on the topic. Second, it forced much of the research that did exist to spend its efforts refuting secularization theory rather than building knowledge on the relationship between religion and politics.

Studies examining the presence of articles on religion in political science journals consistently demonstrate a lack of articles on religion in mainstream journals until recently. Wald and Wilcox (2006) examined articles in the *American Political Science Review* between 1960 and 2002 and found that the discipline's most prestigious journal published only 25 articles – less than one a year – that included religious terms in their title or abstract, and many of these did not, on closer examination, treat religion to be of central importance. Philpott (2002) similarly examined four major international relations journals between 1980 and 1999 and found only four of 1,600 articles treated religion as a serious influence on international relations. Ver Beek (2002) found no reference to religion in three major development journals between 1982 and 1988. In a response to the 9/11 attacks, Robert Jervis (2002: 37), a prominent political scientists, provides perhaps the most succinct and accurate description of this phenomenon: "terrorism grounded in religion poses special problems for modern social science, which has paid little attention to religion, perhaps because most social scientists find this subject uninteresting if not embarrassing."

Of course, this does not mean that there was no research on religion among political scientists before the new millennium. However, it tended to be in journals that focused on more narrow issues such as the *Journal of Church and State* and were read mostly only by scholars who focused on religion and politics. Typically, these scholars were not located at top-tier universities. Another outlet for research on religion during this period was area study journals that focused on the non-West.

One description of this phenomenon has it that to the extent it was studied, whenever religion influenced politics, it was considered an exception to a more general rule of irrelevance. "Whenever, and wherever, religion in the West manifests itself in a form which is more than a matter of private faith, it will be defined in most Western societies as disruptive and judged to be marginal and deviant" (Beit-Hallahmi, 2003: 11). Many who studied religion in politics did so as a psychologist would study a serial killer. It exists, but it is dangerous, abnormal, and the world would be better off without it.

While Beit-Hallahmi's (2003) description of the social science literature on religion puts it in perhaps its worst light, the influence of secularization theory is undeniable. Two of the first articles in *American Political Science Review*, political science's most prestigious journal, which addressed religion in the post–9/11 era spent a considerable portion of their space discussing and refuting secularization theory and dealing with the issue of why political scientists have neglected religion. Wald et al. (2005: 122–123) argued that until around the mid-1980s, "most scholars in the discipline regarded religion as too exotic or epiphenomenal to warrant sustained interest. Even when religion was considered in systematic studies of political change, it was largely regarded as a problem in need of a solution." Nearly half of the article was devoted to explaining why this was the case. More recently, Philpott (2007: 506) noted that political scientists are "far less nimble with religions" then they are with other topics that "fit easily into disciplinary boundaries like that between comparative politics and international relations but devoted considerably less of his article to explaining this phenomenon."

Even with increasing research on the topic in the 21st century, religion as a political phenomenon is still understudied. An examination of 20 prominent political science journals between 2000 and 2010 reveals that only 1.34% of these articles address religion as a primary topic, and even including religion as a secondary topic brings this total to 2.54%. To put this in perspective, for most journals, this would be about one article or less per year. While this is an improvement over previous decades, religion is still far less studied than topics that are considered central to political science, which tend to be addressed by 8% to 20% of the articles in these journals, depending on the specific topic and keeping in mind that a single article can address multiple topics (Kettell, 2012). Thus, although religion is being addressed, it is still not given the same consideration as issues such as security, regime, and party politics.

Secularism

The preceding discussion sets the stage for the central argument made by the competition perspective: that the term *secularization* should be discarded and replaced with an understanding of *secularism* as an ideology. By this I mean that secularization theory contains useful insights on the causes and consequences of the rise of secularism as an ideology that competes with religion in the political and social arenas. Thus, secularism is a game-changing political, social, and historical factor that helps us understand religion's role in politics, society, and history. However, although this competition is likely to continue for the foreseeable future, there is no reason to believe that secularism is an unstoppable force that will inevitably triumph over religion.

What Does Secular Mean?

Daniel Philpott (2009: 185) identifies nine conceptions of the term secular in the literature:

(1) *Secular* means pertaining to the world outside the monastic sphere. (2) *Secular* means a concept or use of language that makes no specific reference to religion or revelation but is not necessarily hostile to them. (3) *Secular* means a differentiation between religion and other spheres of society (political, economic, cultural, etc.) but not necessarily the decline of religion's influence. (4) *Secular* describes a social context in which religious faith is one of many options rather than an unproblematic feature of the universe (5) *Secularization* is a decline in the number of individuals who hold religious beliefs. (6) *Secularization* is a decline in religious practice and community. (7) *Secularization* is a differentiation between religion and other spheres of society (political, economic, cultural, etc.) in a way that entails, and is part and parcel of, a long-term decline in the influence of religion. (8) *Secularization* involves a decline of religious influence on politics, not because of a general long-term decline in religion but rather because of the intentional efforts of regimes to suppress it. This concept does not imply a decline in religious belief or practice. (9) *Secularism* is an ideology or set of beliefs that advocates the marginalization of religion from other spheres of life.

Most of these conceptions are related to secularization theory and are discussed earlier in the chapter. However, the most salient commonality that emerges from these definitions is that all of them conceive of the secular as something other than religion. The term *secular* is not monolithic and can refer to the antireligious, the decline of religion, or just simply something that is not religion. Yet all of these meanings can be described as being the opposite of religion or at least something other than religion. In fact, like Philpott, I can find no conception of any permutation of the word *secular* that does not reference religion.[4]

Secularism as an Ideology

Without negating the other conceptions of the secular, I focus here on Philpott's (2009: 185) ninth conception, secularism as "an ideology or set of beliefs that advocates the marginalization of religion from other spheres of life." I posit that this conception of secularism as an ideology is the key to understanding the role of the secular in politics as well as an essential element of the *competition perspective*. While Philpott's definition is accurate, my focus is on religion in politics. Accordingly, for the purposes of this discussion, I focus on the

---

[4] For example, Calhoun, Juergensmeyer, and VanAntwerpen (2012), in their edited volume, seek to "rethink secularism." Yet none of the authors in the volume are able to do so without reference to religion.

narrower concept of *political secularism*, which I define as *an ideology or set of beliefs advocating that religion ought to be separate from all or some aspects of politics and/or public life*. This definition focuses on secularism as a political ideology without denying that it can also have nonpolitical manifestations. Casanova (2009: 1051) similarly defines "secularism as a statecraft principle" as "some principle of separation between religious and political authority."

This version of secularism is not monolithic. For instance, Western liberal ideology has multiple conceptions of this type of secularism. A key aspect of Western liberal political ideology is that religion should, at a minimum, be separate from government. Stepan (2000: 39–40), in his classic study of religion and toleration, describes this school of thought as follows:

> Democratic institutions must be free, within the bounds of the constitution and human rights, to generate policies. Religious institutions should not have constitutionally privileged prerogatives that allow them to mandate public policy to democratically elected governments. At the same time, individuals and religious communities... must have complete freedom to worship privately. In addition, as individuals and groups, they must be able to advance their values publicly in civil society and to sponsor organizations and movements in political society, as long as their actions do not impinge negatively on the liberties of other citizens or violate democracy and the law.

One of the most cited versions of this argument can be attributed to Rawls (1993: 151), who argues that we must "take the truths of religion off the political agenda."[5]

It is important to note that this normative argument is not universally accepted within liberal democratic theory. However, even those who argue for a role for religion in democratic government call for a limited role. For example, de Tocqueville is often paired against Rawls to argue that there is room for religion in democracy. In fact de Tocqueville argues that a "successful political democracy will inevitably require moral instruction grounded in religious faith" (Fradkin, 2000: 90–91). However, de Tocqueville does not support the concept of an official religion. Rather, he believes that religion can "facilitate the use of" democracy (quoted in Fradkin, 2000: 88) by preventing it from degenerating into despotism. More specifically:

> since it facilitates the use of freedom, [religion is] ... "indispensable to the maintenance of republican institutions." And there is good reason for this, because "despotism may govern without religion, but liberty cannot." (Wach, 1946: 90 with quotes from de Tocqueville)

Thus, although religion has a role, it is a limited one. The secular concept of limiting religion's public role is still present.

This type of argument for a limited public role for religion in democracy is common. For example, Greenawalt (1988: 49, 55), Durham (1996: 19), and Bader (1999) argue that the liberal concept of tolerance also applies to religion,

---

[5] For additional versions of this argument see, among others, Demerath (2001: 2) and Shah (2000).

TABLE 2.1. *Models for Separation of Religion and State (SRAS)*

	Secularism-Laicism	Absolute SRAS	Neutral political concern	Exclusion of ideals
May the state support religion?	No	No	Yes, if applied equally	Yes, as long as there is no ideological preference for any religion
May the state restrict religion?	Yes, in public sphere and if applied equally	No	Yes, if applied equally	Yes, as long as there is no ideological preference for any religion
May the state restrict using religion in political discourse?	Yes	No	Yes, if applied equally	Yes, as long as there is no ideological preference for any religion
May the religious ideals of a specific tradition influence public policy?	No	Maybe, if there is no support or restrictions	Yes, if there is no unequal treatment	No

and thus it cannot be fully banned from the public sphere. Mazie (2004; 2006), Marquand and Nettler (2000), and Driessen (2010) argue that even supporting an official religion does not violate liberal values as long as governments maintain religious freedom and avoid making a religion mandatory. Even though this is not exactly secularism, it does maintain the concept that there are lines that cannot be crossed with regard to religion.

Those who advocate some form of separation of religion and state (SRAS) within the Western liberal tradition can be divided into four categories. The terms for these models differ across the literature, but I rely on those developed by Fox (2007; 2008), Madeley (2003), and Raz (1986).[6] These categories basically represent different answers to the following questions: (1) May the state support religion? (2) May the state restrict religion? (3) May the state restrict religious discourse and expression in political speech? (4) May the religious ideals of a specific tradition influence public policy? The four conceptions of SRAS are presented in Table 2.1.

The *secularist-laicist* conception bans state support for any religion. In addition, it restricts the presence of religion in the public sphere. This conception

---

[6] For examples of different classification schemes, see Calhoun et al. (2012).

of secularism views religion as something negative that undermines democracy. It is strictly excluded from the public sphere, although religion in the private sphere is acceptable. Accordingly, supporters of this model see religion as a wholly private matter, and the state enforces this through restrictions on public religious activities and on religious institutions (Durham, 1996: 21–22; Esbeck, 1988; Kuru, 2009; Haynes, 1997; Hurd, 2004a; 2004b; Keane, 2000; Stepan, 2000). Because it is religion itself, rather than any particular religion, which is detrimental to the public sphere, any restrictions on religion are placed on all religions equally, including the majority religion. France's 2004 law banning any overt religious symbol in public schools, including the head coverings worn by Muslim women, is a classic example of this model. While someone from another tradition of secularism might consider this law a restriction on religious liberty, from the French perspective, these religious symbols constitute an aggressive encroachment of religion – something that should be a private matter – on the public sphere.

The other three conceptions are variations on the expectation that the state must maintain neutrality toward religion. These models do not require that religion be banned from the public sphere and are, in fact, compatible with a view of religion as a positive public influence, although two of them allow such bans under specified circumstances. This is qualitatively different to secularism-laicism in that secularist-laicist governments consider religion to be a negative public influence that must be relegated to the private sphere. In contrast, this type of conception takes the less extreme stand that the state should not privilege any particular religion.

The second model, *absolute SRAS*, requires that the state neither support nor restrict any religion. This is perhaps the strictest of the three "neutral" models because it bans all government support for religion as well as all government interference in religion. However, within this trend, there are differing opinions on the proper role of religion in the public sphere including civil society and political discourse (Esbeck, 1988; Kuru, 2009). The differences between Rawls and de Tocqueville described earlier are part of this debate. The United States is often considered the prime example of this model. Within the US discourse on the topic, there is general agreement that religion should not be the business of government, but the expression of religion in public life is not only acceptable, it is a positive influence (Kuru, 2009).

The third model, *neutral political concern*, conceives of state neutrality toward religion differently. This conception "requires that government action should not help or hinder any life-plan or way of life more than any other and that the consequences of government action should therefore be neutral" (Madeley, 2003: 5–6). The key to this model is equal treatment for all religions. Thus, government support for religion and interference with religion are acceptable as long as they are applied equally to all religions.[7] *Exclusion*

---

[7] See also Stepan's (2000; 2012: 133–134) concepts of positive neutrality and twin tolerations.

of ideals, the final Western liberal conception of SRAS, has a similar view of neutrality but focuses on intent rather than outcome. It mandates that "the state be precluded from justifying its actions on the basis of a preference for any particular way of life" (Madeley, 2003: 6). Thus, religions can in practice be treated differently as long as there is no specific intent to support or hinder a specific religion.[8]

The West has also produced conceptions of secularism more extreme than this, but not within the liberal school of thought. For example, most communist and some fascist governments take an even more negative view of religion. They ban religion from government, the public sphere, and the private sphere. Thus, these extreme secular ideologies ban religion from all aspects of public and private life.

As Casanova (2009: 1051–1057) points out, the motivations for political secularist ideologies vary. These motivations include the following:

(1) The belief that religion is a thing of the past; it should and will be replaced by modern secular political ideologies.
(2) The belief that religion is a destructive irrational force that is better separated from politics, especially in a democracy.[9]
(3) The belief that religion contributes to society in a positive way but is best left out of the public discourse.

In sum, secularist political ideologies are not monolithic but have an important commonality. They all, to varying extents, advocate keeping religion out of government. Some of them also restrict religious expression in the public sphere, and a few restrict even the private expression of religion. This type of political secularism became common in the 20th century. Toft et al. (2011: 72) estimate that 50% of world's population lived under antireligious regimes at some point between 1917 and 1967. This does not include the less restrictive forms of political secularism in which religion is kept out of government but is otherwise not significantly restricted. In fact, it is possible for an individual to be personally religious but still believe that a government should stay out of religion. Gill (2008) argues that minority religions tend to prefer exactly this type of policy because it affords them the highest level of religious freedom. Thus, we must distinguish between secularism as a political ideology and secularism as a personal ideology.

Given this, secularism as a political ideology is not necessarily hostile to religion (Casanova, 2012: 79). It encompasses a spectrum of beliefs with regard to the desired government policy toward religion. In its more mild forms, the minimum requirement is a belief that the government should be neutral with

---

[8] For a review of the Western intellectual history of the concept of separation of religion and state, see Laycock (1997) and Witte (2006).
[9] Some, including Calhoun (2012: 90), Ebaugh (2002), Hadden (1987), and Thomas (2005), argue that this dislike of religion was the motivation for the development of secularization theory.

regard to religion. Farther along the spectrum is the US version, for example, which has the government avoiding all entanglements with religion. But this version includes avoiding limiting religious freedom and an acceptance of religion in public life outside of government. Even farther along the spectrum is the French version, which views religion as a private matter that should be actively kept out of public space. The most extreme versions tend to be found in nondemocratic governments, especially Communist governments, where religion is considered a negative influence and the government seeks to limit even the private expression of religion. This is a wide spectrum of beliefs that have little in common other than the belief that governments must limit their role in supporting religion.

Despite this diversity, this one commonality is profound. It distinguishes political secularism from the overt choice to privilege one or more religions. As I demonstrate in the following chapters, the line between governments who privilege certain religions and those that do not is a significant one.

The Secular-Religious Competition Perspective

Given all of this, I argue that *secularization theory* should be discarded as an explanatory theory and replaced with a focus on *secularism*. By this I mean that secularization theory has insight into significant and real social and political processes, but it contains a set of flaws that can be traced to its focus on religion's *inevitable* demise. By removing this aspect of secularization theory and recognizing secularism as an ideology, it is possible to build a new perspective on religion's role in society and politics that I call the secular-religious competition perspective, or competition perspective. I do so using the following principles, which in this context I limit to describing secularism's political manifestations, although they can arguably be applied more widely.

First, political secularism is, among other things, a family of political ideologies that advocates that governments must at the very least remain neutral on the issue of religion. Some forms of this ideology also mandate that the government restrict religion in the public sphere or even the private sphere. These secularist political ideologies challenge and compete with religion to influence government policy. Other than the fact of this competition between secularist and religious ideologies, I make no long-term predictions with regard to the outcome of this struggle.

Second, the bulk of the secularization theory literature, which focuses on the social and political processes that undermine religion's influence, is accurate. That is, all of the processes and influences I described earlier in the chapter challenge religion in exactly the manner predicted by secularization theory. However, the fact of this challenge does not necessarily mean religion will disappear or decline. Rather, this literature describes the social and political processes that contributed to the genesis and rise to political prominence of secularist political ideologies.

Third, all of the manifestations of secularization discussed by secularization theorists, which again I listed earlier in the chapter, exist. However, they are not manifestations of religion's demise in politics and society. Rather, they are expressions the influence that political secularism has had on society. That is, in some countries, political secularism has had success in replacing religion as a basis for knowledge and legitimacy and in inspiring the rise of secular institutions that fulfill social and political roles that were formerly the purview of religion. However, this success is neither absolute nor unidirectional. Secularism competes with religion in the political realm on a daily basis and does not always win.

Fourth, the politics of religion can be seen, in part, as a struggle between religious and secular ideologies. The supporters of each set of ideologies have a political agenda. Setting the diversity within each set of ideologies aside for the moment, secular political ideologies at their most basic level advocate limiting or eliminating the role of religion in government, politics, and sometimes the public and private spheres. Political manifestations of religious ideologies seek to increase the influence of religion in all of these arenas. This is perhaps among the most massive of oversimplifications, yet it is accurate in describing the general boundaries of the struggle between religion and secularism over politics.

Using these principles, secularization theory and its prediction of religion's inevitable decline or demise can be set aside while retaining much of its content as part of the competition perspective. This perspective focuses on the rise of a potent and significant political ideology that challenges religion's public role. This perspective does not require a prediction regarding the strength of this challenge or the extent of the success of this challenge, in both the past and the future. But it does acknowledge a fundamental shift in religion's public role. Religion has changed from the dominant form of political ideology to one among two types that compete in the public sphere. The relative power and influence of religious and secular ideologies is an important question, but it is one that requires empirical enquiry to answer.

Taylor (2007) calls this a form of secularization. This description is also not dissimilar to the concept of functional differentiation, a school of thought within sociology described earlier in this chapter (Achterberg et al., 2009; Bruce, 2009; Dobbelaere, 1985; 1999; Kaspersen & Lindval, 2008; Lambert, 1999: 319–320). Thus, it is possible to call the competition perspective a new type of secularization theory.

I argue that to do so would be a mistake. Clearly modernity has given rise to a new phenomenon – secularism – that, in its political manifestation, has fundamentally changed the role of religion in politics. Some would argue it has also fundamentally changed the nature of religion itself. This is a critically important insight. However, it is not secularization. The term *secularization*, as it has come to be known among social scientists, implies both that religion will decline and that this decline is *inevitable*. Yet there is nothing inevitable about religion's decline or demise. Put differently, secularization theory with the element of inevitability removed has lost something so essential that it can no longer remain secularization theory. While parts of the theory can, should, and are retained in the competition perspective, secularization theory has, nevertheless, been left behind. Thus, the competition perspective includes parts cannibalized from secularization theory, but it is a new construct.

The struggle between secularism and religion has certainly changed society and led to an evolution in religious practices and institutions, as well as in their political role. This is certainly a critically important, game-changing, and evolutionary shift, but even if one were to argue that it makes possible a decline in religion, this decline is neither predetermined nor inevitable. In fact, it is possible to argue that the challenge has strengthened religion and, in the long run, has increased religion's overall influence in society and politics. It has led to new forms of religion, such as fundamentalism, which through actively defending religion against modernity and secularism has increased religion's social and political influence (Fox, 2013: 109–121). The evidence provided later in this book demonstrates that religion remains relevant to politics across the world and that this relevance has been increasing over a period of nearly two decades.

Monica Duffy Toft, Daniel Philpott, and Timothy Shaw, in their book *God's Century* (Toft et al., 2011: 49–78), describe a perspective on history consistent with this view of religion and politics. In premodern times "relationships between religious and political actors tended to involve significant mutual dependence for the sake of overall social order and reliance on each other for the maintenance of rule" (Toft et al., 2011: 52). Around 1450, this power relationship began to change. There was a shift from the balance in premodern times when religion shared power with the state to one in which the state became dominant. In a "friendly takeover" of religion, the increasingly powerful state both protected the existing religious monopoly by both enforcing and financing religion. In doing so, it created a new relationship in which the state was clearly superior to religious institutions. Why did this occur? As the state became more powerful, it was less inclined to share power. With the Reformation, the power of the pope declined. In addition, the Protestant Reformation weakened the Catholic Church and gave rise to political theologies that supported state power. This forced Catholics to depend on rulers to enforce religion. The Treaty of Westphalia established the principle that religion was an internal matter to the state as an element of sovereignty, undermining the ability of outside actors to influence state religion policy. Finally, nationalism began to rise as an alternative legitimating ideology for the state. From the late 18th century through the late 20th century, the state became more hostile to religion. Religion became fully subordinated to the state and was often restricted in the public sphere. In extreme cases, such as some Communist and fascist states, religion was banned altogether.

Beginning in the 1960s, secular regimes began to have setbacks and religion began to regain some of its former political power. Essentially, secularism did not succeed in delivering the "coup de grace" to religion. Rather, the rise of the secular state forced religion to become independent from the government. Religious institutions found nonstate sources of financial support. Until the 1960s, people remained religious but usually focused that religion inward. From the 1960s, a combination of the failures of the secular state and the increasing strength of the now independent religious institutions led these institutions to begin to become politically assertive. Two additional trends have facilitated this process. First democratization has made it easier for religion to compete in the political arena. Second, globalization has made many of these religious actors transnational actors, improving their negotiating position with regard to the state. Thus, religion has returned, not as the partner of the state that existed in premodern times but as a powerful, influential, independent, and often global actor with a political agenda (Toft et al., 2011: 49–78).

It is possible to quibble with the specifics of this historical description, but the general outline of secularism rising as a challenge to religion followed by a resurgence of religion in politics is an increasingly popular one. For example, Mark Juergensmeyer (2012: 197) dates the decline of religion

> at least to the twelfth century, when John of Salisbury... held that rulers should be subject to charges of treason and could be overthrown – violently if necessary – if they violated their public trust; and William of Ockham, in the fourteenth century, argued that a "secular ruler need not submit to spiritual power."

That being said, this is not inconsistent with the argument by Toft et al. (2011) in that they focus on the political decline of religion while Juergensmeyer looks at the intellectual roots that contributed to this decline. Juergensmeyer (1993) attributes the recent rise of religion to the failures of "secular nationalism," the term he uses for secular political ideologies such as liberalism, socialism, communism, and fascism in combination with nationalism. Governments, especially those in the Third World, espousing these ideologies failed to deliver the economic prosperity and social justice they promised. As a result, they suffer from a crisis of legitimacy that has allowed religion, an inherently legitimate and indigenous ideology, to return to fill this power vacuum.

Toft et al. (2011) date this resurgence of religion in politics earlier than do most, who usually date it to the 1970s with the rise of the religious right in US politics and the Iranian revolution (e.g., Demerath, 2001; Haynes, 1997; Juergensmeyer, 1993; 2008; Zubadia, 2000). Huntington (1993, 1996) dates it to the end of the Cold War around 1990. Yet the general principle that religion remains relevant and is competing with secularism in the political marketplace is consistent across this literature.

Beyond the Secular-Religious Competition Perspective

I argue that the secular-religious competition perspective is essential to understanding religion and politics in the modern era, but this is not to say that it is the only influence. As I noted earlier in the chapter, the secular camp is not monolithic, and there are multiple interpretations of the concept of political secularism. Pushing for a more secular government policy can mean removing all religion from public space and discourse. It can mean asking the government itself not to get involved in religion but allowing religion to be present in public space and discourse. It can also mean allowing government support for religion as long as the government treats all religions equally. There is no agreed on "secular policy" among supporters of political secularism.

Among supporters of religion, there is certainly no agreement. As we will see, especially in Chapter 6, religions regularly compete with other religions. Huntington (1993; 1996) argues that this will be the essential clash of the post–Cold War era. Huntington's argument is based on the importance of culture, arguing that large cultural groupings will be the dominant forces in politics. Grim and Finke (2011) come to a similar conclusion looking at more microlevel societal factors. They argue that societal prejudice and discrimination is often a harbinger of discriminatory policies by governments. Although this study does not precisely focus on either religious conflict or societal pressures, Chapter 6 does focus on religious discrimination, which is when a state – often linked to one religion – places limitations on religious minorities. In addition, within each religious tradition, there is no agreement over the proper interpretation of religious doctrine much less whether, how, and to what extent the state should enforce this doctrine. This clash between and within religions is ubiquitous and permeates most elements of state religion policy.

Finally, it is important to remember that the political class also participates in this process. Gill (2008) argues that religion policies are to a great extent molded by the interests of politicians. Politicians seek to hold onto power and keep that power at the lowest cost possible. The support of a dominant religion can be a strong source of support, and it can also be a potent tool of social control. Religion can also be a drain on resources. Thus, a politician must decide whether supporting religion is less expensive than using other forms of social control. Part of this calculation is that the dominant religion often wants to maintain its dominance through state repression, which also has its costs. So, for Gill, the question is one of how a politician sees the cost-benefit ratio for supporting religion. Sarkissian (2010: 493) similarly argues that

> it is in the interests of both insecure regimes and insecure religious groups to pursue religious establishment. For the insecure regime, the support of a hegemonic religious organization can give it popular legitimacy. For a religious organization, establishment brings both benefits from the state, and access that allows it to cement its monopoly status and limit religious competition.

Contemporary Religion and Politics

In sum, I propose that the secular-religious competition perspective is a useful tool for understanding religion's current role in politics and society. Religion and politics is largely but not exclusively defined by the competition between secular and religious ideologies. In the context of this study, I examine how this plays out in government religion policy. This contest between ideologies is not a simple one because neither religion nor secularism is monolithic, and each is better described as a family of ideologies rather than a single one. As noted earlier, there are a several strains of secularist political ideologies. Secularists often argue among themselves over basic issues such as whether the government should support and even fund religion (on an equal basis) and the extent to which government must avoid and/or restrict religion in the public sphere.

Religious ideologies are, if anything, more diverse. There are many religions in the world and many include multiple denominations. Even within a single denomination of a religion, interpretations of the religion can differ. R. Scott Appleby (2000) calls this the ambivalence of the sacred. He argues that religious traditions include complex and diverse texts and dogmas that can be interpreted in many ways. Although his discussion focuses on how religions support both violence and peace, this concept is certainly applicable to other aspects of politics.

Thus, the political struggle between religious and secular ideologies is also complemented by struggles between subsets of these ideologies. Perhaps the most common are conflicts between religious denominations. In most cases, this takes the form of a dominant religion in a state restricting or repressing minority religions, a topic I discuss in great detail in Chapter 6.

This struggle is unavoidable. Every government has no choice but to have a religion policy. This religion policy involves several dimensions. First, a state must decide whether to support religion and, if so, whether it will support all of them, some of them, or only one. States that support religion must also decide on the extent of this support, including how this support will be divided between different religions, assuming the state chooses to support more than one religion. Second, states must decide whether and to what extent to restrict, regulate, and control religion in general in the public sphere as well as the private sphere. As the evidence provided in later chapters shows, many states both support and limit the same religions, so these two aspects of policy are not mutually incompatible. Third, states must decide on their policy toward minority religions. Are they to be treated the same as the majority religion or differently? Different treatment almost always involves restrictions on minority religions. In most states, the treatment of minority religions is different from religion to religion.

Having no policy is not an option because having no policy is essentially deciding to have a neutral policy, which is a form of secularist policy. As is discussed in more detail throughout this book, truly neutral policies are rare and difficult to maintain.

Whatever a state's policy, there are almost inevitably forces within society dissatisfied with the status quo. No matter how strongly a state supports a single religion, there will be those who feel that this support is not strong enough. For example, in Saudi Arabia, which arguably supports Wahhabi Islam more strongly than any other state in the world supports its majority religion, there exists an opposition that seeks to bring the state into greater conformance with Islam. In any state that supports a religion, there will also be both those who feel that this support is too strong and religious minorities unhappy with their disadvantaged position, even if they have full religious freedom and this disadvantage is limited to not having all the benefits given to the majority religion. Similarly, in a secular state, there will always be elements that consider it insufficiently secular as well as those who would like religion to have a greater influence.

Essentially, every country is a battleground. Whatever the status quo, there will be, within the majority group, forces seeking to make the state more religious as well as forces seeking to make it more secular. There will be religious minorities who are influenced by state religion policy with their own agenda. There will also be politicians who seek to find the formula that best benefits their own interests. Given these cross-pressures, it is no surprise that state religion policy across the globe is in a constant state of flux. Between 1990 and 2008, 148 (83.6%) of the 177 countries included in this study in some way changed their religion policy.

Thus, struggle and change is the norm in this contest between (and within) religious and secular ideologies. This is a struggle that has been continuing for centuries and is likely to continue to play out for centuries. This study examines state religion policy for a brief 19-year period of this historical process. The results presented in this book demonstrate that there is a competition between religion and secularism across the globe, and, at least for the period covered by this study, the influence of religion is increasing.

3

Establishment, Support, Neutrality, or Hostility

The Varieties of Official Religion Policy

In 1995, after decades of discussion and debate, the government of Sweden and the (Lutheran) Church of Sweden decided to separate from one another, a separation that took place officially in 2000. This decision had numerous practical results. Local parishes and the government had to appraise and divide vast amounts of property. The Church received significantly less government support, which forced it to drastically cut its budget. The king was no longer required to be a Lutheran, and the government no longer appointed the Church's bishops. Children of at least one Lutheran parent are no longer automatically Church members. To join the Church, they must be baptized into it.

Even so, this was not a total victory for the advocates of political secularism. Like most cases of shifts in state religion policy, which are part and parcel of the secular-religious competition perspective, neither Sweden's starting point nor its ending point were absolute support for religion or total secularism. Rather, it was a shift from one point on the spectrum between the two to another. Many states support religion more than Sweden did before it disestablished the Church of Sweden, and the new separation was not a complete one. For example, the Church still receives fees through taxes but gets these funds on an equal basis with other religions. Taxpayers may choose to divert the tax to the religious group of their choice or receive a tax reduction.

As we will see in this chapter, a shift of this magnitude in state religion policy is rare, but it illustrates one of the most basic choices involved in government religion policy – whether to have an official religion. Yet like most choices involved in state religion policy, this choice is not as black and white as it seems. There are significant differences among states with an official religion as there are among states with no official religion. As we will see in Chapter 4, states with an official religion still vary widely in the extent to which they support it and the role they allow religion in the state. Policies among states with no official religion can vary from strongly supporting religion to being overtly hostile to it. Neutrality is also an option.

To capture this diversity, I divide these state religion policies into 14 categories. These categories are based on the overall structure of a state's policy toward religion and include multiple gradations of policy for states in each of the following categories: (1) states that establish a religion, (2) states that support religion without declaring an official one, (3) states that are neutral toward religion, and (4) states that are hostile to religion. A clear majority of states are in the first two categories and either officially or unofficially support one or a few religions more than others. Most states did not change this aspect of their policy between 1990 and 2008, but among those who did, more moved toward greater support or less hostility to religion than the opposite.

Although this is consistent with the expectations of the competition perspective outlined in Chapter 2, as we will see in Chapters 4 through 6, this perspective is more strongly supported by the shifts in the more specific aspects of state religion policy. It is also important to emphasize that this aspect of state religion policy is an important guideline, but it is not absolute. Within each of the 14 categories, there is significant variation in a state's policy in practice, which is the focus of Chapters 4 through 6. For example, it is not unusual for a state to have no official religion but, in practice, more strongly support a single religion than many states that do have official religions.

Liechtenstein and Sudan provide an illustrative example of this principle. Liechtenstein's constitution declares that "The Roman Catholic Church is the State Church and as such enjoys the full protection of the State." However, beyond this, it takes few concrete actions to support and uphold the state religion. It funds the Catholic Church from the state budget, but it also does so for other religions including Muslim, Orthodox Christian, and Protestant organizations. There is also religious education in public schools. Until 2003, the choices were between Catholicism and Protestantism. In 2003, a nonconfessional "religion and culture" class was added as were classes in Islam in 2007. Even before 2003, exemptions to these classes were regularly granted on request. This may seem to some a substantial level of state support for religion, but as I demonstrate in Chapter 4, it is relatively low, even for a state with no official religion.[1]

---

[1] The following are used as general sources for the country information presented in this and subsequent chapters: Amore (1995); Barret et al. (2001); Morigi et al. (2003); US Department of State International Religious Freedom Reports 2000–2009 and Human Rights Reports, 1994 to 2009; UN Abortion Policies webpage, www.un.org/esa/population/publications/abortion/profiles.htm; "Abortion in Law History and Religion" *Childbirth by Choice Trust*, 1995, www.cbctrust.com/homepage.html; Susheela Singh, Deirdre Wulf, Akinrinola Bankole, and Gilda Sedgh, *Abortion Worldwide: Uneven Progress*, www.guttmacher.org/pubs/AWWfullreport.pdf; Daniel Ottoson, "A World Survey of Laws Prohibiting Same Sex Activity between Consenting Adults," 2009 ILGA, The International Lesbian, Gay, Bisexual, Trans and Intersex Association, http://old.ilga.org/Statehomophobia/ILGA_State_Sponsored_Homophobia_2010.pdf; "Religious

In 2005, Sudan, as part of a peace agreement intended to end a violent civil war that began a process of separation between the country's Northern and Southern regions, removed all references to an official religion from its constitution. Yet in practice, all 20 types of state support for religion measured by the Religion and State project (RAS) dataset (and discussed in more detail in Chapter 4) that existed before this constitutional change remained in place in Sudan's north. Essentially, the change in Sudan was primarily a change in name only. It remains a state that strongly supports Islam even though it no longer declares Islam its official religion.

Liechtenstein is among the weakest supporters of religion among states with an official religion, and Sudan is among the strongest supporters among states without one. Nevertheless, they, along with Sweden, illustrate three important points that are critical to understanding the nature and diversity of state religion policies. First, the basic decision on whether to endorse a religion officially can have a substantial impact on the lives of citizens. Second, there is a wide amount of variation in applied policies among both states that declare an official religion and those that do not. This is true to the extent that there is considerable overlap in levels of actual support for religion between the two categories. Third, while declared policy has a substantial impact on the actual level of state support for religion, not all states follow their declared policy in practice. I examine the statistical link between declared policy and actual policy in more detail in Chapters 4 and 8.

In this chapter, I examine the wide range of official religion policies among the world's governments. This includes the types of policies that exist, how many states follow each type of policy, factors that influence the type of policy, and how these policies have changed between 1990 and 2008.

Why Support a State Religion?

Although this study focuses on the details of state religion policy, a brief discussion of the motivations for supporting a state religion will help place the findings in context. Perhaps the most obvious reason is religious ideology. To the extent that leaders and their constituents believe in a religion, states will

Freedom World Report," *International Coalition for Religious Freedom*, www.religiousfreedom.com/wrpt/Europe/ireland.htm;www.religioustolerance.org; "Freedom in the World" Freedom House, www.freedomhouse.org; The Religion and Law Consortium, www.religlaw.org; World Religions and Cultures, http:wrc.lingnet.org "Religious Freedom in the Majority Islamic Countries, 1998 Report: Saudi Arabia," *Aid to the Church in Need*, www.alleanzacattolica.org/acs/acs_english/acs_index.htm; "Handbook on Religious Liberty around the World," http://religiousfreedom.lib.virginia.edu/rihand; European Studies on Religion and State Interaction, www.euresisnet.eu/Pages/Religion-State.aspx; International Coalition for Religious Freedom, www.religiousfreedom.com; Human Rights without Frontiers, www.hrwf.net; International Christian Concern (ICC), http://persecution.org. Subsequent notes include only sources in addition to these.

be more likely to support that religion (Stark, 2001; 2003). Gill (2008) argues that political leaders will also do so for practical reasons. A state religion can support the legitimacy of a government. This lowers both the costs of ruling and social unrest. When people believe a government to be legitimate, they are less likely to oppose it and cause social unrest.

Another possible reason is cultural. That is, even people who are not particularly religious and find no realpolitik benefits for supporting a state religion may do so because they value religion as an essential part of a national culture that is worth preserving. Religion is generally considered an essential element of identity (Breakwell, 1986; Gurr, 1993; 2000; Horowitz, 1985; Little, 1995) and is a central element of many nationalist ideologies (Friedland, 2001: 129–130; Smith, 1999; 2000). In fact, Juergensmeyer (1993; 2008) argues that religious and secular ideologies compete for defining the nature of national identity in a manner consistent with the competition perspective.

Types of State Religion Policies

I divide state religion policies into 14 categories. This includes 4 types of policies for states with official religions and 10 types for states without official religions. The distribution of states based on these types of policies for 1990 (or the earliest year for which information is available) and 2008 is presented in Table 3.1. Table 3.2 provides a brief explanation for each category and a listing of the states in the category. Unless otherwise noted, the discussion here focuses on the status in 2008.

States with Official Religions

The most basic division between types of government religion policies is whether a state has an official religion. Official religions are generally declared in constitutions (which I discuss in more detail in Chapter 8) but can be declared in some other format such as a law or long-standing tradition. For example, the Dominican Republic signed a Concordant with the Catholic Church in 1954 declaring the Church the state's official religion. Overall, in 2008, 41 of the 177 countries included in this study declared official religions; 33 of these states make this declaration in their constitutions.

Once declaring an official religion, a state must decide on several additional aspects of state policy toward the official religion. Setting aside for the moment how the state relates to all religions other than the official religion (the topic of Chapter 6), these decisions include the following: (1) the extent to which it will support the official religion, (2) the extent to which it will enforce the religion, and (3) the extent to which it will control, regulate, and restrict the religion. I discuss all of these types of policies in more detail in Chapters 4 and 5. For the most part, these decisions are what differentiate between the four categories of official religions in this study. I discuss these categories beginning with those that most strongly support, enforce, and control their official religions.

TABLE 3.1. *World Distribution of Official Religion Policies 1990 (or Earliest) and 2008*

	1990 or earliest		2008	
	N	%	N	%
Religious state: religion mandatory for all	2	1.1	2	1.1
Religious state: mandatory for majority	8	4.5	8	4.5
State controlled religion: positive attitude	7	4.0	7	4.0
Active support	25	14.1	24	13.6
Total for official religions	42	23.7	41	23.2
One religion preferred	29	15.8	28	15.8
Multitiered: one religion preferred	11	6.2	16	9.0
Multitiered: multiple religions preferred	6	3.4	7	4.0
Multiple religions preferred (cooperation)	27	15.3	26	14.7
Total for preferential treatment, no official religion	73	41.2	77	43.5
Total for preferential treatment and official religion	115	65.0	118	66.7
Total for official religion and one religion preferred	82	46.3	85	48.0
Supports all religions equally	9	5.1	8	4.5
Accommodation (supports no religion)	34	19.2	35	19.8
Total for neutral policies	43	24.3	43	24.3
Separationist (mild hostility)	9	5.1	7	4.0
Nonspecific hostility	1	0.6	1	0.6
State controlled religion: negative attitude	6	3.4	7	4.0
Specific hostility	3	1.7	1	0.6
All hostile policies	19	10.7	16	9.0

These three criteria help define the extent to which a state's government becomes entangled in religion. By this I mean the extent to which a state becomes involved in supporting and controlling a religion and its institutions – and to an extent is itself and supported and controlled by those institutions – can vary considerably. However, this relationship among states with official religions can be understood by placing them into four categories. I discuss these categories starting with the highest level of entanglement.

Religious states are states that strongly support and enforce the majority religion to the extent that observing the religion is considered mandatory. There currently exist on this earth no states more intertwined with religion than these. Religious states are further divided into two categories. The most strict of these are those states where the majority religion is mandatory for everyone in the state. This technically includes members of minority religions.

TABLE 3.2. *How States Were Categorized in 2008*

Category and Definition	States in the Category
States with official religions	
Religious state: The state strongly supports and enforces the majority religion. Observing the religion is mandatory.	Afghanistan, Brunei, Iran, Kuwait, Malaysia, Maldives, Oman, Pakistan, Qatar, Saudi Arabia
State-controlled religion, positive attitude: The state both supports a religion and substantially controls its institutions but has a positive attitude toward this religion.	Bahrain, Egypt, Jordan, Libya, Tunisia, United Arab Emirates, Yemen
Active state religion: The state actively supports a religion, but the religion is not mandatory and the state does not dominate the official religion's institutions.	Algeria, Argentina, Bangladesh, Bhutan, Bolivia, Cambodia, Costa Rica, Denmark, Djibouti, Dominican Republic, Finland, Greece, Iceland, Iraq, Israel, Liechtenstein, Malta, Mauritania, Morocco, Norway, Somalia, United Kingdom, Western Sahara, Zambia
States with no official religion	
Preferred religion: No official religion, but one religion receives unique recognition or benefits. Minority religions all receive similar treatment to each other.	Andorra, Armenia, Bahamas, Belize, Bulgaria, Cape Verde, Chile, Comoros, Cyprus (Turkish Government), El Salvador, Equatorial Guinea, Georgia, Guatemala, Guinea, Haiti, Honduras, Ireland, Ivory Coast, Macedonia, Moldova, Myanmar, Nicaragua, Panama, Paraguay, Peru, Sudan, Syria, Venezuela
Multitiered preferences – one religion: One religion receives the most benefits. There is one or more tiers of religions receiving less benefits than the preferred religion but more than others.	Belarus, Colombia, Croatia, India, Indonesia, Italy, Mongolia, Poland, Portugal, Romania, Russia, Serbia, Slovakia, Spain, Sri Lanka, Thailand
Multitiered preferences – multiple religions: Same as above except the top tier is occupied by multiple religions.	Austria, Bosnia, Cyprus, Czech Republic, Hungary, Latvia, Lithuania
Cooperation: Multiple religions receive benefits that others do not.	Albania, Belgium, Chad, Germany, Ghana, Kazakhstan, Kenya, Lebanon, Liberia, Kenya, Lebanon, Liberia, Luxembourg, Madagascar, Malawi, Mauritius, Montenegro, Nigeria, Papua New Guinea, Philippines, Slovenia, Solomon Islands, Swaziland, Sweden, Switzerland, Tanzania, Togo, Ukraine, Vanuatu

Category and Definition	States in the Category
Supportive: The state supports all religions equally.	Brazil, Gambia, Jamaica, Nepal, New Zealand, Senegal, Suriname, Trinidad and Tobago
Accommodation: Minimal support for religion and no religion is preferred. The state has a positive attitude toward religion.	Angola, Australia, Barbados, Benin, Botswana, Burkina Faso, Burundi, Cameroon, Canada, Central African Republic, Congo-Brazzaville, Ecuador, Estonia, Fiji, Gabon, Guinea Bissau, Guyana, Japan, Lesotho, Mali, Mozambique, Namibia, Netherlands, Niger, Rwanda, Sierra Leone, Singapore, South Africa, Taiwan, Timor, Uganda, United States, Zaire, Zimbabwe
Separationist: Minimal support for religion. The state has a negative attitude toward religion and relegates it to the private sphere.	Azerbaijan, Eretria, Ethiopia, France, Mexico, Turkey, Uruguay
Nonspecific hostility: Religious organizations restricted in a manner similar to other nonstate organizations.	Cuba
State controlled religion, negative attitude: The state sets up an official religious organization, which it controls. All religious outside of this institution is restricted. The purpose is to control rather than support religion.	China, Kyrgyzstan, Laos, Tajikistan, Turkmenistan, Uzbekistan, Vietnam
Specific hostility: The government restricts or bans all religion for ideological reasons.	North Korea

These states also substantially control all religious institutions in the country. Only Saudi Arabia and the Maldives fit into this category.

In Saudi Arabia, Islam is the state's official religion, the public practice of any other religion is prohibited, and all citizens must be Muslim. The only non-Muslims allowed are tourists, diplomats, and temporary residents. The government declares that Sharia (Islamic) law is the country's only legal code. This law is strictly enforced, including with regard to strict separation of men and women, dress code, the criminal code, family law, and inheritance. Any public criticism or questioning of the country's official interpretation of Islam can result in detention, harassment, and deportation. The government controls all mosques, including private mosques. All imams of these mosques are approved by the government and are employees of the Ministry of Islamic Affairs. The religious police, called the Mutaww'ain, enforce religious dress codes, separation of the sexes, and others violations of Islamic law.[2]

In the Maldives, Islam is the official religion. The 2008 constitution declares that "Islam shall be one of the bases of the laws of the Maldives," that "no law contrary to any tenet of Islam shall be enacted in the Maldives," and that "a non-Muslim may not become a citizen of the Maldives." Civil and criminal law are subordinated to Sharia law, and Sharia law is applied in cases where civil law is silent. The 2000 Family Act declares Sharia family law the law of the land but adds some additional protections for women. The government enforces religious practices such as fasting on Ramadan, daily prayer, and a ban on alcohol. Citizens must use government-approved religious practices and facilities. For example, performing the Islamic ritual *namaz* prayer in a non-government-approved way can lead to arrest. The public practice of any religion other than Islam is also banned. The government directly controls all mosques, and only those individuals licensed by the government may preach.[3]

In an additional eight countries, Afghanistan, Brunei, Iran, Kuwait, Malaysia, Oman, Pakistan, and Qatar, the state religion – which in all of these cases is Islam – is mandatory, but only for members of the majority religion. This means it is technically not illegal to be a member of a minority religion but, in practice, all of these states severely limit the religious freedom of minorities. For example, Iran's constitution specifically states that "Zoroastrian, Jewish, and Christian Iranians are the only recognized religious minorities, who, within the limits of the law, are free to perform their religious rites and ceremonies, and to act according to their own canon in matters of personal affairs and religious education."[4] However, in practice all of these religions suffer from high levels of restrictions including bans on publically practicing minority religions

---

[2] Brian Hershorin, "The Separation of Church and State: Have We Gone Too Far?" www.expertlaw.com/library/misc/first_amendment-2.html#O; "Vicious about Virtue: Saudi Arabia," *The Economist*, June 23, 2007; Saudi Arabia Divorce and Family Law, www.international-divorce.com/d-saudi.htm; Mohammed Jamjoom and Saad Abedine, "Saudis Order 40 Lashes for Elderly Woman for Mingling" CNN International, March 9, 2009, http://edition.cnn.com/2009/WORLD/meast/03/09/saudi.arabia.lashes; "Women Lose Out, Regardless of Religion," *The Toronto Star*, March 11, 2009; Michael Theodoulou, "Saudi Professor Faces Lashes for Having Coffee with Female 'Student'," *The Times Online*, February 26, 2008, www.timesonline.co.uk/tol/news/world/middle_east/article3439642.ece.

[3] Odd Larsen, "Almost No Religious Freedom for Migrant Workers," Forum 18, June 23, 2009, www.forum18.org/Archive.php?article_id=1316; Odd Larsen, "Maldives: Religious Freedom Survey, October 2008," Forum 18, October 15, 2008; Maldives 2008 Constitution, www.presidencymaldives.gov.mv/Index.aspx?lid=5; Maldives 1968 Penal Code, www.lexadin.nl/wlg/legis/nofr/oeur/lxwemdv.htm; Maldives 2000 Family Act, www.lexadin.nl/wlg/legis/nofr/oeur/lxwemdv.htm; "'Creeping Islamization' in Maldives," *BBC Monitoring South Asia (Political)*, October 1, 2007; "Maldives Bans Popular Religious Leaders from Leading Prayers," *BBC Monitoring South Asia (Political)*, October 12, 2005.

[4] Iranian Constitution, www.servat.unibe.ch/icl.

Establishment, Support, Neutrality, or Hostility

among Muslims, harassment of those who attend religious services, especially Christians, and the inability to achieve high-level positions in the government and military.[5]

These states typically include Sharia law in state law to varying extents and enforce Islam through the state apparatus. Most also control the country's religious institutions. For example, in Kuwait, the government controls and monitors sermons delivered by imams and preachers. Several religious leaders have been banned from giving sermons – including the Imam of the Grand Mosque – after they did not comply with government regulations. Unlicensed mosques are especially subject to governmental monitoring. Imams and preachers must also sign a "mosque compact," promising to stay within certain boundaries when delivering sermons.[6]

The next category is a *state-controlled religion, positive attitude*. This is when the state both supports a religion and substantially controls its institutions while having a positive attitude toward this religion. This distinguishes it from the other state-controlled religion category I discuss later. The seven states in this category are all Middle Eastern Muslim-majority states. They all control and support the state religion but do not go as far in enforcing it as do the states in the previous categories. These states typically take part in the appointment process for clergy, monitor or regulate sermons by clergy, control religious education, and otherwise influence the workings of religious institutions. Although they support Islam and incorporate elements of Sharia law into state law, they do so to a lesser extent than states categorized here as religious states. Their governments are also more independent from religious institutions than those of the religious states. Thus, while they are heavily involved in religion, this involvement including the level of enforcement is less than that of religious states. These governments are also more firmly in control of their relationship with religion than those of the religious states. This power relationship is a significant distinction.

For example, Jordan's constitution declares Islam the official religion, and the king must be a Muslim born to two legitimate Muslim parents. Sharia law determines family and inheritance law for Muslims, although the law gives women more rights in divorce than traditional Sharia law. Religious minorities have their own tribunals that officiate and oversee marriages and divorces. Some other religious laws are enforced publically. This includes bans on insulting Islam, proselytizing by non-Muslims, and conversion away from Islam. Ramadan fasting laws are enforced, including the closing of restaurants during

---

[5] Anuj Chopra, "In Iran, Covert Christian Converts Live with Secrecy and Fear," *U.S. News*, May 8, 2008, www.usnews.com/articles/news/world/2008/05/08/in-iran-covert-christian-converts-live-with-secrecy-and-fear.html?PageNr=1.
[6] "Kuwait to Launch Media Drive to 'Cure Extremist Ideologies' after Attacks," *BBC Monitoring Middle East*, January 31, 2005; U.S State Department Report on Religious Freedom, 2006, 2007, 2008, www.state.gov/g/drl/rls/irf/2006/71425.htm.

the day unless specifically exempted by the government, such as restaurants that cater specifically to tourists. Preachers and teachers in mosques must have licenses issued by the Ministry of Religious Affairs. The government sets the Islamic education curriculum in schools, which is mandatory for all Muslim children. The Ministry of Religious Affairs and Trusts essentially controls all Muslim institutions in Jordan. They manage Islamic institutions, supervise the construction of mosques, appoint and pay the salaries of imams, direct Islamic clergy training institutions, and subsidize certain mosque-sponsored events. Furthermore, the government monitors sermons and forbids criticism of the Royal Family and the instigation of social or political unrest. The Political Parties Law prohibits houses of worship from being used for political activity.[7]

The final category of official religion is an *active state religion*. These 24 countries declare an official religion and actively support it. However, government control and regulation of religious institutions, although present in many of these states, is significantly lower than that of the previous category. This gives the religious institutions therein a substantially higher level of independence than those in the previous categories. Thus, while these governments tend to be significantly involved in religion, this lower level of control gives them a bit more distance from religion than can be found in states in the previous categories.

Denmark, for example, declares in its constitution that "the Evangelical Lutheran Church shall be the Established Church of Denmark, and, as such, it shall be supported by the State." The government heavily subsidizes the church through a tax it collects from Church members, a subsidy exclusive to the state church. The Church is responsible for registering all civil births, deaths, marriages, and divorces, as well as for the management of cemeteries (including secular ones). Blasphemy is illegal, but no one has been charged with this crime since 1971. The public school curriculum includes a "Christian studies" class, which focuses on the state religion but also covers other religions. The government does not substantially interfere in the internal affairs of the state church. Also, other than the rarely enforced blasphemy law, which prohibits the mockery or insult of any legally recognized religion, it does not substantially enforce the majority religion.[8]

Similarly, Argentina's constitution states that "the Federal Government supports the Roman Catholic Apostolic religion." The Catholic Church receives

---

[7] Constitution of Jordan, www.kinghussein.gov.jo/constitution_jo.html; "Jordan: Restaurants Forced to Close for Ramadan," www.adnkronos.com/AKI/English/Religion/?id=1.0.13170 18982; "Jordan: Change to Law Grants Woman a Historic Divorce," *National Post*, May 14, 2002, p. A14; "Jordanian Minister Denies External Pressure Behind Curricula Changes," *Al-Sharq al-Awsat*, November 30, 2004; Nicolas Pelham, "Jordanian Blasphemy Verdict Shakes the Free Press," *The Christian Science Monitor*, February 18, 2003.

[8] Constitution of Denmark, www.servat.unibe.ch/icl; Irene Maria Briones Martinez, "Women and Freedom of Speech in Denmark: Three Crucial Factors for a Healthy Society," Center for Studies on New Religions, www.cesnur.org/2006/sd_martinez.htm; Zambeta (2008).

millions of dollars in direct government subsidies and tax exemptions that are not available to the other religious groups. Since 2007, the Church also receives exclusive licensing preferences for radio frequencies, a large degree of autonomy for parochial schools, and school subsidies. The government does not get involved in the internal affairs of the Catholic Church or enforce its doctrine.[9]

States without Official Religions
States that have no official religions essentially have the same policy options as those with official religions. They can choose whether to support, enforce, and regulate religion. However, the lack of an official religion means that there is a much wider range of discretion when making these choices. The policies of countries in this category range from supporting a single religion as if it was the official religion to overt repression of all religion. I divide this range of policies into 10 categories, which are based on three related dimensions. First, is the state supportive, neutral, or hostile toward religion? Second, among supportive states, to what extent does it single out one religion or a few religions for special privileges? Third, among hostile states, what is the extent and nature of the hostility?

States with *preferred religions* are those that, although not declaring an official religion, in practice single out one religion for support in a manner similar to a state with an official religion. In these states, no other religion is singled out for any special privileges or benefits. This distinguishes these states from those in the following category. The extent of state support for and regulation of the majority religion varies widely among these 28 states, and they have little in common other than this unofficial endorsement of a single religion. However, most of them support religion less than the average state with an official religion, even the average state categorized as having an active state religion. There are certainly exceptions, but the fact that a state does not declare an official religion is also of considerable significance.

As noted earlier, Sudan has fit into this category since 2005, strongly supporting Islam without declaring it the official religion. Article 13 of Bulgaria's constitution declares that "religious institutions shall be separate from the State" but also states that "Eastern Orthodox Christianity shall be considered the traditional religion in the Republic of Bulgaria." The 2002 Religious Denominations Act reiterates both separation of religion and state and the Bulgarian Orthodox Church's (BOC) "traditional" status. Thus, although there is no official religion, one religion is considered to have a special place in Bulgaria. While the government provides funds to several religions, the bulk of these funds go to the maintenance and renovation of BOC property as well as supporting BOC churches abroad. The government has also supported the BOC in a dispute with a splinter church called the Bulgarian Orthodox

---

[9] Constitution of Argentina, www.servat.unibe.ch/icl.

Alternative Synod. (The group is the same as the BOC in most respects, save for the acceptance of a particular church leader.) The 2002 Denominations Act prevents religious groups from using the same name as an existing group or claiming its properties, a clause many believe was written to single out the Alternative Synod. The government has evicted the Alternative Synod from hundreds of churches and otherwise harassed its clergy and members. The dispute continues despite declarations in 2009 and 2010 by the European Court of Human Rights that these actions are a violation of religious rights.[10]

While Peru does not have an official religion, Article 51 of its constitution states that "within a regime of independence and autonomy, the State recognizes the Catholic Church as an important component of the historical, cultural and moral formation of Peru, and gives its collaboration." Church rites play an important role in state events. For example, the president's inauguration includes a High Mass, followed by Holy Week events and then the celebration of major Peruvian saints' days and festivals. The Catholic Church receives preferential tax and education benefits. All schools are required to teach Catholicism, which is mandatory unless parents specifically request their children to be exempted. The teachers are subject to the approval of the local Catholic bishop. Parents may organize non-Catholic education in schools at their own expense. The country's 52 bishops and those priests whose ministries are located in towns and villages along the country's borders receive government payments, and each Catholic district receives a monthly institutional subsidy from the government. The government does not substantially interfere with the inner workings of the Catholic Church.[11]

The next category of state religion policy is *multitiered preferences – one religion*. This is a case in which the state establishes a hierarchy of religions with each tier on the hierarchy receiving different benefits and status and the top tier is occupied by a single religion. I posit that this type of policy is less preferential to a single religion than the preferred religion policy because although it still singles out one religion as the most important in a state, it also recognizes other religions as important, even if they are not as important as the dominant religion. Thus, while the state still prefers a single religion, this

---

[10] Constitution of Bulgaria, www.parliament.bg/en/const; Religious Denominations Act, adopted by the National Assembly of the Republic of Bulgaria, 39th National Assembly on December 20, 2002, original Bulgarian version published in State Gazette Issue No. 120 of December 29, 2002 (Bulgaria). Translation by Kalina Miller; Dony K. Donev, "Church and State in Bulgaria Today" *East-West Church and Ministry Report*, 13 (3), 2005; "Mosque in Bulgaria Torched to the Ground," *The Sofia Echo*, October 8, 2009; "Bulgaria to Send Sectional Churches to Diaspora Communities," Sofia News Agency, January 4, 2010; Felix Corley, "Bulgaria: Legal Problems Continue for Ahmadi Muslims and Alternative Orthodox," Forum 18 News Service, February 27, 2007; "Strasbourg Court Issues Second Ruling in Favor of Bulgaria's Alternative Synod," *Society*, September 16, 2010.

[11] Constitution of Peru, www2.congreso.gob.pe/sicr/RelatAgenda/constitucion.nsf/constitucion; Jimmy Sturo, "Religion in Peru" *Ezine*, http://ezinearticles.com/?Religion-In-Peru&id=429475.

dominant religion shares this preferential status on a lesser basis with other religions.

Romania, for example, officially has a three-tier system. It recognizes 18 religions as religious "denominations." These recognized denominations have the right to establish classes in their religion in public schools and tax-exempt status. They also receive government funds to build and repair churches, pay clergy salary, and subsidize their housing expenses. They may also broadcast religious programming on radio and television. Officially, all of these 18 religions are the same, but in practice the Romanian Orthodox Church is favored by the state. The 2006 law that outlined the hierarchy of religions in Romania mentions specifically the important role of the Romanian Orthodox Church, which receives the same benefits as other recognized religions but gets the lion's share of state funding. It is the only religious organization that receives government support for its overseas activities. Religious associations, the second official tier, are recognized as legal entities and receive the tax status of religious entities but otherwise have no special benefits. These associations must have at least 300 members and go through a bureaucratic approval process. They also may apply to the Ministry of Culture and Religious Denominations to gain denomination status. This requires proof that they have been operating as a religious association for at least 12 years and proof of membership equal to at least 0.1% of the population as well as a declaration of faith and a copy of the organizations bylaws. Religious groups, the lowest tier, receive no tax exemptions and may not participate in business activities.[12]

Thailand's hierarchy is less formal but nevertheless present. Although there is no official religion, Buddhism is given a clear preferential status. The constitution declares that the king must be a Buddhist. Buddhist monks have special privileges including free public transportation. In 2009 and 2010, the government subsidized programs to encourage the training and ordination of Buddhist monks. The government established the National Buddhism Bureau in 2002 as an independent state agency. It oversees Buddhist clergy, approves the content of Buddhist education, and sponsors educational and public relations programs that promote Buddhism. The state subsidizes the country's three largest religions, Buddhism, Islam, and Christianity, effectively creating a second tier in the hierarchy for Muslims and Christians. Muslims and Buddhists receive subsidies for education, salaries for administrative officials, and the renovation of temples and mosques. There are classes in Buddhism and Islam in public schools. Subsidies to Christians are mostly for social welfare projects.

---

[12] Law 489/2006 on the Freedom of Religion and the General Status of Denominations Published in the Official Journal, Part I, Issue #11/January 8, 2007, www.religlaw.org; Submission to the UN Universal Periodic Review by Human Rights without Frontiers International," May 15, 2008, www.hrwf.net; Felix Corley, "Romania: Controversial Law Promulgated; Legal Challenges Planned," Forum 18, January 3, 2007; Oana Dan, "Draft Law on Religious Freedom Close to Being Completed," *Bucharest Daily News*, April 12, 2006.

In theory, other religions may register to receive government support if they have 5,000 adherents, a uniquely recognizable theology, and are not politically active. In practice, however, no new religion has been registered since 1984. These unregistered religions constitute the third tier in Thailand's hierarchy and are able to practice freely, with the exception of the Falun Gong, which the government occasionally restricts in what appears to be an effort to appease China.[13]

Multitiered preferences – multiple religions is the next type of policy and is similar to the previous category except that the top tier of the hierarchy is occupied by more than one religion, all of which receive roughly equal treatment. Hungary, has a three-tiered system. The top tier is occupied by the country's four "historical" religions, the Catholic, Lutheran, and Reformed Churches and Judaism. These religions receive the overwhelming majority of state funding. Other than this, their rights are similar to those of the second-tier, registered religions. Any religion with 100 members may register. Hungarian citizens may donate 1% of their income taxes to any registered or historical religion of their choice. The government funds the salaries of clergy in small communities for the four historical religious and some registered religions. Any registered or historical religion may provide religious education in public schools taught by representatives of the religions if requested by students or their parents. Unregistered groups may practice freely but receive no state support or recognition.[14]

Austria has a three-tiered system defined by a 1998 law. Thirteen officially recognized religious societies occupy the top tier. These religions may benefit from the government's religious tax collection program, receive financial support for religious teachers in public and private schools, receive tax exemptions, and may import religious workers and engage in religious education. To achieve this status, a group must have been present in Austria for at least 20 years, including 10 of these years as a "confessional community," and have a membership of at least 0.2% of Austria's population. Groups with this status previous to the law, most of which do not meet these criteria, were allowed to keep their status as recognized societies. Confessional communities, the second tier, are recognized legal entities and must have at least 300 members. Smaller groups may register as an association that has similar rights but is not recognized as a religion. Groups the government considers cults, such as Scientologists and Jehovah's Witnesses, the Unification Church, Hare Krishnas, and some foreign Protestant churches, are denied official status, making

[13] Constitution of Thailand, www.constitutionalcourt.or.th/english; Weena Kowitwanij, "Satellite TV to Train 100,000 Buddhist Monks," *AsiaNews*, January 19, 2010; "Thailand to Ask Falun Gong Members to Leave before APEC Summit," *BBC News*, October 3, 2003; Samuel Albany, "Five Falun Gong Still Detained in Thailand; Legality of Arrests in Doubt," *The Epoch Times*, January 4, 2006.

[14] Schanda (2002); Uitz (2006); "Religious Freedom in the World: Report 2008," Aid to the Church in Need International, 2008.

them the bottom tier. These groups are sometimes harassed and placed under surveillance by government officials and local police. Also, because they lack status as a legal entity, they may not buy or rent property.[15]

While the 23 countries that have one of the multitiered policies are to be found in all world regions with Christian, Hindu, Muslim, and Buddhist majorities, they are most common in the Christian countries of the former Soviet bloc, 12 of which have this type of policy. In this region, these policies seem aimed at protecting and supporting religions that have a long-standing presence in the country and, in some cases, making it difficult for new religions to enter the religious marketplace. These policies are apparently motivated by a desire to preserve the country's historical culture in general rather than an effort to maintain and support religion per say.

Twenty-six states are classified as having *cooperation*. These states give privileges and support to multiple religions on a roughly equal basis that are not given to all religions but do not have multiple tiers of support. Togo's constitution declares the country secular, but the government recognizes Catholicism, Protestant Christianity, and Islam as "state religions," which is a form of official recognition short of being an official religion as defined in this book. Other religions must register as associations whose rights are not substantially different from those of state religions.[16] Belgium makes a clear distinction between eight recognized religions and unrecognized religions. Recognized religions, which include a secular humanist body called Laïcité, receive direct subsidies and funds for places of worship and clergy salaries. Their clergy have preferred access as chaplains to the military and prisons. These religions also may teach religion classes in public schools. The funds are collected via a religious tax in which taxpayers can designate one of these eight religions to receive their taxes. The tax is compulsory even for those who profess no religion or belong to a nonrecognized religion. To become a recognized religion, a group must meet vague criteria including having a "sufficient" number of members and having existed in the country for a "long" time. Nonrecognized religions can register as nonprofits, but not as religions, and receive tax exemptions.[17]

Countries that support all religions equally are classified here as *supportive*. These eight countries, Brazil, Gambia, Jamaica, Nepal, New Zealand, Senegal, Suriname, and Trinidad and Tobago, have little in common other than their religion policies. They include Muslim, Christian, and Hindu majority countries and are found in all world regions other than the Middle East. While most

---

[15] Miner (1998); Federal Law of Austria Concerning the Legal Status of Religious Belief Communities BGBl. I Nr. 19/1998, http://spcp.prf.cuni.cz/dokument/rakusan1.htm.

[16] Constitution of Togo, www.unhcr.org/refworld/country,LEGAL,,LEGISLATION,TGO,456 d621e2,48ef43c72,0.html.

[17] "Denial of Spiritual Assistance to Prisoners Not Professing a State-Recognized Religion," Human Rights without Frontiers, www.hrwf.net; "State Funding of Religion in the UK and Belgium," www.rasmusen.org/x/2006/02/16/state-funding-of-religion-in-the-united-kingdom-and-belgium.

of them are democratic, Gambia is not. Their 2008 per capita gross domestic product ranges from $465 for Nepal to $29,878 in New Zealand. These countries typically provide low levels of support for all religions.

Senegal provides a good example. Despite the country's 94% Muslim majority, Article 1 of Senegal's constitution declares the country secular and declares the equality of all citizens regardless of their religion. Article 4 bans political parties based on religion. The government provides funds to all religions for maintaining places of worship and special events. It supports both Muslim and Christian pilgrimages. Islam and Christianity classes are taught in public schools on an optional basis when requested by parents. To have the legal status necessary to own property and open a bank account, groups must register as nonprofits, but registration is rarely refused.[18]

Thirty-four countries are classified as having policies of *accommodation* – supporting no religion but maintaining a positive attitude toward religion in general. Although, as is discussed in more detail in Chapter 4, countries that do not in any way support religion are rare, these countries have particularly low levels of support for religion. For example, the United States is classified as having three types of support for religion. The first is restrictions on activities during religious holidays including the Sabbath. This is coded because at least 14 US states regulate or forbid the selling of alcohol on Sunday, and at least 3 states regulate retail activity on Sundays, Thanksgiving, and Christmas. Other prohibitions on Sundays found in some localities in the United States include horseracing, hunting, and car sales. Second, since the 2001 Community Solutions Act was passed, the United States funds religious charitable organizations in that these organizations can compete for funding on an equal basis with secular organizations for providing social services. Finally, since 2002, some US states began providing funds to religious schools through "voucher" programs.[19]

Some of these countries regulate religion, but in most cases, this regulation constitutes limitations on religious hate speech and participation of clergy and religious organizations in politics. For example, Article 76 of Mozambique's constitution states that "political parties shall be prohibited from using names containing expressions that are directly related to any religious denominations or churches, and from using emblems that may be confused with national or

---

[18] Constitution of Senegal www.gouv.sn/spip.php?rubrique17.
[19] Americans United for Separation of Church and State, www.au.org/site/News2?page=NewsArticle&id=9047&news_iv_ctrl=0&abbr=resources; Linda Greenhouse, "The Supreme Court: The Louisiana Case; Justices Approve U.S. Financing of Religious Schools' Equipment," *New York Times*, June 29, 2000; "Public Funds Used to Purchase Instructional Equipment for Private and Religious Schools," CivilRights.org, www.civilrights.org/publications/monitor/vol11_no4/art4p1.html; "Faith-Based Initiatives," *Theocracy Watch*, www.theocracywatch.org/faith_base.htm; Anne Farris, "The Tale of Two HR 7's," *The Roundtable on Religion and Social Welfare Policy*, October 7, 2003, www.religionandsocialpolicy.org/news/article.cfm?id=952.

religious symbols." The constitution also declares the state secular, specifically declares public education secular, and bans religious participation in trade organizations.[20]

Separationist policies maintain separation of religion and state but view religion as something negative that must be controlled and limited to the private sphere. These countries may still support or finance religion on some small level, but this is overwhelmed by their regulation of religion. This categorization of policy conforms closely to the *secularist-laicist* philosophy of separation of religion and state discussed in more detail in Chapter 2, which discusses France's 2004 ban on religious symbols in public schools as an example of this policy.

A *nonspecific hostility* policy is one in which the government restricts religion because the government restricts any organization, religious or otherwise, that it considers a potential challenger to the government. In 2008, only Cuba fit this description. The Cuban government places significant restrictions on religion in general, although because most of the country's pre-Communist population was Catholic, this primarily falls on the Catholic Church. Cuba's Ministry of the Interior uses methods such as surveillance, infiltration, and harassment of religious professionals and laypersons to control and monitor the country's religious institutions. While apolitical worship is allowed in government-approved sites, doing so usually invites government surveillance and harassment. The government regularly monitors all religious publications and controls the importation of religious publications such as the Bible. The level of harassment and monitoring of approved religions has dropped since 1999 but remains present. However, unapproved religions are experiencing higher levels of harassment. To be legal, religious groups must register, and registration is often denied.[21]

A *state controlled religion – negative attitude* policy is one in which the state sets up an officially recognized religious organization or organizations, which it dominates and controls. Yet no religion is declared the official religion of the state. The state has an extremely negative attitude toward religion but is unable to eliminate religiosity among its citizens, so it instead allows religious expression but only in the context of religious organizations run and tightly controlled by the state. Thus, although the state is supporting religious organizations, the purpose is not to support religion, much less declare an official religion. Rather, the purpose is clearly to limit and control religion.

---

[20] Constitution of Mozambique, www.unhcr.org/refworld/category,LEGAL,,,MOZ,4a1e597b2, 0.html.

[21] Lena Lopez, "Cuba: Draconian New Restrictions on 'Home Religious Meetings'," Forum 18, September 15, 2005, www.forum18.org/Archive.php?article_id=652; "Cuba OKs Organized Religious Services in Prisons," *Human Rights Without Frontiers*, 2009, www.hrwf.net/index .php?option=comcontent&view=article&id=179:news-2009&catid=38:freedom-of-religion-and-belief&Itemid=90; Howard Friedman, "Cuba Improves Relations with Vatican as Castro Attends Beatification Mass," Religion Clause delivered by Newstex, December 3, 2008.

China's religion policy fits this description. The government recognizes five religions, Buddhism, Taoism, Islam, Catholicism, and Protestantism. For each of these faiths, the government has established a "patriotic" association that monitors, registers, and supervises all religious activities for the faith. The leaders of these organizations have a close working relationship with the government, are sometimes paid by the government and support the leadership of the Communist Party. The government funds activities by these organizations including building and repairing places of worship. The State Administration of Religious Affairs (previously the Religious Affairs Bureau) supervises these organizations. The Public Security Bureau monitors and enforces religious regulations and acts against religious behavior that violates laws or regulations, including the establishment of religious organizations not recognized by the state. The extent of harassment of unregistered religions varies by region in China, with small unregistered groups sometimes tolerated but larger groups generally harassed and pressured to join the existing patriotic associations. The draconian repression of the Falun Gong in China is precisely because it was able to organize a massive protest under the Chinese government's radar and is, accordingly, seen as a political threat.[22]

The final category, *specific hostility*, refers to governments that oppose all religion in the state for ideological reasons. Currently, only North Korea fits this profile, but before 1990, most countries in the Soviet bloc likely also belonged in this category. The country supports a secular national ideology called *Juche* (translated as "self-reliance"). The core principle of the ideology is that "man is master of everything and decides everything." It focuses on three separate principles: independence in politics, self-sustenance in the economy, and national self-defense. The ideology focuses on the person of leader, instilling him as the spiritual head of the nation. The leader becomes a "god," and citizens are constantly exhorted to glorify Kim Jong-il and his father. Although many might consider this a national religion, for the purposes of this project, I consider this a nonreligious nationalist ideology. Traditional religions are highly limited in North Korea. The extent of this limitation is unclear due to conflicting reports. One set of reports claims that small numbers of individuals whose families were religious before the rise of the Communist regime or who were personally religious before then can gather for worship without leaders or religious materials. However, these people are segregated from the rest of the population and persecuted. Other reports state that no religion is tolerated

---

[22] Carlson (2005); Huanzhong (2003); Lai (2006); "White Paper – Freedom of Religious Belief in China," Embassy of the People's Republic of China in the United States, October 1997, www.china-embassy.org/eng/zt/zjxy/t36492.htm; Magda Hornemann, "State-Imposed Religious Monopolies Deny China's Religious Reality," Forum 18, December 5, 2006, www.forum18.org/Archive.php?article_id=883; Magda Hornemann, "State Attempts to Control Religious Leaderships," Forum 18, June 15, 2005, www.forum18.org/Archive.php?article_id=584; Magda Hornemann, "How the Public Security System Controls Religious Affairs," Forum 18, September 29, 2004, www.forum18.org/Archive.php?article_id=422.

other than among foreigners. Although there are officially sanctioned churches, defectors claim that the official churches were "just buildings" used for show to create a pretense of religious freedom to visitors and diplomats. There are multiple reports that members of unrecognized religions have been beaten, arrested, and executed, as well as subjects in biological warfare experiments. While detailed information is difficult to obtain, reports estimated that between 50,000 and 100,000 people were imprisoned in 2000 because of their religious beliefs.[23]

Persistence and Change in State Religion Policy

Between 1990 and 2008, 21 of the 177 states in this study made sufficiently significant changes to their religion policy that they switched between the 14 categories described in the preceding section. Fifteen of them began supporting religion more strongly or became less hostile to religion, and six lowered their level of support for religion. Thus, the shifts in religion policy one would expect in a world where secular and religious interests compete are present. However, the overall religion policy of 88.1% of countries did not change during this period. This is a remarkable level of stability. As will be seen in Chapters 4, 5, and 6, many more states than this made some form of change in their policy, but, based on the findings presented here, most of these changes were smaller ones within the context of a more stable overall policy.

The changes in policy in which states lowered their support for religion in a sufficiently substantial manner to result in a category change were as follows:

- As noted earlier, Sweden removed its official religion in 2000, resulting in a policy change from active support to supportive.
- In 2007, Nepal underwent a fundamental regime change with the rise of a Maoist government, which included the end of the monarchy and a new constitution. As part of this change, its religion policy changed from Hinduism as the preferred religion to a supportive policy.
- In 1992, Paraguay enacted a new constitution that declared the country has no official religion, removing Catholicism as the country's official religion. As a result, it changed from a policy of active support of Catholicism to Catholicism as the preferred religion. Put differently, in this case, little

---

[23] Magda Hornemann, "Religious Freedom Non-existent, but Much Still Unknown," Forum 18, March 29, 2006, www.forum18.org/Archive.php?article_id=752; Magda Hornemann, "Christians Murdered, Sources State," Forum 18, October 14, 2004, www.forum18.org/Archive.php?article_id=431; "White Paper on Religious Freedom in North Korea," Database Center for North Korean Human Rights, 2009, www.uscirf.gov/north-korea.html; Christian Caryl and B.J. Lee, "Houses of the Hidden," *Newsweek*, September 24, 2007; Examining the Plight of Refugees: The Case of North Korea," United States Senate Judiciary Committee Testimony, June 21, 2002, www.uscirf.gov/north-korea.html; Kim Hyung-jin, "Does Genuine Religious Freedom Exist in Communist North Korea," *Yonhap News*, May 18, 2007.

changed other than the official declaration of Catholicism as the official religion.
- As noted earlier, in 2005, Sudan removed Islam as the official religion, resulting in a change in policy of active support of Islam to Islam as the preferred religion. Here, too, little changed in practice other than the declaration of an official religion.
- As a result of the invasion of Iraq by allied forces, it underwent a significant regime change. This included a change from a policy of state-controlled religion – positive attitude to active support of Islam.
- In 2001, Portugal passed the Religious Freedom Act, which created a recognition system for religions that would give them the same rights and benefits as Catholicism, but, in practice, Catholicism is still preferred over these other religions. This resulted in a policy change from preferred religion to multitiered, one religion preferred.

The following are the 15 states that changed their religion policy to more strongly favor religion or be less hostile to it:

- A 1998 Austrian law establishes a multitiered recognition system adding two intermediate tiers to the system established by an 1874 law, which already recognized religious "societies" that have extensive rights. The new law establishes "confessional communities" and "religious associations," which have fewer rights and privileges than religious societies. This resulted in a policy change from cooperation to multitiered preferences – multiple religions.[24]
- A 2002 Czech Republic law established a two-tier registration system for religions. Entry-level registration requires 300 signatures and gains limited benefits. A top-tier registration requires 10 years registered at the entry level and membership of at least 0.1% of the population. Top-tier religions are eligible for more benefits including government funding. This resulted in a policy change from cooperation to multitiered preferences – multiple religions.[25]
- A series of negotiated agreements between Luxembourg and Roman Catholic, Greek and Russian Orthodox, Jewish, and some Protestant denominations' religious institutions, which came into effect in 1998, grants these institutions privileges including government funds that are not granted to other religions. This resulted in a policy change from supportive to cooperation.
- In 2001 Slovakia signed a Concordant with the Vatican giving the Catholic Church special privileges not given to other religions. This resulted in a

---

[24] 1998 Austrian Law on Legal Personalities for Confessional Communities, www.religlaw.com.
[25] Law on Churches and Religious Societies, No. 3/2002 of November 27, 2001.

Establishment, Support, Neutrality, or Hostility

policy shift from multitiered – multiple religions preferred to multitiered – one religion preferred.[26]

- While a 1991 law passed in the Ukraine shortly after independence declares freedom of religion, a 1993 amendment to this law limits religious freedom for "nonnative" religions. The law is, in practice, applied to several minority religions. This resulted in a policy change from supportive to cooperation.[27]
- In 1991, Vietnam, which had previously repressed all religion, began allowing religious practices through closely supervised but recognized religious organizations. This resulted in a policy change from specific hostility to state-controlled religion-negative attitude.[28]
- In 2001, Yemen began a process in which it took control of all Islamic education in the country to eradicate teachings encouraging religious extremism and sectarianism. In 2003, it began dismissing religious figures who preached against the regime. This resulted in a policy change from active support to state controlled religion-positive attitude.[29]
- Until 1994 the constitution of Zaire (now the Democratic Republic of Congo) allowed significant government regulation of religion. The 1994 and later constitutions provided for religious freedom, and since then the government has engaged in minimal regulation of religion and support for religion. This resulted in a policy change from separationist to accommodation.[30]
- In 1992, Cuba changed its constitution to remove references to scientific materialism and atheism. It still heavily regulates and restricts religion. This resulted in a policy change from specific to nonspecific hostility.[31]
- A 1996 amendment to the Zambian constitution declared the country a Christian nation, establishing an official religion. This represents a policy change from Christianity as the preferred religion to active support for Christianity.[32]
- In Equatorial Guinea, a 1992 presidential decree declares an official preference for the Catholic and Reformed Churches. However, in practice, Catholicism is preferred, including in the areas of education and representation at official state events. This represents a policy change from cooperation to Catholicism as the preferred religion.

---

[26] "Slovakia, Vatican Concordant Still Controversial," CWNews.com/Keston, www.cin.org/archives/cinjub/20001 1/0225.html.

[27] Law of Ukraine on Freedom of Conscience and Religious Organizations, www.religilaw.com.

[28] Seth Mydans, "Thi Cau Journal; Vietnam, a Convert Pursues Capitalism Devoutly." *New York Times*, April 5, 1996; "Vietnam's New Ordinance on Religion," Human Rights without Frontiers, www.hrwf.net/religiousfreedom/news/2004PDF/ Vietnam_2004.pdf.

[29] Day (2008); "Yemen Curb Extremism in Religious Teaching," United Press International, July 15, 2004.

[30] Constitution of the Democratic Republic of Congo, www.presidentrdc.cd/constitution.html.

[31] Constitution of Cuba, http://pdba.georgetown.edu/Constitutions/Cuba/cuba.html.

[32] Constitution of Zambia, www.religlaw.org.

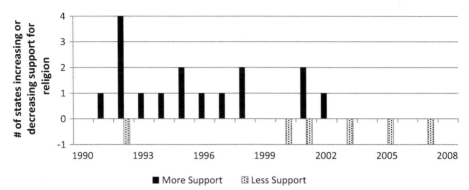

FIGURE 3.1. Number of States Changing Their Religion Policy, 1990 to 2008.

- Yugoslavia's 1992 constitution made radical changes in state religion policy from one that was separationist to one that was supportive of religion in a multitiered preferences – multiple religions format. This policy carried forward when Yugoslavia formally became Serbia.[33]
- Mongolia changed its religion policy twice. In 1992, a new constitution declared religious freedom, which began a transition from a policy of nonspecific hostility to a separationist policy. After an amendment to the state religion law in 1995, the government began supporting Buddhism, leading to a multitiered preferences – one religion policy.[34]
- Russia's 1997 Law on Freedom of Conscience lists Christianity, Judaism, Islam, and Buddhism as "traditional" religions and recognizes the "special contribution of Orthodoxy to the history of Russia and to the establishment and development of Russia's spirituality and culture." This resulted in a policy shift from cooperation to a multitiered preferences – one religion policy.[35]
- Somalia is a complicated case that is difficult to classify. In the 1990s, Islamic courts began to assert more power, and, in time, Muslim militant militias also exerted influence, on and off depending on the state of the internal military situation. While Islam was always dominant in Somalia, in 1995, a draft constitution declared Islam the official religion, as do subsequent draft constitutions. The RAS project codes Somalia as having a preferred religion until 1995 when it began actively supporting Islam as an official religion.[36]

These shifts show an interesting pattern, which is presented in Figure 3.1. The majority of increases in support for religion (or decreases in hostility) took

[33] The various constitutions of Yugoslavia and Serbia are available at www.religlaw.com.
[34] Law on the Relationship between the State and Religious Institutions, www.religlaw.org; Constitution of Mongolia, www.wipo.int/wipolex/en/text.jsp?file_id=183021.
[35] Russian Law on Freedom of Conscience and Religious Associations, 1997, www.religlaw.org.
[36] "Somalia; Islam Is Official Religion, Conversion Is Banned," *Africa News*, September 21, 2006; www.chr.up.ac.za/index.php/documents-by-country-database/somalia.html.

place in the 1990s, and the majority of decreases in support occurred between 2000 and 2007. However, this is not reflected in the other variables examined in Chapters 4, 5, and 6.

That being said, the overall pattern in official religion policies is one of stability. Relatively few countries changed their religion policies sufficiently to change categories, and even fewer changed sufficiently in a manner that can be considered radical. Only five switched between having and not having an official religion. As we will see in the next three chapters, most states did change aspects of their religions policies by increasing or decreasing levels of religious support, regulation, and discrimination. However, these changes mostly took place within the context of a more stable overall policy.

For example, in 2007 Argentina increased its level of support for the Catholic Church by giving it licensing preferences for radio frequencies, a large degree of autonomy for parochial schools and school subsidies. However, none of this changed its overall policy of active support. None of these types of support constitute more government institutional control over the Catholic Church, nor do they involve enforcing the religion on the population. Rather, they involve support of the general type that the government had already been providing. Thus, there was an increase in the level of support but no change in the meta-policy.

Conclusions

A state's official religion policy is a critical element of how it deals with religion. Yet this is a topic that has been neglected in the comparative literature. Previous discussions of the issue are most often philosophical discussions of what a state ought to do and usually focus on what the term *separation of religion and state* should mean.

The comparative studies that take official religion policy into account tend to simply differentiate between states that have official religions and those that do not (e.g., Barret et al., 2001). I argue here that this distinction is simplistic and, more important, that it masks a complex reality. Each of the 14 categories of policy I examine here, 4 of which involve official religions and 10 of which do not, is recognizably distinct from all of the other categories. That is, the states in each category have chosen to relate to religion in a manner that is identifiably and significantly different from those in all of the other categories. For example, placing *religious states* in the same category as those with an *active state religion* undermines our ability to understand that there are critical differences in the policies of these states, even though all of them declare an official religion. Put bluntly, Afghanistan and Costa Rica should not be in the same category just because both have official religions. Their policies are vastly different. The same is true of pairings such as Iran and Iceland, Pakistan and Norway, and Saudi Arabia and Denmark.

Even within a single category, there can be considerable diversity, as has been discussed in detail in this chapter. In some cases, the categories can even be said to overlap. This is especially true of the overlap between the *active state religion* and *preferred religion* categories. In practice, many of the states that have *preferred religions* – supporting a single religion but not declaring an official one – support religion more strongly than do states with *active state religions*.

Because of this, it is possible to argue that it would be desirable to completely ignore whether a state has an official religion and simply look at its policy in practice. Although there is merit to this argument, I posit that paying heed to the official religion element is important for at least five reasons. First, the official religion element is one of the few distinctions that already exists in the comparative literature (e.g., Barret et al., 2001; Barro & McCleary, 2005; Madeley & Enyadi, 2003). Its centrality to the literature means that dropping it may be too radical a departure from current thinking. Second, the fact that a state declares an official religion is in and of itself important. It is not the only factor that determines religion policy in practice, but it is a significant influence. Third, declaring an official religion has significant normative implications. Saying a state has an official religion is a statement of the state's decisions regarding not just religion but also culture, ideology, and ethics. Fourth, it requires a formal decision, usually involving amending the country's constitution, to back out of this policy while a policy of unofficial support for religion can be ended by a series of smaller decisions to stop engaging in a number of more specific policies that cumulatively result in supporting a religion.

Finally, the results presented here show a significant amount of change in this aspect of state religion policy with 21 states changing their policies in a manner that caused them to shift categories. This supports the competition perspective in that we would expect the struggle between political secularism and religious political actors to produce some shifts in policy. As we will see in following chapters, these shifts are the tip of a large iceberg made up of smaller but significant changes in state religion policy. The 14 categories used here are helpful in producing this result in that if this study were limited to the traditional distinction between states with and without official religions, only five states would have been found to shift policies.

Again, it is important to emphasize that these results also show that most states support, either officially or unofficially, one or a few religions more than others. From the prism of Gill's (2008) argument that religion policy is dependent on the interests of politicians, this means state support for religion is widely seen as a useful policy. Its mechanisms for social control are effective and less expensive than using force and repression to maintain social order. It also means that politicians see the costs of supporting religion worth the value they receive from it. However, it is difficult to argue that belief plays no role in this finding.

Overall, the categorization system discussed in this chapter is designed to help understand the official meta-policies on religion that exist in the world today. However, this type of examination remains too abstract and general to fully understand state religion policy. In fact, the RAS project has identified 51 ways a state can support religion; 29 ways it can control, limit, or regulate majority religions; and 30 ways it can restrict the religious practices and institutions of minority religions. A state's stance on these 110 more specific potential policies constitutes the lion's share of what determines a state's religion policy. The next three chapters examine these 110 policies.

4

State Support for Religion

"Do as I say, not as I do" is an old saying often used to describe hypocrisy by the clergy. It also highlights the fact that there is often a significant difference between theory and practice with regard to religion. This distinction is critical in understanding the extent of state support for religion. In the previous chapter, I examined official religion policies of states – whether they have an official religion and, if not, to what extent do they institute a formal regime that privileges some religions or limits all religion. The analysis in this chapter demonstrates that while official religion policy is related to actual levels of support for religion by governments, it is by no means fully determinative.

Unlike a state's overall official religion policy, which changes rarely, change in these more specific laws and policies is common. As described in more detail later in the chapter, 92 (52.0%) of the countries in this study changed their level of support for religion, as opposed to the 21 (11.9%) that changed their official religion policy, making changes in religious support 4.4 times more common than changes in official religion policy. This implies that the tensions between the religious and the secular forces in society described in the secular-religious competition perspective appear to more often cause movement in specific types of government support for religion than in the overall official religion policy. Put differently, a victory in this competition is most likely to be the passing or revocation of a specific law or policy rather than an overall change in the government's formal religious regime.

More important, in this competition, those seeking more state support for religion are having more victories. The analysis in this chapter demonstrates that the contest between political secularism and religious actors described in the competition perspective is active in this policy area. Both sides have had successes, but overall, the religious forces are making significant inroads. There are certainly instances of decreases in government support for religion, but the 72 countries that increased their levels of support outnumber the 20 that decreased it by a ratio of 3.6 to 1. This general pattern is, with a few exceptions, consistent across specific categories of government support for religion as well as specific laws and policies. In fact, of the 51 types of law and policy examined here, 35 were more common in 2008 than in 1990, and only 6 were less common.

Some of the more common changes include providing religious education in public schools (added by 11 countries), the funding of private religious schools (added by 10 countries), and the establishment of a religious affairs department in the government (added by 19 countries but removed by 2). The only type of law to decrease dramatically was bans on either being homosexual or engaging in homosexual sex. This type of ban was dropped in 12 countries but instituted in 1. No other category of law was removed by more than 4 countries. Overall, among 177 states between 1990 and 2008, 192 new laws, policies, and practices supporting religion, as measured by Round 2 of the Religion and State (RAS2) dataset, were instituted and 57 were repealed or ended. Thus, these laws are a major battleground between religious and secular political actors, and at least between 1990 and 2008, the religious actors have had the upper hand.

All of this means that government support for religion is on the rise. This increased support spans the entire spectrum of ways a state can support religion. The following discussion examines each of the 51 types of law and policies that in some way support religion and religious institutions. I divide these laws and policies into categories based on the subject matter of the law or policy. This includes religious precepts guiding or determining law or policy, which I further divide into the following subcategories based on the topic of these laws and policies: relationships, sex, and reproduction; restrictions on women; and other religious precepts. It also includes the enforcement of religion, funding religion, the entanglement of religious and government institutions, and other forms of support for religion.

Support versus Control

Supporting religions through legislation and policy is inexorably intertwined with control. That is, when a government supports a religion, that religion becomes to some degree dependent on the government and more susceptible to government control even if control was not the original motivation for the support. On the other side of the coin, a good tactic to control religion is to support it and make that support dependent on some element of government control (Cosgel & Miceli, 2009: 403; Demerath, 2001: 204; Grim & Finke, 2011: 207). The category of state-controlled religion – negative attitude described in the previous chapter is an example of this phenomenon.

This link between support and control also applies to specific types of support. For example, when a government supports religious education, it can control who teaches these classes and exactly what is taught. Similarly, if a government supports a religious institution, it can control aspects of that institution's inner workings such as the appointment of religious officials such as bishops (Kuru, 2009: 8; 166–167; Roy, 2007: 27–28).

Toft et al. (2011: 34–35) discuss this relationship by outlining six factors that influence a religion's independence from the state. They argue that three activities that support religion undermine its independence: the establishment of a state religion, state control over religious finances, and giving religious leadership a formal part in the political process.[1] If we expand the definition of establishment to include legislating aspects of religious doctrine as law, financing religion, and the creation of government bodies to enforce religious precepts, nearly all of the 51 types of support for religious legislation are included in this general observation. Thus, even when not intended as such, support for religion nearly always involves some element of control.

Given this, while support for religion, as measured by the RAS2 dataset, is a good measure of the extent to which a state actually supports religion, it is not a perfect one. The same activity may be intended to support religion in some states but intended to control it on others. Also, it is likely that even states that genuinely wish to support religion are also, at least in part, motivated by control. In some states, such as China, which is discussed in detail in Chapter 3, the motivation – in this case, control – is clear. But in others, it is less clear.

Kuhle (2011) documents this dynamic in the five Nordic states of Denmark, Finland, Iceland, Norway, and Sweden. All of these states have a positive attitude toward Christianity in general and the Lutheran Church in particular, with all of them except Sweden supporting it as the official religion. All of them finance religion and the churches perform tasks for the state such as maintaining graveyards. Yet as Kuhle (2011: 211) notes, "A close relationship between state and church entails a risk of the state interfering with what some would regard as 'internal' religious questions." These governments have, with some success, pressured the churches to adopt their doctrines on issues such as gay marriage and the ordination of women.

Thus, a law supporting religion cannot on its own be considered prima fascia evidence that a state intends to support religion. However, it is proof that religion is something important in that state – sufficiently important that a state wants to support it, control it, or both. Put differently, whatever the state's true motivation, supporting religion is a clear indication that religion is not irrelevant politically. Also, given a sufficient number of types of support, the contention that a government's motivation is only to control religion becomes less tenable.

More important, there are a number of measures a government can take that are more directly focused on controlling religious institutions and limiting their political influence. The presence of support with low levels of direct control

---

[1] The other three factors are freedom of worship, who selects the religious leadership, and that transnational religious organizations tend to be more independent from state control.

Legislating Religious Precepts as Law

The concept of legislating religious precepts involves governments taking religious doctrines and laws and legislating them into state law or enforcing them in some other manner. Put differently, this refers to when states either directly or indirectly base a law or policy on holy scriptures such as the Bible or Koran, or formal bodies of religious law such as Sharia law. Because of the large number of laws in this category, I subdivide it into three categories: (1) laws on relationships, sex, and reproduction; (2) laws restricting women; and (3) other laws that enact religious precepts.

This type of law is one of the less ambiguous forms of support for religion. Legislating a religious law, dogma, or precept is to use the apparatus of the state to enforce a religion. Although this inevitably entails an element of control, other policies such as financing religion and controlling religious institutions are likely more effective if the intention is to control religion rather than support it. Thus, the presence of these types of laws is arguably a good indicator of a government desire to support religion. One hundred and forty-one states (79.7%) have at least one of these laws, 93 (52.0%) have at least two types, and 30 (15.8%) have at least five types. Thus, most states to some extent support religion in this manner, but only a minority do so extensively.

Relationships, Sex, and Reproduction

Laws focusing on relationships, sex, and reproduction are particularly important because the vast majority of human beings will at some point in their lives marry, have sex, and have children. These are basic aspects of human existence.

As shown in Table 4.1, religious precepts influence legislation on these matters in the overwhelming majority of states. This table, as well as the next several, is designed to examine the number of states that engage in each of the 51 types of support for religion examined by the RAS project. This also includes change in support between 1990 (or the earliest year available) and 2008 as well as how this support differs across religious traditions.

Personal status defined by religion or clergy: Personal status refers to laws regarding marriage, divorce, and burial. This is a basic aspect of government policy and all states legislate on this issue. Throughout the study period, 19.2% of states based all or some of these laws on religious precepts. While this religious influence is present in states whose majorities belong to other religious traditions, Muslim-majority states are the most likely to base personal status on religious law. Interpretations of Sharia law regarding marriage and divorce differ, but it contains a number of provisions that are common to most interpretations. Men have little difficulty divorcing their wives, even without cause or the woman's consent, but it is difficult to impossible (depending on the

TABLE 4.1. *Legislating Religious Precepts: Laws on Relationships, Sex, and Reproduction*

	All States			Majority Religion (2008 results)					
				Christian					
	1990*	2008	Catholic	Orthodox	Other Christian	Christian Total	Muslim	Other Religions
Personal status defined by religion or clergy	19.2%	19.2%	2.3%	7.7%	4.9	4.1%	53.2%	15.6%
Marriages performed by clergy of at least some religions are given automatic civil recognition, even in the absence of a state license	21.5%	23.2%	36.4%	23.1%	17.1%	26.5%	21.3%	15.6%
Restrictions on interfaith marriages	15.3%	15.3%	0.0%	0.0%	0.0%	0.0%	53.2%	6.3%
Restrictions on intimate interactions between unmarried heterosexual couples	4.0%	4.5%	0.0%	0.0%	0.0%	0.0%	17.0%	0.0%
Laws that specifically make it illegal to be a homosexual or engage in intimate homosexual interactions	39.0%	32.8%	4.5%	0.0%	41.5%	19.4%	59.6%	34.4%
Prohibitive restrictions on abortion	69.5%	67.2%	72.7%	7.7%	65.9%	61.2%	78.7%	68.8%
Restrictions on access to birth control	4.0%	4.0%	0.0%	0.0%	2.4%	1.0%	8.5%	6.3%
% of countries with at least one of these laws	80.2%	75.7%	84.1%	23.1%	75.6%	72.4%	85.1%	71.9%
% of countries with two or more of these laws	51.4%	49.2%	31.8%	15.4%	48.8%	36.7%	78.7%	43.8%
% of countries with three or more of these laws	19.2%	19.2%	0.0%	7.3%	7.3%	3.1%	51.0%	21.9%
Mean number of laws	1.72	1.66a	1.16	0.38	1.32	1.12	2.91	1.47

* In some countries, this represents the first available year.

interpretation) for a woman to divorce without her husband's consent. Muslim men may marry non-Muslim women, but Muslim women may not marry non-Muslim men. When divorces occur in these mixed marriages, the women are rarely granted custody of their children to ensure that the children are raised as Muslims. Sharia law allows men to have up to four wives, although many Muslim-majority states prohibit polygamy. For example, in Malaysia, marrying a second wife requires specific judicial permission, which is rarely granted (Reddy, 1995: 620). In most cases, these Muslim-majority countries allow religious minorities to use their own laws to determine personal status or have a civil code on the matter that applies only to non-Muslims.

Many cases of non-Muslim countries that are coded as basing personal status laws on religion are cases in which Muslims living in these countries are given some level of autonomy to use Sharia law as the basis for their family law. For instance, in the Philippines, the Code of Muslim Personal Laws recognizes Sharia law as part of national law, but it applies only to Muslims and does not include criminal law. Singapore's constitution states that Sharia law and courts determine personal status for Muslims.[2] In Tanzania, if both parties agree, marriage and divorce can be determined by Sharia.

In some countries, the application of religious law is more general. For example, in Israel all marriages are guided by Jewish, Christian, or Muslim law. There is no option for civil marriage, but divorce is possible in the civil courts. In Bhutan, family law is determined by Buddhism, but the Hindu minority may use Hindu traditions. In India, both Hindus and Muslims are subject to their own religion's laws for personal status (Mahmood, 2006: 765; Stephens, 2007: 256; Yildirim, 2004: 913). The 1923 Treaty of Lausanne gives Muslims in Thrace the right to use Sharia law to determine family law, but this does not apply in the rest of Greece. However, in Greece, all burials are religious.[3] In Sri Lanka, personal status is determined by the customary law of one's ethnic group. This includes Sharia law for Muslims.

Marriages performed by clergy of at least some religions are given automatic civil recognition, even in the absence of a state license. This type of law, which is present on a roughly equal basis across religious traditions, goes beyond allowing clergy to perform marriage ceremonies. In these countries, a religious ceremony is sufficient to be legally binding without any government certification or license. For example, in Spain, three religions recognized as "well-known deeply rooted beliefs" have bilateral agreements with the government, giving them privileges including automatic civil validity to weddings that these organizations perform.

Restrictions on interfaith marriages. These restrictions are found almost exclusively in Muslim states and refer to the Sharia restrictions on Muslim

---

[2] "Secularism, the Singapore way," *The Straits Times* (Singapore), October 30, 2007, http://academic.lexisnexis.co.il.proxy1.athensams.net/Bar-Ilan-University/academicuniverse.
[3] Helena Smith, "Greek Church Stirs Holy War over ID Cards," *The Observer*, May 28, 2000.

women marrying non-Muslim men. One interesting exception is Israel. Because all marriages in Israel are under religious auspices, interfaith marriages are effectively impossible. However, Israel's Interior Ministry recognizes marriages performed outside of Israel that are valid in the country where they were performed. These "foreign" marriages are popular to the extent that more Israelis get married in Cyprus – perhaps the most popular destination for Israelis seeking a civil marriage – than do Cypriots and Cyprus's application forms for marriage are available in Hebrew.

Restrictions on intimate interactions between unmarried heterosexual couples. Put simply, this category refers to a ban on premarital sex. This type of law is found exclusively in Brunei, Iran, Kuwait, Malaysia, the Maldives, Pakistan, Saudi Arabia, and the United Arab Emirates (UAE), all conservative Muslim countries. In Saudi Arabia, not only is premarital sex banned, there is full gender segregation. Public spaces such as busses are fully segregated, and it is a crime for members of opposite genders who are not related to be alone.[4] Iran similarly segregates the genders in public spaces. Women are forbidden from mixing with unmarried men and those who are not relatives. Women have separate seating on public busses and separate entrances into public buildings. Women are also restricted from attending male sporting events. In the UAE, adultery, prostitution, consensual premarital sex, and pregnancy outside marriage are all illegal and can result in a sentence of flogging from Sharia courts. Pakistan's 1979 "Hudood" ordinances legislate several aspects of sharia including extramarital sex (Imran, 2005: 80). In both Pakistan and Saudi Arabia, there have been instances in which victims of rape were convicted of having extramarital sex.

Laws that specifically make it illegal to be a homosexual or engage in homosexual intimate interactions. This category focuses on laws that make homosexuality itself illegal and not whether homosexuals have equal rights. Between 1990 and 2008, this type of restriction has become less common. Twelve countries, 11 of them Christian-majority countries, ended this type of limitation on homosexuals, and 1, Bhutan, instituted them. Nevertheless, in 2008, 58 countries still considered being homosexual or engaging in homosexual sex illegal. The countries that dropped this type of law include six former Soviet bloc states – Armenia, Belarus, Georgia, Lithuania, Romania, and Russia – which dropped Communist era restrictions. In Latin America, Chile, Nicaragua, and Panama dropped these restrictions. In Nicaragua, for example, under 1992 legislation that was repealed in 2008, "anyone who induces, promotes, propagandizes or practices sexual intercourse between persons of the same sex commits the crime of sodomy and shall incur one to three years' imprisonment." This law not only criminalized same-sex relationships but was vague enough to allow

---

[4] Saudi Arabia Divorce and Family Law, www.international-divorce.com/d-saudi.htm.

prosecution for activities such as campaigning for LGBT rights or anyone providing sexual health information or services.[5]

All but 9 of the 58 states which still have this type of law are either Muslim states or in sub-Saharan Africa. These laws typically mandate prison terms for homosexuality. For instance, in Tunisia, the 1913 penal code makes all acts of sodomy illegal and punishable by imprisonment. In Egypt, homosexuality is not technically illegal, but homosexuals are often charged under other laws including one against "obscene behavior" and a law against the "contempt for religion." Sentences for these transgressions range from between 3 months and 5 years imprisonment.[6] In Swaziland, male-to-male relationships are punishable by 10 years imprisonment, but female-to-female relationships are not illegal. Cameroon bans sexual activities between persons of the same sex. Violations are punishable by 6 months to 5 years imprisonment and a fine of 20,000 to 200,000 francs.

Restrictions on abortion are the most common type of law in this category. The proportion of countries that restricted abortion dropped from 69.5% to 67.2% during the study period. I discuss this issue in more detail, including why I consider it an issue that is strongly correlated with religion, in Chapter 7.[7]

Restrictions on access to birth control exist in eight states. For example, in Myanmar, the government restricts the importation of all contraceptives. In Chad, contraceptives are not banned, but they are heavily restricted. A 1920 French colonial era law banning contraceptives altogether was rescinded in 1993. However, the government continues to heavily regulate the sale and distribution of contraceptives. Women may not acquire contraceptives without the consent of their spouses. Also, the government allows only authorized pharmaceutical companies to import contraceptives, and the sale of contraceptives requires a specific permit.

Laws regulating sex, reproduction, and relationships are unique for at least two reasons. First, they involve government intervention into aspects of people's lives that are among the most intimate and private. Second, they are the only category of religious law examined here that became less common between 1990 and 2008, dropping from being present in 80.2% of countries to 75.7%. This rare overall decrease in state support for religion is primarily attributable to a number of states removing restrictions on homosexuality and, to a lesser extent, reduced restrictions on abortion. In the other five categories, levels remained constant or increased.

---

[5] J. Roberts, "Nicaragua to Decriminalize Gay Sex," *Pink News*, 2007, www.pinknews.co.uk/news/articles/2005-6081.html.

[6] Dyan M. Neary, "Egypt Cracks Down on Homosexuality," The Earth Times.org, November 21, 2001, www.earthtimes.org/nov/humanrightsegyptcracksnov22_01.htm.

[7] The numbers presented in Chapter 7 are slightly different because they include more strict criteria, which include partial and limited restrictions.

That being said, in 2008, more than three-quarters of the world's countries intervened in this issue in a manner influenced by religion. Nearly half (49.2%) have at least two of these types of laws, and nearly one in five (19.2%) have laws in at least three of the seven categories examined here. This is important because it is likely that, with the possible exception of women's rights, these areas of policy are the subject of the most international political pressure by secular forces. Although this explains why this area of policy is the only topic examined here in which secular political forces have made significant inroads, it also demonstrates the resilience of religious political forces to maintain their influence on the state.

Laws Restricting Women

This category refers to restrictions on the freedom of women that are not imposed on men. Although several of the items in the previous category, especially restrictions on abortion, primarily limit women, they also apply to men. For example, even though it affects women more than men, abortion involves reproduction, a process that involves men. While restrictions on abortions do not influence a man's control over his body in the way it does a woman's control over hers, they can result in unwanted children, which can also significantly influence the lives of those children's fathers.

In contrast, the restrictions in this category do not restrict men at all and apply exclusively and directly to women. As can be seen in Table 4.2, these four types of legislation are nearly exclusively found in Muslim-majority states and mostly relate to how Sharia law treats women.

Women may not go out in public unescorted. In 2008, this form of restriction is present only in Saudi Arabia and Sudan. It was also present in Afghanistan while it was ruled by the Taliban regime. In Sudan, this was coded because of partial bans in some parts of the country. For example, in October 1996, the Khartoum state government passed the 1996 "Public Order Law," which separates the sexes and prevents "inappropriate acts" between them. Some of its provisions included a requirement that women may only engage in late-night shopping or ride a bus in the company of a male relative. The law also includes provisions such as compulsory separation of men and women at weddings, parties, and picnics as well as a ban on women wearing jewelry and perfume in restaurants.[8] In Saudi Arabia and Afghanistan (when it was applicable), the ban on women being in public without a male relative is more absolute.

Restrictions on the public dress of women other than the common restrictions on public nudity. This type of law requires the modest dress of women beyond what would be expected in most countries and always involves a manner of dress that has its basis in religious modesty laws. These laws range from requirements to cover one's hair to the full body and face coverings required in Saudi Arabia. These laws are mostly found in Muslim-majority countries

---

[8] "Sudan's Capital Bans Mixing of Sexes in Public," *New York Times*, October 27, 1996, p. A-4.

TABLE 4.2. *Legislating Religious Precepts: Laws Restricting Women*

| | All States | | Majority Religion (2008 results) | | | | | | |
| | | | Christian | | | | | | |
	1990*	2008	Catholic	Orthodox	Other Christian	Christian Total	Muslim	Other Religions
Women may not go out in public unescorted	1.7%	1.1%	0.0%	0.0%	0.0%	0.0%	4.3%	0.0%
Restrictions on the public dress of women other than the common restrictions on public nudity	2.3%	5.1%	0.0%	0.0%	2.4%	1.0%	17.0%	0.0%
Female testimony in government court is given less weight than maletestimony	10.7%	10.7%	0.0%	0.0%	0.0%	0.0%	40.4%	0.0%
Restrictions on women other than those listed above	11.3%	10.2%	0.0%	0.0%	2.4%	1.0%	34.0%	3.1%
% of countries with at least one of these laws	14.7%	15.8%	0.0%	0.0%	4.9%	2.0%	53.2%	3.1%
% of countries with two or more of these laws	7.9%	7.9%	0.0%	0.0%	0.0%	0.0%	29.8%	0.0%
% of countries with three or more of these laws	3.3%	3.8%	0.0%	0.0%	0.0%	0.0%	10.7%	0.0%
Mean number of laws	0.26	0.27	0.00	0.00	0.05	0.02	0.96	0.03

* In some countries, this represents the first available year.

and enforce some interpretation of Sharia law requirements for modest dress. Interestingly, only three countries – Brunei, Iran, and Saudi Arabia – had such laws in 1990. The other six that had such laws enacted them between 1990 and 2008. In Indonesia, Malaysia, and Nigeria, these laws are not national laws. Rather, they have been enacted by local governments. In Indonesia, the first such law was a 2002 law that required "Islamic dress" and was enforced sporadically. Other similar laws were subsequently passed by several regional and local governments in Indonesia. In some cases, these laws were limited to Fridays or to civil servants and in most cases they were enforced sporadically (Bush, 2008: 176–177; Crouch, 2006). Swaziland is an interesting case because it is the only non-Muslim-majority state to enact this type of law. Swaziland's king, Mswati III, believes that women wearing pants is part of a decline in Christian morality and has therefore banned such attire.[9]

Female testimony in government court is given less weight than male testimony. This type of law exists only in 19 Muslim-majority countries and comes directly from Sharia law. Sharia law mandates that in court, a woman's testimony is valued as half that of a man's. Thus, the word of two women is considered equal to that of one man. This puts women at a disadvantage in any legal dispute, whether it involves criminal, family, or civil law. In most of these countries, such as Egypt, Iran, Mauritania, and Saudi Arabia, this is applied in all courts. However, in some, such as Indonesia and Nigeria, this type of law applies only to Sharia courts, which are not always given jurisdiction of all aspects of law.

Other restrictions on women. This category is meant to encompass ways governments restrict women that are related to religion but do not fit into any of the other categories. Accordingly, the variable is coded for various reasons. In Algeria, women are considered minors under the guardianship of their husbands or fathers. In Kuwait, women are banned from jobs requiring them to work past 8 PM. In many Muslim-majority countries, women may not engage in certain activities without the permission of a male relative. These activities include the following:

- Traveling outside of the country (UAE, Syria, Libya, Kuwait, Jordan, Gabon, and Egypt)
- Working outside the home (UAE)
- Applying for a driver's license (Qatar)
- Taking out a loan (Lesotho)[10]

---

[9] Bill Ferguson, "Swazi King: Blessed Are the Skirt-Wearers," *The Macon Telegraph*, June 7, 2003.
[10] Bennoune (1995); "Catholics Free to Worship in Kuwait, Says Bishop," *Catholic News Agency*, June 22, 2007, www.catholicnewsagency.com/new.php?n=9701; "Empowering Women in Lesotho: Actions toward Gender Equality," Millennium Challenge Corporation and Making Headway, March 10, 2010, www.mcc.gov/documents/press/headway-2010002010901-ls-maleribe.pdf.

This sampling of the variety of restrictions against women does not include the more severe restrictions present in countries such as Iran, the Sudan, Saudi Arabia, and Afghanistan during Taliban rule, which include severe segregation of the sexes, among other restrictions.

Religious laws restricting women are mostly due to interpretations of Sharia law in some Muslim-majority countries. Only Saudi Arabia has all four types. Brunei, Iran, Nigeria, and Sudan have three types. They are present in just over half of Muslim countries but, unlike other aspects of religious legislation, are not substantially increasing. Few countries are adding new restrictions, and those that do so are balanced by countries removing them. Mostly, however, these laws are stable in that they tend to remain present where they exist and are rarely enacted where they do not. They are likely heavily linked to cultural attitudes toward women that are justified by religious dogma, which arguably contributes to their stability.

Other Instances of Legislation Religious Precepts

Nearly half of the types of religious precepts that countries commonly legislate are not easily broken down into smaller categories. As shown in Table 4.3, this type of religious legislation increased from being present in 50 to 55 states between 1990 and 2008.

Dietary laws. Ten Muslim-majority countries and Israel enforce religious dietary laws. In the case of Muslim countries, this generally refers to requirements that meat be slaughtered according to Islam's Halal requirements. In Israel, the official Rabbinate – which is a government agency – enforces standards for restaurants and food producers that want to be considered Kosher, but non-Kosher food is generally available and not illegal. Although it is illegal to raise pork "on" the land of Israel, pigs are commonly raised on platforms, creating a legal loophole where they are technically "above" the land of Israel.

Restrictions on the sale of alcoholic beverages. This category refers to a total ban on such sales and not restrictions on selling alcohol on the Sabbath. It is currently found only in Muslim countries and is related directly to a Sharia law ban on alcohol. This type of ban is increasing. In 1990, 21 countries had this type of ban. By 2008, Comoros, Indonesia, Nigeria, and Sudan had enacted a ban on alcohol. In both Nigeria and Indonesia these bans are by local and regional governments enacting various aspects of Sharia law due to pressure by local groups seeking to make their countries less secular.

Laws of inheritance are defined by religion. This involves cases in which inheritance is determined by religious laws. This type of law is present in the same 36 countries in 1990 and 2008. Thirty-one of these cases involve Muslim-majority countries applying Sharia law to inheritance. These laws disadvantage women but involve an equitable distribution of an estate among male heirs. In Kenya, this was coded because despite being a minority, inheritance laws for Muslims follows Sharia law. Similarly, Muslims in Tanzania may use Sharia

TABLE 4.3. *Legislating Religious Precepts: Other Laws*

	All States			Majority Religion (2008 results)						
					Christian					
	1990*	2008		Catholic	Orthodox	Other Christian	Christian Total	Muslim	Other Religions	
Dietary laws	6.8%	6.8%		0.0%	0.0%	0.0%	0.0%	23.4%	3.1%	
Restrictions or prohibitions on the sale of alcoholic beverages	11.9%	14.1%		0.0%	0.0%	0.0%	0.0%	53.2%	0.0%	
Laws of inheritance defined by religion	20.3%	20.3%		0.0%	0.0%	7.3%	3.1%	66.0%	6.3%	
Religious precepts used to define crimes or set punishment for crimes	5.6%	6.8%		0.0%	0.0%	0.0%	0.0%	25.5%	0.0%	
The charging of interest is illegal or significantly restricted	3.4%	2.8%		0.0%	0.0%	0.0%	0.0%	10.6%	0.0%	
General laws on public dress or appearance other than bans in public nudity and those applied specifically to women	0.6%	1.1%		0.0%	0.0%	0.0%	0.0%	2.1%	3.0%	
Restrictions on conversions away from the dominant religion	11.9%	13.6%		0.0%	0.0%	0.0%	0.0%	42.6%	12.5%	
Significant restrictions on public music or dancing other than the usual zoning restrictions	0.6%	2.8%		0.0%	0.0%	0.0%	0.0%	10.6%	0.0%	
Mandatory closing of some or all businesses during religious holidays including the Sabbath or its equivalent	8.5%	9.0%		2.3%	7.7%	12.2%	7.1%	14.9%	6.3%	
Other restrictions on activities during religious holidays including the Sabbath or its equivalent	7.3%	9.0%		0.0%	0.0%	9.8%	4.1%	23.4%	3.1%	
% of countries with at least one of these laws	28.2%	31.1%		2.3%	7.7%	26.8%	13.3%	72.3%	15.0%	
% of countries with three or more of these laws	11.9%	14.1%		0.0%	0.0%	0.0%	0.0%	51.0%	3.1%	
% of countries with five or more of these laws	6.8%	7.3%		0.0%	0.0%	0.0%	0.0%	27.6%	0.0%	
Mean number of laws	0.77	0.86c		0.02	0.08	0.29	0.14	2.70	0.34	

* In some countries, this represents the first available year.

law if both parties agree. In India and Sri Lanka, the laws of inheritance are determined by one's religion. In Ghana, tribal law, which includes religious elements, determines inheritance of land.

Religious precepts are used to define crimes or set punishment for crimes. The states that enact this kind of legislation are exclusively states that use Sharia law as the basis for their criminal law statutes. In 1990, 10 states followed this practice. By 2008, Iraq discontinued the practice but Nigeria, Somalia, and the Sudan began using Sharia law to define elements of criminal law. In Nigeria and Somalia, this imposition of Sharia criminal law is at the level of regional governments. In 1992, the Sudanese government adopted a new penal code based on traditional Islamic punishments, which included provisions for measures such as amputation and stoning for several violations.[11]

The charging of interest is illegal or significantly restricted. This type of law is based on Sharia law and is found only in Afghanistan, Mauritania, Saudi Arabia, Somalia, Sudan, and Yemen, all Muslim-majority states. Afghanistan dropped this restriction after the fall of the Taliban regime.

General laws on public dress or appearance other than bans on public nudity and those applied specifically to women. This type of law is rare, only found in two countries. Saudi Arabia requires modest dress of men, although not to the extent it requires modest dress of women. In Bhutan, a Buddhist-majority state, a 1999 decree requires that all citizens wear the Drukpa national dress.

Restrictions on conversions away from the dominant religion. This type of law is found mostly in Muslim states and is increasing. In 1990 (or the earliest year available), 21 states had such laws. By 2008, three more had added this type of law. This includes two Muslim states. Sudan banned conversion away from Islam as part of the 1991 Criminal Act. The proscribed punishment is death. This imposition of the death penalty for conversion away from Islam is present in other countries such as Saudi Arabia and Iran. Uzbekistan's 1998 Law on Freedom of Conscience and Religious Organizations bans "actions aimed at converting believers of one religion into another (proselytism) as well as any other missionary activities are prohibited."[12] However, this is enforced sporadically.

While 20 of the 24 states that restrict conversions are Muslim majority, 3 Buddhist- and 1 Hindu-majority states also restrict conversions. A 2007 royal decree in Cambodia bans using money or other incentives to bring about a conversion, but this rule does not apply to Buddhists. In Myanmar, while conversion away from Buddhism is not technically illegal, local governments regularly

---

[11] Hedges, Chris, "Sudan Presses Its Campaign to Impose Islamic Law on Non-Muslims," *New York Times*, June 1, 1992, p. A-6.

[12] Felix Corley, "Prisoners of Conscience Numbers Increase," Forum 18, Human Rights without Frontiers, July 29, 2008, www.hrwf.net/index.php?option=com_content&view=article&id=105:news-2008-catalogued-by-country&catid=38:freedom-of-religion-and-belief&Itemid=90.

harass such converts and engage in campaigns to reconvert them to Buddhism. This is part of a larger government campaign to convert non-Buddhists to Buddhism. Similarly, in Vietnam, there is no law against converting away from Buddhism. However, because religion is listed on identity cards, converts must apply for a new identity card with their new religion. Despite this, many converts do not apply for a new national identification card because the procedure is cumbersome and they fear government retribution. Local officials in rural communities often discourage conversion away from Buddhism by threatening converts with refusal of new identity documents and loss of education and social welfare allowances. In India, there is no national anticonversion law, but a number of Indian states have passed such laws. Many of these new state-level laws are post-1990.[13] I discuss this issue further in Chapters 6 and 7.

Significant restrictions on public music or dancing other than the usual zoning restrictions. This form of restriction is uncommon and exclusively found in Muslim-majority states but increasing. In 1990, it existed only in Saudi Arabia, but by 2008, this type of ordinance had been enacted in Indonesia, Malaysia, the Maldives, and Pakistan. In the Maldives, the Ministry of Islamic Affairs was created in 2008 and immediately began to engage in a number of activities to impose Islamic standards on the state including the closing of discos. In the other countries, these laws are not national laws and are, rather, laws passed by local governments. In Indonesia, beginning in 2002, a number of local governments began requiring entertainment facilities such as nightclubs to be closed during the Muslim month of Ramadan.[14] In Malaysia, this type of law is also at the local level. This first instance of such a law was a 1995 Kelantan State Government ban on all song and dance performances not

---

[13] Orissa (India) 1967 Freedom of Religion Act, http://indianchristians.in/news/content/view/1469/43; Madhya Pradesh (India) 1968 Dharma Swantantrya Adhiniyam Act, http://tinyurl.com/6jrwjsl; Chhattisgarh (India) 2006 Freedom of Religion (Amendment) Act, http://tinyurl.com/5rte9t7; Gujarat (India) 2003 Freedom of Religion Act, www.lawsofindia.org/single/alpha/13.html; Tamil Nadu (India) 2002 Prohibition of Forcible Conversion of Religion Ordinance, indianchristians.in/news/content/view/1509/43; Arunachal Pradesh (India) 1978 Freedom of Religion Act, http://tinyurl.com/6fjt3qm; Rajasthan (India) 2006 Freedom of Religion Bill., http://tinyurl.com/5w9gsvv; Himachal Pradesh (India) 2006 Freedom of Religion Act http://www.racindia.com/1073; "State Admits Few Complaints of 'Forced' Conversions," *Compass Direct News/International Christian Concern*, July 17, 2008, www.persecution.org/2008/07/20/state-admits-few-complaints-of-forced-conversions; "Rajasthan Passes New 'Anti-conversion' Bill," *Compass Direct News/International Christian Concern*, March 24, 2008, www.persecution.org/2008/03/25/rajasthan-passes-new-anti-conversion-bill; "'Anti-conversion' Law in Force in 4th State," *Compass Direct News/International Christian Concern*, October 8, 2007, www.persecution.org/2007/10/09/anti-conversion-law-in-force-in-4th-state; Nirmala Carvalho, "State Assembly Adopts anti-conversion Law in Gujarat," *AsiaNews/International Christian Concern*, September 20, 2006, www.persecution.org/2006/09/20/state-assembly-adopts-anti-conversion-law-in-gujarat.

[14] Crouch (2006); "Ramadan in Indonesia brings closure of nightclubs, saunas and pinball parlors: Report," Associated Press Worldstream, November 6, 2002.

directly religious in nature.[15] In 2003, Pakistan's Northwest Frontier Province passed a law limiting the sale of music and videos. This law has resulted in numerous arrests and store-closings but is enforced inconsistently.

Mandatory closing of some or all businesses during religious holidays including the Sabbath or its equivalent. This is the only type of general religion law found in all categories of states examined here. This is one of the few types of religious legislation found in the United States, as was discussed in more detail in Chapter 3. This type of law increased slightly with one country removing such a ban but two countries adding this type of law. Fiji had such a ban between 1989 and 1995. The ban prohibited organized sports, movies, nightclubs, and other businesses on Sundays.[16] Beginning in 2002, a number of local governments in Indonesia began banning activities during the month of Ramadan (Crouch, 2006). In 2002, Liberia began enforcing an old law forbidding the opening of business on Sundays.

Croatia is an interesting case for this type of law. In 2004 and 2008, the Catholic Church successfully pressured the government to ban Sunday shopping. In both cases, the courts declared the ban unconstitutional[17] because article 41 of Croatia's constitution declares separation of religion and state. This is an interesting example of a clash between the power of religious political actors and secular constitutional principles.

Other restrictions on activities during religious holidays including the Sabbath or its equivalent. In 1990 (or the earliest year available), 13 states engaged in this type of restrictions. By 2008, three more had enacted this type of restriction. In 2004, Comoros began arresting people for eating food, drinking alcohol, and smoking during the day during Ramadan. In Malaysia, beginning in 1996, a number of local governments passed similar laws enforcing bans on eating, drinking, or smoking in public during Ramadan. Many Muslim-majority states have similar laws that predate 1990. In Lebanon, the government ordered the closing of shops in Sidon on Fridays. These types of restrictions are also present in Christian countries. For example, in Switzerland, not only are stores closed on Sundays, work is generally prohibited. Aside from special professions, government approval is needed to work on Sunday.[18]

Overall, these instances of "other" religious precepts being enforced by governments are by far more common in Muslim-majority states. However,

---

[15] "Malaysia; Getting Serious about Fun; Recent Edicts by Kelantan's Ruling Party Draw Fire," *Asiaweek*, November 10, 1995.
[16] "Sunday Ban Delay," *The Dominion*, March 4, 1995; "Sunday Tee Time Angers Fijian Church," *Washington Post*, July 25, 1995.
[17] "Secular Croatia in the Grip of Catholic Church," *OneWorld See, News from South East Europe*, June 15, 2009, http://oneworldsee.org/node/18701.
[18] Labor Law of Switzerland, http://docs.google.com/gview?a=v&q=cache:oYMvqzRyebAJ:www.ch.ch/private/00551/00553/index.html%3Flang%3Den%26download%3DM3wBPgDB/8ull6Du36WenojQ1NTTjaXZNqWfVp3Uhmfhnapmmc7Zi6rZnqCkkIN2g3Z/bKbXrZ6lhuDZz8mMps2gpKfo+sunday+law+switzerland&hl=en.

there are many instances of them being present in non-Muslim states. In 2008, 34 Muslim-majority states had at least one of these laws, but so did 21 non-Muslim-majority states. Also, 13 Muslim-majority countries – Albania, Azerbaijan, Burkina Faso, Chad, Gambia, Guinea, Kyrgyzstan, Niger, Senegal, Tajikistan, Turkey, Turkmenistan, and the Turkish government of Cyprus – had no such laws. Not surprisingly, all of these countries are among those Muslim-majority countries with no official religion.

More important, overall these types of ordinance are increasing. In 1990 (or the earliest year available), 136 such laws or policies existed across 50 states. By 2008, 153 existed across 55 states, an increase of 12.5%. Thus, while the majority of the world's states do not have this type of policy either nationally or to a significant extent locally, the number of countries where such laws or policies exist is increasing, as are the number of such laws and policies in these countries.

Many of these laws and policies are not national but rather are enacted by a significant number of local governments; much of the increase in this type of policy is at this level. This indicates a grassroots support for the imposition of religious law as state law. This large-scale effort to influence regional and local governments is potentially a harbinger of future efforts and perhaps success at enacting these types of laws at the national level. This combined with the increase of laws in this category between 1990 and 2008 indicates that the trend is likely to continue into at least the immediate future. It is also evident that the struggle between political secularism and religious actors described in the competition perspective is active at the regional and local levels within many states and that religious actors are having considerable success at these levels.

General Patterns in Legislating Religious Precepts

Looking at the broader category of legislating religious precepts as law, there are at least two striking findings. First, with the notable exceptions of blue laws and laws restricting abortion and homosexuality, these types of laws are found most commonly, and often exclusively, in Muslim-majority states. This is not due to a lack of religious precepts that could be legislated in other religions such as Christianity, Hinduism, and Buddhism. Rather, in the 1990 to 2008 period, Muslim-majority states chose to support Islam in this manner much more often than non-Muslim-majority states. Among Muslim-majority states, this behavior is most common in states that declare Islam the official state religion.

Second, with the notable exceptions of limits on abortion and homosexuality, these types of laws have remained relatively stable over time but increased slightly. Much of the notable increases are due to activity by local and regional governments rather than national governments. Thus, at least at the national level, this aspect of religion policy is much the same in 2008 as it was in 1990. However, as already noted, the rise on regional- and local-level legislation may be a forerunner to future legislation at the national level.

Government Institutions or Laws That Enforce or Protect Religion

The presence of institutions, laws, and policies that enforce or protect religion are another form of support for religion. The enforcement aspect represents a specific devotion of resources to religion. Laws can be on the books, but they must be enforced to be effective. Police have numerous laws to enforce and will often prioritize the enforcement of some types of laws over others. Courts make similar decisions, and, in addition, when interpreting laws they will often balance various legal priorities (Beatty 2001; McConnell 1992). For example, protecting a religion from criticism might be balanced against the right to free speech. Police and courts whose mandate is specifically and exclusively to enforce religious laws and protect the religion do not have these mixed priorities. They are guided primarily or even exclusively by religious precepts. This constitutes a significant level of support, as do laws protecting religion from criticism. Religious institutions and precepts that are protected from criticism have a freer hand in society, thereby increasing their influence. The RAS2 dataset contains five variables measuring this phenomenon. These types of support are listed in Table 4.4.

Blasphemy laws, or any other restriction on speech about majority religion or religious figures. These laws, although most common in Muslim-majority states, can be found in many Christian-majority and other majority states. In 1990 (or the earliest year available), 39 states had this type of law. By 2008, Iraq, Mauritania, and Trinidad and Tobago dropped this type of law, but Bosnia, Lithuania, Nigeria, Romania, Russia, and Sudan enacted it, bringing the total to 42. For example, Article 29 of Russia's 1993 constitution states that "propaganda or campaigning to incite social, racial, national or religious hatred and enmity is impermissible. The propaganda of social, racial, national, religious or language supremacy is forbidden."[19] While the language is egalitarian, this clause has in practice been used to ban religious speech and texts considered critical of or at odds with the Orthodox Church.[20]

In some Muslim countries the blasphemy laws and enforcement are more severe. For example, in Pakistan blasphemy is a criminal offence punishable by 10 years imprisonment. Desecrating the name of Mohammed can, in theory,

---

[19] Constitution of Russia, www.rg.ru/2009/01/21/konstitucia-dok.html.
[20] Geraldine Fagan, "34 Jehovah's Witness Publications and One Congregation Banned," Forum 18, December 8, 2009; "Jehovah's Witness Gets Two Years in Prison for Possession of 'Extremist Literature'," *Asia News*, September 22, 2010, www.asianews.it/news-en/Jehovah%E2%80%99s-Witness-gets-two-years-in-prison-for-possession-of-%E2%80%9Cextremist-literature%E2%80%9D-19529.html; "Forbidden in Russia," *New York Times*, July 19, 2010; Sophia Kishkovsky, "Art Trial Reveals Clash of Russian Cultures," *New York Times*, July 8, 2010; Ben Judah "Russian Curators Anger Church but Escape Jail," *Reuters*, July 12, 2010; "What Happens When You Display Forbidden Art," *The Economist*, June 24, 2010; "Russian Church Condemns Jesus Christ Superstar," Mosnews.Com, May 2010 www.mosnews.com/society/2009/05/04/1457; "Russia Bans Books by Scientology Founder L. Ron Hubbard," AFP, April 22, 2010; "Surgut Extremist Case," Human Rights without Frontiers, September 11, 2010, www.hrwf.net.

TABLE 4.4. *Government Institutions or Laws That Enforce Religion*

	All States		Majority Religion (2008 results)					
			Christian					
	1990*	2008	Catholic	Orthodox	Other Christian	Christian Total	Muslim	Other Religions
Blasphemy laws, or any other restriction on speech about majority religion orreligious figures	22.0%	23.2%	9.1%	23.1%	9.8%	11.2%	57.4%	12.5%
Censorship of press or other publications on grounds of being anti religious	12.4%	13.6%	0.0%	7.7%	0.0%	1.0%	44.7%	3.1%
Presence of a police force or other government agency that exists solely to enforce religious laws	2.8%	4.5%	0.0%	0.0%	0.0%	0.0%	14.9%	0.0%
Presence of religious courts which have jurisdiction over matters of family law and inheritance	16.4%	18.1%	4.5%	7.7%	2.4%	4.1%	46.8%	28.8%
Presence of religious courts which have jurisdiction over some matters of law other than family law and matters of inheritance	6.2%	6.2%	0.0%	0.0%	0.0%	0.0%	23.4%	0.0%
% of countries with at least one of these laws	29.4%	31.1%	13.6%	23.1%	12.2%	14.3%	70.2%	25.0%
% of countries with two or more of these laws	16.4%	18.1%	0.0%	15.4%	0.0%	2.0%	57.4%	9.4%
% of countries with three or more of these laws	7.9%	8.5%	0.0%	0.0%	0.0%	0.0%	32.0%	0.0%
Mean number of laws	0.59	0.65	0.14	0.38	0.12	0.16	1.87	0.34

* In some countries, this represents the first available year.

result in a death sentence. Although death sentences have been handed out, no one has been executed. Because of pressure by religious extremists, including death threats to judges, acquittal of those accused of blasphemy is rare. Both Muslims and religious minorities in Pakistan are regularly charged with blasphemy.[21] While in most of the 27 Muslim-majority states with blasphemy laws, blasphemy is a criminal offense punishable by imprisonment, the death penalty for blasphemy is only present in Afghanistan (also post-Taliban), Iran, Pakistan, and Saudi Arabia. In many conservative Muslim countries such as Oman and Kuwait, these laws, although on the books, are enforced sporadically.

Censorship of the press or other publications on grounds of being antireligious. These laws are different from blasphemy laws in that they specifically apply to publications and involve government review and censorship of the printed word. In addition, this censorship does not need to be because of blasphemy. Rather, it can be any speech against religion, religious institutions, or religious figures. In 1990 (or the earliest year available), 22 countries engaged in this type of censorship. By 2008, Iraq had dropped this practice, but it was instituted in Afghanistan and Bangladesh. Other than Russia and India, all of the states with religious censorship policies or laws are Muslim-majority states.

Presence of a police force or other government agency that exists solely to enforce religious laws. In 1990 (or the earliest year available), Brunei, Iran, Libya, and Saudi Arabia had police forces or government departments devoted to enforcing religious laws. By 2008, Indonesia, Malaysia, and Nigeria formed these governmental units. In Malaysia, local governments, and eventually the prime minister's office, began forming police "snoop squads" tasked with investigating and enforcing conformance with religious practices, although since 2007, they have been limited by privacy laws to only to investigating public practices (Ling-Chien Neo, 2006: 108). In other countries such as Saudi Arabia, these police forces are more pervasive and strict.

Presence of religious courts that have jurisdiction over matters of family law and inheritance. This does not include cases in which the general courts enforce religious laws. Rather, it applies to cases in which separate religious courts exist that have jurisdiction over matters of family law and inheritance. This type of court was present in 29 countries in 1990 (or the earliest year available), which increased to 32 by 2008. Most of these countries are Muslim majority. Nearly half of Muslim-majority states (46.8%) have this type of religious court. However, 10 of these cases are in non-Muslim-majority countries. Many of these cases are coded because Sharia courts within those countries have been given jurisdiction in matters of family law and/or inheritance for their Muslim minorities. Ethiopia, Greece, Kenya, the Philippines, and Singapore have such

---

[21] Nicholas Kristof, "Watch What You Say," *New York Times*, June 21, 2002; "Muslim Attacks on Christianity Intensify," *Sunday Business Post*, September 9, 2001.

courts.[22] Yet there are cases of non-Muslim religious courts. Malta has granted the Catholic Church the right to form tribunals with jurisdiction over civil cases concerning family law. In Bhutan, Buddhist monks decide issues of family law. In Bosnia, churches and religious communities may act as arbitrators of family law, in conformity with state laws.[23] In Israel, all three recognized religions, Judaism, Christianity, and Islam, maintain courts with jurisdiction over family law.

Presence of religious courts that have jurisdiction over some matters of law other than family law and matters of inheritance. Religious courts with jurisdiction over matters other than family law and inheritance are rarer and in 2008 existed in only 11 countries, all of them with Muslim majorities. For example, in the UAE Sharia courts have jurisdiction of family law and criminal matters, but there are secular courts for civil law. Nigeria's constitution allows states to use Sharia courts for any legal matter.[24] Around 2000, several of Nigeria's states began to give Sharia courts jurisdiction over criminal matters.

Government institutions and laws protecting and enforcing religion are by far most common in Muslim-majority states, although they are certainly present in other states, especially with regard to blasphemy laws. Between 1990 and 2008, institutions and laws enforcing religion have increased slightly from being present in a total of 52 states (including all states and all laws and institutions) to 55, an increase of 5.8%. These are serious forms of support that can potentially influence basic elements of everyday life, including what people may say about religion, how people may behave in public, family life, and both what is considered criminal and the consequences of criminal activity. Thus, although such institutions, policies, and laws are present in only a minority of states, where they are present, their influence is felt profoundly.

Funding Religion

The most common type of support for religion, and a significant one, is the funding of religion. In forming a budget, a government must prioritize and select from multiple and competing demands for funding. The choice to fund religion requires decisions to not fund or to give less funds to other competing demands and constituencies. This makes it one of the most tangible forms of support. Put differently, in giving money to support religion, a government demonstrates in one of the most unambiguous ways possible that religion is

---

[22] "Tension Mounting over Islamic Courts," Human Rights Without Frontiers, 2003, www.hrwf.net/religiousfreedom/news/kenya_2003.html; "Secularism, the Singapore Way," *The Straits Times* (Singapore), October 30, 2007, http://academic.lexisnexis.co.il.proxy1.athensams.net/Bar-Ilan-University/academicuniverse.

[23] Law on Freedom of Religion and Legal Position of Churches and Religious Communities in Bosnia and Herzegovina, Inter-religious Council of Bosnia and Herzegovina, 2004, www.mrv.ba/en/contact.

[24] Nigeria Constitution (1999), www.religlaw.org/common/document.view.php?docId=927.

supported by the state. Essentially the state is putting its money where its mouth is. These types of funding are listed in Table 4.5.

As noted earlier, this type of support is also the type that is most associated with control. Government funds often come with conditions. Also, dependence on government funds makes religious institutions more vulnerable to government efforts to influence and control them. For instance, funding religious education may result in government input into the content of that education. Yet these funds still, in practice, support religious institutions and activities and usually further significant goals of these institutions. In the case of education, government funding usually results in more citizens being educated in a religion's precepts, which directly influences the number of active adherents.

None of the 11 individual types of funding examined by the RAS2 project is present in a majority of states. However, when taken as a whole, funding is very common. In 1990 (or the earliest year available), 136 of the 177 countries in this study funded religion using at least 1 of the 11 types of funding for religion included in the RAS2 dataset. This included 349 individual types of funding among these countries. By 2008, this increased to 147 countries and 448 individual types of funding, an average of just over three types of funding among those countries that fund religion. More interesting is that each of these 11 types of funding became more common between 1990 and 2008. This makes the funding of religion the most rapidly increasing form of support.

Government funding of religious primary or secondary schools or religious educational programs in nonpublic schools. In 1990 (or the earliest year available), 71 countries engaged in this type of funding. By 2008, this had increased to 81. This is by far, the most common form of funding for religion. In some cases, this involves funding only schools belonging to the majority religion. For example, Argentina began subsidizing Catholic parochial schools in 2007. In other cases, the funding is more widespread across religions. For instance, since the passage of its 2006 law on religion, all recognized religions in Romania may request state funding for the teachers' salaries in theological educational institutions.[25] Similarly, since 2008, Nepal's government provides funding to any parochial school that meets the national funding requirements.[26]

Government funding of institutions which train clergy. In 1990 (or the earliest year available), 26 countries funded this type of institution. By 2008, this had increased to 29. This type of funding is particularly common in Orthodox Christian-majority states. Russia provides this type of funding for the Orthodox

---

[25] Romania, Law 489/2006 on the Freedom of Religion and the General Status of Denominations, Published in the Official Journal, Part I, issue #11/January 8, 2007, www.religlaw.org.
[26] Kalpit Parajuli, "Islamic, Buddhist, Hindu and Catholics Schools to Be Integrated into Nepal's education system," *AsiaNews/International Christian Concern*, June 27, 2008, www.persecution.org/2008/06/29/islamic-buddhist-hindu-and-catholic-schools-to-be-integrated-into-nepals-education-system.

TABLE 4.5. *Funding Religion*

	All States		Majority Religion (2008 results)						
			Christian						Other
	1990*	2008	Catholic	Orthodox	Other Christian	Christian Total	Muslim	Religions
Government funding of religious primary or secondary schools or religious educational programs in nonpublic schools	40.1%	45.8%	50.0%	38.5%	51.2%	49.0%	36.2%	50.0%
Government funding of institutions that train clergy	14.7%	16.4%	6.8%	38.5%	7.3%	11.2%	27.7%	15.6%
Government funding of religious education in colleges or universities	15.3%	18.6%	4.5%	7.7%	24.4%	13.3%	36.2%	9.4%
Government funding of religious charitable organizations	13.0%	13.6%	6.8%	7.7%	22.0%	13.3%	12.8%	15.6%
Government collects taxes on behalf of religious organizations	9.0%	10.2%	13.6%	0.0%	14.6%	12.2%	12.8%	0.0%
Official government positions, salaries or other funding for clergy other than salaries for teachers of religious courses	28.8%	32.2%	38.6%	30.8%	22.0%	30.6%	44.7%	18.8%
Direct general grants to religious organizations	24.9%	27.7%	31.8%	61.5%	19.5%	30.6%	27.7%	18.8%
Funding for building, maintaining, or repairing religious sites	33.9%	36.7%	20.5%	84.6%	17.1%	27.6%	55.3%	37.5%
Free air time on television or radio or license preferences provided to religious organizations on government channels or by government decree	20.3%	23.7%	18.2%	16.2%	24.2%	24.5%	27.7%	15.6%
Funding or other government support for religious pilgrimages such as the Hajj	11.3%	14.1%	2.3%	7.7%	0.0%	2.0%	38.3%	15.6%
Funding for religious organizations or activities other than those already listed	10.2%	14.1%	18.2%	23.1%	14.6%	17.3%	8.5%	12.5%
% of countries with at least one of these laws	76.8%	83.1%	79.5%	100.0%	75.6%	80.6%	89.4%	81.2%
% of countries with three or more of these laws	35.0%	39.5%	31.7%	61.5%	31.5%	35.7%	55.2%	28.8%
% of countries with five or more of these laws	15.8%	18.1%	22.6%	30.7%	14.4%	16.3%	25.4%	12.4%
Mean number of laws	2.20	2.53c	2.11	3.46	2.17	2.32	3.28	2.09

* In some countries, this represents the first available year.

Church as well as other religions including Buddhism and Islam.[27] Similarly, since 1992 (when it was still Yugoslavia), Serbia has funded higher theological education for the country's "traditional" religions. In a few cases this funding goes primarily to minority religions. For example, the Netherlands' government funds the training of Islamic clergy to counter foreign influences. The training includes training in the Netherlands' norms and values. In addition, the government requires all Imams recruited from Muslim-majority countries to complete a year-long integration course before permitting them to practice in the country. This policy is an excellent example of how funding religion can be directly related to control.

Government funding of religious education in colleges or universities. In 1990 (or the earliest year available), 27 countries funded this type of institution. By 2008, this had increased to 33. For example, in 2000, the Slovakian government created a Catholic university in the town of Ruzomberok and provided the majority of its operating budget. Germany funds university studies of Christian theology, Jewish studies, and, as of 2009, Islam.[28]

Government funding of religious charitable organizations. This type of funding involves supporting charitable work by religious organizations that create a public good. This can include a wide range of activities that have a general social benefit such as hospitals and welfare. In essence, this is government funding of religious organizations to perform functions often performed by governments. In 1990 (or the earliest year available), 23 governments funded religious charitable organizations. This increased to 24 by 2008. In 2001, the United States began allowing "faith-based" organizations to compete with other nonprofit organizations for federally funded social services contracts. By the end of the Bush administration in 2008, these organizations had received 10.6 billion dollars in funding.[29] In Papua New Guinea, a small Christian-majority country in the Pacific, the government has neither the funds nor personnel for social services. Because of this, many social services including hospitals are run by religious organizations and receive government subsidies. This pattern of governments ceding authority over social services to religious organizations is present in a number of underdeveloped states. This is a natural development because before modern times, most social services, including welfare and health care, were the province of religious organizations (Toft et al., 2011).

The government collects taxes on behalf of religious organizations. All types of funding other than this one involve a government giving funds to a religious organization out of the state budget. This represents a separate tax specifically

---

[27] Michael Shwirtz, "With an Assist from Moscow, Islam Flourishes," *New York Times*, December 17, 2007; Anna Nemtsova, "Russian Government Funds Select Islamic Schools to Stem Radicalism," *The Telegraph*, September 1, 2010.
[28] "Germany to Set Up First Islamic Theology Department," *Earth Times*, June 26, 2009.
[29] Michelle Boorstein and Kimberly Kindy "Faith-Based Office to Expand Its Reach; Goals Will Include Reducing Abortion," *Washington Post*, February 6, 2009.

earmarked for religion. In 1990 (or the earliest year available), 16 governments collected these taxes. By 2008, this increased to 18. Interestingly, 11 of these countries can be found in Western Europe. This tax is mandatory for everyone in Belgium and Iceland but can be directed to multiple religions as well as secular organizations such as the University of Iceland. In Austria, Denmark, Finland, and Germany, one can avoid the tax by officially withdrawing from religious membership. In Italy, Portugal, Spain, and Sweden, taxpayers can check a box on tax forms to direct a portion of their income taxes to a religious organization. Although most of these states collect the tax for multiple recognized religions, Denmark and Portugal collect this tax only for the state religion, and Finland collects it only for the state religion and the Orthodox Church. Many of Switzerland's cantons collect religious taxes, but the specific policy varies from canton to canton.

The two states that enacted religious taxes during the study period were Indonesia and Malaysia. A 1999 Indonesian law makes the zakat, a Muslim religious tax, obligatory for all Muslims. According to Article 6 of the same law, the management of zakat is done by the Amil Zakat charity established by the government.[30] Since 1993, the Malaysian government has been responsible for collecting zakat taxes in the federal territories of Kuala Lumpur, Putrajaya, and Labuan.[31] The other states that collect religious taxes are Hungary, Brunei, Pakistan, Saudi Arabia, and Sudan.

Official government positions, salaries, or other funding for clergy. This does not include funding for teachers or government chaplains in places such as military bases and prisons. It also does not involve tax breaks for clergy. Rather, it focuses on the funding of traditional clergy who serve the population in general. In 1990 (or the earliest year available), 51 countries funded clergy in this manner, which increased to 58 by 2008. This funding involves the full salaries of all clergy only in a minority of cases and is usually somewhat selective. For example, in 2001 Hungary began funding clergy from recognized religions in towns of less than 5,000 people. Similarly, beginning in 2005, Lithuania began subsidizing the social security and health care of clergy from "traditional" and "state-recognized" religious groups. Slovenia pays the social insurance for one religious employee per 1,000 members of a religious community. However, sometimes countries, such as Egypt, fund clergy more universally. Egypt pays the salaries of the imams who run most of the country's mosques, with the exceptions of some private mosques and unauthorized mosques.

Direct general grants to religious organizations. This represents cases in which the government transfers funds from its budget to a religious organization without specifying how the money should be spent. In 1990 (or the

---

[30] Crouch (2009); Indonesia 1999 Law 38 on Zakat (translated online from original Indonesian December 22, 2010), www.legalitas.org/proses/uu.php?k=1999&n=30-45.
[31] Malaysia 1993 Administration of Islamic Law (Federal Territories) Act 1993 (No. 505), www.commonlii.org/my/legis/consol_act/toc-1993.html.

earliest year available), 44 countries gave these grants, which increased to 49 by 2008. Costa Rica and Spain both stopped this type of funding. In 2004, Costa Rica stopped including a grant to the Catholic Church in the national budget. In 2008, Spain did the same. However, both countries continue to engage in other forms of funding. Seven countries began this type of funding since 1990. For example, since 2005 Georgia has given grants to the Georgian Orthodox Church as well as additional funds when requested by the church's patriarch. Beginning in 2005, the Ivory Coast began allotting money to 20 major religious organizations.

Funding for building, maintaining, or repairing religious sites. This is the second most common form of funding for religion. It is particularly common in Orthodox- and Muslim-majority countries. In 1990 (or the earliest year available), 60 countries provided this type of support, which increased to 65 by 2008. In some cases, such as Albania, this funding is to restore past damage done under less religion-friendly regimes. In 2008, Albania agreed to fund the restoration of the religious property of all major religions.[32] In other cases, the funding is more comprehensive. For example, Mexico's 1917 constitution declared all religious property to belong to the state.[33] This remained in effect until a 1992 amendment.[34] In practice this means that the government maintains most religious property in existence before 1992. Similarly, Belgium subsidizes the building and maintenance of places of worship for all of its "recognized" religions.

Free airtime on television or radio. This type of support is common and increasing. It increased from 32 to 46 states during the study period. The only country that eliminated this type of support was Iraq as a consequence of the overthrow of the Saddam Hussein regime. For example, Argentina began giving the Catholic Church preferential access to licenses for radio frequencies in 2007. In 2000, the state-run Croatian State Radio and Television agreed to provide regular, extensive coverage of Catholic events (as many as 10 hours per month). Other denominations receive approximately 10 minutes of broadcast time per month or less. In 2004, Guyana granted a license and frequency free of cost to an all-faith television station.

Funding or other government support for religious pilgrimages such as the Hajj. This form of support, which increased from 20 to 25 countries during the study period, is most common in Muslim-majority states. This is not surprising given that although the concept of pilgrimages is present in many religions, in Islam it is a religious duty considered the fifth pillar of Islam. All seven non-Muslim states that supported religious pilgrimages – China, Guinea-Bissau,

---

[32] "Albania: Secularism Holds Its Ground," *One World South East Europe*, June 16, 2009, http://oneworldsee.org/node/18709.
[33] Mexican Constitution (1917), www.ilstu.edu/class/hist263/docs/1917const.html.
[34] 1992 amendment to Article 27 of the Mexican Constitution (1917), http://info4.juridicas.unam.mx/ijure/fed/9/28.htm?s.

India, the Ivory Coast, the Philippines, Russia, and Thailand – supported the Hajj by members of their Muslim minorities.[35]

Other forms of religious funding. Governments can be inventive when it comes to funding. Funding religion is no exception because the number of governments that engaged in some form of funding that is different from the categories mentioned above increased from 18 to 25 between 1990 (or the earliest year available) and 2008. For example, Andorra funds the Catholic Church to maintain historical birth and marriage records. In 2007, the Romanian government began funding overseas cultural activities by the Romanian Orthodox Church. In 2008, Angola began supporting a Catholic music school.[36]

Funding religion is the most common form of support for religion both in general and for each religious denomination analyzed in this study. It is increasing more than any other type of support. It is also the only type of support in which each of the individual categories shows an overall increase. In essence more governments are pouring more money into religion in a wider variety of ways than they have in the past. This represents perhaps the most clear and measurable example of the overall increase in government support for religion.

That being said, the funding of religion is not distributed equally among states. Simply put, states with more money are more likely to fund religion. For example, among Christian-majority states, those in the Third World engage in an average of 1.25 types of funding as opposed to 3.52 types for Christian-majority states in Western Democracies and the former Soviet bloc. This link between wealth and funding is not surprising, but it is significant.

The Entanglement of Religious and Government Institutions

This category represents policies and laws that blur the lines between government and religion. These primarily constitute cases in which government and religion become entwined in a manner that can allow religion more influence in government or in a way that brings religious and governmental institutions closer together. However, several of them also have the potential to facilitate significant levels of government control over religion. These categories are listed in Table 4.6.

Some religious leaders are given diplomatic status, diplomatic passports, or immunity from prosecution by virtue of their religious office. This form of support is relatively rare with only six countries providing it in 2008, an increase of

---

[35] Carleson (2005); Michael Shwirtz, "With an Assist from Moscow, Islam Flourishes," *New York Times*, December 17, 2007; China 2005 Regulations on Religious Affairs, www.amitynewsservice.org/page.php?page=1289; India 1959 Hajj Committee Act, vlex.in/vid/the-haj-committee-act-29630788.

[36] "Angola; Government Donates Music Instruments to Church," *Africa News*, November 15, 2008.

TABLE 4.6. *The Entanglement of Government and Religious Institutions*

	All States		Majority Religion (2008 results)						
			Christian						Other Religions
	1990*	2008	Catholic	Orthodox	Other Christian	Christian Total	Muslim		
Some religious leaders are given diplomatic status, diplomatic passports, orimmunity from prosecution by virtue of their religious office	2.8%	3.4%	6.8%	15.4%	0.0%	5.1%	0.0%		3.1%
Presence of an official government ministry or department dealing with religious affairs	44.6%	54.2%	45.5%	61.5%	34.1%	42.9%	87.2%		40.6%
Certain government officials are also given an official position in the state church by virtue of their political office	2.8%	2.8%	0.0%	0.0%	2.4%	1.0%	8.5%		0.0%
Certain religious officials become government officials by virtue of their religious position	3.4%	4.0%	2.3%	0.0%	2.4%	2.0%	10.6%		0.0%
Some or all government officials must meet certain religious requirements to hold office	13.6%	13.6%	0.0%	0.0%	7.3%	3.1%	40.4%		6.3%
Seats in legislative branch and/or cabinet are by law or custom granted, at least in part, along religious lines	6.2%	8.5%	2.3%	0.0%	7.3%	4.1%	17.0%		9.4%
% of countries with at least one of these laws	51.4%	61.6%	55.5%	69.2%	41.5%	51.0%	91.5%		50.0%
% of countries with two or more of these laws	15.3%	16.9%	2.3%	7.7%	7.4%	5.1%	46.8%		9.4%
% of countries with three or more of these laws	6.2%	6.8%	0.0%	0.0%	4.9%	2.0%	21.3%		0.0%
Mean number of laws	0.73	0.86b	0.57	0.77	0.54	0.58	1.64		0.59

* In some countries, this represents the first available year.

one from the beginning of the study period. It is one of the few forms of support not present in any Muslim-majority countries. This immunity is usually limited to a few senior clergy members. For example, a 2002 concordant between Georgia and the Georgian Orthodox Church gives the patriarch legal immunity. In Lithuania, the most senior clergy of the country's four "traditional" religions are eligible for diplomatic passports. In Moldova, the archbishop of Chisinau holds a diplomatic passport. Burundi gives diplomatic status to the heads of major religions in the country. The Ivory Coast gives diplomatic passports to major religious chiefs. Finally, Panama gives the country's Catholic archbishop the same privileges and immunities given to government officials.

Presence of an official government ministry or department dealing with religious affairs. This is the fourth most common form of government support for religion and the most quickly increasing with an increase from 79 in 1990 (or the earliest year available) to 96 in 2008. The designation of a government department devoted to religion demonstrates that religion is a significant policy issue. These departments can engage in a variety of activities including regulation, advocating, enforcing, and funding religion. They also can potentially be a significant instrument of control. Thus, while this type of support overlaps with other categories discussed here, it is most congruous with the entanglement between government and religion.

Some of these organizations have nominal powers. For example, in 2007, Chile created the Office of Religious Affairs to work with all religions to guarantee the implementation of constitutional religious freedom rights. Others extensively blur the lines between religion and government. For instance, in 2002, Mali's government created the High Council of Islam centralizing several existing Islamic bodies. It serves several functions, including serving as a liaison between the government and local Muslim groups, providing the government with legal opinions on Sharia law, issuing fatwas (binding religious decrees), and standardizing sermons in mosques so they are consistent with Mali's constitution. Also, along with similar bodies from other religions, it is often consulted on important national issues.[37]

Certain government officials are also given an official position in the state church by virtue of their political office. This form of entanglement is present in six states during the study period. In some cases, such as the United Kingdom, this represents a symbolic joining of religion and state. In the United Kingdom, the monarch is the symbolic head of both the state and the state church. In Brunei, the sultan is similarly the head of the state religion, but this appointment is not symbolic. A 1984 law gives the sultan the power to regulate Islam in Brunei.[38] The current sultan is largely responsible for bringing the country's laws into greater compliance with Sharia law.

---

[37] "Mali Plans Setting Up High Islamic Council Tuesday," PanAfrican News Agency Daily Newswire, January 10, 2002.
[38] Brunei 1984 Religious Council and Kadis Courts Law, www.lexadin.nl/wlg/legis/nofr/oeur/lxwebri.htm.

Certain religious officials become government officials by virtue of their religious position. This form of support increased from six to seven states during the study period. Perhaps the most important example is Iran where the "supreme leader," the "Assembly of Experts," and "Guardian Council" are essentially religious offices with veto power over nearly every aspect of Iran's government, including the ability to overrule elected officials and otherwise influence policy. In other instances, the power of these officials, while present, is more limited. For example, in Comoros, the Islamic religious leader, the grand mufti, is attached to the Ministry of Islamic Affairs. He officially councils the government on matters of Islamic faith and ensures that Islamic laws are respected.

Some or all government officials must meet certain religious requirements to hold office. At the beginning and end of the study period, 24 countries had this requirement, but several added and dropped it between 1990 and 2008. This category does not to apply to religious officials such as the heads of the state religion or government religion departments. Rather, it focuses on general government positions such as head of state, the legislative branch, and the cabinet. Most often this is a requirement that the head of state be a member of the majority religion. For example, until 1994 and 1992, respectively, the presidents of Argentina and Paraguay had to be Catholic. In some countries the requirement is more extensive. In the Maldives, the president, vice president, and members of the cabinet must be Muslim.[39] In Yemen, most officials including the president and members of parliament must be Muslims. The only non-Muslim countries to have this type of requirement in 2008 were Denmark and Norway, both of whose monarchs must be members of the state religion.

Seats in the legislative branch and/or cabinet are by law or custom granted, at least in part, along religious lines. This type of entanglement increased from 11 to 15 countries between 1990 (or the earliest year available) and 2008. In some cases, this involves reserved seats for representatives of religious organizations. For example, according to Madagascar's 1992 constitution "one-third [of the Senate] shall consist of members representing economic, social, cultural, and *religious groups* appointed by the President of the Republic upon nomination by legally constituted organizations and groups."[40] Similarly, a 2002 amendment to Belize's constitution states that one senator "shall be appointed by the Governor-General acting in accordance with the advice of the Belize Council of Churches and Evangelical Association of Churches."[41] In other cases, this involves the apportionment of seats to members of minority religions. In Iran, religious minorities have five reserved seats (two for Armenian Christians and

---

[39] Maldives 2008 Constitution, www.presidencymaldives.gov.mv/Index.aspx?lid=5; Odd Larsen, "Reform Excluded Freedom of Religion or Belief," Forum 18, February 18, 2009, www.forum18.org/Archive.php?article_id=1257.

[40] 1992 Constitution of Madagascar, International Constitutional Law, www.servat.unibe.ch/icl/ma00000_.html.

[41] Constitution of Belize, Ministry of the Attorney General, Belize, www.belizelaw.org/e_library.html.

one each for Assyrian Christians, Jews, and Zoroastrians) in the parliament but are barred from every other representative body. Likewise, the king of Jordan traditionally appoints some Christians to the legislature's Upper House.

In 2008, 109 countries had at least one of these forms of government-religion entanglement, an increase of 18 countries over the study period. Much of this entanglement is due to the presence of religion departments and ministries in governments. Setting this factor aside, in 1990 (or the earliest year available), 57 countries had at least one of these forms of entanglement, which increased to 60 in 2008. In either case, a substantial and increasing number of states blur the lines between religious and government institutions. This increase includes four of the six categories analyzed here and the other two remained stable. This is consistent with the larger pattern of increasing government support for religion presented in this chapter.

Other Forms of Government Support for Religion

This category covers eight forms of support that do not fit into any of the previous categories. They are listed in Table 4.7. Overall, this type of support increased from 86.4% of states to 93.8% during the study period and was common in states with all types of religious majorities.

Religious education is present in the public schools. This second most common type of support represents a serious form of support in that one or several religions, always including the religion of the country's majority, are taught in the public schools. This does not refer to courses in comparative religion but, rather, refers to when schools teach religious doctrine or theology or otherwise include religious indoctrination in their curriculum. This form of support is common and increasing. This type of religious education was present in 107 countries in 1990 (or the earliest year available), increasing to 118 by 2008. With the exception of the "other religions" category, a majority of states within each religious tradition engaged in this practice in 2008. There is a wide diversity of policies with regard to this type of support, which I discuss in detail in Chapter 7.

Official prayer sessions in public schools. This is considerably less common than public school religious education, with 19 states engaging in the practice at the beginning of the study period, increasing slightly to 20 by 2008. In half of these countries, the prayer sessions were optional. For example, in Canada's Ontario province, public schools can elect to read from scriptures of various religious and secular sources. They also may include a period of silent reflection in place of, or in addition to, the readings.[42] However, in 10 cases, it is mandatory for at least some students. For example, in 2008, Thailand's government started a pilot project of bringing a Buddhist ethics class to troubled schools. Students in selected schools are taught Buddhist meditation

---

[42] Ontario Consultants on Religious Tolerance, www.ReligiousTolerance.org.

TABLE 4.7. *Other Forms of Government Support for Religion*

	All States		Majority Religion (2008 results)						
			Christian						
	1990*	2008	Catholic	Orthodox	Other Christian	Christian Total	Muslim	Other Religions
---	---	---	---	---	---	---	---	---
Religious education is present in public schools	60.5%	66.7%	75.0%	69.2%	75.6%	74.5%	70.2%	37.5%
Presence of official prayer sessions in public schools	10.7%	11.3%	2.3%	30.8%	17.1%	13.3%	6.4%	15.6%
Public schools are segregated by religion or separate public schools exist for members of some religions	7.9%	8.5%	2.3%	0.0%	4.9%	3.1%	21.3%	6.3%
The presence of religious symbols on the state's flag	20.9%	21.5%	9.1%	23.1%	14.6%	12.2%	42.6%	15.6%
Religion listed on state identity cards or other government documents that most citizens must possess or fill out	14.1%	12.4%	2.3%	0.0%	2.4%	2.0%	29.8%	18.8%
A registration process for religious organizations exists that is in some manner different from the registration process for other nonprofit organizations	51.4%	59.9%	68.2%	92.3%	56.1%	66.3%	40.4%	68.8%
Blasphemy laws protecting minority religions or religious figures	7.9%	10.7%	6.8%	7.7%	7.3%	7.1%	19.1%	9.4%
Other religious prohibitions or practices that are mandatory	12.4%	16.9%	25.0%	0.0%	4.9%	13.3%	29.8%	9.4%
% of countries with at least one of these laws	86.4%	93.8%	97.7%	100.0%	87.8%	93.9%	97.9%	87.5%
% of countries with three or more of these laws	31.1%	34.5%	27.3%	38.5%	7.3%	30.5%	27.7%	14.7
% of countries with five or more of these laws	4.0%	4.5%	0.0%	2.4%	10.7%	1.0%	6.2%	4.5%
Mean number of laws	1.86	2.08c	1.91	2.23	1.83	1.93	2.60	1.81

* In some countries, this represents the first available year.

techniques and precepts once a week.⁴³ In Myanmar, students recite a Buddhist prayer. In some schools, Muslim students are allowed to leave the room but at others, non-Buddhists are forced to recite. Similarly, at some Romanian public school events, all students, regardless of their religious affiliation, must attend Orthodox religious services.

Public schools are segregated by religion or separate public schools exist for members of some religions. Fourteen countries followed this policy at the beginning of the study period, which increased to 15 when Bahrain opened a separate public school for Shi'i Muslims. Most of Ireland's school system is denominational, and the government provides funding for schools of all denominations. School boards are partially governed by trustees within that religious denomination. Religious education is usually part of the core curriculum of most schools, but parents may excuse their children from such classes. While in theory a school can refuse to admit members of other denominations or faiths subject to proof that this is essential to the maintenance of the "ethos" of the school, there are no reports of this right having been invoked.⁴⁴

The presence of religious symbols on the state's flag. This form of support for religion, although mostly symbolic, is still significant because it associates what is arguably the most central and well-known symbol of a state with a particular religion. In 1990 (or the earliest year available), 37 states had religious symbols on their flags. Since then, only Georgia added religious symbols to its flag. In 2004, Georgia replaced its tricolored flag with one that has one large red cross and four smaller crosses. Religious symbols are by far most common on the flags of Muslim-majority states.

Religion is listed on state identity cards or other government documents that most citizens must possess or fill out. This form of support for religion is important for three reasons. First, it allows state officials to easily identify a citizen's religious identity. Second, it requires a government official to approve one's official religious affiliation, including when people switch religion. Third, it can facilitate both enforcement of the majority religion and discrimination against religious minorities.

At the beginning of the study period, 25 countries engaged in this practice. By 2008, four had dropped the practice and one had instituted it. After massive demonstrations, in 2000, Greece discontinued this practice, which had been instituted during the Nazi era.⁴⁵ In Latvia, passports include ethnicity, which includes religious groups such as Jews. In 2002, this became optional. In 2006,

---

⁴³ Simon Montlake, "Thai Schools Use Dance Class, Prayer to Curb Violence," *The Christian Science Monitor*, November 20, 2008.

⁴⁴ "Schools and the Equal Status Act," *The Equality Authority*, Ireland, 2005, www.equality.ie/index.asp?locID=106&docID=66.

⁴⁵ B.A. Robinson, "Religious Intolerance in Greece," Religious Tolerance.org, December 15, 2000, www.religioustolerance.org/rt_greec.htm; "Greece Says Nazis First Put Faith-Designation on ID Cards," AFP, May 30, 2000, http://religiousfreedom.lib.virginia.edu/freedomalert/ HRWF_Greece/000602Greece.htm; "Poll Boosts Church ID Referendum Plan," Human Rights

Romania removed a section on religion from its national identity card application form. Laos removed religious affiliation from its national identity cards in 2003. In 1999, Thailand's national identity cards began to include religious affiliation. In most of these countries, the identification had few consequences. However, in other countries, they have practical consequences. For example, Malaysia uses these cards to determine whether an individual is Muslim and, thus, subject to religious law. Malaysia does not allow citizens to change their religious identity from Islam to another religion without the approval of a Sharia law court, which is almost never granted. Changes after conversions to Islam are generally approved.

A registration process for religious organizations exists that is in some manner different from the registration process for other nonprofit organizations. This form of support overlaps with issues of control and entanglement with religion but is, in my assessment, not necessarily either of these. Essentially this requirement constitutes government recognition that religious organizations are different from other organizations. This can be both to religion's benefit and detriment. It can facilitate many of the forms of support discussed in this chapter as well as restrictions on religious organizations. It also usually involves a distinct bureaucracy that registers and sometimes monitors religious organizations. In most countries with official or favored religions, the favored religion or religions are automatically recognized without having to register. All things being equal, this tends to get governments involved in religion usually in a positive manner for the larger religious denominations in a state and often also for smaller ones. This type of support is becoming increasingly common, increasing from 91 states at the beginning of the study period to 106 in 2008. I discuss this issue further in Chapter 6.

Blasphemy laws protecting minority religions or religious figures. While many types of support can be applied to minority religions, this category is the only one that involves explicit support for minority religions. Fourteen countries had this type of support in 1990 (or the earliest year available). By 2008, Afghanistan, Bosnia, Italy, Romania, and the Sudan added this type of law. It usually takes the form of a general protection against denigrating all religions, which applies, at least in theory, equally to the majority and minority religions. Israel is the only country to have this type of protection for a minority religion but not the majority religion. Acts denigrating Islam, such as putting up posters depicting the prophet Mohammed as a pig, are prosecuted by the state, but there are no similar prosecutions for denigrating Judaism.

Other religious prohibitions or practices that are mandatory. This category is intended to allow the RAS project to code types of support that do not fit into any of the other 50 categories and are too uncommon or unique to be the basis for an additional category. Countries coded in this category increased

without Frontiers, June 30, 2000, http://religiousfreedom.lib.virginia.edu/freedomalert/HRWF_Greece/000630Greece.htm.

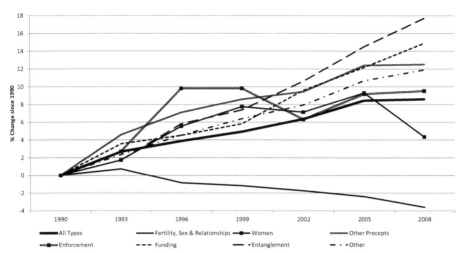

FIGURE 4.1. Change over Time in Support for Religion.

from 22 to 30 during the study period. The activities covered in this category vary considerably. In Bolivia, the Catholic Church effectively participates in running aspects of the nation's education, health, and social welfare functions, which constitutes a significant entanglement between government and religion. Honduras similarly consults with the Catholic Church on policy issues and occasionally appoints Catholic leaders to quasi-official commissions on major issues of mutual concern, such as anticorruption programs. In Djibouti, anyone who does not claim another faith is automatically designated by the government to be Muslim.

Trends

The most important trend in the RAS2 data on support for religion is its consistent and significant increase over time. As illustrated in Figure 4.1, this trend is mostly consistent over time and types of support. As discussed earlier, other than the sex, relationships, and fertility category, all categories of support increased over time. Furthermore, this increase has been consistent throughout the 1990 to 2008 period; by this I mean that in nearly every year, the overall level of support was the same or higher than the previous year. The one exception to this is laws restricting women, which began to drop toward the end of the period.

Examining the data from other perspectives further demonstrates the robustness of this finding. Thirty-seven (72.5%) of the 51 individual types of support became more common between 1990 (or the earliest year available) and 2008, 8 (15.7%) remained the same, and 6 (11.8%) became less common. Also, as shown in Table 4.8, 72 (40.7%) countries increased their overall levels of

TABLE 4.8. *Change over Time in Support for Religion*

	Change between 1990* and 2008		
	Lower	Same	Higher
All support	20 (11.3%)	85 (48.0%)	72 (40.7%)
Religious precepts			
Relationships, sex, and reproduction	18 (10.2%)	152 (85.9%)	7 (4.0%)
Restrictions on women	2 (1.1%)	169 (95.5%)	6 (3.4%)
Other religious precepts	3 (1.7%)	161 (91.0%)	13 (7.3%)
The enforcement of religion	4 (2.3%)	161 (91.0%)	12 (6.8%)
Funding religion	3 (1.7%)	133 (75.1%)	41 (23.2%)
The entanglement of religious and government institutions	5 (2.8%)	149 (84.2%)	23 (13.0%)
Other forms of support	5 (2.8%)	134 (75.7%)	38 (21.5%)

* In some countries, this represents the first available year.

support as opposed to 20 (11.3%) that decreased their levels of support. This finding is also consistent across the different categories of support. Again, with the exception of the relationships, sex, and reproduction category, the number of states increasing support outnumbered those decreasing support across categories.

As shown in Table 4.9, the trend is also mostly robust across religious denomination. Overall, support for religion increased for all religious denominations. It also increased or remained stable across denominations when looking at the specific categories of support, again with the exception of the relationships, sex, and reproduction category. In addition, there were small drops in two additional categories in countries with "other Christian" majorities in the context of an overall increase in support. The increases were the highest among Orthodox Christian states, which is not surprising given that most of these states spent much of this period transitioning from the antireligious policies of the former Soviet bloc.

The second trend – that the highest levels of support are found, in general, in Muslim-majority states – is discussed in more detail earlier in the chapter. It is important to note that these results are not driven by the Middle East. In fact, mean levels of support for religion is higher among the Muslim-majority states in Asia that were not part of the former Soviet bloc – Afghanistan, Bangladesh, Brunei, Indonesia, Malaysia, the Maldives, and Pakistan – with a mean of 26.9 types of support as opposed to 19.1 in Middle Eastern Muslim-majority states. However, this is not a finding that can be generalized to all Muslim-majority states. For example, Albania, Azerbaijan, Burkina Faso, Kyrgyzstan, Niger, Tajikistan, and the Turkish government in Cyprus all have four or less forms of support. Thus, this result is driven by high scores in the majority of Muslim-majority countries, but Muslim-majority states have diverse religion policies,

TABLE 4.9. *Change in Mean Level of Religious Support between 1990 and 2008 Controlling for Majority Religion and Official Religions*

	All Support	Religious Precepts						Other Support
		Relationships, Sex, and Reproduction	Women	Other	Enforcement	Funding	Entanglement	
Catholic	10.1%	−7.3%	0.0%	0.0%	20.0%	17.7%	25.0%	12.0%
Orthodox Christian	20.3%	−50.0%	0.0%	0.0%	66.7%	36.4%	11.1%	26.1%
Other Christians	3.2%	−5.3%	0.0%	−7.7%	0.0%	15.6%	−4.3%	7.1%
Islam	8.1%	−0.7%	4.7%	13.3%	6.0%	7.7%	26.2%	11.0%
Other	10.5%	4.4%	0.0%	37.5%	22.2%	15.5%	11.8%	13.7

including several states that are among those with the lowest levels of support for religion in the world.

The final trend, shown in Table 4.10, is that although support for religion is related to official state religion policy, this relationship is not fully determinative. For instance, support for religion is not absent in states with official religions, but there are several that are not particularly supportive of religion. Using the categories of official religion policy described in Chapter 3, it is clear, and unsurprising, that stronger official support for religion results, on average, in more support for religion as measured by the 51 types of support examined by the RAS2 dataset. However, support is present even in states that are officially neutral or hostile to religion. In fact, in 2008, the only state with none of the 51 types of support was South Africa. The only state with only one type of support was Albania. Thus, support for religion can be said to be nearly fully ubiquitous in the world in 2008.

In addition, an examination of the ranges of scores for support – based on how many categories of support are present in state policy – provides even stronger evidence that the influence of a state's official policy is not nearly as determinative as one might think. For example, the difference in mean levels of support between states with official religions and states that "prefer" one religion without designating an official one is large. But on closer examination, this is driven by the results from a few states. In both categories of states, there exist states that only engage in two types of support in practice. Liechtenstein has an official religion but only engages in two types of support. The same is true of Andorra, El Salvador, and the Turkish government of Cyprus, all countries that prefer a single religion. The range of support for states that prefer a single religion – again without declaring an official one – reaches as high as 28 types of support, Indonesia's score. Only five states with official religions score higher: Egypt (29), Brunei (31), Pakistan (32), Malaysia (33), and Saudi Arabia (42). Thus, all other states that prefer a single religion without having an official one have, in practice, policies with levels of support that are in the same range as 38 of the 43 states with official religions.

Similarly, only five of the states with a single preferred religion – India, Indonesia, Sudan, Syria, and Thailand – score higher than the highest scoring state with multiple preferred religions, although one of the states with multiple preferred religions – Albania – scores lower than any state with a single preferred religion. This overlap is profound to the extent that all states that are hostile to religion have levels of support that overlap with the 10 lowest scoring states in the official religion category. This means that 23.3% of states with official religions have levels of support that are similar to states that are hostile to religion altogether.

While the nature and quality of that support as well as the motivations behind it are likely quite different between states in these two categories – as I discussed in more detail in Chapter 3 – the fact that the actual levels of support partially overlap is still counterintuitive. This evidence demonstrates

TABLE 4.10. *Mean Level of Religious Support in 2008 Controlling for Official Religion Policy*

	All Support			Religious Precepts			Means			
				Relationships, Sex, and Reproduction	Women	Other	Enforcement	Funding	Entanglement	Other Support
	Mean	Low	High							
Official religion	16.78	2	42	2.98	0.85	2.71	1.80	3.66	1.71	3.17
One religion preferred	8.23	2	28	1.34	0.16	0.48	0.43	2.70	0.75	2.34
Multiple religions preferred	7.85	1	13	1.27	0.15	0.36	0.39	3.12	0.73	1.94
Equal treatment	4.28	0	11	1.38	0.02	0.14	0.18	1.08	0.32	1.20
Hostile	5.11	2	8	0.22	0.00	0.22	0.00	2.44	1.11	1.22

that official religion policy is not nearly as predictive of the actual policy as many might assume. Consequently, studies of state religion policy should focus more on policy in practice than policy in theory.

It also means that the motivations behind these policies can be as important as the policies themselves. Nevertheless, whatever the motivation of these support policies, they do demonstrate that governments consider religion important.

Conclusions

Religion, like the air we breathe, is all around us. Support for religion is so common that other than South Africa, every state in this study supported religion in at least some small way in 2008. Setting the patterns and trends, which I discussed earlier, aside, this has some important general implications. First, if one wants to define the concept of separation of religion and state (SRAS) strictly to include no government support for religion, and as noted in Chapter 2, many do not define it in this manner, few states have SRAS. The average Western democracy engages in 7.46 types of this support. The average European Union country engages in 8.48 types. This is a significant level of support for countries that follow liberal democratic policies, which many believe should include SRAS.

Second, while showing that state support for religion is common and increasing is not by itself enough to disprove secularization theory, it certainly paints a picture that is inconsistent with predictions of religion's decreasing public influence. This snapshot of religious support between 1990 and 2008 is more consistent with the competition perspective, which describes a world in which secularism and religion contend for influence, and religion – at least for the moment – is gaining on secularism. Although support for religion can also involve control, this still implies that religion is something sufficiently important and influential that it needs controlling.

Third, although the contest between secular and religious political actors is active and the religious forces are having significantly more successes, it is important to emphasize that this rise in support for religion is not monolithic. Collectively there were 192 new forms of support during this period, but 57 were repealed. While 72 countries had more forms of support in 2008 than they had in 1990, 20 had less. These numbers show support for religion increasing but also that secularist political forces have also had their successes. All of this supports the contentions of the secular-religious competition perspective.

Fourth, many of the changes in support for religion are occurring at the local level. Especially in non–Middle Eastern Muslim-majority countries such as Indonesia, Malaysia, and Nigeria, many new laws are being passed by regional and local governments. Often these changes are opposed, with varying levels of success, by national governments. This represents a phenomenon in which people at the grassroots level want changes that national political elites are reluctant to support. Yet these types of movements are often, although certainly not always, the harbingers of future change at the national level, especially in democratic states.

They also represent some of the best evidence that the changes in policy documented in this chapter are a direct result of religious pressure. This is because these local and regional shifts in religion policy can be more easily attributed to religious pressure groups, political parties, and politicians at the regional level. However, the considerable number of policy shifts toward more support for religion also implies significant successes at the national level, even when it less simple to trace the motivations for these policy shifts. Although it is certainly possible, or even likely, that some of these policy shifts have other motivations, the sheer number of new policies supporting religion makes it difficult to believe that pressure from religious political actors played anything other than a significant role in many if not most of these increases in support for religion.

Finally, it is important to reiterate that although the RAS2 project can measure actions, it is difficult to measure motivations. The same actions that support religion can also be linked to controlling it. There are three indicators that can suggest the motivation for support is actual support. First, the more forms of support, the less likely that the motivation for this support is exclusively control. Second, the enforcement of religious precepts category is a type of support that is less likely motivated by control issues. Third, if there are low levels of regulation of the type discussed on Chapter 5, it is more likely that the government's intention is to support religion. However, as I discuss in more detail in Chapter 5, governments can wish both to support and to control religion. These indicators indicate that there is a desire to support religion, but they do not mean that there is not also a desire to control it.

Overall, the results of this chapter especially show support for religion in a state of flux, exactly as predicted by the *competition perspective*. Most of these policies can be changed by the passage of a law or other types of decisions by leaders, officials, and bureaucrats. They do not require fundamental changes in policies or national constitutions. Thus, all of them are subject to political pressure by both those who want to increase state support for religion and those who wish to decrease it. Given this, state support for religion is likely to remain politically "in play" for the foreseeable future.

5

Regulation, Restriction, and Control of the Majority Religion or All Religions

Thomas Beckett became archbishop of Canterbury in 1162 with the support of King Henry II, who hoped that Beckett, who was until then the king's close advisor and chancellor, would use his position to support the king's rule and prerogatives. This did not prove to be the case, and Beckett sought to defend and expand the power of his religious office. This lack of control led Henry to wish Beckett dead. While there is no agreement on his exact words, many claim they were: "Will no one rid me of this turbulent priest?" This led directly to Beckett's assassination. Henry II is neither the first nor the last head of state to try and limit religion's political power. This chapter focuses on contemporary policies that regulate, restrict, and control religion.

The previous two chapters wrestled with the issue of whether supporting religion also implies an element of control and, if so, to what extent. The discussion in this chapter is free of this conundrum. It is certainly arguable that it is not possible to support religion without an element of control coming into play. However, there is little doubt that a state can have policies that control, restrict, and regulate religion without supporting it. This chapter focuses on this aspect of state religion policy. The 29 specific policies examined in this chapter are all examples of policies that focus on regulating, restricting, or controlling religion within the state and do not imply support for religion.

Of course, in the larger picture, control rarely exists without support. As demonstrated in Chapter 4, all states in this study save South Africa support religion in at least some small way. Thus, all of the 146 (82.5%) states that restricted, controlled, and regulated religion in 2008 also supported it. This finding that no state regulates, controls, or restricts religion without also supporting it in at least some small way is perhaps the most surprising and interesting finding in this chapter. It implies that many governments have mixed feelings about religion and that control, regulation, and restriction are inevitably intertwined with support. Perhaps this is because, as I argue in Chapter 4, one of the best ways to control religion is to support it.

That being said, it is important to define what I mean by control, restriction, and regulation. The Round 2 Religion and State Project (RAS2) dataset makes an important distinction focusing on to whom policies of restriction, control, and regulation apply. Specifically this study distinguishes between whether the government engages in these types of actions toward minority religions on one hand, and the majority religion or all religions in the state on the other hand. This distinction is critical because actions that can be quite similar have considerably different implications depending on the object of these policies. This is a distinction that is not generally included in other data collections such as Grim and Finke (2011) and Abouharb and Cingranelli (2006). In fact, the ability to distinguish whether a government limits the majority religion as compared to minority religions is unique to the RAS dataset.

Consider, for example, a government restricting the ability to build a place of worship. If this restriction is applied only to some or even all minority religions in a country but not all religions and certainly not the majority religion, this has several possible implications. Perhaps the most important is that this does not indicate that the government is antireligion in general. The fact that it does not restrict the majority religion in this way demonstrates that the implications of this policy have little to do with general hostility to religion and more to do with how minorities are treated.

There are several common reasons that a government might choose to restrict a minority religion, which are discussed in more detail in Chapter 6; these can include a desire to privilege the majority religion and that the government perceives the minority religions to be some form of threat. In contrast, when a government applies the same type of restriction to the majority religion and perhaps also all religions in the country, the implications are quite different. This indicates hostility or wariness toward religion or a desire to control religion in general. Thus, although government restrictions on minority religions and majority religions may often be similar, the distinction in motivation is so critical and clear-cut that the RAS2 dataset treats them separately. The laws, policies, and government actions discussed in this chapter are only those that are applied to the majority religion in the state and usually apply to minority religions as well, although application to the majority religion alone is sufficient for them to be coded.

There are numerous possible motivations for a policy like this. As I discussed in Chapter 2, antireligion political ideologies such communism are a clear motivation, but in today's world, the number of states with this type of ideology is dwindling. One explanation for states that support religion but still restrict it is a fear or wariness of religion's political power. Religion's political power is useful to politicians or sufficiently important that it cannot be ignored but at the same time politicians want to maintain their power and consider religion a potential threat to that power or at least a check on it (Gill, 2008).

Demerath and Straight (1997: 44) point out that "while religion is often an ally in the pursuit of power, once power has been secured, religion can become an unwelcome constraint in the quite different processes of state administration." Accordingly, regulation of religion is often "an effort to coopt and nullify it as an independent power base" (Demerath & Straight, 1997: 44).

A similar but distinct motivation is the desire to maintain control of or limit any large organization that is not directly part of the state so it cannot challenge the state. Sarkissian (2012: 502) argues along these lines that religious regulation in Muslim-majority states is "aimed at preventing the development of an independent sector of society that can challenge the state." However, some argue that while regulation may be necessary to meet this type of objectives, only limited regulation is necessary. For example, Driessen (2010) argues that as long as the government can make decisions without religious forces having a veto over those decisions, no more regulation is necessary. Finally, regulation of religion might be an effort to limit religiously motivated violence and disorder (Grim & Finke, 2011: 207–212).

Gill (2008) does not directly address what happens when a religious institution poses a political threat to the state. Rather, he focuses on religion's bargaining power and the interests of politicians in either supporting a religious monopoly or religious freedom. However, his observation that politicians seek to remain in power and maintain order at the lowest possible cost can be extrapolated to arrive at a similar conclusion as Demerath and Straight (1997), Grim and Finke (2011), and Sarkissian (2012). If religion is a challenge to political power or a cause of disorder, this would be a strong motivation to regulate it. As we will see later in this chapter, none of the motivations for controlling, regulating, and restricting religion discussed here are incompatible with supporting religion.

While much of the discussion in this chapter focuses on the presence or absence of the 29 types of policy in this category, it is important to note that each of these policies is coded in RAS2 on a weighted scale:

0. No restrictions.
1. Slight restrictions including practical restrictions or the government engages in this activity rarely and on a small scale.
2. Significant restrictions including practical restrictions or the government engages in this activity occasionally and on a moderate scale.
3. The activity is illegal or the government engages in this activity often and on a large scale.

This chapter divides these types of policy into four categories: (1) restrictions on religion's political role, (2) restrictions on religious institutions, (3) restrictions on religious practices, and (4) other restrictions. The policies in each of these categories have different implications for the motivations behind them. With some notable exceptions, most of these policies were more common in 2008 than in 1990. Nearly half of the world's countries changed this aspect of their religion policies, with most increasing the extent to which they regulated, controlled, and restricted religion.

Restrictions on Religion's Political Role

The five types of restrictions listed in Table 5.1 all relate to preventing religion from entering the political realm. As such they express a desire to maintain separation of religion and state (SRAS). This can be due to hostility toward religion, an anticlerical political philosophy, or simply a manifestation of the belief that government should stay out of religion that is popular among many modern liberal democratic theorists such as Rawls (1971; 1993). These policies can also represent a fear of religion's potential political power. In fact, they conform well to Sarkissian's (2012: 502) observation that "religious regulation is likely motivated more by political considerations than theological ones, for it imposes restrictions on those religious activities that may lead to oppositional mobilization."

Restrictions on religious political parties are rapidly increasing from 42 to 63 states during the study period. Much of this increase took place in sub-Saharan Africa, where 17 countries began restricting or banning religious political parties since 1990.[1] In some cases, this is based on a policy or law. For example, in Eritrea a 1995 proclamation bans involvement in politics by religious organizations. In many cases, this policy is part of a country's constitution. These constitutions usually ban political parties that are not inclusive of all citizens including parties based on religion. For example, Burundi's 1992 constitution forbids "political parties to identify themselves in the form, in action or any other way, including an ethnic group, region, religion, a sect or sex."[2] Burundi's 2001 constitution similarly states that political parties "must be open to all Burundians and ... must not advocate violence or hatred based, among other things, on membership of an ethnic group, regional origin or religion."[3] The Republic of Congo's 2002 constitution states that "political parties have a national character and do not identify themselves in form, in action, or in any other way with an ethnic group, region, religion, or cult."[4] The constitutions of the Central African Republic,[5] Sierra Leone,[6] and Uganda[7] have similar clauses. However, in some cases, the intent is clearly to ban religious political parties. Mozambique's constitution prohibits political parties "from

---

[1] This does not include countries that ban political parties or opposition parties altogether.
[2] Constitution of Burundi, 1992, www.religlaw.org/common/document.view.php?docId=1808.
[3] Burundian Transitional Constitution, 2001, www.chr.up.ac.za/hr_docs/constitutions/docs.
[4] 2002 Constitution of the Republic of Congo, www.chr.up.ac.za/index.php/documents-by-country-database/congo.html.
[5] 2004 Constitution of the Central African Republic, http://www.law.yale.edu/rcw/rcw/jurisdictions/afm/centralafricanrepublic/car_const.htm.
[6] Constitution of Sierra Leone, www.religlaw.org.
[7] Constitution of Uganda, www.wipo.int/wipolex/en/text.jsp?file_id=170004.

TABLE 5.1. *Restrictions on Religion's Political Role*

	All States		Majority Religion (2008 results)						
			Christian						
	1990*	2008	Catholic	Orthodox	Other Christian	Christian Total	Muslim	Other Religions
---	---	---	---	---	---	---	---	---
Restrictions on religious political parties	23.9%	35.6%	15.9%	46.2%	22.0%	22.4%	57.4%	43.7%
Restrictions on trade or civil associations being affiliated with a religion	4.5%	3.4%	2.3%	7.7%	0.0%	2.0%	4.3%	6.2%
Restrictions on clergy holding political office	11.3%	13.0%	22.7%	7.7%	4.9%	13.3%	6.4%	21.9%
Restrictions or monitoring of sermons by clergy	22.0%	23.2%	6.8%	7.7%	2.4%	5.1%	61.7%	21.9%
Restrictions on clergy or religious organizations engaging in public political speech, propaganda, or activity	20.9%	24.9%	13.6%	38.5%	17.1%	18.4%	36.2%	28.1%
% With at least one type	43.5%	53.7%	38.6%	53.8%	34.1%	38.8%	80.9%	59.4%
% With at least two types	24.9%	29.4%	15.9%	38.4%	9.7%	16.4%	53.2%	34.4%
% With at least three types	10.2%	13.6%	4.5%	15.3%	2.4%	5.2%	27.7%	18.8%
Mean number of types	0.82	1.00c	0.61	1.08	0.46	0.61	1.66	1.01
Mean score	2.05	2.51c	1.50	2.77	1.10	1.50	4.23	3.06

* In some countries, this represents the first available year.

using names containing expressions that are directly related to any religious denominations or churches, and from using emblems that may be confused with national or religious symbols."[8]

Restrictions on trade associations or other civil associations being affiliated with a religion. These restrictions are relatively rare and were present in only seven states in 2008, one less than at the beginning of the study period. Many of these bans are contained in constitutions. For example, Mozambique's constitution states that "professional associations and trade unions shall be independent from employers, from the State, from political parties and from churches or religious denominations."[9] Similarly, Haiti's constitution states that "unions are essentially nonpolitical, nonprofit, and nondenominational.[10]

Restrictions on clergy holding political office. This type of restriction increased from 20 to 22 states during the study period. For example, in Barbados, "a clerk in holy orders or other minister of religion" may not be elected as a member of the House of Assembly.[11] Guatemala's constitution bans clergy from serving as the president, vice president, ministers of state, judges, and magistrates.[12] Similarly Bolivia's 1967 constitution bans clergy from the offices of president and vice president.[13] Its 2009 constitution states that "ministers of any religious affiliation who have not resigned at least three months prior to the day of the election" may not run for public office.[14]

Restrictions or monitoring of sermons by clergy. While this category can include monitoring for doctrinal correctness, in most cases, governments monitor sermons for political content. In 1990 (or the earliest year available), 39 countries monitored sermons by clergy. This increased to 41 by 2008. This activity is particularly common in Muslim majority countries, especially in the Middle East where every government other than Israel and Lebanon monitors sermons. However, some non-Muslim-majority countries also monitor sermons. Equatorial Guinea monitors all political speech by clergy and has been known to arrest clergy perceived as antigovernment. This is mostly in the context of limitations on any antigovernment speech.[15] This fits a larger

---

[8] Constitution of Mozambique, www.unhcr.org/rcfworld/category,LEGAL,,,MOZ,4a1e597b2,0.html.
[9] Constitution of Mozambique, www.unhcr.org/refworld/category,LEGAL,,,MOZ,4a1e597b2,0.html.
[10] Constitution of Haiti, www.religlaw.org/countryportal.php.
[11] The Barbados Independence Order 1966, 2:44:1:c. Online, Religious Law International Documents Database: www.religlaw.org/template.php?id=935.
[12] Constitution of Guatemala, www.religlaw.org.
[13] 1967 Bolivia Constitution, http://pdba.georgetown.edu/Constitutions/Bolivia/bolivia1967.html
[14] 2009 Constitution of Bolivia, http://pdba.georgetown.edu/constitutions/bolivia/bolivia.html.
[15] Freedom of Expression: Equatorial Guinea," Freedom House, 2006, www.unhcr.org/refworld/country,,,,GNQ,,473451b925,0.html; Alex Vines. "Well-Oiled: Oil and Human Rights in Equatorial Guinea, Human Rights Watch, www.hrw.org/reports/2009/07/09/well-oiled-0; "Archbishop of Canterbury Welcomes the Release of Pastor from Five-Year Detention," June 25, 2008, Archbishop of Canterbury Home Page, www.archbishopofcanterbury.org/1867.

pattern in which non-Muslim-majority countries monitor sermons tend to be autocratic ones such as China, Cuba, Laos, and Myanmar.

Restrictions on clergy or religious organizations engaging in public political speech, propaganda, or activity. This category covers bans on political activity by clergy or religious institution other than sermons. Like the previous category, it is common and increasing from 37 to 44 countries during the study period. Unlike the previous category, this type of ban on political activity is common in states with all types of religious majorities and is present in several democratic states. For example, in the United States, religious organizations that endorse political candidates can lose their tax-exempt status, although this provision is rarely enforced. In most cases, these restrictions are stricter. For example, India's 1988 Law on Religious Institutions states that "no religious institution or manager thereof shall use or allow the use of any premises belonging to, or under the control of, the institution... for the promotion of any political activity."[16] In Macedonia, it is illegal to use religious gathering, services, schools, and instruction for political aims.[17] Similarly, Mongolia's constitution states that "religious institutions shall not pursue political activities."[18]

Overall, restrictions on political activity by clergy and religious institutions is increasing. Between 1990 and 2008, the number of states engaging in at least some of these restrictions increased by 18 countries from a minority of 43.5% to a slight majority of 53.7%. This rise in restrictions on religion's role in politics is also true of four of the five categories of restrictions examined here. As noted earlier, these policies are often enshrined in constitutions or the very laws that protect religious freedom. Thus, for many governments, the concept of religious freedom does not include the right of religious institutions or clergy to interfere in politics.

This type of regulation of religion is particularly important because it represents government recognition and perhaps fear of religion's political power. These laws and policies are directly designed to check this power. Thus, the significant increase in presence of such laws and policies, overall from 146 to 177 (a 21.2% increase) during the study period, likely represents either an increase in religion's actual political power or an increasing recognition by governments that this power exists. It also likely represents, at least in part, a desire by political classes to protect their territory from encroachment by religious elites. Put differently, all of the countries with these policies also support religion, many of them to a considerable extent. Yet they draw a line between supporting religion and allowing religious institutions and actors unbridled political influence.

---

[16] India 1988 Religious Institutions (Prevention of Misuse) Act, www.mha.nic.in/pdfs/Religious-InstitutionsAct1988.pdf.
[17] Macedonia, 1997 Law on Religious Communities and Religious Groups, www.religlaw.org/document.php?DocumentID=1757.
[18] Constitution of Mongolia, www.wipo.int/wipolex/en/text.jsp?file_id=183021.

Religious Institutions

The nine types of regulation, control, or restrictions on religious institutions, listed in Table 5.2, all represent either hostility toward religion or recognition of religion's influence in society and politics. This manifests as either government restrictions on religious institutions themselves, often institutions outside of government control, or efforts to control the institutions themselves or the clergy who run these institutions.

Religious institutions are clearly a potential political threat to governments. In fact, religious institutions across the world regularly engage in political activities, often mobilizing their followers to participate. This often includes opposition to governments or government policies. Although the primary purpose of religious institutions is rarely political activity nor are they designed for this purpose, they nevertheless are often well suited and placed to engage in political activity. This is why those who govern often see them as a potential threat (Fox, 2013: 84–93; Johnston & Figa, 1988; Wald et al., 2005).

However, unlike the previous category, which focuses only on the participation of religion in politics, the restrictions, regulation, and control of religious institutions can be more far reaching than simply limiting religion's political influence. Restricting religious institutions can influence their internal workings and organization. It can even influence their theology or at least how that theology is interpreted. For example, the ability to appoint clergy allows a government to appoint clergy whose theological views are in line with those of the government.

The regulation, restriction, and control of religious institutions can also transform them into a political asset that supports the state. These policies also constitute serious government penetration into the religious arena. This can involve government control over which institutions are allowed to function and who will control or even serve in these institutions. Religious institutions are vital to the survival of a religion and its ability to propagate itself from generation to generation. Thus, government involvement in religious institutions constitutes state control over one of religion's basic foundations. This has potential consequences far beyond simply limiting the political influence of religious institutions.

The government restricts or harasses members and organizations affiliated with the majority religion but who operate outside of the state-sponsored or recognized ecclesiastical framework. In all of these cases, the government supports a set of institutions associated with the majority religion and bans or limits religious organizations that are not part of the official or recognized religious network. This includes states with official religions such as Egypt, Morocco, and the Maldives; states that unofficially prefer a single religion such as Belarus, Myanmar, and Indonesia; or states that have more negative attitudes toward religion such as Azerbaijan, Laos, and Vietnam. In the Maldives, Islamic institutions outside of government control are forbidden. The government controls all

TABLE 5.2. *Restrictions on Religious Institutions*

	All States		Majority Religion (2008 results)					
			Christian					
	1990*	2008	Catholic	Orthodox	Other Christian	Christian Total	Muslim	Other Religions
The government restricts or harasses members and organizations affiliated with the majority religion but who operate outside of the state-sponsored or recognized ecclesiastical framework	15.3%	24.3%	4.5%	46.2%	4.9%	10.2%	59.6%	15.6%
Restrictions on formal religious organizations other than political parties	11.3%	14.7%	0.0%	7.7%	2.4%	2.0%	31.9%	28.1%
Restrictions on access to places of worship	4.5%	7.9%	0.0%	15.4%	0.0%	2.0%	19.1%	9.4%
Foreign religious organizations are required to have a local sponsor or affiliation	4.5%	5.6%	6.8%	15.4%	0.0%	5.1%	4.3%	9.4%
Heads of religious organizations (e.g., bishops) must be citizens of the state	5.1%	5.6%	2.3%	30.8%	2.4%	6.1%	6.4%	3.1%
All practicing clergy must be citizens of the state	1.7%	1.1%	2.3%	0.0%	0.0%	1.0%	0.0%	3.1%
The government participates in the clerical appointment process	20.3%	20.9%	11.4%	30.8%	7.3%	12.8%	42.6%	15.4%

(*continued*)

TABLE 5.2 (continued)

	All States		Majority Religion (2008 results)						
			Christian						Other Religions
	1990*	2008	Catholic	Orthodox	Other Christian	Christian Total	Muslim		
Other than appointments, the government legislates or otherwise officially influences the internal workings or organization of religious institutions and organizations	12.4%	14.7%	2.3%	38.5%	4.9%	8.2%	25.5%		18.7%
Laws governing the state religion are passed by the government or need the government's approval before being put into effect	6.2%	5.6%	0.0%	0.0%	2.4%	1.0%	12.8%		9.4%
% With at least one type	37.3%	44.5%	25.0%	76.9	17.1%	28.6%	76.6%		40.6%
% With at least two types	20.3%	25.4%	4.5%	53.8%	4.9%	11.3%	55.3%		25.0%
% With at least three types	11.9%	16.9%	0.0%	38.4%	2.4%	6.2%	36.2%		21.9%
Mean number of types	0.81	1.01b	0.30	1.85	0.24	0.48	2.02		1.13
Mean score	1.78	2.16a	0.55	3.15	0.41	0.84	4.70		2.44

* In some countries, this represents the first available year.

mosques. All imams must be licensed by the government after being educated in government-controlled institutions. The government even writes the sermons that imams may use in mosques.[19] In 1990, Myanmar's government banned all Buddhist organizations other than the nine state-recognized monastic orders that are controlled by the State Monk Coordination Committee. Laos similarly controls all religious activity in the country overseeing Theravada Buddhism, the country's majority religion. Its clergy, temples, and training all operate in close conjunction with government officials. Registration is mandatory to practice a religion, and no other Buddhist organizations have been allowed to register. In Azerbaijan, non-government-sponsored organizations exist but are severely harassed. This is primarily part of a campaign against what the government perceives as radical and political Islam. Independent Islamic organizations are often banned and their members harassed. The government is particularly hostile to foreign Islamic missionary activity, which it sees as trying to spread political Islam and sometimes as connected to terrorist activities (Wilhelmsen, 2009). This type of policy is becoming increasingly common increasing from 27 countries in 1990 (or the earliest year available) to 43 by 2008.

Restrictions on formal religious organizations other than political parties. This represents restrictions on even the mainstream religious organizations. These restrictions are sometimes pressed even by governments that support these organizations in some ways. This type of restriction was present in 20 states in 1990 (or the earliest year available). By 2008, Mexico had dropped its restrictions, but eight states began this type of policy. Mexico's 1917 constitution, which was amended in 1992, contained several anticlerical provisions including bans on the establishment of religious orders and the denial of legal status to the Catholic Church, among many other restrictive provisions.[20] Perhaps the most extreme example of restrictions on religious organizations is North Korea. While North Korea has a national religion-like ideology called *juche* in which the country's leader is arguably worshipped, traditional religions are essentially banned altogether. There exist government-controlled religious organizations, but they are mostly used for propaganda purposes and are closed when there are no foreign visitors.[21]

---

[19] Odd Larsen, "Almost No Religious Freedom for Migrant Workers," Forum 18, June 23, 2009, www.forum18.org/Archive.php?article_id=1316; Odd Larsen, "Maldives: Religious Freedom Survey, October 2008," Forum 18, October 15, 2008, www.forum18.org/Archive.php?article_id=1203; "Maldives Bans Popular Religious Leaders from Leading Prayers," BBC Monitoring South Asia (Political), October 12, 2005.

[20] 1917 Constitution of Mexico, www.latinamericanstudies.org/mexico/1917-Constitution.htm.

[21] Magda Hornemann, "Christians Murdered, Sources State," Forum 18, October 14, 2004, www.forum18.org/Archive.php?article_id=431; "North Korea: Faith and Famine," *Washington Times/International Christian Concern*, October 8, 2008, www.persecution.org/2008/10/08/north-korea-faith-and-famine; Magda Hornemann, "Religious Freedom Non-existent, but Much Still Unknown," Forum 18, March 29, 2006, www.forum18.org/Archive.php?article_id=752; Magda Hornemann, "Mystery of the Last 'Hermit Kingdom'," Forum 18, February 25, 2004, www.forum18.org/Archive.php?article_id=261; Kim Hyung-jin, "Does Genuine

Restrictions on access to places of worship. Although this could also be considered a restriction on religious practices because it focuses on access to the physical embodiment of religious institutions, I place this policy in this category. In 1990 (or the first year available), eight countries engaged in this practice. By 2008, six countries – Algeria, China, Georgia, Mauritania, Tajikistan, and Uzbekistan – began this type of policy. In 2001, Algeria began banning the use of mosques for meetings other than religious services. This was mostly intended to restrict their use for political purposes. Since the mid-1990s, Uzbekistan has repeatedly closed mosques suspected of supporting militant activity. The government also restricts the access of children to mosques. Children may not attend nighttime Ramadan prayers or visit mosques during school hours. In 2006, the government distributed instructions to imams expressing the undesirability of children attending prayers at mosques.[22]

Foreign religious organizations are required to have a local sponsor or affiliation. This is the first of three types of policies that focus on limiting foreign religious organizations and foreign influence on religious organizations. This policy was present in eight countries at the beginning of the study period with Belarus and Madagascar adding it by 2008. In some cases these restrictions are minimal. For example, in Honduras foreign missionaries must be sponsored by a Honduran institution or individual, but the government generally grants permits to anyone with such a sponsor. In others, these constraints are very strict. For example, in Oman, foreign Muslims are prohibited from preaching, teaching, and leading worship.

Heads of religious organizations (e.g., bishops) must be citizens of the state. This type of restriction ensures that foreigners cannot lead religious organizations, a significant check on foreign influence. In 1990 (or the earliest year available), nine states engaged in this practice. By 2008, Belarus and Estonia had added this type of policy, but Mexico had discontinued it. Estonia's 1993 Church and Congregations Act states that only citizens and legal residents may be members of a congregation's management board and that congregation leaders must be Estonian with at least five years residence in the country.[23] Turkey similarly requires all religious community leaders to be Turkish with the exception of Catholics and churches attached to the diplomatic community (Yildiz, 2007).

Religious Freedom Exist in Communist North Korea," *Yonhap News*/ International Christian Concern, May 18, 2007, www.persecution.org/2007/05/18/does-genuine-religious-freedom-exist-in-communist-north-korea; Uwe Siemon-Netto, "Covert Church in North Korea Growing," *United Press International*, February 21, 2002; "Life Inside North Korea," Senate Foreign Relations Committee Subcommittee on East Asian and Pacific Affairs Hearing, June 5, 2003, www.uscirf.gov/north-korea.html.

[22] Mushrig Bayram, "Muslim and Christian Worship Attacked," Forum 18/ Human Rights without Frontiers, September 18–19, 2009.

[23] Estonia, Church and Congregations Act 1993, translation, http://religlaw.com/document.php?DocumentID=128.

All practicing clergy must be citizens of the state. This practice was only present in China, Mexico, and Panama, with Mexico discontinuing the practice in the context of its 1992 constitutional reform. In Panama, foreign clergy are not banned but are limited through a strict visa procedure, which is less strict for rabbis and Catholic priests. In China, the only legal religious institutions are sponsored by the state and all clergy must be Chinese. Foreign religious organizations may provide social services but may not proselytize.

The government participates in the clerical appointment process. This is when the government appoints, approves appointments, or otherwise takes part in the appointment process for at least some clergy, usually senior clergy. This type of government control of religious organizations is surprisingly common with 36 states engaging in this practice in 1990 (or the earliest year available), which increased to 37 by 2008. However, there was considerable turnover in this category with five countries ending this practice and six instituting it. An example of very low-level intervention in the appointment process is Luxembourg. Luxembourg's constitution maintains that

> [s]tate intervention in the appointment and installation of heads of religions, the method by which religions appoints and dismiss ministers of religion, the right to correspond with superiors and publicize their acts, and Church-State relations are subject to agreements to be submitted to the Chamber of Deputies for the provisions requiring it intervention.[24]

In practice, little intervention occurs. In contrast, Kuwait's government appoints the country's Islamic leader the Grand Mufti. Egypt's and Jordan's governments appoint most imams.

Other than appointments, the government legislates or otherwise officially influences the internal workings or organization of religious institutions and organizations. This refers to a wide variety of ways in which a government can control or influence religious organizations. Countries that engage in this type of practice increased from 22 to 26 during the study period. For example, the Greek government has considerable influence over the Greek Orthodox Church, the state's official religion. The government has the right to modify the church charter, introduce regulations, and suspend noncompliant synods.[25] Similarly, until 2000, when Sweden divested of its official religion the Church of Sweden, the parliament approved all changes in Church law.[26] A more extreme case, as was noted earlier, is China, which controls all recognized religious organizations in the country.

Laws governing the state religion are passed by the government or need the government's approval before being put into effect: This category represents

---

[24] Constitution of Luxembourg, www.wipo.int/wipolex/en/text.jsp?file_id=194538.
[25] Karagiannis (2009); Anthee Carassava, "Greek Church Struggles to Quell Raft of Scandals Involving Clergy," *New York Times*, February 5, 2005.
[26] T.R. Reid, "Sweden Separates Church, State," *Washington Post*, December 30, 2000.

governments that to some extent control even the doctrine of a religion. For example, Brunei's constitution makes the sultan the head of Islam in the country and gives him absolute power to regulate Islam in the country (Roberts & Onn, 2009; Talib, 2002). In 1990 (or the earliest year available), 11 countries engaged in this practice. This dropped to 10 in 1998 when Iceland transferred the power to pass Church laws for the Evangelical Lutheran Church from the Althing – Iceland's legislature – to an annual Church assembly.

Overall, the regulation, restriction, and control of religious institutions is increasing. At the beginning of the study period, 66 countries engaged in at least one of these nine practices. This increased to 77 by 2008. Most countries engaging in these practices engaged in multiple types during this period. Seven of the nine types became increasingly common during this study period, and the other two were already among the least common of these practices. This is consistent with the lager pattern of increasing government involvement in religion between 1990 and 2008.

Another interesting pattern is that other than the requirements that all clergy be citizens and that foreign religious organizations and clergy require a local sponsor, seven of these practices are most common among Muslim-majority states. Because Muslim-majority states on average support religion more strongly than other states, this is further evidence of the entanglement between support and control. The link between state support for religion and state control of religion is analyzed in more detail later in this chapter.

Restrictions on Religious Practices

This category of regulation, restriction, and control of religion focuses on limitations on the freedom to practice one's religion. At first glance, this would seem to indicate that hostility to religion or at least a fear of its power on some level is the primary motivation, especially given that this set of variables focuses on the treatment of the majority religion or all religions in a state. In fact, while control is frequently a motivation, there are often other motivations for this type of practice. Some of the countries coded in these categories, which are listed in Table 5.3, restrict members of the majority religion who operate outside of state-approved institutions. In these cases, this type of restriction indicates a desire to control religion by making sure all religious people use state controlled or approved institutions. In other cases, it represents a fear that unrestricted religion can be potentially dangerous or strengthen the political opposition.

Restrictions on the public observance of religious practices, including religious holidays and the Sabbath. While at both the beginning and end of the study period, 12 countries followed this practice, several states changed their policies during this period. Until 2008 in Macedonia, Orthodox Christian religious practices outside the auspices of the Macedonian Orthodox Church were restricted by banning more than one organization per religion and banning

TABLE 5.3. *Restrictions on Religious Practices*

	All States		Majority Religion (2008 results)						
			Christian						
	1990*	2008	Catholic	Orthodox	Other Christian	Christian Total	Muslim	Other Religions
Restrictions on the public observance of religious practices, including religious holidays and the Sabbath	6.8%	6.8%	2.3%	7.7%	7.3%	5.1%	4.3%	15.6%
Restrictions on religious activities outside of recognized religious facilities	8.5%	10.2%	4.5%	7.7%	9.8%	7.1%	10.6%	18.7%
Restrictions on the publication or dissemination of written religious material	11.9%	11.3%	0.0%	7.7%	2.4%	2.0%	29.8%	12.5%
People are arrested for religious activities	4.5%	4.5%	0.0%	0.0%	0.0%	0.0%	10.6%	9.4%
Restrictions on religious public gatherings that are not placed on other types of public gathering	5.1%	5.6%	4.5%	0.0%	2.4%	3.1%	6.4%	12.5%
Restrictions on the public display by private persons or organizations of religious symbols, including (but not limited to) religious dress, the presence or absence of facial hair, nativity scenes, and icons	5.1%	10.2%	4.5%	0.0%	2.4%	3.1%	27.7%	6.2%
Conscientious objectors to military service are not given other options for national service and are prosecuted	15.3%	8.5%	2.3%	23.1%	2.4%	5.1%	10.6%	15.6%
% With at least one type	29.4%	30.5%	13.6%	30.8%	19.5%	18.4%	55.3%	31.2%
% With at least two types	14.1%	13.0%	4.5%	15.4%	7.3%	7.2%	21.3%	18.7%
% With at least three types	7.9%	6.2%	0.0%	0.0%	0.0%	0.0%	10.7%	11.9%
Mean number of types	0.57	0.57	0.18	0.46	0.27	0.26	1.00	0.91
Mean score	1.06	1.00	0.25	0.77	0.32	0.35	1.68	2.00

* In some countries, this represents the first available year.

public and private services by unregistered religions. The 2008 Law on Religious Freedom ended this policy.[27] In 2003, Syria stopped banning prayers by soldiers in military facilities (Zisser, 2005). A 1998 Uzbek law bans religious activities outside of state-controlled institutions. The law has several vague provisions that can be used to restrict religious expression including a ban on wearing religious clothes outside places of worship for anyone other than clergy and bans on "religious fanaticism and extremism" as well as on antistate activities and actions creating "hostility" between religions.[28] In 2003, several of India's regional governments began banning Trishuls, which are traditional Hindu symbols similar to a trident that can be used as weapons.

Restrictions on religious activities outside of recognized religious facilities. In 1990 (or the earliest year available), 15 states had this type of policy. This increased to 18 by 2008. Macedonia was the only state to eliminate this type of policy in the context of the 2008 law discussed earlier. A rarely enforced 1995 Angolan law bans "cult demonstrations" outside of authorized locations. Niger's minister of the interior set a policy in 2006 that required Islamic preachers to "ask for authorization before organizing sermons in public places."[29] In 2000, several of Nigeria's northern states began banning open-air religious services held away from places of worship including preaching, public religious processions, rallies, demonstrations, and meetings in public places. This ban is due to fears that these activities would heighten interreligious tensions, which had already resulted in violence. Zimbabwe has on several occasions used a public order ordinance to ban public prayer meetings it believes are covers for opposition activities and sometimes arrest the participants.[30] The most restrictive policies of this nature are in North Korea and China, both of which ban religious activities outside of recognized facilities altogether.

Restrictions on the publication or dissemination of written religious material. This includes all written religious material especially foundational works such as the Bible or Koran. Twenty countries restricted religious publications at both the beginning and end of the study period. Turkmenistan's policy is particularly strict. The government must approve all religious publications, whether

---

[27] Law on Religious Communities and Religious Groups, original Macedonian version published in the Official Bulletin of the Republic of Macedonia (No. 35 of July 23, 1997) (Macedonia). Translation by Zorica Angelovska-Kovacevik.

[28] The Law of the Republic of Uzbekistan on Freedom of Worship and Religious Organizations, 1998, www.religlaw.org/document.php?DocumentID=10; Felix Corley, "Prisoners of Conscience Numbers Increase," www.forum18.org/Archive.php?article_id=1158.

[29] "Niger: Authorities to Regulate Islamic Sermons in Public Places," *BBC Monitoring Africa*, September 10, 2006.

[30] "Under a Shadow: Civil and Political Rights in Zimbabwe," Human Rights Watch, June 6, 2003, www.hrw.org/legacy/backgrounder/africa/zimbabwe060603.htm; "Could Zimbabwe's Churches Have Done More to Counter the Excesses of Mugabe's Regime?" *The Times* (London), March 9, 2002; "Pray and Walk Protest Puts Irish Priest in Jail in Bulawayo," *Irish Times*, March 20, 2002.

published in the country or imported. Only registered groups may publish or import such material, and the number of copies is limited to the number of registered members. Unauthorized materials are regularly confiscated.[31] In Vietnam, the government must approve all religious publications and requires that they be published through a government owned or approved publishing house. In practice, this limitation is not drastic, and a range of Buddhist sacred scriptures, Bibles, and other religious texts and publications are printed and openly distributed by these organizations.

People are arrested for religious activities. Eight countries engaged in this type of practice between 1990 and 2008. North Korea restricts all religious activity in the country. Four of them – China, Turkmenistan, Uzbekistan, and Vietnam – significantly restrict religious expression outside of state-approved institutions, which are designed to limit religion in the state. The other three – Iran, Oman, and Qatar – are Middle Eastern Muslim-majority states that support an official version of Islam and generally support Islam. Iran restricts the practices of Sufi Muslims who consider themselves to belong to Iran's Shi'i majority, while the government believes that they deviate from proper religious practices.[32] Qatar and Oman occasionally arrest people for setting up illegal religious organizations or criticizing government religion policy.

Restrictions on religious public gatherings that are not placed on other types of public gathering. In 1990 (or the earliest year available), nine states had this type of policy. In 2004, Pakistan instituted this type of policy by banning all public gatherings by "extremist" organizations. Rwanda limits nighttime religious meetings because in the past, rebels used such meetings as a guise for mobilizing to attack nearby targets. Since 2003, it has allowed such meetings but with a government permit.

Restrictions on the public display by private persons or organizations of religious symbols, including (but not limited to) religious dress, the presence or absence of facial hair, nativity scenes, and icons. In 1990 (or the earliest year available), nine countries had this type of policy. By 2008, this doubled to 18, all but five of which were Muslim-majority states. Perhaps the most notorious example of this in a non-Muslim country is France's 2004 law banning all overt religious symbols in schools. Although it is arguable that the main target of this law is the traditional head coverings of Muslim women, the law was specifically and intentionally applied to any overt religious symbol from any religion including large crosses, turbans worn by Sikhs, and Jewish skullcaps. The Maldives began a series of policies regulating Islamic dress in 2007. It banned wearing a Muslim veil in court because it can hide a woman's identity. Female police officers could not wear a head covering

---

[31] Felix Corley, "I Want to Know If I Can Import Religious Books," Forum 18, May 12, 2009, www.forum18.org/Archive.php?article_id=1294.
[32] Roxana Sabari, "Growing Popularity of Sufism in Iran," *BBC News*, April 25, 2006.

without permission, which was often denied and even revoked. The government also ordered the state-run television network not to employ women who cover their face.[33]

Conscientious objectors to military service are not given other options for national service and are prosecuted. This type of policy dropped from being present in 27 states to 15 states during the study period, which is the largest drop of any of the 29 types of restriction control or regulation of religion. Albania, Georgia, Greece, Iraq, Kazakhstan, Latvia, Lithuania, Macedonia, Russia, Serbia, Taiwan, the Turkish government of Cyprus, and Vietnam all dropped this type of policy, and no country added it during this period. Interestingly, the only region of the world where this policy was not present at all is sub-Saharan Africa.

Overall, only a minority of countries restrict religious practices. In 1990 (or the earliest year available), 52 countries did so, which increased to 54 by 2008. These countries engaged in a combined 101 types of restrictions at both the beginning and end of the study period. If we discount the conscientious objectors category, restrictions on religious practices increased substantially. Be that as it may, this category is both the least common form of religious restrictions, regulation, and control and the only one that has not increased substantially.

Perhaps this is because the practical political motivations to engage in this type of policy are the weakest. Certainly ideologically antireligious states might be motivated to engage in these policies but, as is discussed in Chapter 3, such states are rare and getting rarer. Many of the existing restrictions, as noted anecdotally in this section, are motivated by a desire to limit and control religion's political power or its use to facilitate political opposition. The policies listed in the previous two categories are likely more efficient at achieving this goal and are, accordingly, more common. Thus, in the larger scheme of things, these policies are a poor choice for a government that wants to limit religion's political influence. Specifically, this type of policy is likely to enflame antigovernment sentiment among religious people, and there are other policies available that are no more likely to cause upset but are more effective at limiting religion's political influence. Thus, of all the types of regulation, restriction, and control of religion, this is the type that is most likely to be motivated by ideology.

Yet I posit that these policies are sometimes selected to control religion for three reasons. First, governments often do not select the most efficient policy to achieve a goal. Second, many of these policies are a reaction to specific circumstances in which a specific action is seen as a threat. Thus, in these cases, there is no general policy of restricting religion. Rather, the policy

---

[33] "Maldives Rights Body Opposes Ban on Veil in Courtroom," *BBC Monitoring South Asia* (Political), November 12, 2007; MEL Gunasekera, "Maldives Moves against Veiled Women, Jihadis on TV," *Agence France Presse*, November 14, 2007.

represents more narrow circumstances with more limited goals, such as limiting the influence of a specific opposition group that uses open-air prayer meetings to organize. Third, these policies are often enacted in states that also engage in many of the more "efficient" means to limit religion. However, the perceived threat is so great that the state enacts these less efficient policies in addition to the other ones.

This postulation is supported by the nature of the states that most restrict religious practices. Azerbaijan, China, Cuba, North Korea, Turkmenistan, Turkey (through 2008), Uzbekistan, and Vietnam all have at least four types of restrictions on religious practices and score at least 35 on their overall religious regulation score. All of them, other than perhaps Turkey, are nondemocracies that are overtly hostile to religion in general, and combined they account for 36.6% of the world's restrictions on the religious practices of the majority religion.

Other Types of Regulation, Restriction, and Control

This category includes the eight types of government regulation, restriction, and control of religion, listed in Table 5.4, that do not fit into the other three categories.

Arrest, continued detention, or severe official harassment of religious figures, officials, and/or members of religious parties. In theory this refers to arrests due to one's religious affiliation, activities, or position. In practice governments that wish to arrest people because of their religious position, activities, or affiliation often come up with pretexts, claiming that those arrested engaged in criminal activities. It is also true that religions are sometimes, in fact, used as covers for criminal activities and that some religious organizations engage in criminal activities. In recent years, religious terrorism has been a prime example of this phenomenon, although by no means the only one. Accordingly, in practice, no arrests, detentions, or severe harassment were coded in this category if it is clear that the real motivation is criminal or illegal activities that would be considered criminal or illegal in most free democratic states.

This activity increased considerably from 17 countries in 1990 (or the earliest year available) to 28 in 2008, 19 of them Muslim-majority states. For example, in 2002, Zimbabwe's government began arresting members of a number of religious groups, although those arrested are mostly those who criticized the government. In many countries, such as Mauritania and Tunisia, the arrests and harassment focus on members of the majority religion who are considered radical. In Mauritania, this began in 2003 and involves multiple arrests.[34]

---

[34] Mauritania Vows Crackdown on Religious Extremism," Pan African News Agency Daily Newswire, May 14, 2003; "Mauritanian PM Denounces "Rampant Danger" of Islamic Extremism," Agence France Presse, May 19, 2003; Ahmed Mohamed, "Mauritanian Authorities

TABLE 5.4. *Other Regulation of Religion*

	All States		Majority Religion (2008 results)						
			Christian						
	1990*	2008	Catholic	Orthodox	Other Christian	Christian Total	Muslim	Other Religions
---	---	---	---	---	---	---	---	---
Arrest, continued detention, or severe official harassment of religious figures, officials, and/or members of religious parties	9.6%	15.8%	2.3%	0.0%	7.3%	4.1%	40.4%	15.6%
Restrictions on public religious speech	6.8%	7.3%	0.0%	0.0%	2.4%	1.0%	17.0%	87.5%
Restrictions on religious-based hate speech	18.2%	26.7%	40.9%	61.5%	39.0%	42.9%	23.4%	37.5%
Restrictions on or regulation of religious education in public schools	16.4%	17.5%	2.3%	15.4%	12.2%	8.2%	46.8%	3.1%
Restrictions on or regulation of religious education outside of public schools or general government control of religious education	16.4%	19.8%	2.3%	7.7%	7.3%	5.1%	40.4%	65.6%
Restrictions on or regulation of religious education at the university level	7.9%	7.9%	0.0%	7.7%	0.0%	1.0%	23.4%	6.2%
State ownership of some religious property or buildings	18.6%	18.6%	15.9%	30.8%	9.8%	15.3%	27.7%	15.6%
Other types of restrictions	22.6%	28.2%	15.9%	30.8%	24.4%	21.4%	40.4%	31.2%
% With at least one type	63.3%	65.5%	63.6%	84.6%	58.5%	64.3%	76.6%	65.6%
% With at least two types	29.4%	35.0%	15.9%	46.1%	26.8%	24.5%	57.7%	37.5%
% With at least three types	15.3%	19.2%	0.0%	15.3%	9.7%	6.1%	40.7%	28.1%
Mean number of types	1.27	1.35	0.80	1.54	1.02	0.99	2.15	1.56
Mean Score	2.63	3.19c	1.41	2.92	1.78	1.77	5.96	3.50

* In some countries, this represents the first available year.

Tunisia regularly harassed and arrested supporters and members of Ad Nadaha, an Islamic political party.

Restrictions on public religious speech. This refers to limitations on religion in public discourse. The presence of this type of policy increased from 12 to 13 states during the study period. For instance, beginning in 1999, several states in Malaysia banned imams from opposition parties from speaking in mosques (Stark, 2004). Similarly, Tajikistan's government often blocks members of the Islamic Renaissance Party from speaking in mosques, even though the party is legal. However, the motivation for this type of policy is not always to limit political opposition. For example, several of Switzerland's cantons prohibit public employees from publically expressing religious opinions.[35] Another example is Cuba where these restrictions are part of the country's general ideologically based policy of limiting religion in the state.

Restrictions on religious-based hate speech. This policy is becoming increasingly common, rising from 50 to 65 states during the study period. Most often this policy is part of a law or constitutional clause banning hatred on several bases including ethnicity, race, and religion. For example, Ecuador's constitution prohibits "advertising that causes violence, discrimination, racism, drug abuse, sexism, religious or political intolerance."[36] However, sometimes the laws are specific to religion. For instance, in Poland offending religious sentiment through public speech is punishable by a fine or three years in prison. Venezuela's constitution specifically prohibits promoting religious intolerance.[37] While the only world region where this policy is absent is the Middle East, 11 non–Middle Eastern Muslim-majority states, such as Albania, Bangladesh, Indonesia, and Malaysia, have this type of law.

Restrictions on or regulation of religious education in public schools. This does not refer to bans on religious education in public schools. Rather it codes countries that somehow control its content or select who teaches religion in public schools. In 1990 (or the earliest year available), 29 countries engaged in this type of control. By 2008, Afghanistan, Malaysia, and Pakistan began this type of policy but Iraq discontinued it after the fall of Saddam Hussein's

---

Detain Several Prominent Islamic Opposition Figures," Associated Press, October 10, 2004; "Mauritania Authorities Arrest Islamist Leader," Associated Press Worldstream, November 2, 2004; Ahmed Mohamed, "Mauritanian Authorities Arrest Five Islamist Leaders," Associated Press, April 25, 2005; "Mauritanian Authorities Crack Down on Islamic Fundamentalists," Panafrican News Agency Daily Newswire, April 26, 2005; "Mauritania Cracks Down on Islamists," Agence France Presse, April 28, 2005; "Searches and Arrests at Mauritanian Mosques," Agence France Presse, May 12, 2005; Ahmed Mohamed, "Mauritania Arrests 7 Men Suspected of Terrorism," Associated Press, October 17, 2007; "Mauritania Arrests Three Suspected Islamists: Authorities," Agence France Presse, January 18, 2008.

[35] "Muslim Teacher Fired for Violating Geneva Laws," December 19, 2002, www.swissinfo.ch/eng/index.html?siteSect=105&sid=1527150.

[36] Constitution of Ecuador, http://pdba.georgetown.edu/Constitutions/Ecuador/ecuador.html.

[37] Constitution of Venezuela, http://pdba.georgetown.edu/Constitutions/Venezuela/venezuela.html.

regime, increasing the number to 31. At 22 states in 2008, this type of policy is most common in Muslim-majority states, For example, Algeria's Ministry of Religious Affairs supervises all schools in the country. Yemen's government began standardizing all religious education in public schools in 2001 and in 2004 began actively eradicating "extremist" ideas from the curriculum.[38] This type of policy is also present in several non-Muslim-majority states. For example, in Germany, one of four Western democracies with this type of policy, the State Ministry of Education controls the curricula of all religion courses.[39]

Restrictions on or regulation of religious education outside of public schools or general government control of religious education. This type of policy is the same as the previous one but applies to religious education outside of public schools. It was present in 29 countries in 1990 (or the earliest year available), increasing to 35 by 2008. Although most common in Muslim-majority states, it was also present in 15 other states in 2008. Essentially, this type of policy is present in two types of states: states that control the religion curriculum in both public and private schools and states that ban religious education in public schools and regulate or ban it elsewhere. Brunei is an example of the former. A 2003 executive order requires that both public and private schools "comply with the National Education Policy ... by incorporating the philosophy of the Malay Islamic monarchy as a compulsory subject into its teaching syllabus."[40] Tajikistan, Turkmenistan, and Uzbekistan are examples of the latter. They ban religious education in public schools and heavily regulate it elsewhere. Tajikistan bans private religious lessons, although this is rarely enforced and parents are allowed to teach their own children. All formal religious education is heavily controlled and regulated by the government.[41] A 2003 Turkmenistan law states that "children may be taught religious dogma at Mosques during off-hours from school for not more than four hours per week, subject to the approval of the Gengesh for Religious Affairs under the President of Turkmenistan and to consent from the parents, substitute persons, legal guardians and the children themselves."[42] Uzbekistan bans religious education in all schools as well as private lessons but allows licensed religious education institutions with licensed teachers.[43]

[38] "Yemen Curbs Extremism in Religious Teaching," United Press International, July 15 2004.
[39] "German State to Teach Islam in Public Schools," Associated Press, September 5, 2006.
[40] Brunei 2003 Education Order, www.agc.gov.bn:81/index.php?option=com_content&view=article&id=61&Itemid=165; Alex Colvin, "Brunei," International Coalition for Religious Freedom, www.religiousfreedom.com/index.php?option=com_content&view=article&id=160&Itemid=29.
[41] Sandra Cheldelin, "Religion and Education in Tajikistan: Toward Tolerant Civic Society," Institute for Conflict Analysis and Resolution, George Mason University, 2007, www.icar.gmu.edu/docs/reports/Religion_Education_Tajikistan.pdf.
[42] Turkmenistan 1991/2003 Law on Freedom of Religion and Religious Organizations, www.unhcr.org/refworld/docid/44a3c4184.html.
[43] Mushfig Bayram and Felix Corley, "Threats, Raids, and Violence against Religious Believers," *Forum 18*/Human Rights without Frontiers, February 24/March 2, 2010, www.hrwf

Restrictions on or regulation of religious education at the university level. This is similar to the previous two categories but applies to higher education and is less common. At both the beginning and end of the study period, 14 countries had this type of policy. Most of these controls are in the context of general controls on religious education. For example, the control noted earlier for Tajikistan, Turkmenistan, and Uzbekistan also apply at the university level.

State ownership of some religious property or buildings. This does not refer to states that maintain chapels and places of prayer on government property. Rather, it indicates state ownership of religious properties that are intended for general use or are otherwise of significance. Throughout the study period, 33 states owned or controlled this type of religious property. In Mexico, all religious property from before 1992 is owned by the government. This is the result of a provision in Mexico's 1917 constitution that was amended in 1992. Similarly, the French government owns and operates all religious buildings that predate the 1905 law separating religion from state. In Kuwait, as is the case in many Muslim-majority countries, the government is responsible for the running and upkeep of all mosques. Also, most former Soviet Bloc countries at the beginning of the study period held large amounts of properties seized during the Communist era. Much of this property has been returned, but in many of these countries, some properties have remained in government hands, often because of disputes over which religious organization is entitled to the property.

Other types of restrictions. While the previous 28 categories cover most state policies that regulate, restrict, and control the majority religion in a state, governments are creative and often engage in policies that are more unique. This category is intended to cover any relevant policy in a state that is not covered by another category. In 1990 (or the earliest year available), 40 states had such policies. This increased to 50 by 2008. A sampling of these policies includes the following:

- Religions may not practice or preach ideas contrary to social norms. (Austria)
- A ban on broadcast advertising for religious causes. (Germany)
- Religious groups may not hold a broadcasting license. (Mexico, United Kingdom, Uruguay)
- A ban on the use of public buildings by religious organizations. (Bulgaria)
- Religious funds may be used only for religious purposes not social purposes. (Czech Republic)

.net/index.php?option=com_content&view=article&id=187:news-archives-2010&catid=38: freedom-of-religion-and-belief&Itemid=90; the Law of the Republic of Uzbekistan on Freedom of Worship and Religious Organizations (1998), www.religlaw.org/document.php?DocumentID=10; Igor Rotar, "State Control of Islamic Religious Education," Forum 18, May 11, 2004, www.forum18.org/Archive.php?article_id=318.

- Students may not study the majority religion outside of the country. (Kazakhstan)
- Religious organizations may collect contributions only in facilities where religious services and activities are performed. (Macedonia)
- Only religious organizations that have been in the country for a set period of time may use that country's name in their official name. (Russia)
- Bans on Muslim call to prayers or Minaret speakers. (Azerbaijan, Tajikistan)
- Clergy may not vote. (Myanmar, Thailand)
- Any religious person is restricted from holding office even if he or she is not clergy. (China, Vietnam)
- Politicians may not appeal for votes using religious affinities or affiliations. (India)
- A ban on foreign chaplains or religious assistance to the military. (Timor)
- A ban on "religious fanaticism." (Congo-Brazzaville)
- A government representative must be present at religious meetings. (Equatorial Guinea)
- Candidates for election must declare their religion. (Mauritius)

During the study period, the eight types of regulation, restrictions, and control in the "other" category increased from 224 to 239, an increase of 6.7%. In 1990 (or the earliest year available), 112 countries had at least one of these types of policies. This increased to 116 in 2008, an increase of 3.6%. However, overall, the mean score for this variable increased by 21.3%. This disparity is due to two factors. First, many countries increased the number of policies in which they engaged. Second, and more important, this variable is coded on a scale and many countries increased the severity of policies already in place.

Trends

Change over Time

As is the case for religious support, the most important trend for regulation, restriction and control is the consistent increase over time. As shown in Figure 5.1, this type of policy increased by 23.2% as measured by the overall score. This increase happened steadily over time and became statistically significant in 1994.[44] Other than the practices category, all of the categories increased over time with statistical significance.[45]

---

[44] The increase compared with 1990 or the earliest year available was statistically significant at the .05 level in 1994; at the .01 level in 1995, 1996, 1997, 1998, and 2000; and at the .001 level in 1999 and from 2001 through 2008.

[45] The increase in political role compared with 1990 or the earliest year available was statistically significant at the .05 level in 1992, at the .01 level from 1993 to 1998, and at the .001 level from 1990 to 2008. The increase in institutions compared with 1990 or the earliest year available was statistically significant at the .05 level in 1999, 202, 2004, and 2006 to 2008 and at the .01 level in 2003 and 2005. The increase in other restrictions compared with 1990 or the earliest

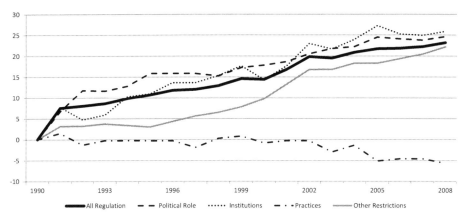

FIGURE 5.1. Change over Time in the Regulation, Restriction, and Control of the Majority Religion or All Religions.

This trend is robust when examining it from other perspectives. At the level of the 29 individual types of regulation, restriction, and control, 20 (69.0%) of them increased over time, 4 (13.8%) remained at the same level, and 5 (17.2%) decreased.[46] As shown in Table 5.5, the number of states that engaged in higher levels of this type of policy outnumber those that engaged in less by a ratio of 3.4 to 1 with nearly half of states changing their policy in some manner. Overall, states added 175 new policies in this category and dropped 59, a ratio of almost 3 to 1. This trend is consistent across categories of regulation, restriction, and control with, again, the exception of restrictions on religious practices.

As presented in Table 5.6, this trend is mostly consistent across religious traditions, although there are some interesting nuances. Restrictions on religious institutions dropped in two of the three Christian categories. The result for Catholic states is largely driven by Mexico's 1992 constitutional reforms, which lowered four categories of restrictions on institutions by a total of 10 points. Other than this, no Catholic-majority state changed its policy other than Rwanda, which in 2002 began occasionally harassing dissident Catholic groups as well as those affiliated with the political opposition. The drop among other Christian states occurred only in Western democracies – Finland, Iceland, Sweden, and Switzerland. Sweden's reduction was the largest and occurred in the context of removing its official religion in 2000. Eritrea and Estonia increased restrictions on religious institutions.

year available was statistically significant at the .05 level in 1997 and 1999; at the .01 level in 1998, 2000, 2004, and 2005; and at the .001 level from 2001 to 2003 and 2006 to 2008.

[46] This calculation is based on the number of states with each type of policy.

TABLE 5.5. *Change over Time in the Regulation, Restriction, and Control of the Majority Religion or All Religions*

	Change between 1990* and 2008		
	Lower	Same	Higher
All Regulation	20 (11.3%)	89 (50.3%)	68 (38.4%)
Restrictions on Religion's Political Role	7 (4.0%)	136 (76.8%)	35 (19.8%)
Restrictions on Religious Institutions	6 (3.4%)	138 (78.0%)	33 (18.6%)
Restrictions on Religious Practices	19 (10.7%)	140 (79.1%)	18 (10.2%)
Other Restrictions	7 (4.0%)	128 (72.3%)	42 (23.7%)

* In some cases, this represents the earliest year available.

The rise in restrictions on religion in politics was disproportionally high in other Christian-majority states. This is due to increased restrictions in eight sub-Saharan African states. No other Christian-majority states lowered political restrictions. Interestingly, in 2008, 12 of the 13 other Christian-majority states that engaged in restrictions on religion in politics were in sub-Saharan Africa. The one exception is Honduras. Thus, this is clearly a regional trend, and it is not limited to other Christian majority states. Twenty-five of the 46 sub-Saharan African states included in the RAS2 dataset increased restrictions on religion in politics. Only 13 states in all other world regions combined also increased political restrictions.

An examination of regulation, restriction, and control by world region, presented in Table 5.6, superficially shows that the regional factor undermines the robustness of the overall rise in this category. However, a closer examination shows that this is due to a small number of states significantly reducing levels of regulation, restriction, and control. Regulation, restriction, and control dropped in three world regions. In Western democracies, this drop was small and driven mostly by the drop on control of religious institutions noted earlier. In the Middle East, the drop was almost exclusively due to the fall of Saddam Hussein's regime in Iraq, which until that point in time was among the most heavy regulators of a majority religion in the world. In Latin America, the decrease was similarly driven by Mexico and Cuba. As noted earlier, Mexico reduced much of its restrictions on Catholicism as part of its 1992 constitutional reforms. Cuba has also significantly reduced its regulation of Catholicism, although heavy regulations and restrictions remain in place. In all of these regions, the number of states increasing levels of regulation, restriction, and control outnumber those decreasing it.

Control versus Support

A second trend is that there is clear evidence of a link between control and support. As shown in Table 5.7, the states that have the most of this type of policy are, unsurprisingly, those most hostile to religion. However, setting

TABLE 5.6. *Change in Mean Level of Regulation, Restriction, and Control, between 1990* and 2008 Controlling for Majority Religion and World Region*

	All, Regulation, Control, and Support	Political	Institutions	Practices	Other
Majority religion					
Catholic	4.5%	4.8%	−25.0%	−26.7%	34.8%
Orthodox Christian	12.6%	44.0%	24.2%	−52.4%	18.7%
Other Christians	24.4%	125.0%	−26.1%	8.3%	14.1%
Islam	24.8%	22.1%	35.6%	12.9%	21.7%
Other	9.2%	7.7%	21.9%	−8.6%	19.2%
World region					
Western Democracies	−5.2%	0.0	−44.8	20.0	12.1
Former Soviet	28.8%	27.0	49.2	−13.6	45.6
Asia	27.4%	17.2	41.7	1.5	37.1
Middle East and North Africa	−5.4%	−5.6	1.0	−21.4	−6.6
Sub-Saharan Africa	84.8%	122.2	184.6	29.4	27.1
Latin America	−10.8%	−8.7	−38.5	−33.3	15.6

* In some cases, this represents the earliest year available.

that category aside, the highest levels of regulation, restriction, and control are found in states that most strongly support religion. Thus, support – which as discussed in Chapter 4 is in and of itself inseparable from control – is also correlated with control. That being said, the level of government support for religion is by no means determinative of regulation, restriction, and control. In each given category of support, the range of regulation, restriction, and

TABLE 5.7. *Mean Level of Regulation, Restriction and Control in 2008, Controlling for Official Religion Policy*

	All Support			Means			
	Mean	Low	High	Political	Institutions	Practices	Other
Official religion	12.15	0	31	3.12	3.46	0.61	4.90
One religion preferred	7.61	0	33	2.41	1.93	0.52	2.75
Multiple religions preferred	4.61	0	19	1.61	0.42	0.42	2.15
Equal treatment	5.14	0	15	1.88	1.04	0.68	1.50
Hostile	36.56	18	54	7.00	9.78	9.00	10.78

control policies is large. Thus, although there is a correlation, states that have an official religion, for example, range from no such policies to extremely high levels of regulation, support, and control.

Given this, the results are consistent with the argument that the regulation, restriction, and control of religion is motivated by a combination of ideological and practical reasons. On one hand, those states with antireligious ideologies regulate, restrict, and control religion the most. Among other states, the more a government supports religion, the more it wants to limit its political influence.

Control and Politics
A third trend is not one that is found solely in the numbers but is strongly supported by the anecdotal evidence presented throughout this chapter. Although determining motivations is difficult and measuring them is nearly impossible, the overall rise in regulation, restriction, and control on the majority religions or all religions across the world is arguably motivated in large part by political concerns. In the case of the rise in restrictions on religion in politics that this motivation is a large part of the equation is a very defensible position. However, the anecdotal evidence presented in this chapter implies that many of the policies in the other categories involve political motivations. Thus, the fear of religion's power in politics arguably leads to restrictions on religious institutions, practices, and other aspects of religion that are not directly linked to political participation.

This indicates a growing perception among political elites that religion can be a potential challenger itself or a potential supporter of the political opposition. This provides indirect evidence of religion's increasing importance in aspects of society and politics that are not directly related to state religion policy.

Who Does Not Regulate Religion?
Twenty-nine states did not regulate religion during the study period. Although it is difficult to find things these states have in common, these states can be described collectively using a tactic that 12th-century rabbi Moses ben Maimon – known also as Maimonides or the Rambam – used to understand that nature of God. He argued that we cannot define God, but we can understand what God is not. Similarly we can best define these states by what they are not or at least what they are mostly not.

First, they are mostly not Western. The only Western states in this category are Australia, Malta, and New Zealand. Second, they are generally not part of the former Soviet bloc. Only Slovenia and Hungary are from the former Soviet bloc. No region has a majority of these states, but Latin America and sub-Saharan Africa combine to include 18 of them.

Third, while it would be incorrect to say these states are democratic, they are mostly not undemocratic. Using the Polity scale, Cameroon and Guinea-Bissau are the only states on this list that are clearly undemocratic. However, they certainly include democracies including Argentina, Australia, Botswana, Cape

Verde, Chile, the Dominican Republic, Hungary, Jamaica, Japan, Lesotho, Malta, Montenegro, New Zealand, Peru, Slovenia, and the Solomon Islands. They also include countries that, although not fully democratic, are more democratic than not, including Benin, Guinea, Guyana, Lebanon, Malawi, Namibia, Papua New Guinea, and Sri Lanka.

Fourth, with the exceptions of Malta, Iraq, the Dominican Republic, and Argentina, none of these states have official religions. Fifth, absolutely none of them are hostile to religion. However, within this range there is some variety. Six of them prefer a single religion, and seven prefer multiple religions over others. Three support all religions equally. Finally, 10 have SRAS with a positive attitude toward religion.

Sixth, they are mostly not Muslim-majority countries. Among Muslim-majority states, only Burkina Faso, Lebanon, and Guinea are on this list. Nineteen (65.5%) of them are Christian, but Christian-majority states are a majority of the world's states, so this is not conclusive.

These identifying factors are by no means absolute. Each of these six criteria has exceptions in that there are a few states on the list that run counter to them. Also, there are many states not on the list that have these qualities. That is, for example, not all states on the list have no official religion, and many states with no official religions engage in religious regulation, restriction, and control. Yet all of the states on this list other than Malta and Iraq have at least five of these six qualities.

Conclusions

The regulation, restriction, and control of the majority religion and all religions in a state is both common and on the rise. There is a group of states that do not engage in these practices and are best described as *not* all of the following: Western, former Soviet bloc, Muslim majority, undemocratic, supporters of official religions, and hostile to religion. However, many other states that meet this description do regulate, restrict, and control religion, as do many or most states in every category examined here. The rise in religious regulation, restriction, and control is also consistent across categories.

Yet as discussed in the previous chapter, control and support are intimately linked. All states that restrict religion also support it. I identify four reasons this is the case. First, many of the states that restrict religion are not antireligious. Rather, they support religion but at the same time want to restrict its political power. Accordingly, they support religion in general but restrict its encroachment into the political arena (Demerath & Straight, 1997: 44; Gill, 2008).

Second, even the most antireligious of states find themselves supporting religion to control it. This is the essence of the state-controlled religion – negative attitude category of policy described in Chapter 3. These states are antireligious but find that the best way to regulate, restrict, and control it is to establish and support official religious institutions that they control and restrict the expression of religion in all other formats. As Demerath and Straight (1997: 50) put it, these states "carefully construct their own religion to frustrate the political mobilization of a genuine religious alternative." While in 2008 only seven states followed this policy sufficiently to be included in this category, the general policy of supporting religion to control it is more widespread.

Third, as I argued in Chapter 4, support for religion is inexorably intertwined with control even when a state does not seek that control. However, beyond this, states that support religion usually want an element of control. To a large extent, this overlaps with the desire of states to keep religion out of politics but also involves efforts to control religious organizations themselves to achieve this. Pre–Arab Spring Egypt, for example, strongly supported Islam. However, it did not appoint all mosque prayer leaders to support Islam. Rather, it did so to make sure that these imams would support the state.

Fourth, in some cases regulation, restrictions, and control are themselves a form of support. This occurs when states restrict alternative religious institutions – religious institutions belonging to the majority religion but other than those supported by the state – to maintain the dominance of the officially recognized institutions.

All of this makes it difficult to sort out whether the policies described in this chapter are related to supporting religion or restricting it. These motivations have religion alternatively as a potent political partner that must be kept in its place, a potentially serious political challenger that requires neutralization in the political arena, and something that is present and potent but undesirable that must be stamped out. However, it is clear that the increase in the regulation, restriction, and control of religion between 1990 and 2008 means that religion is becoming a more significant factor in state policy. Whether states are using these policies to limit religion altogether, restrict religion's influence on politics, or support religion, these policies all imply that governments consider religion to be of increasing political and social importance. Thus, like a black hole, religion's true significance in society and politics is difficult to see through direct observation, but we can discern things about it from how it influences the things around it.

Another indication of this potency is a growing agreement in the recent literature that efforts to control and limit religion, in the long run, often have the opposite result. That is, efforts to repress religion often incubate more violent and intransigent manifestations of religion in society that, in time, can be more potent challengers to the state than the manifestations of religion that preceded them (Grim & Finke, 2011; Toft et al., 2011).

It is also difficult to sort out the relationship among the regulation, restriction, and control of the majority religion with concepts of religious freedom such as those discussed by Grim and Finke (2011). While in some cases it is clear that governments intends to restrict religious freedom, in others the motivation and primary effect is to restrict religious incursions into the political realm.

Yet in practice many of these efforts to limit religion's entry into politics end up also limiting religious freedom and independence. Thus, this aspect of state policy is likely best explained by a combination of the competition perspective and Gill's (2008) arguments regarding the political origins of religious liberty. To make matters more complicated, although it is clear that this type of policy is influenced by the tug of war between political secularists and those who seek a more religious state described in the competition perspective, sorting out the two sides is particularly difficult in this aspect of their competition.

Also, all of this is inconsistent with predictions of religion's decline or demise as a significant social and political force. However, within this context, the rise of religion is certainly not a monolithic one. States that increased their regulation, restriction, and control of religion outnumber those that decreased it by a ratio of 3.4 to 1, but those that decreased this type of policy exist. Almost half of the 177 countries in this study changed their policies in some way, but a bit more than half did not. Thus, efforts to control religion are in a state of flux. Most of these changes do not require a fundamental policy change but rather involve movement within a larger general policy. Nevertheless, the issue of restricting, regulating, controlling religion is very much "in play."

6

Religious Discrimination

Religious freedom has become an important international issue. It is the subject of major international treaties. About 9 in 10 constitutions across the world have language that protects religious freedom. Major government and multistate organizations such as the United States, the European Union, and the United Nations monitor religious freedom and produce reports on religious freedom around the world. It also receives significant attention by human rights organizations including Amnesty International and Human Rights without Frontiers.

Religious freedom can be defined as the right for everyone to be able to practice their religion as well as set up and maintain religious institutions without unreasonable interference from the government or other sources. The term *unreasonable* is an important qualification because every state in the world restricts religion in some manner. Take, for example, the ancient sect of the Baal that was native to modern-day Israel. This sect regularly practiced human sacrifice. Another sect, the Thugs, was native to India. Its religious practices included murdering innocents with a garrote (strangulation rope or wire) then mutilating the bodies. While to the best of my knowledge both of these sects are extinct, in the event there were any modern-day worshippers, no government would allow them to practice these rites. Even under religious auspices, murder remains murder.

US Supreme Court Chief Justice Morrison Waite succinctly explained this principle in the 1879 case *Reynolds v. United States*. He argues that the state may in some circumstances limit religious practices because to do otherwise "would be to make the professed doctrines of religious belief superior to the law of the land, and in effect to permit every citizen to become a law unto himself. Government could exist only in name under such circumstances."

This chapter does not strictly focus on religious freedom. It focuses on religious discrimination. I define religious discrimination as limitations placed on the religious practices or institutions of minority religions that are not placed on the majority religion. This definition is narrower than the more general concept of religious freedom in two respects. First, it applies only to the treatment of minority religions. Second, the minority religion must be limited in some way that the majority religion is not. To discriminate means to differentiate between two or more categories. Limitations on everyone's religious freedom are not discrimination. In the previous chapter, I addressed limitations that are placed on all residents of a state. In this chapter, I focus on the treatment of minorities.

This focus distinguishes the discussion in this chapter from most studies of religious freedom, such as Beatty (2001), Facchini (2010), Farr (2008), Grim and Finke (2011), and Marshall (2000). These types of studies focus on any limitation on religious institutions or practices, regardless of whether these restrictions are placed on everyone or only religious minorities. As I argued in Chapter 5, separating out treatment of all religions or the majority religion from treatment of minority religions, as I do in this study, provides a clearer understanding of both the state of government religion policy and its causes.

Accordingly, this focus on minorities is important because it represents a different aspect of state religion policy than general limitations on religious freedom. A state that limits all religions is most likely seeking to generally control religion or limit its political power, and in a few cases it may be unsympathetic toward or at least wary of religion in general. Religious discrimination is less about a state's general attitude toward religion and more about its attitude toward specific religions. It advantages those religions which are not subject to this discrimination because by limiting some religions, the government in relative terms is privileging those religions not subject to the discrimination. For example, if minority religions are not allowed to build places of worship, the majority religion is given an advantageous monopoly on places of worship. Most states with official religions discriminate against at least some minority religions. Interestingly, even states that are hostile to all religion tend to single out some minority religions for an extra dose of repression. For these states, religion in general is undesirable, but there are some minority religions considered even more undesirable.

Also, religion by its nature claims a monopoly on truth. As Stark (2003: 32) puts it, "those who believe there is only One True God are offended by worship directed toward other Gods." Gill (2005; 2008) similarly argues that religious majorities favor a religious monopoly because religions make universal claims and want them to be believed universally. This can manifest in the form of state-sponsored intolerance of other religions. In fact, there is general agreement in the literature that religious monopolies require force to maintain and generally involve discrimination against other religions (Casanova, 2009; Froese, 2004: 36; Gill, 2005: 13; 2008: 43; Grim & Finke, 2011: 70; Stark & Bainbridge, 1985: 508; Stark & Finke, 2000: 199; Stark & Iannaccone, 1994: 232).

Of course, religious discrimination can have other sources. It can be the result of a social conflict between the majority and a minority, which happens to belong to a different religion than the majority. In this type of case, restrictions on the minority's religion would be just one manifestation of a general battery of political, social, and economic discrimination against that minority (Fox, 2002; 2004). Discrimination can be a manifestation of a state protecting its national culture. In many cases, states feel the need to protect their culture from outside influences.[1] As religion is a part of culture, this can result in limitations placed on religions considered nonnative. Finally, some states restrict what they consider to be dangerous "cults" because they see these cults as a potential threat to citizens. However, I argue that in most cases, restrictions placed on religious institutions and practices that are targeted solely against religious minorities involve an attempt to create an uneven playing field in the state's religious economy and regardless of intention always have this result. As I discuss in this chapter, even in the case of allegedly dangerous cults, the government institutions designed to monitor and control them are often used against religions that are small and new to the country rather than dangerous.

Because of this, religious discrimination is in some ways a better indicator of a state's true attitude toward religion than either religious support or religious regulation. It is an action that is freer of conflicting motives. As noted in Chapter 4, religious support includes an element of control. Many states that technically support religion are truly seeking to control it. Even those states that clearly intend to support religion usually also seek to control it. Religious regulation is not purely about disliking religion. In many cases, it involves a desire to limit religion's political power rather than hostility to the concept of religion itself. That is, the state can be supportive of its population practicing religion but simply desire that religion be kept out of politics. Religious discrimination does not really accomplish either of these goals. While it can be said to be an aspect of control, by definition it does not control the majority religion. Similarly, it does not keep the majority religion out of politics. Essentially, it accomplishes little other than hampering the viability of religions other than the majority religion, a result that is a natural desire for most majority religions which tend to seek a religious monopoly (Gill, 2008; Grim & Finke, 2011).

Thus, both support for religion and religious discrimination can come from the same motivation – to promote the majority religion, propagate its belief system, and support its dominance. However, there is a large practical difference between support and discrimination. Support involves privileging the majority religion. While this can create what Stark and Finke (2000) call an uneven playing field by making minority religions more "expensive" relative to the majority religion, it does not limit the ability to practice a minority religion except in cases in which the majority religion is made mandatory

---

[1] For more on religion's link to national identities and ideologies, see Breakwell (1986), Sorek (2009), Voicu (2011), Seul (1999), and Juergensmeyer (1993).

Religious Discrimination 139

(a factor included in the variables described in this chapter). Religious discrimination, by definition, places explicit restrictions on the religious practices and institutions of minority religions. Thus, the difference between support and discrimination is the difference between being a free minority in a state that clearly supports the majority religion and being a persecuted minority. This is a significant distinction.

All of this places religious discrimination at the center of two contests: the contest between religious political actors and political secularism described in the secular-religious competition perspective on one hand and the contest between different religious ideologies on the other. Actors who seek to get the state to more strongly support religion often also seek to limit and restrict other religions (Gill, 2008; Grim & Finke, 2011). Thus, this is part of their desire both to make the state less secular and to maintain a religious monopoly.

Be that as it may, while the extent of religious discrimination certainly relates to religious equality and freedom in a state, these concepts are not the focus of this chapter. Rather, this chapter focuses on religious discrimination defined narrowly as restrictions on religious practices and institutions placed on minority religions and not the majority religion. It is a distinct aspect of state religion policy. Religious freedom and equality are broader in that they are also influenced by other aspects of state religion policy including religious support (Chapter 4) and religious regulation, restrictions, and control (Chapter 5).

Religious discrimination is common, with 146 (82.5%) countries placing at least 1 of the 30 types of limitations coded in the RAS dataset on at least some minorities in 2008. This is significantly higher than was the case in 1990, supporting the contentions of the competition perspective. Although much of the discussion in this chapter focuses on the presence or absence of this type of policy, it is important to note that each type of religious discrimination is coded in RAS2 on a weighted scale:

0. No restrictions.
1. The activity is slightly restricted for some minorities.
2. The activity is slightly restricted for most or all minorities or sharply restricted for some of them.
3. The activity is prohibited or sharply restricted for most or all minorities

Thus, this scale takes into account both the strength of the restrictions and how widely they are applied across minorities.

This chapter divides these types of policy into four categories: (1) restrictions on religious practices, (2) restrictions on religious institutions, (3) restrictions on conversion and proselytizing, and (4) other types of restrictions.

Restrictions on Religious Practices

These nine types of restrictions, listed in Table 6.1, limit in some manner the ability of minorities to practice their religion. Unlike when this type of restriction is placed on all religions, when it is placed only on minority religions,

TABLE 6.1. Restrictions on Religious Practices

	All states		Majority Religion (2008 results)						
			Christian						
	1990*	2008	Catholic	Orthodox	Other Christian	Christian Total	Muslim	Other Religions
---	---	---	---	---	---	---	---	---
Public observance of religious practices, including holidays and the Sabbath	24.3%	31.1%	6.8%	61.5%	17.1%	18.4%	53.2%	37.5%
Private observance of religious practices, including holidays and the Sabbath	10.2%	15.3%	0.0%	38.5%	7.3%	8.2%	23.4%	25.0%
Forced observance of religious laws of another group	10.2%	11.3%	2.3%	7.7%	4.9%	4.1%	27.7%	9.4%
Making or obtaining materials for religious rites, customs, or ceremonies	8.5%	10.7%	0.0%	23.1%	13.2%	8.2%	14.9%	12.5%
Writing, publishing, or disseminating religious publications	19.8%	23.2%	0.0%	46.2%	7.3%	9.2%	53.2%	21.9%
Importing religious publications	18.6%	19.2%	0.0%	46.2%	0.0%	6.1%	44.7%	21.9%
Access to religious publications for personal use	6.8%	7.9%	0.0%	15.4%	2.4%	3.1%	19.1%	6.2%
Observing religious personal status laws (marriage, divorce, and burial)	14.7%	16.4%	6.8%	46.2%	9.8%	13.3%	25.5%	12.5%
Wearing religious symbols or clothing	9.6%	13.6%	6.8%	23.1%	17.1%	13.3%	12.8%	15.6%
% With at least one type	42.9%	48.6%	15.9%	84.6%	41.5%	35.7%	72.3%	53.1%
% With at least two types	27.6%	34.5%	6.8%	69.2%	19.5%	20.4%	63.8%	34.3%
% With at least three types	17.4%	23.2%	0.0%	61.5%	9.7%	12.6%	48.9%	18.7%
Mean number of types	1.23	1.49b	0.23	3.08	0.78	0.84	2.75	1.63
Mean Score	2.19	2.58a	0.27	4.77	1.22	1.22	5.23	2.81

* In some countries, this represents the first available year.

Religious Discrimination

it is less an attempt to control religion than simply to ban elements of a minority religion. As noted in Chapter 5, when these restrictions are placed on the majority religion, they often involve limiting religious institutions other than those officially recognized or supported by the state. When these restrictions are placed only on minority religions, in nearly every case, the minority as a whole is restricted. Thus, this type of restriction represents an attempt to limit religions considered by the state to be undesirable, usually at least in part because they are not tolerated by the majority religion.

Restrictions on the public observance of religious practices, including holidays and the Sabbath. In 1990 (or the earliest year available), 43 countries restricted minorities in this manner. By 2008, five dropped this type of restriction but 17 added it, bringing the total to 65. Most of these restrictions are selective, applying to some minorities not others. The only countries to impose significant bans on the religious practices of all minority religions are Brunei, Comoros, the Maldives, and Saudi Arabia, all Muslim-majority states. Although more common in Muslim-majority states than Christian states in general, this type of restriction is even more common in Orthodox Christian states. For example, in Belarus, religions that fail to register are banned and may not practice. The country regularly denies registration to a number of religions, such as all Orthodox faiths other than the Belarusian Orthodox Church and Hare Krishnas, effectively making them illegal.[2] The government has also fined registered religious organizations for engaging in public baptisms. While in Orthodox Christian–majority states these bans apply to many religions considered mainstream elsewhere, a good proportion of the bans in other Christian states in the Third World are on witchcraft. For example, in 2005, the Bahamas government banned the practice of Obeah, a Caribbean religion often associated with witchcraft and voodoo. Malawi's 1911 Witchcraft Act similarly makes it an offense to claim to practice witchcraft as well as to accuse another of practicing witchcraft. Claiming to be a witchdoctor or witchfinder is punishable by life imprisonment.[3]

Restrictions on the private observance of religious practices, including holidays and the Sabbath. These restrictions are more severe than the previous category, which focuses on public observance – worship, observances, and ceremonies in official places of worship and other public spaces – as opposed to this category's focus on similar restrictions even in private spaces such as people's homes. In 1990 (or the earliest year available), 18 states restricted at least some minorities in this manner. By 2008, Barbados and Iraq dropped this type of restriction, but 11 states added it, bringing the total to 27. An excellent,

---

[2] Felix Corley, "They Were Not Doing Wrong – Its Just Our Law," *Forum 18*, October 19, 2009; "Evangelicals Vow to Keep Church after Fine," October 2, 2009, www.rferl.org/content/Belarus_Evangelicals_Vow_To_Keep_Church_After_Fine/1841960.html.

[3] "Witchcraft Act Review Program: Issues Paper," Malawi Law Commission, Lilongwe, Malawi, April 2009, www.lawcom.mw/docs/ip_witchcraft.pdf.

if extreme, example is Saudi Arabia. In Saudi Arabia, all non-Wahabbi Islamic practices are illegal, although to some extent the religious practices of its Shi'i minority are tolerated. These restrictions are strictly enforced. The country's security forces, including its religious police, regularly break up private religious gatherings.[4] For example, in 2006, the government broke up a private gathering of Ahmadis – a sect the Saudis consider heretical – and deported all participants.[5] The religious police regularly raid foreigners' homes on suspicion of non-Muslim religious practices. These raids regularly result in deportations.[6] There are more than one million Christian and Hindu foreigners in Saudi Arabia, all of whom must either refrain from practicing their religions or do so in secrecy and fear.

Forced observance of religious laws of another group. In these cases, members of a minority religion are required to observe the religious laws of the majority group. At the beginning of the study period, 18 countries engaged in this practice. By 2008, three countries had removed this type of discrimination, but five had added it, bringing the total to 20. Those dropping it include Ghana, where until 2000 all students in government schools were required to attend assemblies that included Christian prayer. The other two cases were Afghanistan and Iraq, both of which did not continue this behavior when new governments were installed after the US-led invasions. In 2008, Fiji launched a "Christian Anti-Crime Crusade" and has forced all police officers – including Muslim and Hindu police – to attend New Methodist Services.[7] In 2000, several local governments in Malaysia began to enforce Islamic dress code in public and on public servants, regardless of their religion. Most graveyards in Romania are controlled by the Orthodox Church, which often refuses burial to those of other faiths or insists that such burials be conducted according to Orthodox rites, in some cases against the express wishes of the family.[8]

Restrictions on making or obtaining materials for religious rites, customs, or ceremonies. This type of restriction rose from 15 countries in 1990 (or the earliest year available) to 19 by 2008. In Kenya, witchcraft is illegal but rarely prosecuted. Beginning in 2002, there have been sporadic arrests for the possession of witchcraft supplies. In 1998, Sweden banned the Kosher

---

[4] "Saudi Arabia: End Secrecy, End Suffering," Amnesty International, www.amnesty.ca/SaudiArabia/6.php.
[5] "Religious Persecution of Ahmadis," Human Rights without Frontiers, February 2007, www.hrwf.net; "Saudi Arabia: Stop Religious Persecution of Ahmadis," Human Rights Watch, January 23, 2007, www.hrw.org/en/news/2007/01/23/saudi-arabia-stop-religious-persecution-ahmadis.
[6] "Persecution of Christians Grows under New King Abdullah," Human Rights without Frontiers, August 2005, www.hrwf.net.
[7] Sean Dorney, "Fiji Methodists Face Ban," ABC News, June 5, 2009.
[8] Felix Corley, "Romania: Controversial Law Promulgated; Legal Challenges Planned," Forum 18, January 3, 2007.

slaughter of meat, forcing Jews to buy expensive imports. As part of a general harassment campaign of unregistered religions – which under a 1995 law are illegal in Turkmenistan – the police arrest members of these religions often confiscating Bibles and other religious materials.

The next three types of restriction include the following restrictions on religious publications: (1) *Writing, publishing, or disseminating them*, (2) *importing them*, and (3) *access for personal use*. In 1990 (or the earliest year available), these restrictions were present in 35, 33, and 12 countries, respectively, which increased to 41, 34, and 14 by 2008. Publication restrictions are most common in Muslim- and Orthodox-majority states. For example, the Russian government maintains a list of banned "extremist" publications including Islamic religious texts, a series of neo-pagan materials intolerant of other religions (Christianity in particular), more than 30 Jehovah's Witness publications, 28 books and audiovisual materials related to Scientology, and several texts that were deemed explicitly racist or anti-Semitic. Those who publish or distribute the texts face a four-year prison term.[9] Kuwait bans non-Islamic publishing companies but in practice allows several churches to publish religious materials for their congregants. Only one company, The Book House Company Ltd., may import Christian religious materials such as Bibles, CDs, and videos into Kuwait and only for use by the country's recognized churches. All religious imports must be approved by government censors. Customs officials occasionally confiscate non-Islamic religious material from individuals upon their arrival.

These types of bans are also present in other types of states. For example, both Germany and some of Switzerland's cantons have prevented Scientologists from distributing their literature. Singapore bans and seizes all publications by the Jehovah's Witnesses. Possession of banned literature can result in fines and jail.

Restrictions on observing religious personal status laws including marriage, divorce, and burial. This type of restriction increased from 26 to 29 states during the study period. Three states, Comoros, Cyprus, and Iraq, removed this type of restriction, but six states, Belarus, Eritrea, Kyrgyzstan, Mexico, Romania, and Serbia, added it. In 2005, several indigenous areas in Mexico began denying burial to non-Catholics under new laws that allow indigenous communities the power to control their burial customs.[10] According to Article 5 of India's Constitution as well as many of its laws, Buddhists, Jains, and Sikhs are considered part of the Hindu faith. As a result, Hindu personal status law

---

[9] "Russia Bans Books by Scientology Founder L. Ron Hubbard," Associated Foreign Press, April 22, 2010; "Surgut Extremist Case," Human Rights without Frontiers, September 9, 2010, www.hrwf.net.
[10] International Christian Concern, "Evangelical Christian Denied Burial in Mexico," 2005, www.persecution.org/suffering/newsdetail.php?newscode=998.

is applied to members of these religions. The Sikh community, in particular, has objected to this, unsuccessfully demanding that the government codify a Sikh personal status law for their community.[11]

Restrictions on wearing religious symbols or clothing. This type of restriction increased from 17 countries to 24 during this study period. It is, interestingly, one of the few types of restrictions in this category that is least common in Muslim-majority states. Much of the increase is in European democracies, which have begun limiting the wearing of head coverings by Muslim women. In most cases, this is by local or regional governments and applies mostly to students, teachers, and public employees. Unlike France's 2004 and 2011 laws, these laws and policies apply specifically to Muslims. By 2009, at least eight German states passed such a ban. Beginning in 2003, several municipalities in Belgium including, Antwerp and Brussels, enacted bans on head coverings by their employees. In 2007, a number of Bulgarian schools banned the wearing of head coverings by female students. This ban was upheld by Bulgaria's Commission against Discrimination.[12] Several Swiss cantons, including Geneva and Fribourg, have banned head coverings in schools since 2001. Montenegro bans the wearing of head coverings in official identity photos. Western countries are also beginning to ban full facial coverings by Muslim women. In 2008, an Austrian court barred a woman from attending her trial in this type of attire. In 2007, Norway's Ministry of Education allowed schools to prohibit the wearing the niqab, a form of Muslim facial covering.

Restrictions on the practice of religion are the least common form of religious discrimination. It is most common in Muslim- and Orthodox-majority states but, as I discuss at the end of the chapter, discrimination in general is distributed unevenly among Muslim-majority states. While the other categories of religious discrimination are important, this category is perhaps the most significant because these nine types of restriction involve the actual practice of religion or materials necessary for this practice. Imagine being unable to worship in public or even being unable to privately observe basic religious practices without fear of arrest or deportation, being unable to obtain basic religious literature and materials such as the Koran or Bible, and being forced to attend or observe religious rites of a religion not your own. When these types of religious discrimination are enforced in their more severe forms, they make the practice of religion difficult to impossible. While the other categories discussed here involve restrictions that can seriously hamper religion, as a whole they are not as destructive to the ability to practice religion as are the restrictions in this category.

---

[11] India Constitution, http://lawmin.nic.in/coi.htm; Yildirim (2004: 913).
[12] Tsvetelia Ilieva, "Bulgarian Muslims Wonder What EU Entry Holds," Reuters, December 26, 2006; "Bulgaria's Ataka Campaigns against Mosque Loudspeakers," *Sofia Echo*, July 24, 2006; "Freedom of Thought, Conscience, Religion and Belief," Human Rights without Frontiers, April 28, 2007, www.hrwf.net.

Religious Discrimination

Given this, despite being the least common form of religious discrimination, the extent to which they are common and increasing is sobering. In 1990 (or the earliest year available), 76 (42.9%) countries engaged in 217 types of restrictions on religious practices by religious minorities. By 2008, this increased to 86 (48.6%) countries and 256 types – increases of 13.2% and 18.8%, respectively. Taking the magnitude of the discrimination scores into account, in 2008, 15 countries engaged in less of this type of discrimination than at the beginning of the study period, but 39 engaged in more.

The countries that decreased this type of discrimination were not in particular democratic ones. Among Western democracies, only Greece and Cyprus reduced restrictions on religious practices. In 2006, Greece repealed a law banning cremation, which had hampered Buddhist burial rites, as did Cyprus in 2007. However, several nondemocratic states also reduced restrictions. Morocco reduced its enforcement of bans on Baha'i religious practices but did not completely eliminate these restrictions. Sudan, while still extremely restrictive of religious minorities, did ease some of these restrictions in the context of its 2005 peace agreement that allowed autonomy in many non-Muslim regions of the country. The increases are similarly present in liberal democracies. As noted earlier, several European democracies increased restrictions on Muslims. Thus, freedom to practice one's religion is not an issue restricted to minorities in non-Western, nondemocratic states.

Restrictions on Religious Institutions and the Clergy

These five restrictions, listed in Table 6.2, limit religious institutions and clergy. Both institutions and clergy are crucial to the stability, preservation, and propagation of religion and are essential to maintaining a coherent religious community. Accordingly, these restrictions seriously hamper minority religious communities.

Restrictions on building, leasing, repairing, or maintaining places of worship. In 1990 (or the earliest year available), 65 states engaged in this type of restriction. By 2008, five – Iraq, Moldova, Mongolia, Mozambique, and Slovenia – removed it but 13 added it, for a total of 73. In many cases, these are not outright bans but rather denial of building permits and bureaucratic delays. For example, Lesotho's government has since 2003 used this tactic to prevent Muslims from building and expanding mosques. Similarly, this type of tactic is often used by Western local governments against mosques. This includes local governments in Austria, Australia, Denmark, Germany, Greece, Italy, Norway, Spain, and Switzerland. In some cases, these restrictions are at the national level and more direct bans. Saudi Arabia, for example, bans any non-Muslim house of worship. Tunisia, while not closing existing minority places of worship, has rarely allowed new ones to be built since the 19th century.

TABLE 6.2. *Restrictions on Religious Institutions and the Clergy*

	All states		Majority Religion (2008 results)						
			Christian						Other Religions
	1990*	2008	Catholic	Orthodox	Other Christian	Christian Total	Muslim	
Building, leasing, repairing, or maintaining places of worship	36.7%	41.2%	27.3%	76.9%	24.4%	32.7%	61.7%	37.5%
Access to existing places of worship	18.1%	19.8%	9.1%	69.2%	2.4%	14.3%	26.7%	25.0%
Formal religious organizations	19.2%	26.0%	15.9%	30.8%	17.1%	18.4%	36.2%	34.4%
Ordination of or access to clergy	13.0%	14.7%	4.5%	23.1%	7.3%	8.2%	19.1%	28.1%
Minority religions (as opposed to all religions) must register to be legal or receive special tax status	41.2%	46.3%	52.3%	84.5%	36.6%	50.0%	46.8%	34.4%
Access of minority clergy to hospitals, jails, military bases, etc.	19.8%	19.8%	25.0%	61.5%	9.8%	23.5%	14.9%	15.6%
% With at least one type	66.1%	68.4%	65.9%	92.3%	53.7%	64.3%	78.7%	65.4%
% With at least two types	40.0%	46.9%	40.9%	84.6%	24.4%	39.8%	61.7%	46.6%
% With at least three types	23.2%	28.9%	20.4%	9.2%	12.3%	23.5%	38.3%	31.0%
Mean number of types	1.48	1.67c	1.34	3.46	0.98	1.47	2.06	1.75
Mean score	2.66	3.10c	2.16	7.15	1.71	2.63	4.04	3.13

* In some countries, this represents the first available year.

Restrictions on access to existing places of worship. This refers to cases in which a government limits the use or access to places of worship that already exist. At the beginning of the study period, 32 countries engaged in these types of restrictions, which increased to 35 in 2008, with Iraq stopping the practice and Cuba, Nigeria, Eritrea, and Sri Lanka beginning the practice. Until 2005, Cuba allowed house churches to operate, albeit with some harassment. In 2005, it began requiring these house churches to register and limited their hours of operations.[13] In many former Soviet bloc states, such as Belarus, Bulgaria, Georgia, Macedonia, Montenegro, Romania, Russia, and Serbia, governments have failed to return all religious property seized by the government during the Communist era. In most of these cases, properties belonging to the majority religion were returned by 2008 or some other form of compensation was arranged, and only minority properties remain outstanding.

Restrictions on formal religious organizations. This refers to when a religious organization, or in some cases an entire religion, is banned or significantly restricted. In 1990 (or the earliest year available), 34 countries engaged in this restriction. By 2008, four (Barbados, Ghana, Iraq, and Malawi) ended this practice, but 16 added it, for a total of 46. In many cases, the ban is limited to religions many consider "cults," such as Scientology, the Unification Church, and the Jehovah's Witnesses. For example, in 1997, Venezuela banned the Unification Church.[14] Poland similarly restricts the Unification Church. I discuss the treatment of "cults" in more detail later in the chapter. On the other end of the spectrum, religious states such as Saudi Arabia and the Maldives ban all minority religions. Other countries are closer to the midpoint of this spectrum. For example, Turkey bans all Christian institutions that were not present in the country at the time of the signing of its 1923 Treaty of Lausanne with Greece. Thus, organizations such as the Jehovah's Witnesses and the Protestant Free Churches are banned (Yildiz, 2007).

Restrictions on the ordination of or access to clergy. Denying clergy to religious communities can significantly undermine their spiritual health. At the beginning of the study period, 23 countries restricted at least some minorities in this manner. By 2008, Iraq had stopped this behavior, but Mongolia, Russia, Switzerland, and Uzbekistan began restricting clergy, bringing the total to 26. In 2004, Switzerland began limiting permits for Muslim imams to enter the country as clergy, claiming many who applied were "extremist."[15] Mongolia similarly denies visas to Christian clergy. This is significant because many of the churches in Mongolia depend on foreign clergy. In 2001, Uzbekistan's

---

[13] Lopez, L. "Cuba: Draconian New Restrictions on 'Home Religious Meetings'" Forum 18, 2005, www.forum18.org/Archive.php?article_id=652.

[14] Kenneth D. MacHarg. "Venezuela Restricts Unification Church," *Christianity Today*, November 17, 1997, www.rickross.com/reference/unif/Unif27.html.

[15] "Imam Refused Swiss Work Permit," SWI, October 9, 2005, www.swissinfo.ch/eng/front/Imam_refused_Swiss_work_permit.html?siteSect=107&sid=6149521&cKey=1128881439000&ty=st&rs=yes.

government began requiring Christian congregations to replace their foreign pastors with pastors who were Uzbek citizens.

Minority religions must register to be legal or receive special tax status. This variable is only coded if minorities are required to register in a manner not incumbent on the majority religion, and this registration is somehow different from that of nonreligious organizations. In 1990 (or the earliest year available), this type of registration requirement was present in 73 countries, which increased to 82 by 2008. In many cases, this requirement is pro forma. For example, Botswana requires registration, and nonregistered religions can be liable for penalties such as fines and jail time, but no religions are refused registration. Thus, no religion need be restricted.

This type of policy only becomes restrictive when a government both denies registration and restricts nonregistered religions. In 2008, 29 countries did both. As noted earlier, this is the case in Belarus. Similarly, in Egypt nonregistered religions are illegal, and members of such religions are subject to detention, prosecution, and jail. All registrations must be approved by the president, who consults with the Religious Affairs Department. This department can recommend against registration on grounds of national security and objections by the leaders of local Muslim and Coptic communities. No group has successfully registered since 1990.

Many countries also place additional requirements on registration. In 2008, the following additional requirements were present in multiple states: 32 required that the applicant submit a copy of its religious doctrines, 53 required a minimum number of members to apply, and 16 required a minimum period of presence in the state before applying. Russia, for example, requires all three. A 1997 law requires 15 years of presence in Russia, and 10 Russian members before a religion can register. The application must include a list of persons forming the organization; a charter; information about the belief system and practices; the history of the origins of the religion; the forms of its activity; its attitude toward family, marriage, and education; its attitude toward the health of adherents; and restrictions on members and clergy of the organization with regard to their civil rights and duties.[16] While unregistered organizations in Russia are not illegal, their activities can be significantly restricted mostly stemming from their lack of legal status.

Restrictions on access of minority clergy to hospitals, jails, military bases, and other places chaplains may be required. This type of restriction was present in 35 states at both the beginning and end of the study period, but Chile and the Ivory Coast stopped this type of policy, while Bolivia, and Russia initiated it. Many of these restrictions are relatively minor. For example, in one of the few instances of religious discrimination in the United States, the military does not recognize Wicca as a religion and has no Wiccan chaplains. This is part of a larger issue in the US military. There have been several reported instances

---

[16] Russian Law on Freedom of Conscience and Religious Associations, 1997.

of harassment of Wiccans, and until 2007, the government would not allow Wiccan pentacles on military tombstones.[17] In other cases, the limitations are more serious. For example, Peru allows only Catholic military chaplains. Until the passage of a 1997 law, there were no Protestant chaplains in Chile's armed forces, and Protestant chaplains had limited access to hospitals.[18] Even after 1997, non-Catholic ministers reported that local administrators sometimes delayed their efforts to carry out their ministries in hospitals and military units. By 2008, after additional implementation regulations from the government, this type of discrimination seems to have become less common but remains present.

At the beginning of the study period, 117 (66.1%) states engaged in a total of 261 restrictions on religious institutions and clergy. By 2008, this increased to 121 (68.4%) countries and 297 restrictions, increases of 3.4% and 13.8%, respectively. Taking the discrimination score magnitudes into account, 18 countries lowered this type of discrimination between 1990 and 2008, but 43 engaged in more. As with the previous category, the countries that lowered their discrimination were not particularly democratic or Western. They included three each from the Middle East, Latin America, and the former Soviet bloc. The other five were from sub-Saharan Africa. Only Chile and Costa Rica score among the Polity Project's most democratic states in the world.

However, a number of Western democracies are among the states that increased restrictions on minority clergy and institutions, including Austria, Finland, France, Malta, Spain, and Switzerland. Additionally, Bulgaria a European Union member, and Macedonia, a candidate member, had more of this type of discrimination. Clearly, this increase is not exclusive to Western Christian states. Multiple countries from all religions and world regions, both democracies and autocracies, increased this type of discrimination.

Restrictions on Conversion and Proselytizing

Not all religions actively seek converts, but most do at least to some extent, and only a few absolutely refuse to accept them. For many religions, spreading the religion and bringing in new members is a central element of their theology. This is natural in that religions nearly always claim a monopoly on truth. The desire to spread that truth is a normal consequence of that type of belief. On the other hand, this type of belief also can make a religious group wary of other religions that seek to poach its members. Thus, it is not surprising that in 2008, just over half of the states in this study, 52.5%, in some way limit conversions or missionaries or use the power of the state to convert minorities

---

[17] Julia Duin, "U.S. to Allow Wiccan Symbols on Military Graves," *Washington Times*, April 24, 2007; Randy Myers, "Military Casts Wicca in the Shadows," *Contra Costa Times*, August 12, 2004; Pagan Institute Report, www.paganinstitute.org/child_custody.html.
[18] Chilean Law of Worship (1999), www.religlaw.org/template.php?id=813.

to the majority religion. I divide these state efforts into the seven categories listed in Table 6.3.

Restrictions on converting to minority religions is the most common form of restriction on conversion. It was present in 26 states at the beginning of the study period and increased to 29 by 2008 with Cambodia, Sudan, and Turkmenistan adding this type of policy. No Christian-majority state has this type of policy, but more than half of Muslim-majority states do. For example, Sudan's 1991 Criminal Act forbids conversion away from Islam.[19] In Malaysia, conversion away from Islam requires the approval of the Sharia court, which is never granted except when someone who converted to Islam for marriage seeks to revert to their original religion after divorce. In Afghanistan, Iran, Saudi Arabia, and the United Arab Emirates, converting away from Islam is punishable by death, although this penalty is rarely applied. These bans are not always formal. For example, Egypt has no law against conversion, but the government refuses to recognize conversion away from Islam. Also, in 2008, Cairo's administrative court ruled that the freedom to convert does not extend to Muslims. Three non-Muslim states – Cambodia, India, and Laos, also restrict conversion. In Cambodia, conversion itself is not illegal, but a 2007 royal directive bans non-Buddhists from using money or other incentives to induce a conversion. In India, there is no national anticonversion law, but many of India's states have such laws. In Laos, there are no laws regarding conversion, but many local authorities harass converts.

The next three categories deal with government efforts to induce people to convert to the majority religion. They are distinguished by the target population and the extent to which force is used.

Forced renunciation of faith by recent converts to minority religions. States that use force and target members of the majority religion who left the religion increased from 12 to 15 during the study period. For example, Malaysia maintains "rehabilitation" centers for wayward Muslims including those who attempt to convert away from Islam. In a good example of this practice, in 2007, a nonpracticing Muslim woman who married a Hindu was sentenced to this type of rehabilitation. Yemen simply arrests converts and holds them until they recant.[20]

Forced conversions of people who were never members of the majority religion is much rarer, with only five countries engaging in this practice throughout the study period. None of these cases involve putting a gun to someone's head but, rather, involve significant government pressure. Perhaps the most extreme case is Sudan, which engages in a series of practices designed to pressure non-Muslims to convert. Enlistees in Sudan's armed forces are subject to

---

[19] Sudan 1991 Criminal Act, www.ilo.org/dyn/natlex/natlex_browse.details?p_lang=en&p_country=SDN&p_classification=01&p_origin=SUBJECT.
[20] "Official: Yemen Detains 9 People for Converting to Christianity," FoxNews.com, August 19, 2008.

TABLE 6.3. *Restrictions on Conversion and Proselytizing*

	All states		Majority Religion (2008 results)					
			Christian					
	1990*	2008	Catholic	Orthodox	Other Christian	Christian Total	Muslim	Other Religions
Conversion to minority religions	14.7%	16.4%	0.0%	0.0%	0.0%	0.0%	55.3%	9.4%
Forced renunciation of faith by recent converts to minority religions	6.8%	8.5%	0.0%	0.0%	2.6%	1.0%	21.3%	12.5%
Forced conversions of people who were never members of the majority religion	2.8%	2.8%	0.0%	0.0%	0.0%	0.0%	4.3%	9.4%
Attempts to convert members of minority religions that do not use force	9.6%	10.2%	2.3%	7.7%	2.4%	3.1%	17.0%	21.9%
Proselytizing by permanent residents of state to members of majority religion	27.7%	32.2%	6.8%	53.8%	9.8%	14.3%	68.1%	34.4%
Proselytizing by permanent residents of state to members of minority religions	13.6%	16.9%	4.5%	38.5%	7.3%	10.2%	21.3%	31.2%
Proselytizing by foreign clergy or missionaries	39.5%	45.2%	38.6%	69.2%	12.2%	31.6%	70.2%	50.0%
% With at least one type	45.8%	52.5%	45.5%	76.9%	19.5%	38.8%	78.7%	56.2%
% With at least two types	29.4%	33.9%	6.8%	53.8%	7.3%	13.3%	71.3%	40.6%
% With at least three types	20.4%	23.7%	0.0%	38.4%	4.8%	7.2%	52.2%	31.2%
Mean number of types	1.15	1.32c	0.52	1.69	0.34	0.60	2.57	1.69
Mean score	2.19	2.58b	0.61	2.38	0.51	0.81	6.17	3.38

* In some countries, this represents the first available year.

indoctrination in Islam. In prisons, juvenile detention facilities, and displaced persons camps, the government pressures people to convert, sometimes also promising incentives and benefits. In addition to this pressure, children in camps for vagrant minors were required to study the Koran.

Attempts to convert members of minority religions that do not use force are more common. At the beginning of the study period, 17 countries engaged in this practice. In 2002, Belize added this practice when its only prison was taken over by the Kolbe Foundation. Since then, conversion to Christianity has been central to the prison's rehabilitation program for non-Christian prisoners, but no force or coercion is involved. In a number of Nigeria's northern states, Christians attending public schools are indoctrinated in Islam. In addition to overt attempts to convert Christian children, they are required to study Arabic and Islam and to say Islamic prayers.[21]

There are three types of restrictions on proselytizing coded in this category. They are differentiated by on whom the limitations are placed and to whom the proselytizers may proselytize. *Restrictions on proselytizing by permanent residents of state to members of majority religion* rose from 49 to 57 countries during the study period, with Iraq and Guinea stopping this policy and 10 states adding it. *Restrictions on proselytizing by permanent residents of state to members of minority religions* is coded because many states only ban proselytizing to members of the majority religion but do not care about attempts to convert members of other religions. These states also ban proselytizing to minority religions. During the study period, this type of ban increased from 24 to 30 states. Finally, *restrictions on proselytizing by foreign clergy or missionaries* refers to states that specifically limit the ability of foreigners to proselytize, often by denying them visas or entry into the country. At the beginning of the study period, 70 countries engaged in this practice. By 2008, this increased to 80 with Lithuania dropping the practice and 11 other states beginning it. I discuss limits on proselytizing in more detail in Chapter 7.

Overall, restrictions on conversions and proselytizing have become increasing common. In 1990 (or the earliest year available), 81 (45.7%) states engaged in 203 of these types of restrictions. By 2008, this had increased to 93 (52.5%) states and 234 types, an increase of 14.8% and 15.3%, respectively. Taking changes in the intensity of policy changes into account, only 4 (2.3%) states decreased their restrictions in this category, and 27 (15.3%) increased them. The countries increasing this practice include Western democracies such as Denmark, Norway, and Switzerland as well as other Christian democracies such as Costa Rica, Chile, and Panama. Thus, these restrictions can be found in states in all regions of the world, not just nondemocracies.

---

[21] O. Minchakpu, "Islam's Power Grab in Niger State: The Imposition of Shari'a Oppresses the Christians That Make up Half of the Population," Human Rights without Frontiers, 2005, www.hrwf.net/religiousfreedom/news/2005PDF/Nigeria_2005.pdf.

The patterns across religions are also interesting. Christian-majority states engage in extremely low levels of limitations on actual conversions but many limit proselytizing, especially by foreign missionaries. Muslim-majority states engage in very high levels with regard to both proselytizing and conversion.

Other Restrictions

This category includes all types of religious discrimination that do not fit into the previous three categories. They are listed in Table 6.4.

Religious schools or religious education in general. These countries limit the ability of religious minorities to provide formal education to their members. This seriously limits a religion's ability to propagate itself from one generation to the next. Between the beginning of the study period and 2008, this practice increased from 21 to 33 countries. For instance, in 2006, Finland denied five religious groups permits to form religious schools on the grounds that the government was not assured that they would meet the government standards and that schools should not be promoting a single religious truth. Several Muslim-majority states including Brunei, Kuwait, Saudi Arabia, and the United Arab Emirates ban practically all non-Islamic religious education with the possible exceptions of schools for foreigners.

Mandatory education in the majority religion. This means at least some religious minorities in at least some schools are required to study the majority religion with no opportunity to opt out of these classes. Thirty-one countries engaged in this practice at the beginning of the study period, which increased to 35 by 2008. While religious education in Christianity has always been part of Zambia's public school curriculum, in 2007, it became mandatory for all students, including Muslims and Hindus. In Indonesia, religious education is mandatory and, in theory, provided in all five of the country's major minority religions. In practice, few schools offer classes in all faiths so minorities are often required to take classes on religions other than their own.

Arrest, continued detention, or harassment of religious figures, officials, and/or members of religious parties for activities other than proselytizing. This was only coded in cases where it was clear that the arrests or harassment were due to an individual's religion or religious activities. This type of discrimination is one of the fastest growing, increasing from with 35 in 1990 (or the earliest year available) to 55 by 2008. Three states – Djibouti, Iraq, and Trinidad and Tobago – stopped this practice, and 23 (13.0%) states began this practice during the study period. For example, Italy, like a number of Western countries, began detaining and deporting Muslim imams in 2005. In Italy, the stated reason was violation of hate crime laws. In 1998, Kazakhstan began harassing and arresting members of "nontraditional" religious minorities – those religions that are relatively new to the state. These activities intensified in 2006. Beginning in 2000, local governments in Rwanda began to arrest and detain

TABLE 6.4. *Other Restrictions*

	All states		Majority Religion (2008 results)						
			Christian						Other Religions
	1990*	2008	Catholic	Orthodox	Other Christian	Christian Total	Muslim		
Religious schools or religious education in general	11.9%	18.6%	0.0%	38.5%	7.3%	8.2%	38.3%		21.9%
Mandatory education in the majority religion	17.5%	19.8%	2.3%	15.4%	12.2%	8.8%	48.1%		12.5%
Arrest, continued detention, or harassment of religious figures, officials, and/or members of religious parties for activities other than proselytizing	19.8%	31.1%	13.6%	69.2%	14.5%	21.4%	46.8%		37.5%
State surveillance of minority religious activities	14.7%	23.2%	13.6%	53.8%	12.2%	18.4%	26.7%		31.2%
Custody of children granted to members of majority group solely or in part on the basis of religious affiliation or beliefs	7.3%	10.2%	2.3%	23.1%	0.0%	4.1%	27.7%		3.1%
Declaration of some minority religions as dangerous or extremist sects	13.0%	19.2%	27.3%	38.5%	9.8%	21.4%	14.9%		18.7%
Antireligious propaganda in official or semiofficial government publications	19.2%	23.2%	15.9%	76.9%	9.8%	21.4%	27.3%		21.9%
Other restrictions	14.7%	20.9%	13.6%	38.5%	7.3%	14.3%	31.9%		25.0%
% With at least one type	48.6%	57.6%	43.2%	92.3%	36.6%	46.9%	78.7%		58.8%
% With at least two types	28.8%	39.0%	16.0%	76.9%	19.5%	25.6%	63.8%		43.2%
% With at least three types	18.6%	29.4%	13.7%	61.5%	12.2%	19.5%	48.9%		30.3%
Mean number of types	1.19	1.66c	0.89	3.58	0.73	1.17	2.64		1.72
Mean score	2.05	2.76c	1.27	5.54	1.02	1.73	4.72		3.00

* In some countries, this represents the first available year.

members of unregistered denominations such as the Jehovah's Witnesses, Pentecostals, and Seventh Day Adventists.

State surveillance of minority religious activities. This involves monitoring and surveillance of religious activities beyond what is reasonably justifiable by security concerns. This surveillance increased from 26 states to 41 during the study period. In several cases, such as Belgium and France, this surveillance began after an incident of mass suicide. As discussed in more detail later under the context of restrictions on "cults," this surveillance can go well beyond anything justifiable by security concerns. A 2006 Algerian law regulates non-Islamic religions. It protects religious freedom but requires certain conditions including public order and morality. Since the law's passage, government monitoring of Christians has increased. In 2000, Togo set up a government committee to investigate religious groups that harm the welfare of society. In 1996, Uganda began surveillance of Muslim groups in the context of a general campaign of arrest and harassment.

Custody of children is granted to members of majority group solely or in part on the basis of religious affiliation or beliefs. This is a serious restriction because it ensures that when religiously mixed couples divorce, members of the majority religion gain child custody. This has a significant impact on the religious demography of the next generation. In 1990 (or the earliest year available), 13 countries engaged in this practice, increasing to 18 by 2008. In some cases, this refers to limited court decisions. For example, in 2003, a French appellate court denied a Jehovah's Witness custody of her children, citing concerns about her religious affiliation. There are several similar court decisions regarding Jehovah's Witnesses in Armenia in 2008 and in Russia since 2002.[22] In many Muslim countries, the Muslim parent, usually the father, automatically gains custody in cases of divorce. For example, Malaysia not only enforces this but has seized children of people who converted away from Islam to give them to relatives who remained Muslim and in a case involving a non-Muslim couple awarded custody to a parent who converted to Islam.[23] Other Muslim-majority countries that follow this type of policy include Egypt, Jordan, Kuwait, the Maldives, Pakistan, and Saudi Arabia.[24]

---

[22] Gita Elibekian and Seda Muradian, "Armenian Religious Minorities Complain of Discrimination," United Nations High Commissioner for Refugees, February 13, 2009, www.unhcr.org/refworld/country,,,,ARM,4562d8cf2,499a6f200,0.html.

[23] Clarence Fernandez, "Malaysians in Dispute over Sway of Religious Courts," Reuters/International Christian Concern, March 17, 2009, www.persecution.org/2007/03/18/malaysians-in-dispute-over-sway-of-religious-courts; "Woman Battles against the 'forced' Conversion of Her Children to Islam," AsianNews/International Christian Concern, March 14, 2007, www.persecution.org/2007/03/14/woman-battles-against-the-forced-conversion-of-her-children-to-islam.

[24] Roger Elliott, "Egyptian Mother Refuses to Give Child to Christian Mother," Human Rights without Frontiers, January 2009, www.hrwf.net.

Declaration of some minority religions as dangerous or extremist sects. This policy increased from 23 to 34 countries during the study period. Many of the states that added these policies did so after a serious event with a cult. After a mass suicide in 1996, the French government identified 173 groups as "cults." This includes groups considered by many governments to be "cults," such as Church of Scientology, the Unification Church, and Jehovah's Witnesses. But it also includes groups considered more mainstream elsewhere such as Mormons, Seventh Day Adventists, and Pentecostals.[25] After a similar event, Belgium created the "Belgian Sect Observatory" in 1999, which maintains a list of more than 600 sects and cults. This list, like the French list, includes groups considered more mainstream elsewhere, including Seventh Day Adventists, Zen Buddhists, Mormons, Hassidic Jews, and the YWCA. Thus, both lists contain groups that are small and new to the country, whether or not they are actually dangerous. Both France and Belgium have created government institutions to monitor and often restrict groups on the list that have been accused of abuses of religious freedom (Kuru, 2009).[26]

Not all countries that experienced a traumatic event at the hands of a cult overreacted in this manner. For example, in 1995, members of the Aum Shrinyiko sect – which is an offshoot of Buddhism – carried out a deadly attack with saran gas in Tokyo's subway. Understandably, the government has since significantly restricted that specific sect and maintained surveillance on it but has not applied this policy to any other religion. Also, not all antisect policies are due to traumatic events. For instance, Hungary's government maintains a list of groups considered to be a danger to society. However, other than occasional criticism of these groups, mostly of Scientology, the government has taken no actions. Similarly, since 2001, Poland's interior ministry monitors the activities of "new religious groups" and "cults."

Antireligious propaganda in official or semiofficial government publications: In 1990 (or the earliest year available), 35 countries engaged in this policy, increasing to 41 by 2008. This practice is common in a wide variety of countries. Western democracies such as Austria, Belgium, France, Germany, Greece, and

---

[25] Cults in France [report of the National Assembly], December 22, 1995, www.cftf.com/french/Les_Sectes_en_France/cults.html.

[26] "France Moves to Outlaw Cults," BBC News Europe, June 22, 2000; Ontario Consultants on Religious Tolerance, ReligiousTolerance.Org, www.religioustolerance.org/rt_franc.htm; "Public Controversy about MIVILUDES," Human Rights without Frontiers, October 17, 2007, www.hrwf.net; "Religious Discrimination in France: CAP Submission Regarding the Appointment of Mr. Georges Fenech as President of MIVILUDES," Human Rights without Frontiers October 7, 2008, www.hrwf.net; MIVILUDES 2006 Report to the Prime Minister, www.miviludes.gouv.fr/IMG/pdf/Report_Miviludes_2006.pdf; International Coalition for Religious Freedom, World Reports www.religiousfreedom.com; "The Institute on Religion and Public Policy Denounces Defamation of Religion in Belgium at the UN," Human Rights without Frontiers www.hrwf.net; "Defamation of Religions in Belgium," Human Rights without Frontiers; "Institute Report to UN Details Systematic Religious Discrimination in Belgium," International Christian Concern, www.persecution.org.

Switzerland all engage in this type of practice, usually against groups considered "cults" such as Scientologists and Jehovah's Witnesses. This type of practice is present in all world regions and in countries of all major religious traditions.

Other restrictions. This category includes all types of religious discrimination not included in the previous 29 categories that do not exist in enough countries to justify creating a new category. The number of countries engaging in these varied practices jumped from 26 to 36 during the study period. Some of these practices include the following:

- Denial of a religious diet in prisons. (Belgium)[27]
- Limitations on Jewish circumcisions. (Sweden)[28]
- A ban on foreign funding of religious organizations. (Armenia)[29]
- Religious believers may not speak publically on social and public issues. (Belarus)[30]
- Restrictions on public calls to prayer or ringing bells. (Georgia, Kuwait)
- Minority religions may not preach in the native language. (Uzbekistan)[31]
- Minorities must wear the religious dress of the majority group. (Brunei)
- Mandatory contributions to building houses of prayer for the majority religion. (Myanmar)
- Limitations on pilgrimages. (Egypt, Israel, Pakistan)
- Converts to the majority religion inherit all their family's property. (Iran)
- Limitations on the display of religious symbols on houses of worship. (Kuwait, Qatar, United Arab Emirates)

Each of the eight types of restrictions in the "other" religious discrimination category increased over time. In 1990 (or the earliest year available), 86 (48.6%) countries engaged collectively in 210 types of discrimination. This increased to 102 (57.6%) countries and 273 types of religious discrimination, an increase of 18.6% and 30.0%, respectively.

Patterns and Trends

Change over Time

As is the case for religious support as well as for regulation, restrictions, and control, the most important trend for religious discrimination is that it

---

[27] Hindus in Europe Come Together for Common Causes," Human Rights without Frontiers, www.hrwf.net.
[28] "Sweden Restricts Circumcisions," BBC News Europe, October 1, 2001, http://news.bbc.co.uk/2/hi/europe/1572483.stm.
[29] The Republic of Armenia Law on the Freedom of Conscience and on Religious Organization, Adopted 1991, amended 1997.
[30] Geraldine Fagan, "Why Can't Believers Speak on Social Themes?" Forum 18, March 3, 2006.
[31] "Churches told to stop preaching in Uzbek," Barnabas Fund News Service/Human Rights without Frontiers, June 11/June 13, 2002, www.hrwf.net/religiousfreedom/news/uzbekistan2002.HTM.

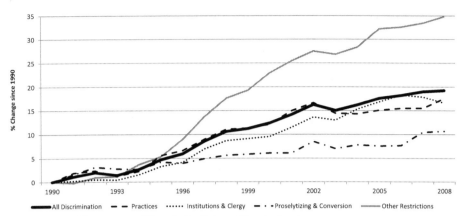

FIGURE 6.1. Change over Time in Religious Discrimination.

is increasing over time. As shown in Figure 6.1, the mean levels of all four categories of religious discrimination increased steadily between 1990 and 2008. The overall score increased by 19.2%. This rise became statistically significant by 1994.[32] The increases in each of the four more specific categories were also statistically significant.

This trend is robust when examining it from other perspectives. Twenty-eight of the 30 specific types of discrimination became more common, and two remained as common in 2008 as they were at the beginning of the study period. None of them became less common.[33] Overall, these countries added 308 individual religious discrimination policies and dropped 79 between 1990 and 2008. As shown in Table 6.5, while religious discrimination decreased in some states, states in which it increased outnumber those in which it decreased by a ratio of 3.6 to 1. This trend is consistent across the four categories of religious discrimination.

As presented in Table 6.6, this trend is mostly consistent across types of majority religion and world region. The extent of the increase varies, but only in the Middle East did it drop. This is mostly due to a large drop in religious discrimination in Iraq after the US invasion. When this is removed from the equation, religious discrimination also increased in the Middle East. Interestingly, the rise in religious discrimination is higher in all three categories of Christian majority states than it is in Muslim-majority and other majority states. Thus, while the actual mean levels are highest in Muslim-majority states, Christian-majority states closed this gap somewhat between 1990 and 2008.

---

[32] From 1994 to 1995, the difference between the mean level of religious discrimination to that of 1990 was significant at the .05 level; from 1996 onward it was significant at the .01 level.
[33] This calculation is based on the number of states with each type of policy.

TABLE 6.5. *Change over Time in Religious Discrimination*

	Change between 1990* and 2008		
	Lower	Same	Higher
All discrimination	23 (13.0%)	71 (40.1%)	83 (46.9%)
Restrictions on religious practices	15 (8.4%)	124 (70.1%)	38 (21.5%)
Restrictions on institutions and clergy	18 (10.2%)	116 (65.5%)	43 (24.3%)
Restrictions on proselytizing and conversion	4 (2.3%)	146 (82.4%)	27 (18.3%)
Other restrictions	10 (5.7%)	107 (60.4%)	60 (33.9%)

* In some countries this represents the first available year.

Who Discriminates Most?

Overall, if one compares just Muslim-, Christian-, and other majority states, the Muslim-majority states discriminate the most. This is true of the entire time period of the study, but this discussion focuses on 2008. The mean level of discrimination in Muslim states is 20.2 compared with 6.3 and 12.3 for Christian-majority and other majority states, respectively. Also, Muslim-majority states discriminate more often on 21 of the 30 specific discrimination measures. However, among Christian-majority states, Orthodox-majority states have levels similar to those of the Muslim majority states with a mean level of 19.8.

There are additional important variations within each majority religion. Within Christianity, as noted earlier, Orthodox-majority states discriminate the most while Catholic and other Christian states discriminate at about the

TABLE 6.6. *Change in Mean Level of Religious Discrimination between 1990 and 2008 Controlling for Majority Religion*

	All Discrimination	Practices	Institutions & Clergy	Proselytizing & Conversion	Other
By Majority Religion					
Catholic	33.6%	50.0%	13.1%	50.0%	83.9%
Orthodox Christian	43.3%	40.9%	40.9%	34.8%	53.2%
Other Christians	54.8%	64.3%	32.1%	200.0%	50.0%
Islam	8.1%	8.8%	5.6%	2.8%	16.2%
Other	17.3%	9.8%	14.9%	6.9%	45.5%
By World Region					
Western democracies	33.1%	42.1%	13.3%	35.7%	64.5%
Former Soviet	53.0%	71.6%	36.6%	16.3%	81.2%
Asia	13.0%	12.3%	4.3%	6.6%	32.9%
Middle East	−4.5%	−9.6%	−3.3%	−2.7%	−3.1%
Sub-Saharan Africa	40.2%	17.4%	56.4%	15.3%	73.0%
Latin America	18.4%	0.0%	14.9%	52.9%	15.8%

TABLE 6.7. *Mean Level of Religious Discrimination in 2008 Controlling for Official Religion Policy*

	All Discrimination			Means			
	Mean	Low	High	Practices	Institutions & Clergy	Proselytizing & Conversion	Other
Official religion	18.31	1	71	4.27	4.05	5.83	4.17
One religion preferred	11.80	0	47	2.45	4.07	2.43	2.93
Multiple religions preferred	7.03	0	22	1.52	2.64	0.88	2.00
Equal treatment	3.62	0	15	0.78	1.18	0.64	1.04
Hostile	31.22	4	47	9.33	6.33	7.78	7.78

same level. Christian states also differ by world region. Christian states in the Third World discriminate significantly less. The means for Christian-majority states in Western democracies and the former Soviet bloc are 6.0 and 14.4, respectively, compared with 1.0, 4.1, and 3.4 for Christian-majority states in Asia, sub-Saharan Africa, and Latin America, respectively. This is particularly interesting because based on liberal democratic theory, we would expect Western democracies to discriminate the least.

Religious discrimination varies widely among Muslim-majority states. The highest levels are found in Asian states that were never part of the Soviet bloc – Afghanistan, Bangladesh, Brunei, Indonesia, Malaysia, the Maldives, and Pakistan – which have a mean level of 30.7. This is slightly higher than the 30.1 scored by the Persian Gulf states, which are generally perceived as the most oppressive in this respect. The rest of the Middle East scores 20.8, which is similar to the 19.3 score of the former Soviet bloc Muslim-majority states. Muslim-majority states in Sub-Saharan Africa scores 7.4, which is not much higher than the score for Western democracies.

Thus, overall the answer to the question of who discriminates the most does not fully follow conventional wisdom when looking within religious traditions.

Religious Discrimination and Official Religions

The official status of religion in a state influences religious discrimination, as presented in Table 6.7. Setting countries hostile to religion aside for the moment, stronger state support for religion is correlated with higher the religious discrimination. This is consistent across categories of religious discrimination. This provides confirmation that an element of state support for religion is restricting minority religions.

However, states hostile to religion by far discriminate the most. This is particularly interesting because hostility implies a uniform hostility to all religion and religious discrimination – as defined here – is restrictions placed on minority religious practices and institutions that are not placed on the majority religion. Thus, states that are hostile to religion not only restrict religion in general (as demonstrated in Table 5.7 of the previous chapter), they also single out minority religions for extra discrimination, creating a distinction between the majority religion and minority religions.

Of course, these results are not uniform. Discrimination varies widely within each category of the official religion variable. Several states that formally treat religion equally still engage in high levels of religious discrimination. Eritrea's government heavily restricts all religions, but the patterns of restriction of the majority and minority religions differ. The same is true of Turkey, but this appears to be changing with regard to hostility toward Islam after the study period.

Who Has No Religious Discrimination?
Twenty-seven countries engaged in no discrimination at any time between 1990 and 2008, but they have few commonalities. They include autocratic states such as Cameroon, Congo-Brazzaville, and Gambia, but a majority lean to the democratic side of the Polity scale. This includes countries such as Papua New Guinea, Burundi, and Namibia, which while not fully democratic lean toward democracy. They also include five Western democracies – Andorra, Canada, Ireland, New Zealand, and Portugal – as well as non-Western democracies including Estonia, the Philippines, the Solomon Islands, South Africa, South Korea, Taiwan, Uruguay, and Vanuatu.

On a regional level, no state in the Middle East is on this list, only Estonia represents the former Soviet bloc, and only Suriname and Uruguay represent Latin America. The most represented region is sub-Saharan Africa with 13 states, or 28.3% of states in the region.

While 55.6% (15) of the states on the list are Christian, so are 55.4% of the states in the study, so this is the expected distribution. Five Muslim states – Burkina Faso, Gambia, Niger, Senegal, and Sierra Leone – are on the list. All of them are located in the same region of Western Africa, indicating a geographic pocket of religious tolerance among Muslim-majority states. Interestingly, of the seven states on the list that are neither Christian- nor Muslim-majority, five – Cameroon, Guinea Bissau, Liberia, and Suriname – have no religious majority. The others are Taiwan (Buddhist and Taoist majority) and Benin (Animist majority).

The one thing all of these countries have in common is that none of them have official religions. However, they vary widely in how they deal with religion. Three – Andorra, Ireland, and Portugal – prefer a single religion, five support some religions over others, four support all religions equally, and 14 are coded as accommodation – separation of religion and state with a positive attitude toward religion. Only Uruguay is coded as separationist – separation of religion and state (SRAS) with a negative attitude toward religion.

It is important to remember that religious discrimination involves limitations on minority religious institutions and practices not placed on the majority religion. 17 of these states regulate, control, or restrict religion in general.[34]

Overall Patterns in State Religion Policy

The results in this chapter, combined with those of the previous two chapters enable a description of patterns in religion policy in general. There are two major trends worthy of note. First, of the 177 states in this study, only one – South Africa – engaged in none of the 110 religion policies covered in this study. This is relatively new to South Africa because in 1990, it had several of these policies. Until 1994, the regime monitored the religious activities of black churches. Male homosexuality was illegal until 1994, as was abortion for economic and social reasons as well as on demand until 1996. Religious education was present in public schools until 2002. While this was not the largest shift in state religion policy, it resulted in the unique situation in which a state has none of the religion policies recorded in the RAS2 dataset. This makes South Africa that rarest of entities: a state with full SRAS. Every other state engages in at least some small amount of support for religion; regulation, restriction, and control of religion, and/or religious discrimination. Most engage in more than a small amount.

The second trend is changes in religion policy over time and is shown in Tables 6.8 and 6.9. There are two aspects of this trend. First, only a minority of 29 states (16.4%) did not change their religion policy between 1990 and 2008. There is no particular pattern in these states. They include states from all major world regions and majority religions. While they lean toward democratic, five of them – Cameroon, Equatorial Guinea, Kuwait, North Korea, and Tunisia – are clearly autocratic. While most of them have no official religion, Kuwait and Tunisia do. Thus, although these states are exceptions to the rule of change, there does not appear to be any common factor explaining this lack of change.

The second aspect of this trend is that among those states that did change their policies, most uniformly increased their involvement in religion. This means between one and three of the three factors examined here – religious support, regulation, and discrimination – rose and none of them dropped. A majority of 98 (55.4%) of states are in this category. In contrast, only 22 (12.4%) uniformly lowered their involvement in religion. This means increases outnumbered decreases by a ratio of 3.5 to 1. Twenty-eight states (15.8%) had mixed changes, which means that they became less involved in religion on at least one of the variables but more involved on at least one other.

---

[34] Practices was significant at the .05 level from 1998 onward. Institutions and clergy was significant at the .05 level from 1995, at the .01 level from 1998, and the .001 level from 2001. Proselytizing and conversion was significant at the .05 level from 1995 and the .01 level from 1997. Other restrictions were significant at the .05 level in 1996, the .01 level in 1997, and the .001 level from 1998.

TABLE 6.8. *Change in Religious Legislation, Discrimination, and Regulation between 1990 (or Earliest) and 2008*

Change in Religious Regulation		Change in Religious Discrimination	
	Lower	Unchanged	Higher
Religious Legislation Lower			
Lower	Greece, Iraq, Latvia (3)	South Africa, Turkish Cyprus (2)	Sweden, Switzerland (2)
Unchanged	Cyprus, Paraguay (2)	Canada, Chile, Liechtenstein, Qatar (4)	Fiji, Japan, Lesotho, Sri Lanka (4)
Higher	Moldova (1)	—	Laos, Nepal (2)
Religious Legislation Unchanged			
Lower	Vietnam (1)	Iceland, Syria, Taiwan (3)	Albania, Armenia, Cuba, Finland, Macedonia, Turkey (6)
Unchanged	Barbados, Guinea, Jordan, Malawi, Slovenia, UAE, Western Sahara (7)	Andorra, Benin, Botswana, Brazil, Burkina Faso, Cameroon, Cape Verde, Colombia, Costa Rica, Equatorial Guinea, Gabon, Guatemala, Guyana, Haiti, Ireland, Jamaica, Kuwait, Mauritius, Montenegro, Namibia, Netherlands, New Zealand, N. Korea, Papua New Guinea, Portugal, Solomon Islands, S. Korea, Suriname, Tunisia (29)	Austria, Bahamas, Belgium, Denmark, Ecuador, Ethiopia, Libya, Norway, Panama, Singapore, Ukraine, Venezuela (12)
Higher	Ghana, Trinidad & Tobago (2)	Burundi, Central African Rep., Congo-Brazzaville, Myanmar, Sierra Leone, Uruguay, Zimbabwe (7)	Algeria, Belarus, Bolivia, Brunei, Egypt, France, India, Israel, Nicaragua, Oman, Saudi Arabia, Spain, Togo, Turkmenistan, United Kingdom, Yemen, Zaire (18)

TABLE 6.8 (continued)

	Change in Religious Discrimination		
Change in Religious Regulation	Lower	Unchanged	Higher
Religious Legislation Higher			
Lower	Bahrain (1)	–	Mexico, Serbia (2)
Unchanged	Morocco, Slovakia (2)	Australia, Bhutan, Czech Rep., Dominican Rep., Guinea Bissau, Honduras, Ivory Coast, Lebanon, Liberia, Lithuania, Luxembourg, Mongolia, Philippines, Senegal, Swaziland, United States, Vanuatu (17)	Argentina, Belize, Bosnia, Cambodia, Chad, El Salvador, Germany, Hungary, Italy, Malta, Peru, Poland, Tanzania (13)
Higher	Comoros, Djibouti, Mozambique, Somalia, Sudan, Timor (6)	Croatia, Estonia, Gambia, Niger (4)	Afghanistan, Angola, Azerbaijan, Bangladesh, Bulgaria, China, Eritrea, Georgia, Indonesia, Kazakhstan, Kenya, Kyrgyzstan, Madagascar, Malaysia, Maldives, Mali, Mauritania, Nigeria, Pakistan, Romania, Russia, Rwanda, Tajikistan, Thailand, Uganda, Uzbekistan, Zambia (27)

Lower (22 countries) = SMALL CAPS; mixed (28 countries) = plain font; no change (29 countries) = underlined; higher (98 countries) = shaded.

TABLE 6.9. *Change in State Religion Policy between 1990 (or Earliest) and 2008*

	Change in Religious Legislation, Discrimination, and Regulation							
	Higher		Unchanged		Lower		Mixed	
	n	%	n	%	n	%	n	%
All Cases	98	55.4%	29	16.4%	22	12.4%	28	15.8%
By Majority Religion								
All Christian	53	54.1%	19	19.4%	12	12.2%	14	14.3%
Catholic	27	61.4%	9	20.5%	4	9.1%	4	9.1%
Orthodox Christian	6	46.2%	1	7.7%	2	15.4%	4	30.8%
Other Christian	20	48.8%	9	22.0%	6	14.6%	6	14.6%
Muslim	28	59.6%	3	6.4%	8	17.0%	8	17.0%
Other	17	53.1%	7	21.9%	2	6.3%	6	18.8%
By World Region								
Western democracies	13	48.1%	5	18.5%	6	22.2%	3	11.1%
Former Soviet Bloc	19	67.9%	1	3.6%	2	7.1%	6	21.4%
Asia	17	58.6%	4	13.8%	2	6.9%	6	20.7%
Middle East	9	45.0%	2	10.0%	6	30.0%	3	15.0%
Sub-Saharan Africa	27	58.7%	9	19.6%	3	6.5%	7	15.2%
Latin America	13	48.1%	8	26.9%	3	11.1%	3	11.1%

Both of these trends are robust. As shown in Table 6.9, these trends are consistent across world region and majority religion. Rising involvement in religion outweighs decreasing involvement, and states with unchanged policies are clearly in the minority for all categories examined here. Of the 110 individual types of religion policy, 85 (77.3%) became more common, 14 (12.7%) became less common, and 11 (10.0%) remained the same. Thus, the overall pattern of increasing government involvement in religion remains consistent.

However, even if they are in the minority, many states have lowered their involvement in religion. Fifty (28.2%) lowered at least one aspect of it. Thus, within this pattern of increasing government involvement in religion, there is a state of flux. Political secularists are sometimes successful in their competition with those who seek to involve governments in religion. All of this is consistent with the dynamics described in the secular-religious competition perspective.

Conclusions

Religious discrimination – government restrictions on the practice of religion by religious minorities or on their religious institutions – is common and increasing. In 1990 (or the earliest year available), 136 countries engaged in

891 types of religious discrimination. By 2008, 146 countries engaged in 1,060 types. These countries include the majority of countries from all world regions, all major religious denominations, and democracies as well as nondemocracies. This ubiquity of religious discrimination is astounding and has important implications.

First, placing restrictions on the practices and institutions of religious minorities is the world norm. This is true despite the presence of religious freedom clauses in most of the world's constitutions (I discuss this in more detail in Chapter 8) as well as multiple international treaties and conventions that protect religious freedom. In fact, if one were to base one's assessment of the world's norms on constitutional documents and international conventions and treaties, the inescapable conclusion is that protecting the religious freedom and rights of religious minorities is the international norm. Yet this examination of what actually happens on the ground shows that in 2008, all but 31 countries did not fully practice this norm. This result arguably demonstrates that if there is truly an international norm of religious freedom, it is based more on rhetoric than a genuine intention to follow the norm.

Second, the majority of Western democracies are among those that engage in religious discrimination, although mean levels tend to be lower than the world average. Yet Christian states in both Sub-Saharan Africa and Latin America, on average, discriminate less than do Western democracies. This runs directly counter to expectations among liberal democratic theorists that liberal democracies should have separation of religion and state. Western democracies are generally considered to be not only the birthplace of liberal democracy, but also the ones that most closely conform to its values. The fact that most of them discriminate demonstrates that liberal ideologies do not always translate into liberal practices. The fact that Christian majority countries elsewhere perform better on this front undermines assumptions regarding which world region is the most free.

Third, the patterns of discrimination conform to the results of previous chapters, which demonstrate that state involvement in religion is in a state of flux. While some states engaged in less religious discrimination in 2008 than they did before, an even larger number engaged in more discrimination. This is consistent with the competition perspective presented in Chapter 2, which posits that secularism and religion compete in the political arena.

Fourth, this is evidence of both the relative success of religious political actors in their struggle with political secularism and increasing tensions between religious groups. Political secularists tend to support religious freedom and equality for ideological reasons. In fact, a ban on restricting religious minorities is one of the few things that the various factions of the secularist camp can agree on. If they support restrictions on religion, they support these restrictions being applied equally to all religions. Religious minorities tend to support religious freedom because this is the environment in which they are best able to practice their religions (Gill, 2008). Thus, the increasing levels of religious discrimination represent shifts in two significant aspects of the world's religious economy.

These findings for religious discrimination are part of a larger trend in which, on all policy fronts, the world's governments are becoming increasingly involved in religion. In the struggle between political secularism and religious political actors described in the competition perspective, the religious actors are logging considerably more victories than defeats. This is consistent across world regions, major world religions, and regime types. It is also largely consistent across the 110 types of specific policies I examine in this study. At least within the realm of government religion policy, religion remains present and, arguably, unavoidable. Remaining fully neutral on all matters related to religion, for a government, is rare and a choice that is difficult to maintain. The competition between religious and secular actors is an active one that few states have been able to fully avoid.

7

Education, Abortion, and Proselytizing

While all aspects of state religion policy are important, a small number of government religion policies are particularly pervasive and contentious across the globe. Religious education in public schools, restrictions on abortion, and limits on proselytizing are among them. These three issues are among the most important and active in the competition between political secularism and religious political actors described in the secular-religious competition perspective. When there are political clashes over state religion policies, these issues are frequently involved. The first two are especially prominent in the United States, involving multiple political and judicial battles at both the federal and local levels. The latter is a prominent issue in many other Western democracies, especially with regard to banning or deporting "radical" Muslim preachers.

In this chapter, I subject these three issues to a more intense examination than I apply to other aspects of state religion policy in previous chapters. I select these issues for heightened scrutiny for at least five reasons. First, each of these policy types is present in a significant majority states, which is true only of these and two other types of policy among the 110 specific policies examined here.[1] This alone is sufficient to demonstrate that they are central issues to religion and politics. Second, there is considerable diversity across states in the specifics of these policies, so simply measuring their presence and absence is not enough to fully understand them. Third, each of these policies involves significant religious principles and substantially influences the lives of large numbers of people. Fourth, as noted earlier, all of these policies are the

---

[1] The others are the presence of a government religion department and the requirement for religions to register. I do not deal with these issues here because the first does not have sufficient variety in policy to warrant a discussion beyond what I present in previous chapters and the second I discuss in detail in Chapters 4 and 6.

Education, Abortion, and Proselytizing

subject of considerable political contention. This makes them excellent case studies of the competition between secular and religious forces in society and politics. Finally, examining these three types of policy can provide additional insight into the nature of state religion policy and how it has been evolving during the 19-year period covered by this study.

Religious Education in Public Schools

Imagine a country where public schools include religious education – not as an academic subject but religion taught as existential truth. These classes are available in several religions, although students have the opportunity not to take these classes and perhaps to take an alternative class. This country is not imaginary. This is the normal state of affairs in public schools in most Western democracies. The US policy of keeping religion out of public schools is among a minority of three: the United States, France, and the Turkish government of Cyprus.

By 2008, 118 countries – exactly two-thirds of the 177 countries in this study – had some form of religious education in at least some public schools. As presented in Tables 7.1 and 7.2, this is consistent across world regions as well as in Christian- and Muslim-majority states but is less common in "other" majority countries. Like most forms of government support for religion, the presence of this policy increased significantly between 1990 (or the earliest year available) and 2008.

To be clear, this type of policy involves classes that focus at least in part on the theology and belief system of a religion in a manner intended to educate believers, not academic and neutral courses in comparative religion. This is a significant form of support because in the modern era, most children are educated in public schools (schools funded and run by the state). Private schools are an option in most states, but they usually require tuition, while public schools tend to be free. Most countries have laws requiring the education of minors, and thus most children attend public schools either due to economic necessity or their parents' financial choices. This means that official state policy is that children are indoctrinated in religion at the state's expense in an institution most children are required to attend. In many cases, the state also influences the content of this religious education.

Religion is taught in the same place, in the same time period, as all other aspects of a child's formal education, placing religion on a par with topics such as math, science, history, and reading. This gives the religion or religions taught in the school an aura of legitimacy and can socially stigmatize children from other religions or those who choose themselves or whose parents choose (when possible) not to take the religion classes. This is a serious form of support for religion.

I examine this policy using three variables, each designed to clarify an important aspect of the nature and impact of this religious education as well as the

TABLE 7.1. *Religious Education Controlling for Majority Religion*

	All States		Majority Religion (2008 results)						
			Christian						
	1990*	2008	Catholic	Orthodox	Other Christian	Christian Total	Muslim	Other Religions
Have Religious Education in Public Schools	60.5%	66.7%	75.0%	59.2%	75.6%	74.5%	70.2%	37.5%
Are the classes mandatory?								
Optional for all or there is a nonreligious alternative	29.9%	36.2%	63.6%	46.2%	51.2%	56.1%	6.4%	18.8%
There is a procedure to opt out of the classes	11.3%	12.4%	11.4%	0.0%	19.5%	13.3%	10.6%	12.5%
Mandatory for some but optional for others	9.0%	9.0%	0.0%	23.1%	2.4%	4.1%	21.3%	6.3%
Mandatory for all	10.2%	9.0%	0.0%	0.0%	2.4%	1.0%	31.9%	0.0%
Are the classes available in all religions?								
Available in all religions with a significant number of students	13.6%	15.3%	15.9%	7.7%	26.8%	19.4%	10.6%	9.4%
Available in some religions with a significant number of students	26.6%	32.8%	45.5%	46.2%	39.0%	42.9%	21.3%	18.8%
Available in one religion but students of other religions exist	20.3%	18.6%	13.6%	15.4%	9.8%	12.2%	38.3%	9.4%
Who selects the teachers?								
Teachers are laypeople selected by the state	38.4%	41.8%	25.0%	46.2%	63.4%	43.9%	46.8%	28.1%
Teachers are clergy or religious institutions take part in the selection.	22.0%	24.9%	50.0%	23.1%	12.2%	30.6%	23.4%	9.4%

* In some cases, this represents the earliest year available.

TABLE 7.2. *Religious Education Controlling for World Region*

	World Region (2008)						
	Western Democracies	Former Soviet Bloc	Asia	Middle East	Sub-Saharan Africa	Latin America
Have Religious Education in Public Schools	88.9%	57.1%	58.6%	95.0%	52.2%	66.7%
Are the classes mandatory?						
Optional for all or there is a nonreligious alternative	66.6%	50.0%	13.8%	5.0%	34.8%	51.9%
There is a procedure to opt out of the classes	25.9%	0.0%	20.7%	10.0%	6.5%	14.8%
Mandatory for some but optional for others	7.4%	7.1%	13.8%	25.0%	6.5%	0.0%
Mandatory for all	0.0%	0.0%	10.3%	55.0%	4.3%	0.0%
Are the classes available in all religions?						
Available in all religions with a significant number of students	37.0%	3.6%	20.7%	15.0%	8.7%	11.1%
Available in some religions with a significant number of students	40.7%	46.4%	20.7%	20.0%	32.6%	33.3%
Available in one religion but students of other religions exist	11.1%	7.1%	17.2%	60.0%	10.9%	22.2%
Who selects the teachers?						
Teachers are laypeople selected by the state	48.1%	25.0%	41.4%	55.0%	43.5%	40.7%
Teachers are clergy or religious institutions take part in the selection	40.7%	32.1%	17.2%	40.0%	8.7%	25.9%

extent to which it is voluntary: whether the religion classes are mandatory, in which religions the classes are available, and who teaches the classes or selects the teachers. As I discuss in detail here, these three variables individually and in combination have a considerable impact on religious education in public schools. They are listed controlling for the states majority religion and world region in Tables 7.1 and 7.2.

Are the Classes Mandatory?
The simple presence of religion classes in public schools is a significant form of support whether or not they are mandatory. When they are mandatory, this constitutes an even more substantial form of support. This means that the religious indoctrination of children is not only convenient, available, and supported by the state but also that anyone who wants to use the state's free education system cannot prevent their children from experiencing this indoctrination. If the state sets the specific content of this education, it also determines which interpretation of the religion is taught. Because most religions have multiple and competing interpretations, this is a significant state intervention in which interpretation will be dominant. This has far-reaching and long-term implications for the nature of religious beliefs, practices, and institutions in a country. In this case, the presence of religious education in public schools is not only a form of support for religion, it is also a form of control.

Among the states that have religion classes in public schools, I found four basic types of policies. First, the classes are fully optional. This manifests in a number of ways. In some cases, students can take the class or not. Those that do not take the class may be free that period or may have to take another course in its place. Typical topics for this substitute course include general philosophy (e.g., Finland), morals (e.g., Rwanda), or culture (e.g., Romania). Jamaica has an arrangement in which students select their courses from a list of options, and religion is one of the available topics.

There are many other manifestations of this type of policy. In the Philippines, religious institutions may sponsor and fund religion classes in public schools. In some cases, the religious education is only provided at the request of the parents. For example Australia's 2004 Education Act states that "if parents of children at a government school ask the principal for their children to receive religious education in a particular religion, the principal must ensure that reasonable time is allowed for their children's religious education in that religion."[2] Estonia and Hungary have similar policies. The Democratic Republic of Congo and Israel, among other states, operate separate religious and secular school systems. Parents may choose which system their children attend. In Brazil, schools are required to offer optional religious education, but each school decides how to apply this. Overall, 64 countries or 54.2% of the

---
[2] Australia 2004 Education Act, www.legislation.act.gov.au/a/2004-17/current/pdf/2004-17.pdf.

countries that have religious education in public schools have this type of policy.

Second, the classes are "mandatory" in theory, but there is a procedure for students to opt out of the class. In these cases, students do not absolutely have to take the class, but the process for not taking it is not automatic and tends to be more cumbersome. It usually requires that the student or her or his parents take the initiative to make a specific request. For example, in Denmark and Peru, parents must make a written request. In Mauritania, the courses are technically mandatory, but informally many students do not attend without any repercussions. In some cases – usually against official policy – these requests are in practice denied. In Costa Rica, although a parental request should be sufficient, schools often require letters from a clergyperson, and in some cases students were required to remain in the classroom during the course, which is in Catholicism. This type of policy is present in 22 countries, or 18.6% of countries that have religious education in schools. Combined with the previous category, in 72.8% of countries with religious classes in public schools students have, at least in theory, a means not to take the class.

Third, the classes are mandatory for some but not others. Usually this means the classes are mandatory for members of the religion or religions in which the classes are taught but not for others. Thus, no one is forced to take classes in a religion other than their own, but the choice of choosing not to study religion is not an option for the majority of students. However, in some cases, there are repercussions for minority students. For example, in Greece, there is no alternative curriculum for students from other religions, so they often must stay in the room for the religion class. In Jordan, although Christian students may leave the room during studies of Islam, mandatory state exams include questions on Islamic poetry and Koranic verses. Sixteen countries with religious classes in public schools (13.6%) follow this type of policy.

Finally, the classes are mandatory for everyone regardless of their religion. This is the policy of 16 states – 13.6% of states with religious education in public schools. With the exception of Zambia since 2007, where the education is in Catholicism and Protestantism, all of these states have Muslim majorities, and the classes are in Islam.

The patterns across majority religion and world region show some diversity in education policy. Few Christian-majority states make religion classes mandatory. Given this fact, it is not surprising that mandatory classes are uncommon in Western democracies, the former Soviet bloc, and Latin America. The same is true for states with "other" majorities. However, this practice is considerably more common in Muslim-majority states, especially in the Middle East.

Are the Classes Available in All Religions?
The implications of religion classes in public schools differ depending on whether they are taught for all religions for which there are students. Whether

optional or mandatory, teaching only one or some religions for which there are a significant number of students is a form of support for these religions. Beyond the issues of equality and religious freedom, which I discuss later in the chapter, this constitutes an official endorsement of a specific religion or specific religions in a manner that is very clear to the students. It is essentially an open declaration of which religion or religions are "in" and which are "out" both politically and culturally. Either you belong to those whose religion the state supports by providing classes or you do not. Both leaving class while the majority of students stay and segregating students by religion for these classes create a clear division among students. This can have social implications and exacerbate interreligious tensions.

Only 27 states, or 22.9% of all states with religious education in public schools, provide this education in all religions for which there are a significant number of students. This includes Western liberal democracies such as Australia, Finland, Iceland, Ireland, the Netherlands, Sweden, and the United Kingdom, but it also includes some autocratic states such as Equatorial Guinea, Gabon, and Syria.

In 58 states, or 49.1% of all states with religious education in public schools, it is available in multiple religions, but not all religions for which there are sufficient students. For example, in Germany classes are available for Protestants, Catholics, and Jews if there are a sufficient number of students. However, many schools do not provide education in Islam even if there are enough students. Schools in Indonesia, by law, must provide education in six religions, which covers all major religions in the country; in practice, however, many schools do not offer education in all six.[3] In the Czech Republic, only registered religions may teach these classes, but because registration is rarely denied, this is not a significant burden. Croatia and Bulgaria have similar requirements but deny registration to some religions. Also, not all Croatian schools respect this right even for registered religions. Similarly, Austria has a multitier registration process, and only the higher tiers may teach religion classes in public schools. In Peru, the schools include education in Catholicism at the government's expense. All other religions must organize their own classes at their own expense.

In 33 states with religious education in public schools (28.0%), this education is available in only one religion; 18 of these states are Muslim-majority states, 13 of them in the Middle East. This does not include states such as Saudi Arabia where no religious minorities attend public schools. Denmark provides classes in Christian studies that focus on the Evangelical Lutheran faith but also cover other world religions and philosophies. They also teach the Catechism, a question and answer type of theological teaching of Christianity.

---

[3] Indonesia 1989 Law 2 on National Education System (translated online from original Indonesian December 22, 2010), www.legalitas.org/proses/uu.php?k=1989&h=Undang-Undang.

TABLE 7.3. *Mandatory Classes versus Availability of Classes in 2008*

	Are the Classes Available in All Religions?			
Are the Classes Mandatory?	No Religion Classes	All Religions	Some Religions	One Religion
No religion classes	33.3%	–	–	–
Optional for all or there is a nonreligious alternative	–	9.0%	23.2%	4.0%
There is a procedure to opt out of the classes	–	2.8%	4.0%	5.6%
Mandatory for some but optional for others	–	1.7%	4.0%	3.4%
Mandatory for all	–	1.7%	1.7%	5.6%

In Bolivia, classes in Catholicism are optional, but there is strong peer pressure to attend the classes. In Cambodia and Myanmar, Buddhism is part of the curriculum.[4] In Myanmar, although students may opt out of this in some schools, all students are required to recite a Buddhist prayer.

Patterns differ across world regions and majority religions. Muslim-majority countries are more likely to be exclusive, but this is largely, although not solely, driven by the results from the Middle East. Among Christian-majority countries, most states with religious education in public schools offer this education in multiple religions, but not all of them for which there are sufficient students. However, each region and majority religion has states in all three categories.

Religious Education and Religious Freedom
When combined, the two variables so far discussed – whether religious education is mandatory and in how many religions it is offered – have significant implications for religious freedom. As noted at several points in this book, there is no agreement on the meaning of the term *religious freedom*. Accordingly, I explore the implications based on multiple interpretations of the term. This discussion is also based on the results presented in Table 7.3.

One concept of religious freedom involves equality. Under this type of definition, which includes the concepts of *neutral political concern* and *exclusion of ideals* discussed in Chapter 2, all religions must be treated equally. Equal treatment includes cases with no religious education (59 states) and cases in which everyone gets the same access to religious education, which includes all

---
[4] Article 68, Cambodian Constitution, http://religlaw.com/country_portal.php?page_id=22&countryID=35.

27 states with religious education in all religions for which there are significant students. Thus, 47.4% of all states and 22.9% of states with public school religious education meet this standard.

A second concept of religious freedom is that no one is forced to take religious education in a religion other than their own. This concept is based on the perspective that if one's religious rights are not directly violated – and these rights include no forced indoctrination in another religion – one has religious freedom. This includes all of the states in the earlier category, the 86 states where religious education is optional or students can by specific request not take the course, as well as the 16 states where the class is only mandatory for members of the majority religion. This leaves only 13 states – 7.3% of all states and 11.0% of states with religious education in public schools – that force members of minority religions to take courses in a religion other than their own. As noted earlier, with the exception of Zambia since 2007, all of these states have Muslim majorities. All of these Muslim-majority states other than Indonesia and Sudan are in the Middle East.

A third concept involves freedom from religion. This means that people have the right not to be exposed to religion. In a strict sense, this would include only the 59 (33.3%) states with no religious education because the availability of these classes can be interpreted as pressure to take them, but an expanded definition can also include the 86 (48.5% of all states and 72.9% of states with religious education in public schools) where the courses are optional or students can opt out. Thus, based on this definition, 81.8% of states have religious freedom in their public education systems.

A fourth concept is that there can be no situation in which any of the above three criteria are violated. This includes 80 states (45.2% of all states) – the 59 states with no religious education and the 21 (18.0%) states where religious education is available in all religions and the classes are optional or students can opt out of them.

A final concept involves the right to religious education in public schools. As a universal right, religious education should be available to all students, which is the case for 27 (15.2%) countries. If we combine this with the freedom from religion criteria, this includes only 21 (11.9%) countries. These countries are mostly Christian majority. Suriname has no majority religion, and Thailand is Buddhist. Afghanistan is included in this category because it has no significant non-Muslim population that attends public schools.

Interestingly, public school religious education policy of each of the 177 countries in this study can be said to be not fully free based on at least one of these definitions. It is simply not possible to meet the criteria of all four definitions. The only states whose policy can be considered unfree under all of the definitions are the 13 in the second concept. Thus, on the basis of one's definition of religious freedom, there is a wide variation in the number of states whose public school religious education policy adheres to concepts of religious freedom. This demonstrates that the concept of religious freedom can be extremely subjective.

Who Teaches the Religion Classes?

This third aspect of public religious education policy is not an element of any of the concepts of religious freedom discussed earlier, but it does reflect strongly on the quality of state support for religion. Allowing religious institutions to select the religion teachers is significant. It allows clergy or teachers appointed or approved by religious bodies direct access to students to whom they teach the tenets of a religion with no filter of any kind. The government basically cedes control over the curriculum of that class. This has significant implications for understanding a state's religion policy because, as noted in Chapters 3, 4, and 5, control of religion is a strong motivation for much of state religion policy. The presence of this type of education policy suggests that a state's support for religion is not primarily about control.

As shown in Tables 7.1 and 7.2, while most states with public religious education do not follow this policy, 44 (37.3%) of these states do. In many cases, the teachers are clergy. This practice is particularly common in Catholic states, half of which have clergy or Church-appointed or -approved teachers teaching Catholicism in public schools. This includes 7 of the 11 Catholic-majority Western democracies: Austria, Belgium, Ireland, Italy, Luxembourg, Portugal, and Spain. In Latin America, this is less common with only 7 of 20 Catholic-majority states – Belize, Bolivia, Chile, Costa Rica, Haiti, Peru, and Trinidad and Tobago – following this policy.

Religious Education and Official Religion Policy

As presented in Table 7.4, state policy on religious education in public schools is highly correlated with the state's official religion policy. The extent of support can be divided into four categories. First, and not surprisingly, states which are hostile to religion have no religious education in their public schools. Second, 42% of states that treat all religions equally, and accordingly do not support one religion over others, still have public school religious education. This is a relatively high number for states whose policies otherwise meet many definitions of separation of religion and state and speaks to the pervasiveness of religious education in public schools. Third, about three-quarters of states with no official religion but selectively support one or more public school religious education. Finally, this level jumps to 97.6% among states with official religions. Thus, as states more strongly support religion in general they are more likely to support public school religious education.

The results are similar for whether the religion classes are mandatory and whether they are available in all religions. However, the issue of who selects the teachers can be divided onto two categories: those states that prefer some religions over others and those that do not. This implies that among states that

TABLE 7.4. *Religious Education controlling for Official Support for Religion*

	Official Religion Policy (2008)				
	Official Religion	One Religion Preferred	Some Religions Preferred	Equal Treatment	Hostile
Have Religious Education in Public Schools	97.6%	75.0%	72.7%	42.0%	0.0%
Are the classes mandatory?					
Optional for all or there is a non-religious alternative	17.1%	50.0%	51.5%	36.0%	0.0%
There is a procedure to opt out of the classes	26.8%	13.6%	12.1%	2.0%	0.0%
Mandatory for some but optional for others	22.0%	4.5%	9.1%	4.0%	0.0%
Mandatory for all	31.27	6.8%	0.0%	0.0%	0.0%
Are the classes available in all religions?					
Available in all religions with a significant number of students	22.0%	13.6%	12.1%	16.0%	0.0%
Available in some religions with a significant number of students	22.0%	40.9%	57.6%	24.0%	0.0%
Available in one religion but students of other religions exist	53.7%	20.5%	3.0%	2.0%	0.0%
Who selects the teachers?					
Teachers are laypeople selected by the state.	634%	43.2%	36.4%	34.0%	0.0%
Teachers are clergy or religious institutions take part in the selection.	34.1%	31.8%	36.4%	8.0%	0.0%

support religion, the issue of control is not strongly linked to the extent of this support.

The Big Picture
Religious education in public schools is one policy among many that relate to religion. Yet it strongly both reflects and illuminates a state's overall religion

policy. Whether religious education is mandatory is a good indicator of whether the majority religion itself is mandatory. The availability of this education in all religions reflects the state's tolerance of minority religions. A state where public religious education is available in only one religion likely has other elements of exclusivity in its religion policy. Finally, allowing religious institutions to select or provide the teachers is a reasonable measure of how much independence the state is willing to give religious institutions.

Thus, while religious education in public schools is largely a form of support for religion, it also involves elements of control. On one hand, it facilitates the propagation of religion and often involves privileged access to some religions. That is, it facilitates a religion's ability to retain worshippers (Gill, 2008: 20). On the other hand, it also allows the state to control the content of religious education. Whatever the mix of control and support in any particular case, the presence of religion in public schools speaks to the relevance of religion.

With this in mind, the presence of public school religious education in two-thirds of states in 2008 is in and of itself an important indicator. Its ubiquity speaks for itself. The only category of state in which this education is completely absent is states hostile to religion and, as noted in Chapter 3, this type of state is becoming less common. On a more philosophical level, theorists specifically link the extent of religious control of education to the extent of religious authority in society (Beit-Hallahmi, 2003: 13; Kuru, 2009; Swatos & Christiano, 1999: 219–220).

It is even present in a large minority of states that are otherwise mostly neutral on the issue of religion. While all of them other than Turkey and Zimbabwe make this education optional or provide a way to opt out, only 8 of these 20 neutral states with religious education in public schools offer it in all religions for which there are sufficient students. All of this reinforces the conclusion that true state neutrality on the issue of religion is very much the exception rather than the norm.

Abortion Policy

A central question in the context of this study is whether abortion is a religious issue. I argue that it is one that is strongly correlated and associated with religion for three reasons. First, abortion is a topic that is addressed in religious theologies and beliefs. More important, these theologies and beliefs translate into political action. In nearly every case in which changes in abortion policy are publically debated across the world, religious institutions and leaders are heavily involved in the debate. As Minkenberg (2002: 227) puts it

The abortion conflict involves a clash of values or even of "absolutes" that counter poses an individual woman's self-determination and the protection of unborn human life. In the political realm, the confrontation between feminists' insistence on a woman's absolute freedom of reproductive choice and the Catholic and, to a lesser extent, Protestant churches' insistence on the absolute priority of human life (which includes the fetus's right after conception) has been met by a variety of authoritative responses from governments and states.

These beliefs run so deep that stopping abortion has been a justification for terrorism (Dolink & Gunartna, 2009: 344–345; Juergensmeyer, 1997: 18; Stern, 2003). Also, many studies link religious identity to political positions on abortion (Hayes, 1995; Norris & Inglehart, 2002: 255; Oldmixion & Hudson, 2008: 131). This makes the worldwide debate and struggle over this issue one of the most pervasive examples of the conflict between supporters of political secularism and religious political actors described in the competition perspective.

This is not to say that all opponents of abortion do oppose it for religious reasons. Nor is it to say that all of those who oppose restrictions on abortion are secular. Rather, abortion is an issue that is addressed by several significant religious and secular ideologies. These ideologies, in turn, influence political advocacy the issue.

Second, as I demonstrate here, state policy on abortion is correlated with both religious denomination and state support for religion. This does not mean that the issue of abortion is exclusively a religious issue. However, it is one that is inextricably intertwined with state religion policy.

Third, in nearly every case when abortion is discussed in the political arena or abortion laws are changed, religious groups are involved, usually in support of restrictions on abortion. For example, when in 2013 Ireland was considering allowing abortions in cases where the mother's life is at risk including risk of suicide, "Catholic Bishops issued a statement condemning [the proposed law] saying that 'no state has the right to undermine the right to life.'" The Catholic Church called on all Catholics, including politicians, to oppose the law.[5] Similarly, secular groups, often international ones, are involved in pressure to ease restrictions on abortion. Thus, on both an ideological and practical level, abortion is a core international flashpoint in the struggle between political secularism and religious actors, although clearly the debate is by no means completely driven by religious-secular contentions.

To examine this issue in depth, I assess whether states restrict abortion in eight circumstances. These categories are based on those developed for the United Nations report on abortion policies around the world.[6] The report lists state policy for a single point in time around 2000 for each country, but the Religion and State (RAS) project data were coded based on a wider range

---

[5] Douglas Dabley, "Ireland to Legalize Abortion in Limited Cases," *International Herald Tribune*, June 20, 2013.
[6] UN Abortion policies webpage, www.un.org/esa/population/publications/abortion/profiles.htm.

Education, Abortion, and Proselytizing

of sources and cover the entire 1990 to 2008 time period.[7] These variables measure whether abortions are restricted in the first trimester of a pregnancy under the following circumstances:

- On request.
- For social reasons.
- For economic reasons.
- In cases of incest.
- In cases of rape.
- To preserve the mental health of the mother.
- To preserve the physical health of the mother.
- To save the life of the mother.

The level of restrictions are coded as 2 if the restrictions are absolute, as 1 if the restrictions exist but abortions are often allowed in practice, and 0 for no restrictions.

This set of variables allows for a more detailed analysis of abortion policies than presented in previous quantitative analysis such as Minkenberg (2002) which tend to include simply whether abortions are restricted under no more than two or three circumstances at a specific point in time. I posit that states that more strongly support religion will place more of these restrictions on abortion. I also argue that as political stands on abortion are linked to theology and religious beliefs, patterns will differ across religious denominations.

Religious Denomination, World Region, and Abortion

The results for restrictions on abortion controlling for denomination are presented in Table 7.5. To control for whether any differences across denominations are influenced by other factors, I also control for world region in Table 7.6. Before discussing patterns across regions and denominations, it is important to note that overall restrictions on abortion dropped during the study period.

There are clear patterns across religious denomination. Within Christianity, Catholic-majority states consistently restrict abortion more often than non-Catholic-majority states with Orthodox states barely restricting them at all. Among Orthodox, states only Cyprus restricts abortions. Cyprus's criminal code allows abortion only to save the mother's physical and mental health or life and in cases of rape, incest, and fetal impairment. In practice, abortions for social or economic reasons are sometimes allowed to preserve the physical and mental health of the mother. Other than in cases of rape, two physicians must certify the justification for the abortion.

A typical Catholic-majority state, such as Burundi, Rwanda, and Costa Rica, restricts abortions in all circumstances other than to save the life of the mother or preserve her physical health. Many Catholic countries, such as Ecuador,

---

[7] The full range of sources used by the RAS project are listed in Chapter 3.

TABLE 7.5. *Abortion Policy Controlling for Majority Religion*

Restrictions on Abortions	All States		Majority Religion (2008 results)						
			Christian						
	1990*	2008	Catholic	Orthodox	Other Christian	Christian Total	Muslim	Other Religions
To save the life of the mother	6.2%	6.2%	13.6%	0.0%	2.4%	6.4%	7.4%	3.1%
To preserve the physical health of the mother	33.9%	32.8%	43.2%	0.0%	17.1%	26.5%	46.8%	31.2%
To preserve the mental health of the mother	44.6%	41.8%	54.5%	0.0%	26.8%	35.7%	53.3%	40.6%
In cases of rape	53.7%	49.7%	54.5%	0.0%	43.9%	42.9%	70.2%	40.6%
In cases of incest	56.5%	50.8%	59.1%	0.0%	43.9%	44.9%	70.2%	40.6%
For economic reasons	64.4%	62.1%	70.5%	7.7%	53.6%	55.1%	76.6%	62.5%
For social reasons	65.0%	62.1%	70.5%	7.7%	53.6%	55.1%	76.6%	62.5%
On request	70.1%	68.4%	75.0%	7.7%	70.7%	64.3%	76.6%	68.7%

* In some cases, this represents the earliest year available.

TABLE 7.6. *Abortion Policy Controlling for World Region*

Restrictions on Abortions	World Region (2008)					
	Western Democracies	Former Soviet Bloc	Asia	Middle East	Sub-Saharan Africa	Latin America
To save the life of the mother	3.7%	0.0%	10.7%	5.0%	4.3%	14.8%
To preserve the physical health of the mother	11.1%	0.0%	37.9%	45.0%	47.8%	48.1%
To preserve the mental health of the mother	11.1%	0.0%	35.2%	45.0%	63.0%	63.0%
In cases of rape	18.5%	0.0%	62.1%	80.0%	69.6%	63.0%
In cases of incest	18.5%	0.0%	62.1%	80.0%	69.6%	70.4%
For economic reasons	25.9%	3.6%	69.0%	85.0%	91.3%	85.2%
For social reasons	25.9%	3.6%	69.0%	85.0%	91.3%	85.2%
On request	44.4%	3.6%	75.9%	85.0%	93.5%	96.3%

Guatemala, and the Philippines, also restrict abortions even if the mother's physical health is at risk. A few, including Chile, Malta, and Timor restrict it even when the mother's life is at risk. One in four, including Austria, Belgium, Croatia, and El Salvador do not restrict it at all.

Typical "other" Christian states such as the Bahamas, Ghana, and New Zealand restrict abortions on request as well as for economic and social reasons. A large minority such as Papua New Guinea, Tanzania, and Uganda, also restrict abortions in cases of rape and incest. Many, such as the Central African Republic, Malawi, and the Solomon Islands, restrict it when the mother's physical and mental health are at risk. Only in Congo-Brazzaville are abortions to save the life of the mother technically illegal but in practice are still performed in government hospitals when the mother's life or health are at risk.

While the specific results differ by category of restrictions, for the most part Muslim-majority states restrict abortions more often than do Catholic states. A typical Muslim state, such as Comoros and Pakistan, restricts abortions except when the mother's physical health or life is at risk. However, many, such as Bangladesh, Iraq, and Senegal, also restrict abortions when the mother's physical health is at risk.

The typical non-Christian non-Muslim country, such as Cameroon and Liberia, restrict only abortions on request and for economic and social reasons. Many, such as Mozambique and Nepal, also restrict it in cases of incest, rape, and when the mother's mental health is at risk. Just under a third, including

TABLE 7.7. *Abortion Policy Controlling for Official Support for Religion*

Restrictions on Abortions	Official Religion Policy (2008)				
	Official Religion	One Religion Preferred	Some Religions Preferred	Equal Treatment	Hostile
To save the life of the mother	7.3%	9.3%	3.0%	4.0%	10.1%
To preserve the physical health of the mother	39.0%	39.6%	30.3%	28.0%	10.1%
To preserve the mental health of the mother	48.8%	47.7%	33.3%	42.0%	10.1%
In cases of rape	69.3%	47.7%	42.4%	48.0%	10.1%
In cases of incest	69.3%	50.0%	43.4%	50.0%	10.1%
For economic reasons	70.7%	61.4%	51.5%	72.0%	10.1%
For social reasons	70.7%	61.4%	51.5%	72.0%	10.1%
On request	81.5%	65.9%	57.6%	78.0%	10.1%

Guinea Bissau and Sri Lanka also restrict it in cases where the mother's physical health is at risk.

World region has a large impact on abortion policy. The only former Soviet state, regardless of majority religion, to restrict abortion at all is Poland, a Catholic-majority state. During Poland's Communist era, abortion was essentially available on request. After pressure from the Catholic Church, a 1993 law banned abortion on request and for economic and social reasons (Byrnes & Katzenstein, 2000: 131). In Western Democracies, restrictions on abortion are present but at a rate that is well below the world average. The most restrictive of these states are Ireland and Andorra, which restrict it in all cases other than to save the mother's life, and Malta, which restricts abortions even in this case. All three are Catholic-majority states.

In the rest of the world regions, restrictions are the norm, although levels in Asia and the Middle East are somewhat lower than those in Latin America and sub-Saharan Africa. All of this indicates a tendency for more developed states to restrict abortion less. I discuss this in more detail in the multivariate analysis that follows.

State Religion Policy and Abortion

An examination of the link between a country's official religion policy and abortion, presented in Table 7.7 shows a strong link between the two. As states more strongly support religion, they also more strongly restrict abortion. However, this relationship is not absolute. Some states with official religions, such as Bahrain, Tunisia, and Greece, do not restrict abortions, and Laos, one of the nine countries coded as hostile to religion, heavily restricts abortion.

The Religious Correlates of Abortion

The foregoing analysis demonstrates that there are multiple factors correlated with state abortion policy. In this section, I analyze factors that influence abortion policy using logistic regressions. I control for the following factors.

As noted earlier, a state's majority religion, world region, and official religion are correlated with abortion policy. I control for *majority religion* with dummy variables for Catholic, Orthodox Christian, other Christian, and Muslim majorities. "Other" majorities are the excluded variable. I control for *world region* using dummy variables for each world region other than the former Soviet bloc, which is the excluded variable. Rather than use the official religion policy variable, I use *religious support* because religious support is a more detailed variable and, as I argued in Chapter 4, it more accurately reflects a state's true religion policy. The version of the variable used here adds the results for 50 of the 51 types of religious support discussed in Chapter 4, which is all types of support other than restrictions on abortion.

I include three additional control variables that previous studies show to significantly influence state religion policy (Fox, 2008). *Religious diversity* is a Herfendahl-based variable measuring the extent to which a country is religiously diverse, which takes into account the proportion of each religious group in the population. I use the version produced by Barro and McCleary (2003). I include the *Polity* variable from the Polity dataset to control for regime type.[8] Given the findings presented earlier of low levels of restrictions on abortion in Western democracies, it is prudent to assess whether this is due to their political regimes or some other element of their culture. Finally, I control for *economic development* using the log of each country's per capita GDP.[9]

The results, presented in Table 7.8, show a link between religion and abortion policy. No variable examined here is statistically significant at the .05 level in predicting restrictions on abortion to save the life of the mother or when her physical or mental health are at risk. In cases of rape and incest, the Catholic, other Christian, and religious support variables all become significant and predict higher levels of restrictions on abortion. The Catholic, religious support, and all of the world region variables are significant in restrictions on abortions for economic and social reasons.

The results for restrictions on abortion on request are, perhaps, the most important because this effectively measures which states place any kind of restriction on abortion. The results are essentially the same as those for restrictions for economic and social reasons.

---

[8] The variable ranges from −10 (most autocratic) to +10 (most democratic). It is based on the regulation, openness, and competitiveness of executive recruitment, constraints on the executive, and the regulation and competitiveness of political participation. For more details, see Jaggers and Gurr (1995) and the Polity Project webpage at www.systemicpeace.org/polity/polity4.htm.

[9] UN Statistical Division, http://unstats.un.org/unsd/default.htm.

TABLE 7.8. *Multivariate Analysis (Logistic Regressions) of Abortion Policies in 2008*

	Save Life of Mother		Physical Health of Mother		Mental Health of Mother		In Cases of Rape	
	B	Sig.	B	Sig.	B	Sig.	B	Sig.
Catholic	2.571	.110	1.619	.094	2.185	.074	3.392	.004
Orthodox Christian	2.060	.999	−15.427	.999	−15.015	.999	−15.162	.999
Other Christian	.953	.540	−.206	.758	−.276	.671	1.914	.011
Islam	2.436	.192	.608	.457	.594	.489	.817	.337
Western democracies	1.260	.999	18.470	.998	17.849	.998	19.469	.998
Asia	20.046	.998	20.655	.998	21.909	.998	22.052	.998
Middle East	18.942	.998	19.939	.998	20.295	.998	22.032	.998
Sub-Saharan Africa	17.922	.998	21.149	.998	22.782	.997	22.297	.997
Latin America	19.541	.998	20.669	.998	21.397	.998	20.729	.998
Religious diversity	1.386	.499	−1.141	.348	−2.614	.063	−.339	.799
Log per capita GDP	−.675	.422	−.426	.316	−.195	.643	−.947	.061
Polity	−.023	.767	−.065	.096	−.029	.465	−.031	.465
Religious support (abortion removed)	−.042	.593	.023	.568	.024	.565	.113	.043
% predicted correctly	93.8%		77.2%		77.8%		79.0%	
Adjusted r^2 (Nagelkerke)	.246		.438		.561		.594	

	In Cases of Incest		For Economic Reasons		For Social Reasons		On Request	
	B	Sig.	B	Sig.	B	Sig.	B	Sig.
Catholic	3.671	.002	4.801	.002	4.801	.002	3.466	.024
Orthodox Christian	−14.933	.999	3.364	.079	3.364	.079	1.691	.375
Other Christian	1.885	.012	1.053	.262	1.053	.262	1.935	.133
Islam	.926	.281	.293	.820	.293	.820	−.448	.765
Western democracies	19.460	.998	3.036	.024	3.036	.024	3.520	.008
Asia	22.291	.997	6.978	.000	6.978	.000	7.018	.000
Middle East	22.249	.997	7.067	.001	7.067	.001	6.937	.002
Sub-Saharan Africa	22.507	.997	8.886	.000	8.886	.000	8.993	.000
Latin America	21.205	.998	6.548	.000	6.548	.000	7.591	.000
Religious diversity	−.038	.978	1.009	.588	1.009	.588	.524	.763
Log per capita GDP	−.868	.085	−.713	.217	−.713	.217	−.720	.241
Polity	−.030	.489	.016	.756	.016	.756	.095	.107
Religious support (abortion removed)	.109	.050	.168	.030	.168	.030	.229	.010
% predicted correctly	80.2%		87.0%		87.0%		85.8%	
Adjusted r^2 (Nagelkerke)	.608		.716		.716		.698	

Interestingly, the variables for economic development, religious diversity, and regime have no influence in any of the eight tests. This means these variables, which influence other aspects of state religion policy, do not influence abortion policy.

Overall, the religious support and religious identity variables are significant in five of the regressions. This indicates a strong link between these two aspects of religion and state abortion policy.

Religion and Abortion
The results presented here clearly indicate that the issue of abortion is strongly associated with religion. In both bivariate and multivariate tests, both state support for religion and the majority's religious denomination group are correlated with abortion policy. Anecdotal evidence that the Catholic Church influences abortion policies in Catholic-majority countries also supports these results.

Muslim countries, which in bivariate tests show strong support for restrictions on abortion, do not seem to disproportionately restrict it when controlling for other factors. The likely explanation for this divergence between the bivariate and multivariate results is that state support for religion, which tends to be high among Muslim countries, is also strongly correlated with restrictions on abortion. Thus, the stands of Catholics on abortion are by themselves enough to influence abortion policy regardless of other aspects of state support for Catholicism, but in Muslim-majority states this only seems to hold when the state more strongly supports Islam.

World region is also associated with state abortion policy. Because the multivariate analysis controls for other factors, this indicates that this result is likely due to each region's unique history and culture. For example, the former Soviet bloc has countries with different levels of support and many different majority religions. Yet none of them other than Poland, which was pressured by the Catholic Church to change its policy in 1993, restrict abortion. The most likely explanation for this is the region's common historical experience during the Communist era.

No variables other than religious and cultural variables are correlated with this cross-country analysis of abortion policy. This includes economic development and regime, which influence other aspects of state religion policy. This provides strong support for the contention that the issue of abortion is strongly influenced by religion.

Anecdotally, it is a key political issue on which secular and religious forces clash, pitting religious views of the sanctity of life from the point of conception against secular views of women's rights. This is also one of the few policy areas where secular forces are gaining ground with fewer countries restricting abortion in 2008 than in 1990 (or the earliest year available). It, as part of the issue of family planning and women's issues, has been the subject of international political events such as the 1994 UN international conference of family planning and development in Cairo. It also is a regular issue at the UN's annual World Conference on Women.

Education, Abortion, and Proselytizing

This means that politically, abortion policy is "in play" worldwide. Secular and religious forces are organizing to pressure governments in international forums as well as in many domestic political arenas. It is also one of the most concrete pieces of evidence that secularism has remained vigorous enough between 1990 and 2008 to make significant inroads on religion on at least some issues. Yet because abortion remains restricted in the majority of the world's states, these inroads are clearly in the context of a contest with religious political actors, who remain powerful and influential. Given all of this, the patterns of change and consistency in abortion policy provide significant support for the competition perspective.

Restrictions on Proselytizing

Restrictions on proselytizing and missionaries were common throughout the study period, as shown in Tables 7.9 and 7.10. In 1990 (or the earliest year available), they were present in 92 states, increasing to 99 by 2008. These restrictions are common across religious traditions and world regions, although "other" Christian and sub-Saharan African states have relatively lower levels than states in other categories. Three states stopped restricting proselytizing during this period. South Korea required foreign missionaries to be registered and licensed until 1999. Until 2001, Lithuanian officials sometimes denied residency to foreign missionaries from "nontraditional" religions. Finally, until around 2000, government officials obstructed missionary activities by Jehovah's Witnesses in Guinea. Conversely, 10 states – Belize, Cambodia, Chad, Chile, Denmark, Ecuador, El Salvador, Eritrea, Norway, and Ukraine – instituted restrictions on proselytizing during this period.

It is important to note that these variables are coded differently from the three proselytizing variables in the religious discrimination index described in Chapter 6. The religious discrimination versions were coded only if policies led to substantial restrictions. Here, any regulation of missionaries and proselytizing was coded. For example, Barbados requires foreign missionaries to obtain special visas, but these visas are easily obtained, and there are no reports of them being denied. Similarly, some provinces in Canada require permits for door-to-door preaching or preaching in public areas, but there are no reports of permits being denied. Croatia, Cyprus, Liechtenstein, Moldova, Niger, Tajikistan, Turkish Cyprus, and Uruguay have similar types of regulation that do not result in substantial discrimination. Accordingly, these activities were coded for the purposes of the variables presented here but not the discrimination variables presented in Chapter 6.

Why Restrict or Regulate Proselytizing and Missionaries?

With the exception of states generally hostile to religion, limits on proselytizing and missionaries almost always apply to minority religions and not the majority religion. The motivation for states that are ideologically hostile to religion for restricting people who wish to spread their religion is self-evident. The

TABLE 7.9. Restrictions on Proselytizing Controlling for Majority Religion

Restrictions on Proselytizing	All States		Majority Religion (2008 results)						
			Christian						
	1990*	2008	Catholic	Orthodox	Other Christian	Christian Total	Muslim	Other Religions
Any restrictions on proselytizing or missionaries	52.0%	55.9%	50.0%	84.6%	22.0%	42.9%	85.1%	53.1%
Specific types of restrictions								
Proselytizing by all religions is illegal	3.4%	3.4%	0.0%	7.7%	0.0%	0.0%	2.1%	12.5%
Proselytizing to members of the majority religion is illegal but proselytizing to members of minority religions is legal	11.9%	11.3%	0.0%	0.0%	0.0%	0.0%	42.6%	0.0%
Proselytizing is legal but it is restricted in practice by the national government	9.0%	11.3%	6.8%	15.4%	4.9%	7.1%	17.0%	18.8%
Proselytizing is legal but it is restricted in practice by local or regional governments or officials	9.6%	14.1%	6.8%	46.2%	12.2%	14.3%	17.0%	12.5%
Proselytizing is legal but entry to the country or visas are often denied to foreigners who wish to proselytize	14.7%	16.9%	18.2%	23.1%	9.8%	15.3%	14.9%	25.0%
Foreign missionaries and religious workers require special visas or permits to proselytize	20.9%	26.0%	34.1%	53.8%	12.2%	27.6%	25.5%	21.9%
Proselytizing is limited to specific locations such as places of worship	2.3%	5.1%	0.0%	15.4%	0.0%	2.0%	4.3%	15.6%
Proselytizing is limited to legally recognized religions	6.2%	6.8	6.8%	15.4%	0.0%	5.1%	0.0%	21.9%

TABLE 7.10. *Restrictions on Proselytizing Controlling for World Region*

Restrictions on Proselytizing	World Region (2008)						
	Western Democracies	Former Soviet Bloc	Asia	Middle East	Sub-Saharan Africa	Latin America
Any restrictions on proselytizing or missionaries	48.1%	60.7%	65.5%	95.0%	28.3%	66.7%
Specific types of restrictions						
Proselytizing by all religions is illegal and not allowed in practice	3.7%	3.6%	13.8%	0.0%	0.0%	2.2%
Proselytizing to members of the majority religion is illegal, but proselytizing to members of minority religions is legal	0.0%	0.0%	17.2%	55.0%	8.7%	0.0%
Proselytizing is legal, but it is restricted in practice by the national government	11.1%	10.7%	13.8%	30.0%	4.3%	11.1%
Proselytizing is legal, but it is restricted in practice by local or regional governments or officials	18.5%	32.1%	13.8%	15.0%	6.5%	7.4%
Proselytizing is legal, but entry to the country or visas are often denied to foreigners who wish to proselytize	18.5%	28.6%	17.2%	20.0%	6.5%	18.5%
Foreign missionaries and religious workers require special visas or permits to proselytize	14.8%	39.3%	24.1%	10.0%	15.2%	55.6%
Proselytizing is limited to specific locations, such as places of worship	0.0%	10.7%	13.8%	0.0%	4.3%	0.0%
Proselytizing is limited to legally recognized religions	0.0%	7.1%	17.2%	0.0%	2.2%	14.8%

motivations in other states are more complicated but are generally related to majority–minority dynamics. They are also similar to the motivations for religious discrimination in general. Thus, the question here is why this type of discrimination in particular?

In Chapter 6, I discuss religious beliefs and protection of culture as motivations for religious discrimination. Both of these motivations are particularly relevant to the issues of proselytizing and missionaries. Religious beliefs usually include that one's religion has a monopoly on truth. Accordingly, missionaries who try to convert people away from their religion are seen as seeking to bring people away from this truth. Gill (2008) similarly posits that most religions prefer a monopoly situation. For these reasons, among others, religions generally seek to increase their numbers of believers and oppose anything that reduces them. In addition, these missionaries are seen as seeking out the weak, gullible, and ignorant, and, whether it is true or not, they are often portrayed as using coercive and deceptive tactics.

On a more political level, efforts to convert members of the majority religion to another religion alter a state's demographic balance. As demonstrated in Chapter 4, majority religions often receive benefits from the state that other religions do not. Thus, poaching members of the majority religion can, in the long term, have very real consequences beyond a diminishing of the number of believers, which, in itself, is a significant consequence. It can also result in a loss of material and ideological support from the government. Thus, it threatens not only a religion's ideological dominance but also its material and political well-being.

Majority religions are also often considered an essential element state culture. So even when religious ideology is not important to a government, maintaining the integrity of national culture may be a significant goal. Accordingly, converting citizens to nonindigenous religions can be seen as a threat to cultural integrity. As noted in Chapter 6, this can also result in anticult institutions and policies.

In all, the motivations for restricting proselytizing and missionaries are congruent with those for religious discrimination in general. Limits on missionaries and proselytizing are likely more common than any other type of restriction on minority religious practices and institutions precisely because these activities represent the manifestation of the worst fears of religious majorities. Taking members away from the majority religion is among the most direct, unambiguous, and visible challenges possible to religious beliefs, the demographic and political dominance of the majority religion, and national culture. Accordingly, it is not surprising that it is also a lightning rod for government regulation and restrictions.

Specific Types of Restrictions and Regulation

There is significant diversity in policies that regulate or restrict proselytizing and missionaries. To capture this diversity, I divide these restrictions and regulations into eight types of policy, which examine both formal and practical limitations and regulation. This distinction between laws and practice is important. Many states have no laws restricting missionaries and proselytizing but in practice arrest and harass proselytizers or otherwise limit their activities. Although most states with laws limiting these activities enforce these laws, there are exceptions. It is important to note that many states engage in more than one type of restriction.

Proselytizing by all religions is illegal. This is the most severe type of ban on proselytizing. Six countries had this type of ban during the study period. Interestingly, five of them are in Asia, and three of them have Buddhist majorities. In Bhutan, even though the government supports Buddhism, proselytizing, even by Buddhists, is restricted. Myanmar similarly prohibits all proselytizing including by the county's majority Buddhists, but this is enforced more strongly against minority religions. Laos bans all proselytizing by foreigners and in theory allows proselytizing by citizens with a permit, but these permits are never granted.[10] Nepal, a Hindu-majority country, states in its constitution that "no person shall be entitled to convert another person from one religion to another." This is strictly enforced.[11] Uzbekistan bans all efforts to convert people from one religion to another. Article 13 of Greece's constitution bans proselytizing.[12] However, this is selectively enforced. Most cases of enforcement in Greece are against Mormons and Jehovah's Witnesses.[13] Thus, other than Greece, the countries in this category are different from others that restrict proselytizing because they ban proselytizing even by members of the majority religion.

Proselytizing to members of the majority religion is illegal, but proselytizing to members of minority religions is legal. This type of policy is found only in Muslim-majority states. For example in Algeria, any proselytizing by non-Muslims is a criminal offense, but Muslims may seek converts. Similarly, in Morocco and the United Arab Emirates, non-Muslims may not proselytize to Muslims but can proselytize to non-Muslims. In 1990 (or the earliest year available), it was present in 21 of these states. The post-Saddam Hussein government in Iraq did not continue this policy.

Proselytizing is legal, but it is restricted in practice by the national government: Laws against proselytizing are not the only means to limit it. Authorities can simply arrest or harass anyone who proselytizes, even in the absence

---

[10] "Laos Detains Listener to Evangelical Radio Station for Preaching Gospel," Persecution.Org International Christian Concern, www.persecution.org/2006/07/05/laos-detains-listener-to-evangelical-radio-station-for-preaching-gospel.

[11] Subedi (1999); Nepal 1990 Constitution, www.servat.unibe.ch/icl/np00000_.html; Nepal 2007 Interim Constitution, www.worldstatesmen.org/Nepal_Interim_Constitution2007.pdf.

[12] Constitution of Greece, www.hellenicparliament.gr/en/Vouli-ton-Ellinon/To-Politevma/Syntagma.

[13] Anderson (2003); Caroline Moorhead, "Jehovah's Witnesses Jailed in Greece for Proselytism," *The Independent*, September 28, 1992.

of any law. At the beginning of the study period, 17 national governments placed practical restrictions on proselytizing, which increased to 21 by 2008. For example, in 2005, Venezuela's government banned proselytizing among indigenous tribes, resulting in the withdrawal of more than 100 missionaries. In Djibouti, proselytizing is not illegal, but the government discourages proselytizing by non-Muslims. However, foreign clergy and religious workers regularly perform charitable and humanitarian activities and also run schools. In Israel, proselytizing is legal, but a 1977 law prohibits offering or receiving material benefits as an incentive to convert to another religion. This law has not been enforced in recent years. The government has an agreement with Mormons in which they agree not to proselytize. In practice, proselytizers, usually Christians, are arrested when the police receive complaints, whether or not they are in violation of the 1977 law. Otherwise proselytizers are left alone.[14]

Proselytizing is legal but restricted in practice by local or regional governments or officials. This is identical to the previous category except local rather than national government officials limit proselytizing. This distinction is key because it signifies a more grassroots hostility to proselytizing. The national government may espouse religious freedom or be concerned about its international reputation but is unwilling or unable to enforce this in at least some localities. At the beginning of the study period, this local-based limitation existed in 17 countries, increasing to 26 by 2008. The nine countries that added this type of policy – Chile, Eretria, Kazakhstan, Kyrgyzstan, Nigeria, Norway, Switzerland, and Ukraine – come from all major religious groupings and four world regions and include both democracies and nondemocracies. For example, in 2007, police in Oslo, Norway, began arresting evangelists who attempted to share their faith in public and refused a police order to stop. The district court in Oslo found that they were effectively engaged in a demonstration, and the police were justified in asking them to move.[15] Similarly, in 2007, the mayor of N'djamena, Chad's capital, banned all "street-corner" evangelizing and preaching.

Proselytizing is legal, but entry to the country or visas are often denied to foreigners who wish to proselytize. This type of restriction is distinct from the previous types in that it applies only to foreigners rather than citizens of a country. Essentially, the government deports or bars entry to those who it does not want to proselytize. In 1990 (or the earliest year available), 26 countries engaged in this practice. By 2008, Cuba and Lithuania had discontinued it, but China, Costa Rica, Denmark, Eritrea, Kazakhstan, and Panama had instituted this type of policy, bringing the total to 30. For example, in Bangladesh, there is no law against proselytizing, but foreign missionaries require visas.

---

[14] Larry Derfner, "A Matter of Faith," *The Jerusalem Post*, April 29, 2005.
[15] "Pastor's Conviction for Preaching Challenged," *Worldline Daily Exclusive*, July 27, 2009, www.wnd.com/2009/07/105163.

Renewals of these visas are often denied to missionaries seen as trying to convert Muslims.

Foreign missionaries and religious workers require special visas or permits in order to proselytize. This type of regulation also applies distinctly to foreigners. The previous category measures whether governments deny visas or entry to foreign missionaries. This can occur whether or not missionaries require special visas. In contrast, this variable measures specifically whether there is a formal requirement for foreign missionaries to acquire a permit or visa that is unique to missionaries or religious workers to proselytize. At the beginning of the study period, 37 countries had this type of requirement. By 2008, South Korea had discontinued this practice, but 10 countries added it, bringing the total to 46. Although it is present in all categories of countries, it is most prominent in former Soviet and Orthodox states.

For example, a 1995 Belarusian law requires foreign missionaries to obtain a "spiritual activities" visa, which must be renewed yearly. People proselytizing without one of these visas are regularly expelled. These visas are often denied even to denominations with a long history in the country. A 2006 Costa Rican law requires missionaries to apply for residency permits in their country of origin and that foreign missionaries be part of a religious organization accredited by the Ministry of Foreign Affairs and Religion. These permits must be renewed annually. Denmark's 2004 immigration law, known popularly as the "Imam Law," requires that foreign religious workers obtain a religious residence visa. The law also requires that visa applicants be associated with a recognized religion, possess a proven relevant background for religious work, and be self-financing. It also limits the number of visas based on the membership of these communities and allows the government to deny a visa if there is "reason to believe the foreigner will be a threat to public safety, security, public order, health, decency, or other people's rights and duties," alluding to Imams who preach ideas contrary to Danish cultural norms.[16] Even in cases where these visas are rarely, if ever, denied, formal requirements that missionaries obtain a special visa indicate that the government in question considers the issue of foreign missionaries significant.

Proselytizing is limited to specific locations, such as places of worship. At the beginning of the study period, this type of restriction was present in four countries – Belarus, China, Sudan, and Vietnam. By 2008, it was also present in Cambodia, India, Kazakhstan, Nigeria, and Ukraine. For example, a 2007 Cambodian Royal decree bans door-to-door proselytizing and distributing Christian literature outside the vicinity of churches. In Belarus, this applies only to foreign missionaries. Since 2000, several of Nigeria's northern states banned proselytizing outside of designated areas. Vietnam prohibits proselytizing by foreign missionaries and unofficially but strictly discourages public

---

[16] Anthony Browne "Denmark to Curb Muslim Preachers," *The Times* (London), February 19, 2004.

proselytizing outside of recognized places of worship, even by Vietnamese citizens. China's policy is similar to Vietnam's, but the ban is more formal (Potter, 2003: 327).

Proselytizing is limited to legally recognized religions. This is an example of a significant consequence of government religion recognition and registration policies. This type of restriction was present in 11 countries in 1990 (or the earliest year available). This increased to 12 in 2006 when Ecuador began requiring religious groups to be licensed or registered to proselytize. Because China and Vietnam, as noted earlier, limit proselytizing to recognized places of worship, this effectively limits it to recognized religions.

Official Religion Policy and Restrictions on Proselytizing

The pattern of restrictions on proselytizing controlling for official religion policy, presented in Table 7.11, is complex. States that are hostile to religion restrict and regulate proselytizing the most. Because these states tend to be ideologically secular, their opposition to people who seek to get people to be more religious is unsurprising. Among states that are not hostile to religion, the more strongly a state supports religion, the more likely it is to restrict or regulate proselytizing. Interestingly, the gap between states that treat all religions equally and states that prefer multiple religions is not large. Thus, among nonhostile states, the key factor seems to be whether the state prefers a single religion over all others.

The Impact and Import of Regulating and Limiting Proselytizing

Although the impact of these eight types of restriction varies, they have a common denominator: an explicit government effort to limit proselytizing. In all but a few cases – mostly states hostile to religion in general – this applies exclusively to minority religions. That is, while the majority religion may seek converts, at least some minority religions are somehow hampered in their efforts to do the same. This is an extremely significant intervention in the religious demography of a state. As of 2008, it was present in a clear majority of 55.9% of states.

Proselytizing is a key element of the contest between secular and religious forces discussed in the competition perspective as well as of the competition between religions. Proselytizers seek new members both among members of other religions and among those who are secular. Thus, proselytizing has the potential to alter the demographic balance between religions as well as between the secular–religious divide. This demographic balance, as already noted, has significant political implications. It can, in its extreme, determine whether a state supports religion in general as well as which religion or religions it will support and restrict.

The number of missionaries in the world is not trivial. Although there is no systematic collection of their numbers, some available evidence is illustrative. Wuthnow and Offutt (2012) document that US Protestant missionary agencies

TABLE 7.11. *Restrictions on Proselytizing controlling for Official Support for Religion*

	Official Religion Policy (2008)				
Restrictions on Proselytizing	Official Religion	One Religion Preferred	Some Religions Preferred	Equal Treatment	Hostile
Any restrictions on proselytizing or missionaries.	87.8%	61.4%	36.4%	32.0%	88.9%
Specific types of restrictions					
Proselytizing by all religions is illegal and is not allowed in practice	4.9%	2.3%	0.0%	2.0%	33.3%
Proselytizing to members of the majority religion is illegal, but proselytizing to members of minority religions is legal	43.9%	4.5%	0.0%	0.0%	0.0%
Proselytizing is legal, but it is restricted in practice by the national government	12.2%	11.4%	12.1%	6.0%	44.4%
Proselytizing is legal, but it is restricted in practice by local or regional governments or officials	7.3%	18.2%	18.2%	12.0%	33.3%
Proselytizing is legal, but entry to the country or visas are often denied to foreigners who wish to proselytize.	22.0%	15.9%	18.2%	8.0%	44.4%
Foreign missionaries and religious workers require special visas or permits to proselytize	22.0%	40.9%	15.2%	20.0%	44.4%
Proselytizing is limited to specific locations such as places of worship	2.4%	6.8%	9.1%	0.0%	22.2%
Proselytizing is limited to legally recognized religions	2.4%	11.4%	0.0%	6.0%	33.3%

sent 47,787 missionaries abroad in 2001, and in any given year approximately 1.6 million US churchgoers participate in short-term missions. In 2010, the Mormon Church reported 52,225 full-time missionaries and 20,813 "Church-service" missionaries.[17]

These partial numbers apply to US-based Christians and Mormons. They do not cover missionaries from other countries or other religions such as Islam, which regularly proselytize. Many religions consider spreading the religion a basic obligation. Except perhaps in the most religiously homogeneous of states, this can be done part time and without foreign travel, person-to-person and over the Internet. It also does not take into account that many clergy who are primarily occupied with serving existing members of their religions will also seek converts when the opportunity presents itself. Furthermore, in almost all of the 177 countries in the RAS dataset, foreign missionaries were reported to be present, including some of the states such as Afghanistan where such activities are expressly forbidden. Given all of this, although the number of people who seek to spread their religion at least once a year is unknown, this number is a most likely at a minimum several million and possibly considerably higher than that.

This ubiquity of proselytizers combined with their potential impact explains why regulating them is so common. Religion is an active political issue in most states and proselytizing can have a significant impact on the religious status quo. In fact, by definition, proselytizers actively seek to change this status quo. When a government takes an interest in this status quo by supporting a religion, it is not surprising that it will be tempted to restrict or regulate those who seek to entice people to forsake that religion in favor of another. As shown in Table 7.11, this is exactly what most governments that support a single religion do.

Conclusions

The three issues of religious education in public schools, restrictions on abortions, and regulation of proselytizing are among the most common types of state religion policy in the world. Only seven states – Cape Verde, Montenegro, North Korea,[18] Slovenia, South Africa, Taiwan, and the United States – have none of these policies; only 27.1% of states have only one of them.

Why are these policies so uncommonly common? I posit that the education and proselytizing policies are pervasive because they are among the most important ways religion propagates itself. Of course there are other modes of propagation such as the family and the work of religious institutions among

---

[17] See www.mormonnewsroom.org/article/2010-statistical-report-for-2011-april-general-conference.
[18] North Korea essentially bans the practice of religion altogether, so there are no specific restrictions targeted specifically at proselytizing.

their own believers. However, these two modes of propagating religion have two qualities that make them different. First, they are a means to spread religion or reinforce it among people who might not otherwise be exposed to it through family and religious institutions. Public schools teach the majority of children in the world, including children whose families are not religious and are uninvolved in religious institutions. Proselytizing, by definition, spreads a religion to people who are not members. Thus, these are two methods that can spread a religion's influence beyond its existing flock.

Second, these are issues that are within government spheres of power. Public education is a government funded and run program. The content of the curriculum is naturally part of a government's purview. Governments to a lesser extent also regulate religious education outside of public schools; 19.8% of governments regulate the content of religious education for the majority religion outside of public schools in some manner (Table 5.4), and 18.6% of governments restrict religious education by minority religions in some manner (Table 6.4). In contrast, banning families from teaching their religion to their children is so rare that the RAS dataset does not include this type of policy. Thus, as private and family-based religious education is farther outside the core of government power and decision making, regulation decreases.

Not all aspects of proselytizing are as firmly within the core of a government's sphere of influence as public education, but limiting foreign missionaries is well within this wheelhouse. A basic government power is control over who can enter its territory. Fifty-nine countries, one-third of all countries and 59.6% of all countries that restrict proselytizing, either require foreign missionaries to have special visas or otherwise restrict foreign missionaries. Thus, restrictions on foreign missionaries are a large portion of restrictions on proselytizing. However, 75 states – 75.8% of states that limit proselytizing – engage in other types of limits on proselytizing. Thus, many states are also willing to limit proselytizing by citizens and legal residents. This is a level similar to the willingness of states to restrict religious institutions in general (see Table 5.2), so this is consistent with general government policy on religion.

Abortion is a contentious issue for different reasons. Many factors influence views on abortion, but a strong element of these involve the clash between the core religious belief in the sanctity of life from the moment of conception and the core secular belief in women's rights. This places the issue of abortion at the forefront of the clash between political secularism and religious political actors described in the secular-religious competition perspective.

As noted in detail in Chapter 4, there are other aspects of women's rights that are also politically important, but none are restricted as often as abortion. This is likely because other types of religious-based restrictions on women are based on religious beliefs regarding gender roles. While these are important, I argue that within Abrahamic religious doctrines they are not as important as the sanctity of life. "Though shalt not kill" is among the Ten Commandments respected by Christianity and Judaism and acknowledged by Islam in that they are considered part of a genuine divine revelation. The Koran also explicitly bans murder. The Ten Commandments do not include "women shall obey their husbands" or any other mention of gender roles with the possible exception of the ban on coveting one's neighbor's wife, although these gender roles can be found elsewhere in the Bible. If restrictions on abortion were motivated primarily by gender role issues, they would likely be less common.

The equality of women is a central element of the modern secular value system, and the right to choose is considered central to this. Thus, the clash on this issue involves secular and religious core values. The prevalence of restrictions on abortions demonstrates the power of religion on this issue. But the fact that between 1990 and 2008, the amount of restrictions has dropped shows that secularism continues to have a significant influence worldwide.

Given all of this, religious education in public schools, restrictions on abortions and the regulation of proselytizing are illustrative of the larger picture. They demonstrate that the tensions between secularism and religion influence state policy. They also demonstrate the pervasiveness of state intervention in religious issues, and especially state support for religion. That all but seven states have at least one of these policies both supports this argument and demonstrates that these three issues are central to religion and politics as well as the ongoing struggle between secularism and religion for ideological dominance.

8

Religion in Constitutions

In theory, laws and especially constitutions determine a state's policy.[1] This is to a great extent true, at least for declared policy. However, governments do not always follow their own rules, even if those rules are set out in constitutions. A specific clause in a constitution can often be ignored without violating the general constitutional framework. US constitutional doctrine, for example, allows considerable room for interpretation. The US Supreme Court ruled in *Griswold v. Connecticut* (1965) that the US Constitution protects the right to privacy, even though no such right was explicitly written into the constitution. Eight years later in *Row v. Wade* (1973), the court extended the right of privacy to include abortions, another issue not contained in the written word of the Constitution. Thus, the written word is not always a perfect guide even in states that respect their laws and constitutions. Many states are less respectful of their own rules and laws than is the United States.

In this chapter, I examine the correlation between religion policies declared in constitutions and state policy in practice. The results in previous chapters demonstrate that official religion policy has an influence on actual religion policy but it is not fully determinative. As demonstrated in Chapter 4, declaring an official religion, for example, makes a state more likely to support religion but many states without official religions support religion more strongly than many states with official religions.

I examine two types of policy in this chapter. The first is declaration or establishment of an official religion (EOR) or separation of religion and state (SRAS). The second is whether the constitution protects religious freedom.

---

[1] Earlier versions of the analyses presented here are available in Fox and Flores (2009; 2012) and Fox (2011a; 2011b).

Overall, I find that while there is link between constitutional principles and actual policy, this link is far weaker than many would assume.

The Link between Constitutions and Policy: Theory and Practice

Evidence already presented in this book suggests that constitutional declarations do not always determine actual policy. In Chapter 4 (Table 4.10), I examined the link between official state policy – usually as declared in the state's constitution – and support for religion. I find a wide variation among states with official religions ranging from two types of support to 42. While, on average, states with official religions more strongly support religion, many states with no official religion – including even some states that are coded as hostile to religion – provide higher levels of support for religion than do some states with official religions.

Similarly, as I discuss later, nearly 90% of the world's constitutions have religious freedom clauses. Yet, as I demonstrated in Chapter 6, 82.5% of all states restrict the religious practices or institutions of minority religions in a manner they do not restrict the majority religion. Hence, it is clear that religious freedom clauses do not necessarily mean that minorities will be free from religious discrimination. Gill (2008: 12), in a comparative analysis, comes to the same conclusion, arguing that "the Devil is in the details," but does not systematically examine the correlation between constitutional protections and religious liberty.

Despite this, many studies of religion take constitutional clauses as proof of a state's policy. For instance, Beatty (2001), in a study of religious freedom, states that

> [i]n the last half of the twentieth century the rule of law established itself as one of the defining ideas in the political organization of modern democratic states. During this period, people all over the world came to insist that their governments had to respect a set of basic human rights of everyone who was affected by their rule.... In this era, as in no other, country after country entrenched bills of rights into their constitutions at the moment of their liberation from arbitrary and despotic regimes.... This proliferation of constitutional bills of rights has had a profound effect on the institutional structures of government.[2]

Beyond this assumption that constitutional clauses, or other declarations of state policy on religion, translate to actual religious freedom, there is little systematic cross-country comparison in the literature between religion policy as declared in constitutions and religion policy in practice. Examinations of

---

[2] Much of the general literature on constitutions also argues that the enumeration of rights sets a standard by which governments can be judged. This enumeration also reflects and shapes the norms and aspirations of a society to protect these rights. See Keith (2002) for a good review of this literature.

religious freedom include broad analyses of constitutional guarantees,[3] analyses of a single state's enforcement of constitutional guarantees,[4] and detailed critiques of the interpretational approaches of individual nations.[5] However, most cross-national studies focus either on constitutional provisions or state practice with regard to religion.

For example, Hendon and McDaniel (2006) summarize major developments throughout the world in church–state affairs, but do not systematically compare these trends to constitutional guarantees. Boyle and Sheen (1997) provide similar summaries but rarely deal with the link between constitutional clauses and religious freedom on the ground. Barret et al. (2001) collected information on whether states have official religions and on the treatment of Christians in more than 200 countries but did not even ask whether these two factors are correlated. Other examinations of religious freedom by Grim and Finke (2011), Freedom House,[6] and the CIRI dataset[7] similarly provide detailed information on religious freedom across the world but do not evaluate how freedoms as declared in official policy translates to actual practice.[8]

Witte (2001) is one of the few that touches on this issue, finding that the last two decades have seen "the best of human rights protections inscribed on the books, but some of the worst of human rights violations inflicted on the ground" (Witte, 2001: 708). Unfortunately, Witte (2001) does not devote significant discussion to the extent and causes of this disparity, focusing instead on ways to involve religious communities in the quest for better enforcement of human rights.

On the specific issues of religious freedom, there is a strong normative element in the literature mandating that states should not engage in religious discrimination. This expectation is tempered by the assumption that this value will be more likely realized in democratic states (Durham, 1996; Fox, 2007). Some go as far as to argue that human rights are only possible in modern secular states (Beit-Hallahmi, 2003: 32; Spickard, 1999; Voye, 1999: 277–278) and that democratization is more likely to occur in states that have strong differentiation between political and religious authority (Philpott, 2007: 510–513).

Why Would States Fail to Follow Their Constitutions?

This failure of the literature to systematically examine whether constitutional principles regarding religion are followed in practice is likely due to a general

---

[3] See, for example, Boyle and Sheen (1997), Ellis (2006), Garlicki (2001), and Olowu (2006).
[4] See, for example, O'Brien (1996) and Motilla (2004).
[5] See, for example, Du Plessis (1996), Poulter (1997), and Witte and Green (1996). For a review of the general human rights literature, see Hafner-Burton and Ron (2009).
[6] See www.freedomhouse.org/issues/religious-freedom.
[7] See http://ciri.binghamton.edu/index.asp.
[8] See also North and Gwin (2004).

acceptance that, at least in theory, constitutions set the guidelines for government behavior. While there is an understanding that not all states follow their constitutions, especially nondemocracies, the standard assumption is that following a constitution is the norm. More important, I empirically demonstrate in this chapter that following constitutional declarations is not the norm for significant categories of states. Yet there is some discussion of why in some instances states do not follow their constitutions. I identify five explanations for this phenomenon.

First, a state must have both the ability and political will to translate constitutional precepts into policy. One or both of these are often lacking, especially in authoritarian states, which often have liberally written constitutions that are rarely followed in practice (Davenport, 1996: 629; Keith, 2002: 113–114). This lack of political will or ability can also be present in democratic states. To function, democracies require protections for minority political parties, a politically neutral and professional civil service, an independent media, a strong independent judiciary, and both a willingness and mechanism to fight corruption (Bugaric, 2008; Fombad, 2007). An absence of any of these institutions can undermine the rule of law, including constitutional law.

Second, constitutional policies often require implementing legislation or the creation of other institutions before a government can apply the policies in practice. These institutions and legislation are not always forthcoming (Goodliffe & Hawkins, 2006: 363–364). For example, in a study of judicial reform in Argentina, Finkel (2004: 58–59) notes that "although the promulgation of constitutional changes may declare profound institutional changes and elegant new principles, these remain in limbo until the passage of the implementing legislation." Van Cott (2000: 208; 2003: 65) discusses similar issues in implementing constitutional protections for indigenous peoples in Bolivia, Columbia, and Venezuela.

Third, anecdotal evidence from previous chapters demonstrates that many local governments enact laws and institute policies on religion that are at odds with national policy. For example, Article 10 of Nigeria's 1999 constitution states that "the government of the federation or of a state shall not adopt any religion as state religion."[9] While the national government generally follows this precept, many local governments do not. Despite opposition by the national government, many of Nigeria's northern Muslim-majority states began adopting aspects of Sharia law as state law in 2000.

Fourth, the interpretation and enforcement by courts of constitutional provisions heavily influences their implementation. A central task of courts is to balance different constitutional clauses, principles and interests when they contradict each other (Beatty, 2001; McConnell, 1992). This means that religion clauses can be considered of secondary importance to other constitutional clauses or principles. A common principle that can trump constitutional clauses

---

[9] 1999 Constitution of Nigeria, www.religlaw.com.

is national security (Davenport, 1996: 629). In some instances, national security concerns lead to a policy of "constitutional avoidance" in which the courts explicitly allow states to ignore or nullify basic civil rights such as religious freedom (Morrison, 2006). All of this assumes courts are willing and able to enforce constitutional principles. Many authoritarian states limit or eliminate judicial review of their actions (Solomon, 2007).

Even in Western democratic states, restrictions that otherwise might not be allowed can be placed on minorities when they are considered a security threat. The level of perceived threat can lift it above ordinary politics and justify extraordinary strategies outside the boundaries of what would normally be acceptable to eliminate the threat (Buzan et al., 1998; Laustsen & Waever, 2000). Many argue that this has been particularly true of Muslims in the West since 9/11[10] (Cesari, 2004).

Fifth, the ability of courts to interpret constitutions is especially significant because, as I discuss in more detail later, constitutional religious freedom clauses often include qualifications and exceptions. For example, the 1966 International Covenant on Civil and Political Rights is often used as a model for constitutional religious freedom clauses and includes the following qualifying language: "Freedom to manifest one's religion or belief may be subject only to such limitations as are prescribed by law and are necessary to protect public safety, order, health or morals or the fundamental rights and freedoms of others."[11] Many constitutions contain more extensive qualifications. This allows courts considerable leeway to limit religious freedoms because nearly any limitation on religious freedom could, at least in theory, be justified by one of these qualifications. Even a court that generally seeks to uphold religious freedom would likely allow some limitations and a court seeking a pretext to allow the government to limit religious freedom would have no difficulty doing so.

All of this raises the question of why states would incorporate religious freedom clauses into their constitutions if they lack the political will or ability to enforce them, or perhaps never intended to follow them in the first place. A number of interrelated trends can help to explain this phenomenon. First, there is considerable international pressure to conform to human rights norms, including religious freedom. The norm of SRAS is also strong among some important international actors. It is likely that the ability to point to the existence of a religious freedom clause in international forums is the reason that many countries incorporate these norms into their constitutions.

Second, these clauses can help to restore or preserve political credibility at home (Fombad, 2007; Ginsburg et al., 2008; Goodliffe & Hawkins, 2006) in a

---

[10] The *Journal of Ethnic and Migration Studies* (2009) devoted an entire issue to this topic; see volume 35(3).
[11] For a general discussion of the incorporation of international law into national constitutions, see Ginsburg et al. (2008).

manner similar to the use of elections by authoritarian regimes (Schedler, 2002: 103). That is, going through the motions even if these motions have no real impact on policy can have political value. Third, some new and unstable democratic governments may create human rights regimes to "lock in" democratic principles that they fear may not be fully observed (Goodliffe & Dawkins, 2006: 362–263). Fourth, constitutions are often written at a time of crisis and under time constraints. This makes it simpler to take an existing model from international law or an existing constitution than to engage in lengthy philosophical and political debates. Finally, a government may genuinely value a principle such as religious freedom or SRAS but feel that "exceptional circumstances" justify deviating from that principle.

Be all of this as it may, the literature tends to consider these circumstances where a state will deviate from constitutional principles exceptions rather than the rule, at least for democracies. The expectation remains that states will follow their constitutional policies with regard to religion.

Constitutions

Before proceeding with the analysis, it is important to discuss the constitutions included in this study. I analyze the constitutions of 172 countries in 2008, the most recent year available in the Round 2 of the Religion and State project (RAS2) dataset. This is because 5 of the 177 countries in RAS2 had no active constitutions in 2008.[12]

Constitutions were primarily taken from the Religion and Law International Document Database,[13] the International Constitutional Law project,[14] the Political Database of the Americas,[15] and the University of Richmond Constitution Finder.[16] In most cases, these sites provided academic or official government translations of constitutions not written in English. Otherwise, I translated the constitutions using Google Translate. To test Google Translate's accuracy, I compared academic and government translations to Google Translate's translation. The translations were never identical, but the differences did not influence the variables' codings. These databases generally include only recent constitutions. Compilations of earlier constitutions exist[17] but are only current through the mid-1990s and are missing some constitutions. Thus, it is not possible to provide comprehensive codings from before 2000 without

---

[12] These countries are Bhutan, Somalia, Timor, the United Kingdom, and the Western Sahara. This poses no selection bias issue because this analysis examines the link between policy and constitutions. States with no constitution in force are outside of the universe of analysis.
[13] See www.religlaw.org.
[14] See www.servat.unibe.ch/law/icl.
[15] See http://pdba.georgetown.edu/Constitutions/constudies.html.
[16] See http://confinder.richmond.edu.
[17] See Keith (2002) for a listing of these compilations.

missing data, which would raise issues of selection bias. Because of the relatively short time period, I do not analyze changes over time in constitutions.

Declarations of EOR and SRAS

As I discussed in more detail in Chapter 2, there is an extensive literature on the concept of SRAS. This literature, while not agreeing on what should be the ideal form of SRAS, does agree that this is the preferred state religion policy. In fact, many consider it a necessary element of liberal democracy and a foundational element of Western liberal democracies. In this section, I analyze which states enshrine this value in their constitutions and whether they practice what they preach. In brief, the results show that SRAS is present only in a minority of states across the world, including a minority of states that declare SRAS in their constitutions. This result holds true even for those states that the normative SRAS literature most expects to have SRAS.

Categorizing SRAS and EOR Clauses

There are three options with regard to official religion policy in constitutions. The constitution can declare EOR, SRAS, or simply not address the issue. The only exception is Bulgaria, which declares both SRAS and EOR in its constitution. Article 13 of Bulgaria's constitutions declares both that "religious institutions shall be separate from the State" and that "Eastern Orthodox Christianity shall be considered the traditional religion in the Republic of Bulgaria." Article 13 also states that "religious institutions and communities, and religious beliefs shall not be used to political ends."[18] Although the weight of these clauses likely leans toward SRAS, given the ambiguity of the situation, I assign Bulgaria to the category of states with constitutions that do not address the issue of official religion policy.

The wording used to declare EOR and SRAS differs across constitutions. Because different wording may imply differences in intent, I account for this in my analysis. Keeping in mind that many constitutions include more than one type of declaration, the most common form of EOR is a declaration that there is a state religion, official religion, or established religion (30 constitutions). For instance, Norway's constitution declares that "the Evangelical-Lutheran religion shall remain the official religion of the State."[19] Malaysia's constitution declares that "Islam is the religion of the Federation."[20] Other wordings are less common. Afghanistan, Bahrain, Iran, Mauritania, Morocco, and Oman declare themselves Islamic states but also include the first type of EOR clause.

---

[18] 1991 Constitution of Bulgaria as amended through 2007, http://www.parliament.bg/en/const.
[19] 1814 Constitution of Norway as amended through 2007, www.stortinget.no/en/In-English/About-the-Storting/The-Constitution/The-Constitution.
[20] 1957 Constitution of Malaysia as amended through 2007, http://cpps.org.my/resource_centre/Perlembagaan_Persekutuan.pdf.

For example, Bahrain's constitution declares it "a fully sovereign, independent *Islamic* Arab State" as well as declaring that "the religion of the State is Islam."[21] Zambia's constitution similarly declares it a "Christian Nation" but has no other type of EOR clause.[22] Argentina and Bolivia constitute their own category. Argentina's constitution states that "the Federal Government supports the Roman Catholic Apostolic religion."[23] Bolivia's 1967 constitution as amended through 2004 (which was amended to declare SRAS in 2009) states that "the State recognizes and upholds the Catholic religion, and Apostolic Roman."[24]

In this analysis, I divide states with EOR clauses into three categories: (1) states with only the first type of EOR clause, (2) states with any other type of EOR clause only, and (3) states with both the first type and another type. The distributions are presented in Table 8.1. Overall, 33 states have EOR clauses in their constitutions.

The different types of SRAS clauses have theoretical import because they are linked to the different philosophies of SRAS discussed in Chapter 2. Specifically, those that declare the state "secular" or "lay" can be linked directly to the laicism doctrine. France and Turkey are among the 41 states with this type of wording, which is important because they are also considered the archetypal laicist states.

The other formulations of SRAS cannot be linked to any particular SRAS doctrine. The most common, found in 33 constitutions, is a declaration that the state and religious organizations are independent, autonomous, or separate from each other. For instance, Italy's constitution states that "the State and the Catholic Church are independent and sovereign, each within its own sphere."[25] Similarly South Korea's constitution declares that "no state religion may be recognized, and church and state are to be separated."[26] Sixteen states ban the government from establishing, instituting, adopting, or recognizing a religion. Examples of this phrasing include the US "establishment clause," which states "Congress shall make no law respecting an establishment of religion" and the declaration that "Uganda shall not adopt a State religion."[27] Ten states simply declare that there is no state religion. For example, Spain's constitution states that "no religion shall have a state character."[28] Similarly Nicaragua's

---

[21] 2002 Constitution of Bahrain, http://www.servat.unibe.ch/icl.
[22] 1996 Constitution of Zambia, www.religlaw.org.
[23] 1853 Constitution of Argentina as amended through 1994, http://www.servat.unibe.ch/icl.
[24] See www.religlaw.org.
[25] 1948 Constitution of Italy as amended through 2007, www.senato.it/documenti/repository/istituzione/costituzione_inglese.pdf.
[26] 1948 Constitution of South Korea as amended through 1987, http://www.servat.unibe.ch/icl.
[27] 1995 Constitution of Uganda as amended through 2005, www.wipo.int/wipolex/en/text.jsp?file_id=170004.
[28] 1978 Constitution of Spain as amended through 1992, www.senado.es/constitu_i/index.html.

TABLE 8.1. *Constitutional SRAS and EOR Clauses Controlling for Religious Support and Official Religion Policy in 2008*

| | n | % All Cases | Mean Religious Support | Official Religion Policy |||||
				Official Religion	One Religion Preferred	Some Religions Preferred	Equal Treatment	Hostile
Official SRAS								
The state shall be secular (lay, etc.) only	75	43.6%	6.03	0.0%	28.0%	21.3%	44.0%	6.7%
	21	12.2%	5.45	0.0%	19.0%	14.3%	66.7%	0.0%
Other wording only	44	25.6%	6.41	0.0%	36.4%	29.5%	27.3%	6.8%
Both types of wording	10	5.8%	6.30	0.0%	10.0%	0.0%	70.0%	20.0%
Official EOR	33	19.2%	17.64	100.0%	0.0%	0.0%	0.0%	0.0%
A religion is declared the state religion, official religion, or established religion	23	13.4%	17.61	100.0%	0.0%	0.0%	0.0%	0.0%
Other wording only	3	1.7%	6.33	100.0%	0.0%	0.0%	0.0%	0.0%
Both types of wording	7	4.1%	22.57	100.0%	0.0%	0.0%	0.0%	0.0%
The constitution does not address the issue of an official religion or includes both types of clause*	64	37.2%	7.52	6.3%	35.9%	26.6%	25.0%	6.3%

* Only Bulgaria's constitution includes both SRAS and EOR clauses.

constitution declares that "the State has no official religion."[29] Japan and Mongolia ban the state from engaging in "religious activity."

In this analysis, I divide states with SRAS clauses into three categories: (1) states that declare themselves secular and have no other relevant clauses, (2) states with any other type of SRAS clause but no "secular" declaration, and (3) states with both secular and other types of clauses. The distributions are presented in Table 8.1. Overall, 43.6% (75) of states declare SRAS in their constitutions, which is more than double the 19.2% (33) that declare an official religion. This leaves 37.2% (64) of states that do not unambiguously address the issue in their constitutions.

EOR, SRAS, Official Religion Policy, and Religious Support

The results in Table 8.1 demonstrate that while constitutional declarations and official religion policy are related, the connection between them is not absolute. Of course all states that have EOR clauses in their constitutions are coded as having official religions and no SRAS. However, 21 of the 75 countries that declare SRAS in practice support one religion more than others. This includes five that declare themselves secular – Guinea, India, Ivory Coast, Russia, and Turkish Cyprus. An additional 16 support multiple religions more than others. This includes Kazakhstan, Madagascar, and Togo, all of which declare themselves secular.

Just under half (49.3%) of states with SRAS clauses in their constitutions support one or several religions more than others which is a significant divergence from one of the concept's most basic tenets – not giving some religions preference over others. This trend is weaker among states that declare themselves secular but is still present among 25.8% of such states and 59.3% of states with other types of clauses. If we do not count states with both SRAS and "other" SRAS clauses, this increases to 65.8%. This is not much less than the 68.8% of states with constitutions that do not address the issue but support one or several religions more than others. This means that unless constitution declares a state "secular," SRAS clauses do not appear to have a great impact on official government religion policy.

Like official religion policy, religious support (described more fully in Chapter 4) is related to constitutional declarations but they are not fully determinative. This is especially apparent with regard to declarations of SRAS. Although states with this type of declaration in their constitution have the lowest mean level of religious support, the average state in this category supports religion in just over 6 of the 51 types of support measured by the RAS2 dataset.[30] While there is some variation based on the phrasing of SRAS clauses with "secular" clauses resulting in the lowest levels of religious support, these differences are not statistically significant.

---

[29] 1987 Constitution of Nicaragua as amended through 2007, http://confinder.richmond.edu.
[30] The difference between this mean and all others has a significance of .000.

As expected, states with EOR clauses in their constitutions have the highest levels of religious support.[31] However, the three states that have alternative wording to the standard type of declaration without also having the standard EOR declaration have levels of religious support similar to states with SRAS clauses in their constitutions. The phrasing of Argentina, Bolivia, and Zambia's constitutional clauses are all noted earlier, and they have religious support scores of 7, 7, and 5, respectively. This indicates that while these wordings do declare an official religion, it is likely that states that intend to strongly support a religion tend to call it the "official," "established," or "state" religion. An even stronger indicator of state support is a declaration like these combined with additional wording. However, three states is too few to make any final assessment in this regard.

The results for states whose constitutions do not address the issue are particularly interesting. On average, they have only one and a half more types of religious support than do states with SRAS clauses. While these states do not explicitly declare support for a religion, nothing in their constitutions prevents them from doing so. Put differently, we would expect a state with a constitutional clause declaring SRAS would support religion at a level significantly lower than the "default" state with no language one way or the other. In reality, the difference between the two categories is small and not statistically significant. In contrast, states with EOR clauses have significantly[32] higher levels of support for religion.

All of this indicates that while EOR clauses have a real and significant impact on state religion policy, the impact of SRAS clauses is much lower than we would expect. As discussed in more detail in Chapter 3, political thinkers expect such states to treat all religions equally and, in many cases, avoid supporting religion altogether. This is clearly not the case for most states with SRAS clauses, even those whose SRAS clauses declare a state secular.

Quantifying SRAS

While the foregoing finding is illuminating, to fully confirm its validity, it is necessary to quantitatively define what standards a state must meet to be considered to have SRAS and then evaluate how many states meet this standard. In Chapter 2, I discussed four theoretical standards for SRAS. As presented in Table 8.2, three of them can be quantified using the RAS data. That is, the official religion policy, support, regulation, and discrimination variables can be used to define which states meet these SRAS standards. States that are within the correct categories of the official religion policy variable and do not exceed maximum levels of the other three variables can be considered to have SRAS based on these doctrines.

---

[31] The difference between this mean and all others has a significance of .000.
[32] The difference between mean levels of religion support in states with no constitutional declaration and those with EOR clauses is .000.

TABLE 8.2. *Quantifying Standards of SRAS*

SRAS Doctrine	Official Religion Policy	Support	Regulation	Discrimination
Secularism-Laicism 1	Accommodation and all hostile codings	Up to 3	No limit	Up to 1
Secularism-Laicism 2	Accommodation and all hostile codings	Up to 4	No limit	Up to 3
Secularism-Laicism 3	Accommodation and all hostile codings	Up to 5	No limit	Up to 5
Absolute SRAS 1	Accommodation only	Up to 3	Up to 1	Up to 1
Absolute SRAS 2	Accommodation and separationist	Up to 4	Up to 3	Up to 3
Absolute SRAS 3	Accommodation and separationist	Up to 5	Up to 5	Up to 5
Neutral Political Concern 1	Supportive, accommodation, and separationist	Up to 3	No limit	None
Neutral Political Concern 2	Supportive, accommodation, separationist, and nonspecific hostility	Up to 4	No limit	Up to 1
Neutral Political Concern 3	Supportive, accommodation, separationist, and nonspecific hostility	Up to 5	No limit	Up to 2

The *secularism-laicism* concept bans state support for any religion and restricts the presence of religion in the public sphere. This means that any category of the official religion policy variable involving support for religion would not meet this standard. However, because this philosophy does not preclude hostility to religion, the accommodation and all of the hostile codings for this variable meet this standard.

In theory, any support for religion would violate this standard. However, as discussed in detail in Chapter 4, in 2008, only South Africa did not support religion based on the 51 types of support measured by the RAS2 project. On this basis, it is arguable that, using an absolutist interpretation, almost no states meet the secularism-laicism standard, or for that matter any standard. Accordingly, I allow low levels of religious support on the theory that a state can have small amounts of support for religion without undermining an overall regime of separation. From this point of view, these low levels are considered exceptions to the more general rule. I apply this principle to religious support, regulation, and discrimination for all three conceptions of SRAS discussed here.

Applying the specific maximum levels of religious support, as well as religious regulation and discrimination, for these variables, involves a fair amount of arbitrariness and ambiguity. Unfortunately, this is unavoidable in applying these cutoffs. To mitigate this, I apply three versions of the secularism-laicism standard as well as the other two standards I quantify. One is intentionally strict, one is as lenient as I believe is possible within the context of this perspective on SRAS, and one is midlevel between the other two.

Returning to the criteria for the secularism-laicism standard, this philosophy does not limit the regulation of religion, so there is no cutoff for this variable. However, there are cutoffs for religious discrimination. This is because the standard represents the philosophy that all religion is inappropriate in the public sphere. To limit some religions but not others both allows some religions to be present in the public sphere and, by not treating all religions equally, essentially expresses an official preference for some religions over others.

The *absolute SRAS* conception allows no government support for religion and no government restrictions on religion. The only coding of the official religion policy variable that fully meets this standard is the accommodation coding because all other codings involve either support for religion or hostility to religion. However, it is arguable that the separationist standard also meets this definition of SRAS because although it implies a hostile attitude, it also mandates strict SRAS. Accordingly, the first quantification of absolute SRAS allows only accommodation, and the others also allow separationism. Religious support, regulation, and discrimination are all limited by this conception because they involve support or restrictions on religion, which this conception specifically prohibits.

Finally, the *neutral political concern* conception requires that the government treat all groups equally. Thus, religion can be supported or limited as long as it is applied equally to all religions. On the official religion variable this allows the supportive coding because it involves supporting all religions equally, the accommodation coding because it involves no support or restrictions on any religion, and the separationist coding because it does not require unequal treatment. In theory, the more hostile codings can also involve equal hostility to all religions, but in practice these levels of hostility tend to come only when a state is aggressively restricting religion and promoting a secular ideology over religion, which violates the spirit of neutrality. However, the extent to which this is part of the definition is unclear. Accordingly, in one quantification, I do not include any coding more hostile than separationist, and in the others, I also include nonspecific hostility. Supporting one religion over others and limiting some religions but not others clearly violates this conception, so there are cutoffs for religious support and discrimination. However, regulating all religions equally does not violate this conception of SRAS.

The fourth conception of SRAS, discussed in Chapter 2, *exclusion of ideals*, is similar to the neutral political concern conception in that it also requires equality, but it requires the intent for equality rather than equality as a result of government policy. Because the RAS2 dataset does not measure government intent and this conception is otherwise similar to neutral political concern, I do not quantify this conception.

Again, all of these quantifications involve a certain level of ambiguity and arbitrariness in their application and are not the only possible quantifications. However, I argue that they meet three key criteria that make them useful in this analysis. First, they represent a good faith attempt to turn a set of philosophies into a quantifiable set of criteria. Second, the range of lenient to strict definitions allows for testing a broad range of measurable conceptions of SRAS. If, as proves to be the case in the analysis that follows, the results for the different conceptions are not dissimilar, this range of quantifications can allow us to draw conclusions regarding the true presence of SRAS in the world. This is especially the case because the most lenient definitions arguably allow a level of government involvement in religion that is as high or higher than a reasonable advocate of these conceptions would likely allow in practice. Finally, although it would be possible to create more quantifications, the nine presented here are a workable number while still allowing a sufficient level of variety.

Constitutional Clauses and SRAS

The relationship between constitutional clauses and the presence of SRAS is presented in Table 8.3. Overall, no matter which of the nine models for SRAS is examined, states with SRAS are in the minority. This holds true even when examining constitutional clauses and regime type. Perhaps the most striking result is that even among states whose constitutions declare SRAS, only a minority meet any of the standards of SRAS. Depending on the standard and the wording of the constitution, between 0.0% and 42.9% of states with constitutions that declare SRAS meet that standard. The 42.9% result represents states with constitutions that declare the state "secular" and meet the secularism-laicism 3 standard. That is, a majority of states with the strongest constitutional SRAS wording do not in practice meet that standard. This incongruence between constitutional declarations and actual policies is exacerbated by the fact that a number of countries with no relevant clauses in their constitutions nevertheless do meet many of these SRAS standards.

Western democracies, democracies in general, and even democracies with a SRAS clause in their constitution do not have high levels of SRAS. In fact, democracies with SRAS clauses are less likely to have SRAS than non-democracies with SRAS clauses. This is theoretically significant due to assumptions that SRAS is a basic element of liberal democratic thinking. That is, if SRAS should be present anywhere, it should be in democracies with constitutions that declare SRAS. That this is not the case runs against mainstream liberal democratic theory.

Only five states – Benin, Burkina Faso, Namibia, South Africa, and Taiwan – meet the strictest version of all three philosophical standards of SRAS. They collectively do not fit the stereotype of Western, economically developed

TABLE 8.3. *Proportion of Countries That Meet SRAS Standards in 2008 Controlling for Constitutional Clauses and Regime*

Control Factor	Near-Absolute 1	Near-Absolute 2	Near-Absolute 3	Neutral Pol. Concern 1	Neutral Pol. Concern 2	Neutral Pol. Concern 3	Secularism-Laicism 1	Secularism-Laicism 2	Secularism-Laicism 3
Constitutional Clauses									
Official SRAS	8.0%	14.7%	21.3%	9.3%	20.0%	26.7%	14.7%	20.0%	28.0%
• The state shall be secular (lay, etc.) only	19.0%	23.8%	38.1%	19.0%	33.3%	38.1%	28.6%	33.3%	42.9%
• Other wording only	4.5%	11.4%	13.6%	6.8%	18.2%	20.5%	11.4%	15.9%	20.5%
• Both types of wording	0.0%	10.0%	20.0%	0.0%	0.0%	30.0%	0.0%	10.0%	30.0%
Constitution does not address issue of an official religion or includes both types of clause*	3.1%	7.8%	10.9%	3.1%	7.8%	14.1%	3.1%	9.4%	12.9%
Official EOR	0.0%	0.0%	0.0%	0.0%	0.0%	0.0%	0.0%	0.0%	0.0%
Regime									
Western democracies	3.7%	11.1%	11.1%	0.0%	11.1%	14.8%	3.7%	3.7%	11.1%
Western democracies with SRAS clause	11.1%	22.2%	22.2%	0.0%	22.2%	22.2%	11.1%	22.2%	22.2%
Polity = 10	8.8%	17.6%	17.6%	5.9%	17.6%	20.6%	11.8%	17.6%	17.6%
Polity = 8 to 10	5.8%	14.5%	14.5%	7.2%	15.9%	18.8%	10.1%	15.9%	15.9%
Polity = 8 to 10 *with SRAS clause*	6.5%	16.1%	16.1%	9.7%	22.6%	22.6%	16.1%	19.4%	19.4%
All countries	4.7%	9.3%	13.4%	5.2%	11.6%	16.9%	7.6%	12.2%	16.9%

* Only Bulgaria's constitution includes both SRAS and EOR clauses.

democracies. Four of them are in Africa and Taiwan is in Asia. Only Taiwan is economically developed on a par with Western democracies, whereas Benin and Burkina Faso are among the poorest nations on the planet. Only Taiwan and South Africa receive the highest scores for democracy on the Polity index but none of them are outright autocracies. Only South Africa and Namibia have Christian majorities. Even more interestingly, while the constitutions of Benin, Burkina Faso, and Namibia have SRAS clauses, the constitutions of South Africa and Taiwan do not address the issue.

If we expand this to countries which meet any one of the strictest versions of the three standards, an additional eight countries – Congo-Brazzaville, Ecuador, Estonia, Guyana, Japan, South Korea, the US, and Uruguay – are added to the list. Yet the stereotype of the developed Western liberal democracy still does not apply to most of them. Only the United States, among these, is a Western democracy. While the United States, Estonia, Japan, South Korea and Uruguay score high on democracy, the others do not. Japan and South Korea do not have Christian majorities. Estonia, Japan, South Korea, and the United States have high levels of economic development, but the others do not.

A multivariate analysis controlling for majority religion, religious diversity, regime type, the country's population, and economic development,[33] presented in Table 8.4, puts an interesting twist on these results. The only statistically significant result is in that six of the tests, the presence of SRAS clauses results in a higher likelihood that a state will have SRAS. This confirms that SRAS clauses do have an impact on state policy but, as demonstrated earlier, it is a limited impact.

However, what is particularly interesting about these results is what is *not* significant. No other factor predicted to influence the presence of SRAS in a state has a statistically significant impact. This means that counter to expectations, democracy, religious identity, and economic development do not influence the presence of SRAS in a state with any statistical significance. This confirms the results of the descriptive and bivariate analyses demonstrating that there is no consistent pattern in states that have SRAS other than that the states that have it are most often not Christian, Western, liberal democracies. It is also consistent with the central findings that a majority of the world's states do not have SRAS and that even among states with SRAS clauses in their constitutions, only a minority have SRAS in practice.

Declarations of Religious Freedom

Not All Declarations Are Equal

Declarations of religious freedom are not the same from constitution to constitution. In some cases, the wording can be quite simple. For instance, the

---

[33] All of these variables other than the population variable are described in Chapter 7. The population variable was downloaded from the World Bank on April 23, 2010.

TABLE 8.4. *Logistic Regression Predicting Presence of SRAS in 2008*

Independent Variables	Near-Absolute 1		Near-Absolute 2		Near-Absolute 3		Neutral Political Concern 1		Neutral Political Concern 2	
	B	Sig.	B	Sig.	B	Sig.	B	Sig.	B	Sig.
Majority Catholic	−19.156	.998	−1.517	.168	−.563	.550	−1.141	.441	−.686	.472
Majority Orthodox Christian	−19.131	.999	−19.896	.999	−19.921	.999	−19.128	.999	−19.834	.999
Majority other Christian	.091	.930	.144	.853	.472	.485	−.251	.793	.396	.620
Majority Muslim	−.450	.731	−1.055	.384	−1.430	.226	−.299	.818	−.307	.759
Religious diversity	1.745	.558	2.354	.289	3.973	.066	3.835	.213	2.318	.231
Polity	.169	.156	.137	.080	.025	.643	.075	.368	.143	.059
Log population	.284	.616	.045	.920	−.137	.736	−.464	.422	.052	.901
Log per capita gross domestic product	.074	.910	.313	.509	.035	.929	.384	.528	.167	.712
Constitutional clause: SRAS, all clauses	1.277	.170	1.058	.113	1.271	.032	1.339	.128	1.693	.013
Constitutional clause: official religion, all clauses	−16.684	.998	−17.545	.998	−17.416	.998	−16.602	.998	−17.399	.998
% Predicted correctly	94.9%		89.9%		87.3%		94.3%		88.6%	
Nagelkerke r^2	.356		.351		.381		.276		.349	

(*continued*)

TABLE 8.4 (*continued*)

	Neutral Political Concern 3		Laicism 1		Laicism 2		Laicism 3	
	B	Sig.	B	Sig.	B	Sig.	B	Sig.
Majority Catholic	−.979	.261	−1.353	.277	−1.353	.383	−.654	.451
Majority Orthodox Christian	−20.358	.999	−19.660	.999	−19.660	.999	−20.133	.999
Majority other Christian	.605	.364	.151	.865	.151	.181	.644	.352
Majority Muslim	−1.083	.253	−.897	.482	−.897	.644	−.561	.521
Religious diversity	2.583	.150	1.909	.439	1.909	.306	3.273	.072
Polity	.070	.189	.099	.203	.099	.073	.074	.171
Log population	−.241	.539	−.124	.802	−.124	.698	−.330	.407
Log per capita gross domestic product	.003	.993	.436	.423	.436	.722	−.383	.319
Constitutional clause: SRAS, all clauses	1.571	.007	2.086	.017	2.086	.029	1.763	.004
Constitutional clause: official religion, all clauses	−17.948	.998	−16.756	.998	−16.756	.998	−17.686	.998
% Predicted correctly	84.2%		91.1%		88.0%		83.5%	
Nagelkerke r^2	.405		.341		.354		.415	

First Amendment of the US Constitution states, "Congress shall make no law respecting an establishment of religion, or prohibiting the free exercise thereof." These 16 words both declare SRAS and protect religious freedom. South Korea has a similarly simple declaration: "all citizens enjoy the freedom of religion."[34] Although the wording of these two declarations is different, one prohibiting the government from interfering in the freedom of religion and the other declaring that such a freedom exists, they accomplish the same task using relatively simple and unambiguous language. However, of the 158 countries with religious freedom declarations in their constitutions, only 12 have this type of simple and unqualified declaration.

Two factors complicate these declarations. The first is declarations of specific types of religious freedom, which are listed in Table 8.5. In addition to a simple declaration of general religious freedom, these constitutions mention specific types of rights or specific aspects of religious freedom which that the government may not abridge. On one hand, this can be seen as providing extra protection for religious freedom. On the other, it can be seen as protecting these specific aspects of religious freedom more than others. The second are qualifications on religious freedom that are present in 111 states and listed in Table 8.6. This language specifically allows states to limit religious freedom in specified circumstances. Because many of these specified circumstances are ambiguous or widely applicable, these qualifications can significantly increase a government's ability to circumvent the religious freedom its constitutions ostensibly protects.

For example, Article 14 of Belize's constitution states:

Except with his own consent, a person shall not be hindered in the enjoyment of his freedom of conscience, including freedom of thought and of religion, freedom to change his religion or belief and freedom, either alone or in community with others, and both in public and in private, to manifest and propagate his religion or belief in worship, teaching, practice and observance... Nothing contained in or done under the authority of any law shall be held to be inconsistent with or in contravention of this section to the extent that the law in question makes provision which is reasonably required (a) in the interests of defense, public safety, public order, public morality or public health; (b) for the purpose of protecting the rights and freedoms of other persons, including the right to observe and practice any religion without the unsolicited intervention of members of any other religion; or (c) for the purpose of regulating educational institutions in the interest of the persons who receive or may receive instruction in them.[35]

As measured by the RAS dataset, these 171 words include eight specific categories of religious freedom as well as eight categories of qualifications that potentially allow Belize's government to limit religious freedom. This is among the most complicated constitutional declarations of religious freedom, but it

---

[34] 1948 Constitution of the Republic of Korea as amended through 1987, http://www.servat.unibe.ch/icl.
[35] 1981 Constitution of Belize as amended through 2002.

TABLE 8.5. *Types of Religious Freedom in Constitutions, 2008*

Types of Religious Freedom Clauses	#	% of all cases	% Countries that Discriminate		Mean Religious Discrimination		
			Has Clause	No Clause	Has Clause	No Clause	Sig.
Freedom of religion or conscience	158	91.9%	81.0%	92.9%	10.34	19.43	.015
Freedom of worship, observance, or to practice religious rituals or rites	106	61.6%	85.8%	75.8%	10.70	11.70	.664
Freedom to change one's religion	26	15.1%	84.6%	81.5%	6.54	11.88	.019
The right to profess (choose, etc.) a religion	42	24.4%	90.5%	79.2%	13.10	10.42	.267
The right not to profess a religion/freedom from religion or be an atheist	19	11.0%	89.5%	81.0%	10.08	19.11	.034
Hold or express religious opinions	5	2.9%	80.0%	82.0%	6.40	11.21	.434
Right not to join or be a member of a religious organization	4	2.3%	100.0%	81.5%	6.00	11.20	.000
The right to propagate or spread a religion	23	13.4%	82.6%	81.9%	13.52	10.70	.353
No one is required to disclose his or her religion or religious beliefs	21	12.2%	81.0%	82.1%	9.95	11.23	.686
Education or instruction in public schools or at the government's expense	15	8.7%	100.0%	80.3%	14.13	10.78	.361
Education or instruction at one's own expense or does not list at whose expense (also right to teach)	45	26.2%	75.6%	84.3%	6.80	12.59	.002
Form religious groups or practice religion in groups. This includes the right to a religious community	51	29.7%	88.2%	79.3%	9.04	11.93	.201
Have a place of worship or own property (for religious organizations)	12	7.0%	83.3%	81.9%	14.08	10.85	.426
Religious organizations may manage their own affairs	27	15.7%	74.1%	83.4%	10.15	11.25	.699
Right to a chaplain in hospitals, the military, etc.	8	4.7%	87.5%	81.7%	.638	11.30	.009
Protection of religious rights even in states of emergency or war	16	9.0%	81.3%	82.1%	7.75	11.42	.117
Freedom from coercion with regard to religion	15	8.7%	80.0%	82.2%	10.92	12.73	.621
In public	37	21.5%	81.1%	82.2%	5.27	14.60	.000
In private	34	19.2%	79.4%	92.6%	4.32	12.74	.000
Other	15	8.7%	100.0%	80.3%	13.67	10.83	.439

TABLE 8.6. *Qualifications on Religious Freedom in Constitutions, 2008*

Types of Qualifications to Religious Freedom	n	% of All Cases	% Countries That Discriminate		Mean Religious Discrimination		
			Has Clause	No Clause	Has Clause	No Clause	Sig.
The constitution qualifies freedom of religion (general)	111	70.3%	82.0%	78.8%	10.32	10.36	.987
National security or defense	15	9.5%	93.3%	79.7%	10.40	10.33	.984
Public defense, safety, interest, common good, or order or prevent public nuisance.	77	48.7%	81.8%	80.2%	9.65	10.99	.510
The law, constitution, or public policy	51	32.2%	86.3%	78.5%	12.18	9.46	.210
Public health	37	23.4%	78.4%	81.8%	9.76	10.51	.753
To protect the rights and freedoms of others	39	24.7%	84.6%	79.8%	7.69	11.20	.092
Affecting/violating the religious beliefs of others	12	7.6%	83.3%	80.8%	4.17	10.84	.003
Cannot be used for political purposes	3	1.9%	66.7%	81.3%	4.67	10.45	.437
Public morals or "good customs"	56	35.4%	85.7%	78.4%	11.12	9.90	.564
In accordance with local customs or culture	6	3.8%	100.0%	80.3%	21.50	9.89	.028
In accordance with the majority religion	2	1.3%	100.0%	80.8%	29.00	10.10	.575
The secularity of the state or separation of religion and state	4	2.5%	50.0%	81.8%	8.75	10.38	.801
Religious rights do not include the right to be a member of a secret society or religions with secret doctrines or rites	2	1.3%	100.0%	80.0%	10.50	10.33	.985
Other	33	20.9%	84.8%	80.0%	12.06	9.88	.465
Two or more qualification clauses	85	53.8%	84.7%	76.7%	10.56	10.07	.808
Four or more qualification clauses	38	24.1%	84.2%	80.0%	9.05	11.80	.477

* All tests are only for the 158 cases of states that have religious freedom clauses in their constitutions.

does make the point that the language of these declarations can be as important as their presence.

Case law can create similar types of qualifications. For example, in the US Supreme Court's decision in *Reynolds v. United States* (1879), the court unanimously upheld antibigamy laws that contradicted the religious beliefs of a member of the Church of Jesus Christ of Latter-day Saints, deciding that

> laws are made for the government of actions, and while they cannot interfere with mere religious belief and opinions, they may with practices.... Can a man excuse his practices to the contrary because of his religious belief? To permit this would be to make the professed doctrines of religious belief superior to the law of the land, and in effect to permit every citizen to become a law unto himself.[36]

Since then, the US courts have allowed limitations on religious freedom in rare cases where there was a compelling public interest to do so, but the extent of this leeway has varied over time. Notable recent cases include *United States v. Lee* (1982), which ruled religious beliefs do not exempt people from taxes, and *Employment Division v. Smith* (1990), which clarified the doctrine that a reasonable law that is not directed against a religion and does not discriminate between religious groups is allowable even if it happens to make illegal the religious practices of a specific group. In this case, the practice was ingesting peyote – an illegal drug – during a religious ritual.

Types of Freedom Clauses and Religious Discrimination

While the RAS dataset does not measure religious freedom, it does measure religious discrimination against minorities. The absence of this discrimination can be considered a good measure for religious freedom. As discussed in more detail in Chapter 6, there are multiple conceptions of religious freedom, but none of them allow religious discrimination. As shown in Table 8.5, constitutional clauses protecting religious freedom influence levels of religious discrimination but clearly do not prevent it. That is, states with religious freedom clauses in their constitutions engage in lower levels of religious discrimination than states with no such clauses, but these levels are still substantial.

Perhaps the most striking result is that 81.0% of states with religious freedom clauses in their constitutions nevertheless engage in religious discrimination, although this is less than the 92.9% that have no clause and discriminate. Similarly, the average state with a religious freedom clause has a religious discrimination score of 10.34. Although this is significantly lower than the score of 19.43 for countries with no such clause, it is still high. As will be recalled, the religious discrimination score consists of 30 specific types of religious discrimination, which are each measured on a scale of zero to three. Thus, a score of 10.34 means that a state engages in at least four separate types of religious discrimination.

---

[36] *Reynolds v. United States*, 98 U.S. 145, 166–167 (1879).

Religion in Constitutions 223

For example, Sweden's constitution states that "every citizen shall be guaranteed the following rights and freedoms in his relations with the public institutions... freedom of worship: that is, the freedom to practice one's religion alone or in the company of others."[37] However, Sweden's 2008 discrimination score is 10, about average for states with religious freedom clauses. This is because of the following activities.

Two practices central to the Jewish religion have been strongly regulated. Sweden's 1998 Animal Welfare Act effectively bans the Jewish ritual slaughter of meat, which makes the meat Kosher. As a result, all Kosher meat in Sweden is imported significantly increasing the price.[38] A 2001 law regulates male circumcision, requiring that it be performed only by a licensed doctor or a person certified by the National Board of Health. Jewish practitioners, called Mohels, can be certified to perform circumcisions, provided they are accompanied by a doctor or nurse who can administer anesthesia.[39] Although in both of these cases the laws are generally applicable and ostensibly secular, in practice they place significant costs and inconveniences on the practice of Judaism in Sweden.

A 2008 Swedish law bans *private* school teachers from inserting religious doctrine into the teaching of secular subjects such as science. For example, biology teachers may not teach creationism.[40] As noted in Chapter 6, all cemeteries and burials in Sweden are controlled by the Church of Sweden. Finally, to receive government benefits, religious groups must register. Registration is sometimes refused, but lack of registration does not otherwise limit freedom of worship.[41]

While none of these limitations create a situation where any religion is banned, it is clear that some religions in Sweden are in a very real way hampered in their ability to practice and support institutions.

Returning to Table 8.5, of the 19 types of specific protections for religious freedom (this does not include the first which represents general protection for religious freedom), 11 make religious discrimination more likely. That is, a larger proportion of states which have these protections in their constitutions engage in religious discrimination than those which have no such clauses. The

---

[37] 1974 Constitution of Sweden as Amended through 2011, www.riksdagen.se/templates/R_Page___6357.aspx.
[38] "Swedish Jews and Muslims Join Forces," *European Jewish News*, November 13, 2005, www.ejpress.org/article/4192.
[39] "Sweden Restricts Circumcisions," BBC News Europe, October 1, 2001, http://news.bbc.co.uk/2/hi/europe/1572483.stm.
[40] "Creationism to Be Banished from Swedish Schools," *The Local: Sweden's News in English*, October 15, 2007, www.thelocal.se/8790/20071015; Bjorn Ulvaeus, "Religion and Schools Don't Mix," *The Guardian*, June 30, 2009, www.guardian.co.uk/commentisfree/belief/2009/jun/30/bjorn-ulvaeus-religion-schools.
[41] "Joyous Court Climax for Madonna of Orgasm Church," *The Local: Sweden's News in English*, November 19, 2008, http://www.thelocal.se/20081119/15786.

presence of five of these types of clauses is associated with a higher mean level of religious discrimination than states without such clauses in their constitutions.

In sum, while there is a correlation between constitutional protections for religious freedom and the actual presence of religious freedom – as measured by the absence of religious discrimination – this correlation is at best limited. States with such clauses in their constitutions regularly discriminate, and no language of any kind is correlated with any more than 25.9% of states engaging in no religious discrimination. Also, counterintuitively, some religious freedom clauses are statistically associated with higher levels of religious discrimination.

It is arguable that religious freedom clauses are one of those types of clauses that are practically mandatory in constitutions because of international norms, even if governments have no intention of respecting these norms. However, if constitutional religion clauses were a primary determinant of government policy, I would expect a higher level of compliance than I found in these results.

Constitutional Qualifications of Religious Freedom and Religious Discrimination

As shown in Table 8.6, 70.3% of constitutions with religious freedom clauses include language qualifying religious freedom. In theory these qualifications can provide an explanation for why states with religious freedom clauses tend to engage in religious discrimination, but in practice there is little correlation between these qualifications and state practice. For example, the presence of a qualification clause makes a state only slightly more likely to engage in religious discrimination and the average levels of religious discrimination are nearly identical in states with and without these qualification clauses. Although many of the specific types of qualification clause make religious discrimination more likely, no less than 78.4% of states that do not have the specific clause in question engage in religious discrimination.

More interestingly, the presence of 7 of the 13 types of qualification clauses makes religious discrimination less likely. That is, states that qualify religious freedom in this manner tend to engage in lower levels of religious discrimination. Counting the number of such clauses also does not help. For example, the presence of four or more qualification clauses is similarly associated with lower average levels of religious discrimination. This further bolsters the result that constitutional language on religious freedom has no more than a limited correlation with government practice.

The Constitutional Correlates of Religious Discrimination

In Table 8.7, I use multivariate analysis to examine the causes of religious discrimination. The control variables are the same as I use in the tests for the causes of SRAS earlier in this chapter. I test only a selection of the clauses from the previous tests that meet the following criteria: they were present in at least 10 constitutions and resulted in statistically significantly differences in religious

TABLE 8.7. *Constitutional Clauses and Religious Discrimination in 2008: Multivariate Analysis*

Independent Variables	Model 1		Model 2		Model 3		Model 4		Model 5	
	B	Sig.	B	Sig.	B	Sig.	B	Sig.	B	Sig.
Majority Catholic	-.091	.236	-.101	.183	-.100	.189	-.090	.217	-.100	.189
Majority Orthodox Christian	.223	.000	.228	.000	.228	.000	.205	.000	.228	.000
Majority other Christian	-.134	.047	-.142	.034	-.140	.036	-.139	.029	-.140	.036
Majority Muslim	-.100	.216	-.102	.201	-.107	.179	-.130	.091	-.107	.179
Religious diversity	-.036	.576	-.008	.900	.000	.995	-.014	.814	.000	.995
Polity	-.467	.000	-.469	.000	-.460	.000	-.442	.000	-.460	.000
Log population	.125	.026	.114	.039	.109	.050	.100	.060	.109	.050
Log per capita gross domestic product	.187	.000	.185	.000	.177	.001	.167	.001	.177	.001
Religious support	.418	.000	.404	.000	.414	.000	.455	.000	.414	.000
Freedom of religion or conscience	—	—	-.124	.014	-.117	.022	-.122	.012	-.117	.022
Freedom to change one's religion	—	—	—	—	—	—	—	—	—	—
The right to not profess a religion, etc.	—	—	—	—	—	—	.186	.000	—	—
Education or instruction at one's own expense	—	—	—	—	-.051	.316	—	—	-.051	.316
Adjusted r^2	.594		.606		.604		.638		.606	

(*continued*)

TABLE 8-7 (continued)

	Model 6		Model 7		Model 8	
	B	Sig.	B	Sig.	B	Sig.
Majority Catholic	-.093	.223	-.097	.205	-.101	.184
Majority Orthodox Christian	.228	.000	.229	.000	.230	.000
Majority Other Christian	-.138	.040	-.139	.037	-.141	.034
Majority Muslim	-.107	.181	-.101	.207	-.103	.199
Religious diversity	-.012	.846	-.002	.973	-.008	.900
Polity	-.471	.000	-.463	.000	-.469	.000
Log Population	.190	.000	.111	.045	.112	.047
Log per capita gross domestic product	.111	.044	.180	.001	.183	.001
Religious support	.404	.000	.406	.000	.405	.000
Freedom of religion or conscience.	-.124	.014	-.121	.017	-.122	.019
In public	-.045	.363	–	–	–	–
In private	–	–	-.026	.609	–	–
Number of qualification clauses	–	–	–	–	-.010	.849
Adjusted r^2	.606		.605		.604	

discrimination. Model 1 is a baseline model that includes no constitutional clauses. Model 2 includes whether there is a general religious freedom clause. Models 3 through 7 test the influence of specific religious freedom clauses. Finally, model 8 tests the influence of qualification clauses.

Overall, the results show that while constitutional declarations of religious freedom are correlated with lower levels of religious discrimination, the actual impact of these clauses on government policy is limited. The adjusted r^2 – which measures how much of the variance is explained (meaning it measures how much of the behavior in question is explained by the variables in the regression) – in model 1 which includes only the control variables is .594. Adding the freedom of religion variable adds .012 to this score, which means that while the other variables combined explain 59.4% of religious discrimination, constitutional freedom of religion clauses explain another 1.2% of the variance in this type of government policy. Even though the constitution variable is itself statistically significant in all models that include it, the totality of the results show that while it has a statistically significant impact, the actual size of this impact is small. This means constitutional religious freedom clauses are statistically significant but not very important.

Models 3 through 8 test the impact of other types of relevant clauses. None of them add much to the level of explanation in model 2 other than model 4, which tests for clauses that protect the right not to profess a religion. This type of clause, which is present in only 19 constitutions, increases the adjusted r^2 by .032, which means its impact on actual levels of religious discrimination is still small but much greater than that of a general religious freedom clause. More interesting, this type of clause is associated with higher levels of religious discrimination.

The factors that most strongly affect religious discrimination are religious identity – with Orthodox states discriminating more and "other" Christian states discriminating less – regime, population size, economic development, and religious support. Not surprisingly religious discrimination against minorities is less common in democratic states and more common in states that more strongly support religion.

Countries that are more economically developed likely engage in higher levels of religious discrimination because they have a greater ability to do so. That is, as Gill (2008) points out, repressing minority religions requires resources. Wealthier states have more resources that can be devoted to religious discrimination. The results regarding population are consistent with general research on population size and repression. Henderson (1993: 8) argues that "growth in numbers of people can create scarcity – a short-fall between what people need and want and what they have. Under this pressure governments may...resort to repression as a coping mechanism." Findings by Henderson (1993), Poe and Tate (1994), and Poe et al. (1999) support this argument.

Constitutions and State Religion Policy

In Table 8.8, I compare the multivariate results for the influence of constitutional clauses on religious support, regulation, and discrimination. I use the same control variables as in the previous tests, except I do not use religious support in the regression in which it is the dependent variable. The results demonstrate that each of the three types of government involvement in religion examined in this book have a different dynamic. Religious support is influenced by constitutional clauses in the manner one would expect: declarations of SRAS make it less likely and declarations of EOR make it more likely. It is more common in developed states, likely because more developed states have more resources to support and enforce religion. It is also more common in Muslim-majority states. Interestingly, it is not correlated with regime. This implies that the decision to support a religion is as likely in a democracy as a nondemocracy. This further undermines philosophical notions that democracy and SRAS are related.

Religious regulation is significantly correlated with only two variables. It is less common in democracies. The other variable, population, I discuss shortly. This indicates that the decision to regulate all religion in a state is based on more idiosyncratic reasons that are unique from state to state.

The results for religious discrimination are similar to those discussed in the previous section. I present them here again to provide a direct comparison across types of religion policy and to emphasize that the patterns between these independent variables and state religion policy are very different for each of the three categories of policy I examine here. This provides empirical support for my argument that, although certainly related, each of these types of policy represents a distinct policy area within state religion policy with its own correlates and dynamics; that is, for example, the decision to support religion does not require that minority religions be restricted.

Interestingly, the only variable that is significant for all three types of policy is the log of the country's population. As countries become more populous, they engage in significantly more support, restrictions, and discrimination. Perhaps this is because larger countries require a stronger central government to maintain a consistent policy across the state. Other than this, no aspect of the literature on religion and politics of which I am aware can explain this finding.

Conclusions

This chapter examines the question of whether states follow the policies set out in their constitutions. The answer is that while constitutions have an influence, this influence is at best limited, and many states engage in religion policies that are at odds with the ideals expressed in their constitutions. This is true of declarations of SRAS and particularly true of declarations of religious freedom.

TABLE 8.8. *Constitutional and Other Correlates of State Religion Policy, 2008*

Independent Variables	Religious Support		Religious Regulation		Religious Discrimination	
	B	Sig.	B	Sig.	B	Sig.
Majority Catholic	-.073	.372	-.083	.355	-.104	.174
Majority Orthodox Christian	.031	.603	.083	.211	.232	.000
Majority other Christian	-.055	.440	-.141	.071	-.141	.034
Majority Muslim	.401	.000	.117	.217	-.087	.281
Religious diversity	-.011	.878	-.055	.488	-.033	.624
Polity	-.046	.472	-.495	.000	-.480	.000
Log population	.230	.000	.316	.000	.186	.001
Log per capita gross domestic product	.187	.001	.092	.157	.124	.026
Religious support	—	—	.061	.477	.429	.000
Constitutional clause: SRAS, all clauses	-.186	.002	-.104	.116	-.050	.373
Constitutional clause: official religion, all clauses	.289	.000	-.092	.252	-.111	.105
Constitutional clause: freedom of religion or conscience.	-.002	.972	.067	.260	-.133	.009
Adjusted r^2	.552		.460		.609	

This is but one example of the many findings that undermine general assumptions regarding state religion policy. Another is that states with SRAS are in the minority worldwide. They are even a minority among states that declare SRAS in their constitutions as well as among the very democracies that originated liberal democratic theory and are therefore assumed to follow SRAS policies.

All of this supports my general argument that religion remains a central element of state policy, and although these policies remain in a state of flux, the current pattern runs toward increasing state involvement in religion. Put differently, in the competition between secular and religious forces described in the competition perspective, the advocates of political secularism have had more success in writing their ideals into constitutions than they have in influencing actual government practices. The scarcity of governments that successfully separate themselves from religion, even among states that declare such separation as an ideal in their constitutions, is case in point. This is also true of the fact that the vast majority of states that declare freedom of religion to be a basic right do not, in practice, provide this freedom for all of their citizens.

In sum, SRAS and religious freedom are the two most central elements of a state policy intended to keep governments out of the business of religion – so basic and common that they are commonly found in constitutions. If even this most basic and fundamental form of declaration does not usually succeed in separating governments from religion, it is arguable that we live in an era when religion is and will remain a central political issue for the foreseeable future.

9

Conclusions

In this book, I have argued that across the world, secular actors are competing with religious actors to influence state religion policy. No matter how much a country supports religion, there are those who feel it does not support religion strongly enough, and no matter how secular a government's policy, there are those who consider it insufficiently secular. While, as I discuss in more detail in this concluding chapter, this argument, which I call the secular-religious competition perspective, is not the only influence on government religion policy, I believe it is perhaps the most significant influence. In every country in the world, religion is a relevant and active issue, and in most of them, governments have actively altered their policies during the 19 years this study covers. This might have been a controversial statement in the past, but today even those who believe religion is declining in importance do not deny its presence and relevance in politics and society.

That being said, the extent and nature of this political relevance remain topics of hot debate. A central goal of this book is to address this debate. In Chapter 3, I demonstrate that states that support religion outnumber those that are generally neutral toward religion by a factor of greater than two to one and that states that are neutral toward religion outnumber those that are hostile to it by a similar margin. In Chapters 4 through 7, I examine the dynamics of 110 distinct religion policy issues, demonstrating that nearly every state in the world, including those that are in general neutral toward religion, has at least some of these policies and that, overall, these policies are becoming more common. Thus, it is clear that religion and politics are intimately intertwined in nearly every corner of the earth.

The dataset from Round 2 of the Religion and State (RAS2) project provides an unprecedented level of specificity that has allowed this analysis to reveal and compare the details of the religion policies across 177 countries to the extent that I posit that this study provides, among other things, a comprehensive

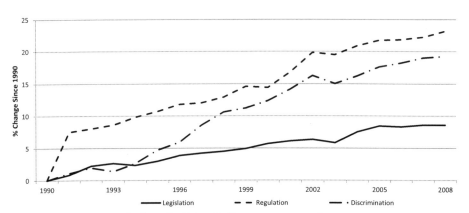

FIGURE 9.1. Increases in State Religion Policy, 1990 to 2008.

lexicon of how governments deal with religion. In this chapter, I seek to move beyond these details and discuss the larger picture. That is, I examine the larger trends and issues that emerge from this detailed examination of specific government religion policies. I also describe how the results of this study fit with the secular-religious competition perspective. Finally, I discuss the complex process that forms a government's overall religion policy.

Trends over Time

As presented in Figures 9.1 and 9.2, states are heavily involved in religion, and this trend has been consistently increasing in strength between 1990 and 2008. This increasing ubiquity in government involvement in religion is perhaps the most obvious and incontrovertible result that emerges from this analysis. It is certainly among the most important. This is not to say that no state has become less involved in religion during this period. However, from all perspectives I examine, new religion policies greatly outnumber religion policies discontinued.

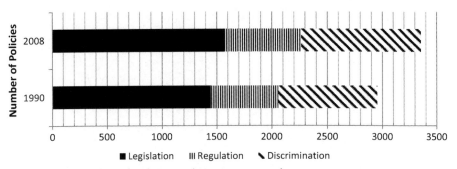

FIGURE 9.2. Number of Religion Policies in 1990 and 2008.

Conclusions

This trend is extensive, deep, and broad. Of the 110 individual types of religion policy, 85 (77.3%) became more common, 14 (12.7%) became less common, and 11 (10.0%) remained stable. Overall, 83.6% (148) of states changed their religion policies in some manner including, 55.3% (98) that did nothing but institute new policies, 12.4% (22) that uniformly dropped policies, and 15.8% (28) that did both. Thus, no matter how one looks at it, overall, states were more involved in religion in 2008 than they were in 1990. Also, as demonstrated in Chapter 8, few states have separation of religion and state (SRAS) based on any definition and quantification of the term. This includes the Western liberal democracies that originated the concept of SRAS as well as states that declare SRAS in their constitutions.

Looking at individual policies (Figure 9.2), the baseline government involvement in religion was already high in 1990. In 1990, or the earliest available year, the average country had 16.67 religion policies, a total of 2,951 such policies across the world. This increased to 18.94 and 3353 by 2008, an increase of 13.6% overall. While there was certainly a great deal of variation in levels of both support and control of religion across countries, the only country to have none of these 110 policies was South Africa from 2003 onward. This is a rare exception in a world where state involvement in religion is ubiquitous and increasing.

Some of the most changed states include the following:

- Eritrea, which around 2001 began a large-scale crackdown on unregistered religions, banning most religious practices by "nonsanctioned" religions.
- Afghanistan, even after the fall of the Taliban regime, has significantly higher levels of religious legislation, regulation, and discrimination than it did in the pre-Taliban era, although these levels are lower than they were during the Taliban era.
- Russia, discounting the changes immediately after the fall of the Soviet Union, has significantly increased its support for the Russian Orthodox Church. The most significant post–Soviet era shift was the 1997 Law on Freedom of Conscience and on Religious Associations,[1] which designates the Russian Orthodox Church as well as Judaism, Islam, and Buddhism as "traditional" religions and severely limits all other religions. Several subsequent laws and policies have strengthened this general policy.
- Other former Soviet states, including Azerbaijan, Belarus, Kazakhstan, Turkmenistan, and Uzbekistan, have significantly increased both the regulation of the majority religion and discrimination against religious minorities.
- Nigeria's northern states began both legislating Sharia (Islamic) law and discriminating against mostly Christian minorities around 2000. This has led to numerous and violent clashes between Christians and Muslims.

---

[1] A copy of this law is available at www.religlaw.org.

- Malaysia and Indonesia, throughout the 1990–2008 period, increased government involvement in religion in all three categories, both more strongly supporting Islam and regulating it as well as increasingly discriminating against religious minorities. These policies are the result of the combined action of central and local governments with the central governments emphasizing regulation more strongly and the local governments more strongly emphasizing support.

These examples should not be taken to mean that no governments have lowered their involvement in religion. The most dramatic drop in involvement was Iraq, with the post-Saddam government significantly less involved in religion than was Saddam Hussein's government in all categories.

While Iraq's change was the result of an invasion, a similarly dramatic change in South Africa was the result of internal processes. The South African government's involvement in religion was never higher than moderate, but a series of actions, which I discussed in more detail in Chapter 6, resulted in South Africa being the only government to have none of the 110 policies reassured by the RAS dataset starting in 2003. Another dramatic lowering of government intervention in religion was Mexico's 1992 constitutional revisions; these significantly eased its anticlerical policy, which had severely limited and regulated religion, especially Catholicism. Similarly, as discussed in Chapter 3, Sweden ended the era in which is supported an official religion in 2000.

These are a few of the more dramatic examples of the 148 states that changed their religion policy between 1990 and 2008. In most of these states, the changes were not earth-shattering but are nevertheless important. Each change represents a conscious decision to change a government policy regarding religion. Much more often than not, these decisions resulted in increased government involvement in religion rather than less. Each of these decisions measurably influenced people's lives, and collectively they constitute a measurable and significant rise of religion's public profile. Whether these decisions are to support religion, regulate it, or both, they show that religion is a topic of public importance and that governments are paying it considerable attention.

An interesting pattern is that a significant portion of the increases are due to actions by local and regional governments. The RAS project only codes such substate level increases when they are present in a significant number of local or regional governments to the extent that the impact is at a minimum similar to a national law that is enforced selectively or sporadically. Local-level changes are often the harbingers of changes in national policy because they represent a grassroots desire to increase government involvement in religion. They are also the type of policy shift that is most easily traceable to religious political actors. Given this, the widespread presence of these local and regional efforts implies that the trend of increased government involvement in religion is likely to continue in the near future.

The Secular-Religious Competition Perspective

I have already noted that depicting the politics of religion as a worldwide competition between political secularism and religion is a gross oversimplification for reasons I discuss in more detail later in the chapter. Yet this oversimplification is a highly useful framework to discuss religion and politics in the modern era. This is because despite its being complicated by numerous factors, there is, in fact, an overt competition between political secularists, who seek to get the governments out of the business of religion, and the political religious camp, which seeks the opposite. These forces compete in the political arena using all the tools that interest groups use to influence government decisions. These include political parties, lobbying, public demonstrations, public information campaigns, and sometimes violence. The focus of this study is not on these groups, but the results of their efforts can be seen in the government policies examined here.

Thus, setting aside for the moment the complexities involved, this study provides abundant evidence of the tensions between religious and secular forces in politics. Toft et al. (2011), among others, are likely right that if we use a perspective that spans centuries, religion's influence on government is less than it was in the past and that this is due in part to the influence of political secularism. But they also argue that religion is coming back in the public sphere and that the 21st century will be "God's century." The evidence presented here is consistent with this broad historical view. In the 19-year period covered in this study, religion has been gaining on secularism, at least in the realm of government religion policy. Yet despite these gains, the data also reveal a give and take in which even while a majority of governments were more involved in religion in 2008 than they were in 1990, many governments are less involved.

That is, if one keeps a global score, religion seems to be currently outperforming political secularism in the arena of government religion policy, but this does not mean political secularism is inactive or defeated. Rather, the politics of government religion policy are local. There is no world governing body that sets religion policy. It is national and local governments that set government religion policy, and these policies influence primarily those living within their jurisdictions. While lobbying and pressure on these issues can be international, the decisions remain at the state and substate levels. This means that each country and often each local government is an arena in which the political struggle between the secular and religious camps can potentially, and often does, take place. For example, the issue of religious education in public schools can be set by state policy, and it can also be influenced at the local level, even on a school by school basis, but it is not set globally by the United Nations or another international body. Perhaps the only exception to this is the European Court of Human Rights, which has multistate jurisdiction in cases where a state's religion policy violates human rights, and even in that case, it involves a check on government power, not the power to create a policy.

From this perspective, while religion is clearly making more gains than political secularism, political secularism has no shortage of victories. During the period examined here, 14 types of religion policies became less common, most notably bans on abortion and homosexuality; 22 states became less involved in religion than they were in 1990 (or the earliest year available); and 195 specific religion policies were eliminated.

Many in the religious camp not only see themselves in a struggle with secularism, they also feel that they are losing. For example, prominent US conservative Baptist minister Pat Robertson expressed this sentiment when he lamented that

fifty-five million aborted babies since *Roe v. Wade*, Bibles taken out of the schools, prayer taken out of the schools, secularism on the rise, and now homosexuality, which was called an abomination in the Bible, has been given the status of a constitutionally protected class, and a justice of the supreme court who says anybody who is against this lifestyle is somehow bigoted.... The defenders of a traditional lifestyle are going to be marginalized very quickly. They are already.... Its been cast as a civil rights struggle and it is no longer a moral issue.... Read the Bible about Sodom and Gomorrah, that's where the term *Sodom* comes from.... Look what happened to Sodom, after a while there wasn't any other way and God did something drastic.[2]

Political secularists feel the same. For example, former US Secretary of Labor Robert Reich wrote that

For more than three hundred years, the liberal tradition has sought to free people from the tyranny of religious doctrines that would otherwise be imposed on them. Today's evangelical right detests that tradition and seeks nothing short of a state-sponsored religion. But maintaining the separation of church and state is a necessary precondition of liberty.... Religious wars aren't pretty. Religious wars never are. But Democrats should mount a firm and clear counter-assault. In the months leading up to Election Day, when Republicans are screaming about God and accusing the Democrats of siding with sexual deviants and baby killers, Democrats should remind Americans that however important religion is to our spiritual lives, there is no room for liberty in a theocracy.[3]

However, the reality is likely more complicated than implied by a simple scorecard of gains and losses for each side of this competition. Monica Duffy Toft, Daniel Philpott, and Timothy Shaw's *God's Century* argument means that the struggle between political secularism and religion is resulting in a new political dynamic among religion, secularism, and politics. Secularism may have made significant inroads into politics over the past few centuries, but it also created an environment in which religious actors evolved, became independent, and relate to politics in a new way. These religious actors have an agenda that they pursue vigorously in the political arena. Nevertheless, we should not "exaggerate the power of religious actors in public life, thereby replacing secularization with

---

[2] Pat Robertson, 700 Club broadcast, June 27, 2013.
[3] Robert Reich "The Religious Wars," *American Prospect*, November 19, 2003, http://prospect.org/article/religious-wars.

sacralization" (Toft et al., 2011: 212). Political secular actors remain potent competitors to the religious actors even as "religious actors... play a larger and more pervasive role than conventional wisdom anticipates" (Toft et al., 2011: 213).

Rodney Stark (1999) argues that this has always been the case. Even in religion's supposed Golden Age, religion was never fully dominant. Thus, from this point of view, the 21st century is no different from the past where religion was significant but religious institutions and actors competed for political influence with political actors more concerned with worldly issues. Political secularism may have changed the nature of at least some of these worldly political elements, but the competition between religious political actors and the nonreligious remains a historical constant.

In fact, as long as religion remains popular among at least a segment of society, it is unlikely to lose its political relevance in the long term. Religious actors often have political agendas. Although these agendas can be repressed in the short term, this is rarely successful in the long run.

This is because government repression of religion does not succeed in making religion go away. Toft et al. (2011: 216) argue that "the more governments try to repress or exclude religious actors from public life in one generation, the more they inadvertently strengthen their [religious actors] capacity to influence public life in the next generation." Or, to paraphrase Nietzsche, whatever does not destroy religion will make it stronger. Past repression of religion resulted in an evolution where religious institutions became less dependent on the state and better able to act on their own to influence politics. This repression has often also resulted in more extremist versions of religion or as Toft et al. (2011: 220) put it "if governments fail to respect the institutional independence of religious actors, especially through systematic repression, the more governments will encourage pathological forms of religious politics, including religion-based terrorism and religious-related civil wars." Perhaps this insight is among the reasons that governments that are truly hostile to religion in general are becoming rarer.

Put differently, religion is a real political force. In the long term, repression has not proven to be an effective method to eliminate religion. This means that it is in the political interests of states to come to an accommodation with religion. Most of today's governments seem to recognize this reality with regard to the state's majority religion. This accommodation can range from benign neutrality to overt support, with all the nuances available within each option, although this support is nearly always mixed with an element of regulation or control. There is no single correct formula for state policy toward religion, but one that seeks to deny and repress religion is, I posit, unsustainable in the long term.

However, most states limit at least some minority religions. While these minorities are unlikely to have the same potential to challenge a state as a majority religion, the lesson of repression leading to radicalization still applies.

Given the increasing number of states that limit at least some minority religions, this avenue for political or violent opposition is potentially relevant in most of the world and will likely become an increasingly significant religious influence on politics in the years to come.

Given this, I do not see secularism triumphing against religion any time soon. That being said, I also do not see political secularism disappearing as an ideology. It has strong roots in many parts of the world, particularly but not limited to Western democracies. It is rooted in the philosophy of science, which itself has a strong constituency. It is also a convenient political ideology for religiously heterogeneous states. On a more practical level, it provides a useful check on the absolutist political ideologies that can become influential among the religious. Thus, for the foreseeable future, I expect the tensions and political struggle between political secularism and political manifestations of religion to continue.

This finding also has some implications for the more recent innovations of secularization theory discussed in Chapter 2. There are essentially five of these new versions of secularization theory. (1) The argument that secularization constitutes the privatization of religion or the shift of religion from the public sphere to the private sphere is contradicted by these results. While there is certainly a concerted effort by those who follow political secularist ideologies to accomplish exactly this, the evidence shows that this result has not been achieved, nor is it likely to be achieved any time soon. (2) The argument that secularism is triumphing in the West is contradicted by the presence of a significant amount of both support for religion and religious discrimination in these states. Chapter 8 in particular demonstrates that only 9 of 27 Western states declare SRAS in their constitutions, and no more than 2 of these 9 have SRAS policies in practice. (3) The Norris and Inglehart (2004) argument that religion is declining in modernized states focuses mostly on individual religiosity, which is not addressed in this study. Otherwise, it is similar to the arguments in the previous form of secularization theory. That is, levels of religiosity notwithstanding, religion remains a political force even in modernized states.

The final two manifestations of secularization theory are on a more philosophical level and do not contradict the concept of a continuing worldwide tension between political secularism and religious political actors. (4) Charles Taylor's (2007) argument that the presence of secularism as an ideology is the true form of secularization is mostly consistent with this argument. The major difference between my formulation and Taylor's is that, as I argue in Chapter 2, I do not believe this constitutes secularization. Secularization implies religion is declining or perhaps disappearing. A continuing clash between secularism and religion does not fit well into this mold. (5) Finally, the neo-secularists do not deny the clash between religion and political secularism. Rather, they are part of this clash, representing the political secularists. They go even farther than many political secularists by arguing that we would be better off without religion altogether and not just in politics.

Conclusions

The Competition Perspective Versus the Interests of Politicians

The competition perspective is not the only one that attempts to explain the state of religion policy in the world. As discussed in more detail in Chapter 2, Anthony Gill (2008) provides one of the most prominent competing explanations. He agrees that religions tend to want a religious monopoly. He argues that politicians grant this monopoly when it is in their interests to do so. Although this theory provides an important insight into how state religion policy is formed, it is an incomplete explanation for state religion policy.

The theory looks at the interests of politicians and accounts for the motivations, interests, and political influence of religion. However, it does not address secularism as a political force. It is certainly possible to build a theory of how politicians acting in their own interests will react to this competing force, but Gill (2008) does not do so, and, more important, no theory based on the interests of politicians can explain state religion policy without also including the competition perspective. For example, such an understanding might argue that politicians will choose to support some form of secularism or SRAS when secular forces in a country have sufficient political influence.

In fact, the competition perspective helps close one of the larger holes in Gill's (2008) theory. He successfully shows that given certain structural situations – which are based on the level of influence a religion has in a country – politicians are likely to behave in certain ways. However, his theory does not predict when these various structural situations will occur. By combining Gill's insights with the competition perspective, we create an approach that can explain all of this.

Thus, although it is certainly true that the interests of politicians play a role in state religion policy, Gill's explanation is incomplete without taking into account other factors including but not limited to the competition perspective. In the following sections, I address in more detail the many influences on state religion policy.

What Kind of Clash?

Another competing theory with regard to religion and politics is Samuel Huntington's (1993; 1996) "clash of civilizations" theory in which he posits that most post–Cold War conflict will be between several civilizations that are religiously homogeneous. That is, he expects competition between religions to dominate international and, to a lesser extent, domestic politics. One of the most prominent, among many, of the critiques of this theory is that subcivilizational conflict will remain more important than intercivilizational conflict (Fox, 2004).

Although this study does not focus on violent conflict, it does focus on a major social and political conflict over how governments deal with religion. In this context, I agree with Huntington's critics. Interreligious conflict is an important issue and, as I discuss later, an important influence on state religion

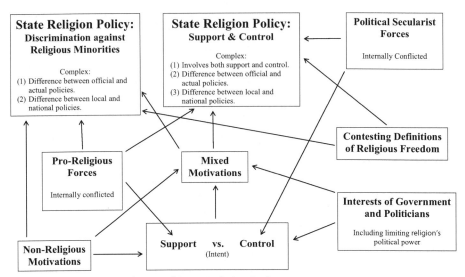

FIGURE 9.3. The Complexity of State Religion Policy.

policy. However, it is important to remember that the clash of civilization argument focuses on identity politics rather than ideological politics. In most states, the political secularists and religious actors competing to influence government religion policy all belong to the same identity group both in the conventional meaning of the term as well as based on Huntington's civilizations construct. Thus, by ignoring the competition perspective's focus on competition within civilizations, Huntington misses a significant part of the overall picture. That being said, as I discuss in more detail later, Huntington's argument that inter-religious competition is a significant factor is accurate.

Complex Religion

The competition perspective's argument that religious politics revolves around a competition between political secularism and politically motivated religious actors is elegant and provides an important insight into the nature of religion and politics in our time. However, on its own it cannot provide a complete explanation for state religion policy. Several additional factors influence state religion policy that, when combined, make for a significantly more complex reality, which I describe next and also show in Figure 9.3.

First, the foregoing discussion essentially revolves around the assumption that political secularism's primary goal is to keep religion out of politics. However, as I discuss in more detail in Chapter 2, political secularism has a number of manifestations. These manifestations each have different implications that can be seen with regard to whether and under what circumstances these conceptions allow religious support, regulation, and discrimination:

Conclusions

- *Absolute SRAS* mandates that the state neither support nor hinder religion in any way. Thus, no support, regulation, or discrimination is allowed.
- *Secularism-Laicism* mandates that the state maintain a secular public space. This means that no support is allowed. Discrimination is also by implication not allowed because this would imply advantaging one or some religions in comparison to others. However, regulation of religion in public spaces is not only allowed, it is mandated.
- *Neutral Political Concern* and *Exclusion of Ideals* both mandate that all religions be treated equally. This allows both support and regulation as long as it is applied equally to all religions. However, because by definition religious discrimination treats some religions unequally, it is not allowed.

Within each of these schools of thought, there exist different trends and subdivisions. In addition, the motivations behind these policies also vary from overt hostility toward religion to a positive attitude toward religion combined with the belief that it is best kept out of politics. Thus, political secularism is not monolithic, and these differences between conceptions of the proper "secular" religion policy can have significant practical applications.

Take, for example, the issue of religion in schools. In the United States, state-supported religion is banned from an absolute SRAS perspective. This means there is no state-supported religious education in public schools. In France, which follows a laicist policy, not only is there no religious education in public schools, since 2004, students may not wear overt religious symbols. From an absolute SRAS perspective, such as that of the United States, one can argue that governments may not take this additional step because it is a government intervention that restricts religion. Many other Western countries use the neutral political concern or exclusion of ideals system and are required simply to treat all religions equally. Thus, countries like Australia and Sweden have religious education in public schools, but it is optional and available in all religions for which there are significant populations in these countries. This policy would violate the conceptions of secularism that dominate both the US and French political systems.

In fact, all of these policies can be considered either secularist or a violation of secular ideals depending on which secularist school of thought one follows. This complicates things in two ways. First, and perhaps most obvious, secularism means different things to different people. Thus, in the conflict between political secularism and religion, there is no unity in what should be the proper secular policy. One practical consequence of this is how one views regulating all religion. As noted earlier, depending on how one views political secularism, it can be mandated, permitted under some circumstances, or banned. Second, some conceptions of secularism allow policies that overlap with supporting religion. As long as this support does not support a single religion, the neutral political concern and exclusion of ideals conceptions allow support for religion.

The second form of complication is that religion is, if anything, less monolithic than political secularism. While the majority of the world's population is Christian, Muslim, Buddhist, or Hindu, there are many more religions in the world, most of which interact with the political. Furthermore, within most traditions there are multiple divisions, denominations, and interpretations, not to mention views within each of the above on how much one's religion should influence political views and actions as well as the content of that influence. This means that there is no agreement on what religious principles might be pursued in the political arena much less to what extent and how they should be pursued. Thus, even within a single tradition, those who seek to get governments to more strongly support religious values are often divided. This also means that the competition between religions is far more complex and occurs at a much more micro-level than can be encompassed Huntington's (1993; 1996) theories.

That being said, Huntington is correct in that another aspect of this complication is the clash between religions. At the same time as religious actors seek to increase state support for their religion, they also often seek to get the state to restrict some or all other religions. I deal with this issue in detail in Chapter 6, which focused on religious discrimination, defined therein as restrictions the religious institutions or practices of minority religions that are not placed on the majority religion. This is the only type of state religion policy disallowed by any conception of political secularism because it, by definition, involves a state intervention in religion that advantages some religions over others through the unequal treatment of some religions. This also makes it among the most unambiguous ways in which a state can express a preference for one or some religions over others.

Religious discrimination is ubiquitous and in 2008 was present in an overwhelming majority of 82.5% of states. This means that this type of interreligious clash is extremely common and is an element of religious politics that is arguably as central as the clash between political secularism and religious political actors described in the competition perspective. This creates a situation in which the secular and religious camps are fighting a battle with each other while at the same time each is engaged in a multiside civil war within their own camp. The result is a complex set of actors engaged in an even more complex multisided set of political maneuvers.

Although this alone can be sufficiently confusing, the next six types of complication create a situation in which it is often unclear how this complex struggle is unfolding. They reveal that states often have mixed motivations for their policies, that the nature of these motivations is often unclear, and that policies are often contradictory.

The third complication is the question of what constitutes supporting religion and what constitutes controlling it. As discussed in detail in Chapters 3 and 4, the same governmental actions that support religion also involve control. To the extent governments supports a religious institution, the institution becomes more vulnerable to government efforts at control. In some cases, these forms of support are specifically designed to create a situation of control.

Also, as demonstrated in Chapter 5, this relationship is even more complex. Many governments that genuinely want to support religion also seek to limit its viability as a political challenger to the government. That is, these governments have a positive attitude toward religion itself but want religion to either support the government or at least be unable to facilitate opposition. More interestingly, there is no government that controls religion without at least in some small way supporting it. Also, one of the most effective forms of control is to support an official version of a religion but also control it, and restrict all expression of that religion outside the auspices of the state-supported network. Thus, while the RAS2 data can measure government actions, the motivation behind these actions is often unclear or mixed.

The fourth form of complexity also involves this tension between supporting religion and limiting the political influence of religion. Most states both simultaneously support and control religion. While since 2003 all states other than South Africa engaged in at least some of the 51 types of support for religion included in the RAS2 data, 82.5% also engaged in at least 1 of the 29 types of regulation, restriction, and control of religion included in the dataset. In fact, the correlation between the two in 2008 was .643 (significance = .000), which means that on average, the states that most strongly support religion are also among those that most forcefully regulate it. This policy of supporting religion, and thus gaining the benefits religious institutions often confer on governments that support them while at the same time regulating these institutions, likely to prevent them from politically challenging the government, is consistent with Gill's (2008) view of a state religion policy designed to benefit the political elite.

The fifth complication is that macro-level policies do not always translate as one would expect into micro-level policies. In Chapters 4, 5, and 6, I compared the macro-level policies set out in the official religion policy variable (discussed in Chapter 3) to the actual policies of states as defined by 51 types of religious support; 29 types of regulation, restriction, and control; and 30 types of religious discrimination. I consistently found that while these specific policies are related to the macro-level policy, that policy was not fully determinative. For example, many states with official religions supported religion less than many states with no official religion. On average, states with official religions supported religion more, but 126 states with no official religions supported religion more than at least some states with official religions.

As demonstrated in Chapter 8, the same is true of constitutional declarations. While constitutional declarations of official religions are strongly correlated with support for religion, again with some exceptions, constitutional declarations of SRAS result in actual SRAS only in a minority of cases. This means that declared policy is a sufficiently poor indicator of actual policy that no serious examination of a state's religion policy can rely exclusively on declared policy and must include an in-depth analysis of all aspects of that policy in practice.

A sixth, and closely related, form of complication is the gap between national and local policies. Although I collected no systematic data on this issue, anecdotal evidence suggests that many local governments have policies that are different from national-level policy. That is, many local governments support the majority religion or restrict minority religions in ways not present in national policy. For example, most, but not all, restrictions on Muslim women wearing head coverings and on mosques in the West are by local rather than national governments.

The seventh form of complication is that not all state religion policies are motivated by religion or religious issues. Regulation and discrimination in particular can have nonreligious motivations. Religious minorities are often also ethnic minorities who are at odds with the government (Fox, 2002; 2004). A common manifestation of this is separatist issues or other political activities the state perceives as a threat. In these cases, religious discrimination may be part of a general pattern of conflict between ethnic groups. The state may see these institutions as potential rallying points for rebels and limit them for this reason. Also, the state may simply repress these institutions and perhaps religious practices as part of a range of repressive conduct intended to punish the minority for its political behavior.

Governments similarly restrict the religious practices and institutions of the majority religion. Governments can often perceive religious institutions and movements as competitors. In many cases, these perceptions are accurate. Nevertheless, accurate or not, this perception of competition can result in repression of religious institutions and often religious activities.

For example, Kyrgyzstan, Tajikistan, Turkmenistan, and Uzbekistan all, with some justification, fear challenges by fundamentalist Muslim groups. As a result, all of them have set up state-supported and -controlled religious institutions and repress any institution outside of state control. This repression does not stop at the institutional level. Kyrgyzstan, Tajikistan, and Turkmenistan also arrest and harass suspected members of fundamentalist groups who are often identified through their religious activities. Thus, in effect, practicing certain interpretations of Islam can result in government repressive activities in these countries. Yet this repression is not primarily motivated by ideology. Rather, it is intended to repress a perceived threat to the government's rule.

Another nonreligious motivation for repression is a state's desire to protect its culture from outside influence. Because religion is an element of culture, religions that are perceived as foreign to the state can suffer from religious discrimination, while the indigenous religions gain special benefits and privileges. The goal in these cases is less to privilege indigenous religions as such but, rather, to ensure that outside influences do not dilute or change a state's traditions and culture.

Conclusions

For example, Hungary recognizes the Catholic, Lutheran, and Reformed Churches as well as Judaism as "historical religions" that receive privileges and benefits given to no other religion. Latvia similarly recognizes and gives benefits and privileges to seven "traditional" religions,[4] as does Lithuania with nine "traditional" religions. In all of these cases, the goal is at least in part to ensure that the state's traditional culture, which includes those religions with a long-standing presence in the state, remains intact.

Even support for religion can have nonreligious motivations. As noted earlier, states can support a religion or a group of religions as part of an effort to support national culture. Also, as Gill (2008) argues, politicians often decide to support religion for purely practical reasons such as the usefulness of religion in maintaining peace and order in society. Gill argues that using religion to accomplish this end is often more effective and less expensive than repression.

A final form of complexity is the concept of religious freedom. As I discussed earlier in this chapter, this concept has multiple and contradictory definitions. It can include the requirement to treat all religions equally, that an individual's or group's rights to practice not be infringed, the freedom from religion, and the right to state support for one's religion. It is not possible for a state to construct a policy that is consistent with all of these definitions, and which of them is the proper one is a subjective issue. Thus, states such as the United States and South Africa, which largely avoid intervening in religion, can be said to have religious freedom because they remain neutral on the issue of religion and do not interfere with the ability to practice religion. At the same time, their unwillingness to be supportive of religion can be considered a violation of religious freedom because, from this perspective, religion requires state support to thrive. Thus, contesting definitions of religious freedom, which are not unrelated to the competition between secular and religious political forces, create an additional source of tension over state religion policy.

As summed up in Figure 9.3, the nature of state religion policy is complicated. It often centers around conflicts between political secularists and religious political actors, as described in the competition perspective, but both of these camps have their divisions. These divisions within camps can result in political conflicts that are potentially more serious than the secular-religious conflict in a state. States often have conflicted policies both supporting and limiting religion at the same time, as well as local governments that engage in policies that are different from those of the national government. Stated policies are not always followed faithfully in practice. Finally, it is often unclear whether a policy is intended to support or restrict religion or even whether the policy has a religious motivation at all.

This complexity is endemic to state religion policy and states with noncomplex policies are few and far in between. Yet, even given this complexity, the results clearly support the basic finding that states regularly become involved in

---

[4] 1995 Latvian Law on Religious Organizations, as amended though 2000.

religion and that this involvement has been increasing. Whatever the complexities found in these policies and the motivations behind them, it is clear that religion remains an important issue over which governments devote significant time and resources.

Parts Making a Whole

Nineteenth-century neo-impressionist George Seurat is known for a painting style, known as pointillism, in which he used nothing but little dots to create a large picture, particularly in his most famous work *A Sunday Afternoon on the Island of La Grande Jatte*. If you look closely at the painting, all you can see are the dots. When you move away and look at the entire painting a detailed picture emerges. Yet it is the many dots that give the painting its quality.

While the focus in this chapter is on the bigger picture, it is important not to forget that this picture is made of many individual observations. In fact, setting aside the variables discussed in Chapters 7 and 8, the 110 specific religion policies, plus the official religion policy variable, were coded for 177 countries for a period of 19 years. Taking into account that not all countries were included for all years, usually because of the nonexistence of the state or a viable government in a given year, the RAS2 dataset includes 367,410 individual observations.

One of the goals of this study is to create a comprehensive lexicon of all of the ways states can become involved in religion. The result has produced a list of 51 types of support for religion, 29 ways states regulate all religions or the majority religion, and 30 types of religious discrimination – which again is defined as limitations on the religious institutions or practices of minority religions that are not placed on the majority religion – as well as a variable for official government policy. The RAS project has been in existence since 2000. Through thousands of hours of work, which includes a minimum of dozens of hours devoted to each of the 177 countries in the study, the project has identified and codified all of the ways states commonly deal with religion.[5] Thus, this list includes categories for all ways that multiple states engage religion as well as the "other" categories designed to include the many ways that some states uniquely engage religion.

This means that, at least for the 1990 to 2008 period, we arguably have all the dots to make a painting of the landscape of state religion policy. That is, the picture that emerges from all of these specific pieces of information is a comprehensive and accurate one. It is not based on selecting some examples and ignoring others. Nor is it based on looking at only some aspects of state religion policy at the expense of others. Hence, this methodology gives this study a level of validity and a more solid foundation than has, to my knowledge, ever been

---

[5] I estimate that over the course of the project, research assistants have engaged in approximately 14,000 hours of data collection research.

achieved by previous studies. The trends I identify are real and are based on all possible policies in all relevant states.

These many individual observations come together to reveal the trends I discuss in this chapter as well as all the complexities. Each datum is important in and of itself, but arguably the relationship between these 367,410 individual observations creates a result that is greater than the sum of its parts.

The Consequences of State Religion Policy

While this study focuses on describing, understanding, and explaining state religion policy around the world, it is important to briefly note that this policy area has important political and social consequences. The competition perspective is based explicitly on the fact that state religion policy is a topic of competition and even conflict. This conflict often becomes violent when forces that do not get their way are unwilling to accept the outcome of more peaceful political processes (Fox, 2013). Some policies, in and of themselves, create the potential for conflict. For example, Grim and Finke (2011: 2–3), among others, argue that religious persecution is a potent instigator of conflict. That being said, religion is not only a cause of conflict but also a potential cause of stability. Gill (2008) argues that politicians often support religion precisely because widely popular religions can increase political stability and decrease the costs of ruling.

A large sociological literature argues that supporting a religious monopoly results in a less religious population for three basic reasons. First, when there is less freedom to choose between religions, people are less likely to find a religion that suits them and, accordingly, refrain from religious practice. Even when a government does not repress minority religions, supporting a national religion makes it less costly to congregants because it is already supported by the government. In contrast, members of minority religions must support their religious institutions out of their own pockets. These financial costs may discourage potential members. Second, when a state supports a religion, clergy are often more beholden to the state for their jobs than to their congregants. This gives them less incentive to serve their congregants than someone who is employed by and accountable to the congregants. Thus, privately supported religions provide a better service and are more likely to attract congregants. Third, people resent being told what to do. State enforcement of religion can cause resentment against it (Finke & Iannaccone, 1993; Fox & Tabory, 2008; Iannaccone, 1995; McCleary & Barro, 2006; Stark & Finke, 2000; Stark & Iannaccone, 1994).

Finally, it is important not to forget that state religion policy can substantially influence day-to-day lives. Religious freedom is felt most in its absence. State policies that are hostile to religion and those that restrict religious minorities can have a profound influence on the lives of people who wish to observe any religion or the wrong religion, depending on the specific state policy in question. Similarly states that enforce a religion can negatively influence the lives of those who do not wish to follow that religion or any religion at all. Finally, as noted earlier, supporting a state religion can significantly influence the quality of that religion and its institutions.

Some Final Thoughts

This book focuses on only one element of religion's intersection with society and politics – state religion policy. There are certainly other relevant and important aspects of religion worthy of study, but given the enormity of my chosen task, I feel justified in restricting my efforts to this section of the religious economy. While the results are limited to this select topic, they have wider implications.

This study has produced three central and interrelated results. First, the governments of nearly every state in the world are involved in religion. Neutrality is the exception and is arguably the policy choice that is most difficult to maintain. Second, states have been becoming more involved in religion. Whether this involvement is to support religion or to regulate, restrict, and control it, this is evidence of religion's continuing political relevance. Third, while state religion policy is complex and influenced by multiple factors, one of the most significant driving forces in today's religious policy landscape is the clash between the advocates of political secularism and religious political actors, which I describe in the secular-religious competition perspective.

An important implication of this increasing ubiquity and centrality of religion to politics is that it likely reflects a similar importance of religion in other sections of the religious economy. The presence of religious political actors pressuring governments to more strongly support religion and sometimes repress other religious groups demonstrates both that there are active religious political actors in most countries and that at least a segment of the population is both religious and considers religion politically relevant.

These constant pressures help to explain why state religion policy is in a state of flux. While this study focuses on a brief, 19-year period, the evidence indicates that this has been the case for centuries, and it is likely that this will remain the case for the foreseeable future. Neither political secularism nor religion will be disappearing any time soon. Each of these sets of ideologies has a large, if divided, base of constituents who are highly motivated to shape state policy in the direction of their choosing.

The competition between, as well as within, these camps has been present for centuries and will likely remain a central element of politics for even longer. While each side will have its victories and it is impossible to predict the tides of this competition in the future, it is unlikely that either side will succeed in exterminating the other, although it is likely both sides will continue to evolve. Political secularism at its highest point of influence did not succeed in delivering a killing blow to religion. For example, religion is now thriving in the former

Soviet bloc where for decades – in some cases as many as seven decades – Communist governments sought to stamp out religion. Toward the end of the Cold War era, many thought that they had succeeded, but history has proven this supposition wrong. It is similarly unlikely that any religion or combination of religions will succeed in destroying secularism.

Thus, for the foreseeable future, the clash between religion and political secularism, as described in the secular-religious competition perspective, will remain a fixture of the political landscape, as will likely clashes between religions and disagreements among political secularists. State religion policies will continue to evolve. There will likely be periods when religion is seen to have the upper hand and those in which secularism is gaining on religion. However, these will likely be short-term rises and ebbs in the tide of a long-term competition. Currently, religion has evolved to meet the challenges of secularism and is gaining, at least within the political realm. I expect that in time secularists, including political secularists, will themselves evolve more effective responses. When this happens, I suspect many may revive the argument that this decline in religious influence is permanent and inevitable. However, it is more likely that this will be just one more shift in the tides of a competition that will continue indefinitely.

Appendix

Data Collection and Reliability

This appendix discusses the methodology for the construction of the three central variables in this study – religious support, discrimination, and regulation. It then evaluates their validity. The content of these variables is discussed in detail in Chapters 4, 5, and 6.[1]

Data Collection Procedures

All 175 countries that were included in Round 1 of the Religion and State Project (RAS1) are included in Round 2 (RAS2). Timor and Montenegro were added because they had recently gained independence, so 177 countries were included in RAS2.[2]

In RAS2, as was the case in RAS1, each country was assigned to a research assistant (RA), who wrote a report based on the country. These reports cover 2003–2008 and are meant to supplement and update the RAS1 reports, which cover 1990–2002. These reports used the following sources:

- Primary sources such as constitutions and the texts of legislation and government policy papers regarding religion. In cases in which laws were not available in a language that the RA understood, Google Translate was used. A sampling of constitutions and laws that were available both in translation and in the original language were tested to see whether the Google Translate results matched the human translation. Although the texts were rarely identical, the Google Translate texts did not result in any inaccuracies that would have influenced the codings.

---
[1] This appendix is an edited and abridged version of Fox (2011c). For a full discussion of RAS1 including the construction of the variables and a comparison with other datasets, see Fox (2008).
[2] This section is based on the RAS2 codebook, which is available online at the Religion and State project webpage: www.religionandstate.org.

- News articles, mostly from a search of the Lexis-Nexis database but also obtained from other sources.
- Academic resources such as journal articles and books.
- Government and intergovernmental organization reports such as the US State Department International Religious Freedom (IRF) reports and the United Nations Abortion Policies reports, among others.
- Reports by nongovernmental advocacy groups and academic organizations such as Human Rights without Frontiers and Amnesty International, among many others.

As project director, I vetted all RAS2 reports and often required several rounds of revisions. Each report used all available sources. While sources were more common for some countries than others, there was sufficient information to code all cases. In general, even among undeveloped peripheral countries, when general reports such as the US State Department IRF reports indicated that there was significant religious discrimination, regulation, or legislation, there tended to be significant amounts of information in other primary, academic, media, and advocacy group sources. The research that was involved in writing the reports inadvertently revealed that religion is a sufficiently important topic that various organizations devote considerable resources to documenting governments that either support or restrict religion anywhere in the world. Thus, there do not seem to be any informational backwaters when states either restrict or strongly support religion.

While this additional information provides considerable advantages over relying on a single source, some of the sources, such as nongovernmental organizations' human rights reports and press coverage, are published only sporadically. This raises the issue of whether the information that is available is partially determined by international attention. Although it is impossible to fully discount this issue, the advantages of multiple sources outweigh relying on a single source that consistently covers nearly all countries, such as the US State Department IRF reports.[3] This is true for several reasons.

First, as has already been noted, additional sources brought in additional in-formation that increases the accuracy of the data. I argue that this alone is sufficient to justify the practice.

Second, multiple sources allow for cross-checking for accuracy. There was a high level of consistency of information between sources and few cases of contradicting sources. In cases of contradicting sources, the RAs sought additional sources and performed a reliability assessment of all of the sources in question.

Third, as was noted earlier, international attention seems to be highly correlated with the presence of government activity in the field of religion. In cases in which the general sources (those that prepared a report on all countries

---

[3] The one country that is glaringly absent from the US State Department reports is the United States itself.

Appendix

regardless of their policy) indicated large amounts of religious discrimination, regulation, and/or legislation, there tended to be considerably more information in the other sources than there was when the general sources indicated lower levels of religious legislation, discrimination, and regulation. That is, in cases that the general sources showed to be important, researchers were more likely to find more academic, media, and advocacy group sources. This demonstrates both a consistency in coverage among sources and that international attention tends to be attracted when governments take codable actions. This was true even of countries that would otherwise be considered peripheral and less likely to attract media and nongovernmental organizational attention. In other words, the squeaky wheels seem to be getting the grease. Because the project is seeking out squeaky wheels, this is arguably an advantage. The general sources provided a good description of a state's policy, but in most cases, the additional sources provided details that were not included in the general sources.

Fourth, the legitimacy of any single source can be challenged. This is the case with the US State Department IRF reports. These reports prove to be accurate when tested (Grim & Wike, 2010). My evaluation of the IRF reports confirms this. I found almost no instances of inaccurate information. The few instances of inaccuracies involved failures to note a change in policy in a timely manner; that is, a government began or stopped taking some action, but the reports, which are produced yearly, failed to notice immediately. This occurred rarely, and the change was generally noted in a later report. I found no other instances of information that was demonstrably incorrect.

It is important to emphasize that the RAS project went over every word of every IRF report from 1999 (the year of the first report) onward. Given the wide range of sources we used for every case, in essence every IRF report was checked for accuracy. Although the original intention of the RAS project was not to assess the accuracy of each and every IRF report, in practice the project did exactly this. While the IRF reports are not perfect, they have a high standard of accuracy that, in my assessment, despite some limitations I note next, meets or exceeds the standards applied to refereed academic publications.

Nevertheless, the connection of the IRF reports to a political entity leaves them open to attack on the grounds of bias. Even if this type of criticism is unjustified, it can undermine the acceptance of a data collection within the academic community. I have experienced this and found that even when I explain why I believe the information in the IRF reports to be accurate, a significant portion of the academic community seems unwilling to accept any evidence, no matter how convincing, that any branch of the US government can produce an unbiased report. Again, I believe, on the basis of my comparison between the IRF reports and other sources, that the reports meet high standards of accuracy and can provide the basis for a data collection, even one that is based solely on these reports. However, the legitimacy issue creates a situation in which any research that is based solely on these reports is unlikely to be accepted by a significant portion of the academic community. Even if this bias is not based on the facts, it is a significant drawback for any dataset.

Many of the other sources can be similarly criticized for being produced by organizations or individuals that have an agenda. Again, by this I mean that it is possible to make such an accusation, not that the accusations are necessarily justified. Nevertheless, such criticisms can gain acceptance among at least a portion of the academic community even if they are not accurate. Thus, the issue in this case can often be one of perception rather than fact. Using multiple sources effectively neutralizes this issue by showing agreement among different sources that have no common agenda.

Fifth, a significant problem with the US State Department IRF reports was missing or incomplete information. For example, in many cases, the IRF reports would note the presence of a law on religion and some general attributes of that law. In these cases, more often than not, a reading of the actual law provided more information that influenced the coding but was not included in the IRF report. This is true of many activities that are reported in the IRF reports: the reports provided a basic summary of an event, policy, action, or law, and other sources provided additional details that influenced codings. Because of this, when preparing the RAS2 reports, RAs were often instructed to seek out additional details of events that were reported in the IRF reports and copies of laws that were mentioned in the IRF reports. Also, in many cases, the IRF reports simply missed significant activities. In most cases, these were low-level (with respect to the codings) activities in peripheral regions of a country. Thus, while I found no instances of incorrect information in the reports, there were many instances of incomplete information.

This does not appear to reflect any ideological or political bias; rather, in my estimation, it is the result of less-than-perfect research by the IRF reports' authors. However, this bias is problematic in that it is not a consistent one. That is, there is no standard threshold across the country reports such that events or details that do not meet the threshold for importance are not included. Rather, some reports appear to have been the result of more industrious work. When compared with other sources, the information in some IRF reports is more complete than that in others. To put it bluntly, if the RAS researchers using open sources can find information, there is no reason why someone with the resources available to the US State Department cannot find the same information.

This means that while the information in the reports is almost never inaccurate, the reports are inconsistent in their thoroughness. Nevertheless, in my assessment, these issues, although worthy of note, are not sufficient to undermine the validity of studies that rely on the US State Department reports. Even with their imperfections, they are high-quality pieces of research and are, in my estimation, the most complete, detailed, and accurate individual source available if one wants to use a single source for research on government religion policy. This type of inconsistency is present in most of the sources used by the RAS project that cover multiple states and demonstrates that using multiple sources is not only the best way to get the most complete information possible, it is the only way.[4]

The RAS2 report, along with the RAS1 report (which was collected using the same methodology), provided the basis for filling out the code sheets. I reviewed all code sheets to ensure that the code sheets were filled out accurately and that all RAs were using the same interpretation of the code sheet. No matter how specifically worded, items on the code sheet can be subject to multiple interpretations. This policy of a single individual reviewing all code sheets is, among other things, intended to reduce the influence of differing interpretations on the codings. Differences between countries in codings need to be based on real differences rather than on differences in interpretations of similar actions by different coders. Overall, 14 RAs worked on the project, and they coded between 1 and 42 cases each.

This system had an additional advantage. In many cases, I questioned specific codings and received an illuminating reply from the RA. That is, the RA would give an answer that revealed information that was not clear in the report. In these cases, the RA was instructed to clarify the report; the result was a more accurate report. This also emphasizes the reason behind the project policy that the RA who wrote the report is the one to fill out the code sheet. The one who invested tens of hours in researching a case will have more insight into the details of the case than will someone who only reads the report.

Data Reliability

All cases were coded a second time by a backup coder. The backup coders were two senior RAs on the project, one senior coder from RAS1 and a colleague associated with the project. These coders used the RAS1 and RAS2 reports as the basis for filling out the code sheets. I did not review the backup code sheets because I had taken part in the primary codings. All of the senior coders were responsible for collecting the primary data on at least 25 cases for either RAS1 or RAS2, which gave them sufficient experience and knowledge of the coding scheme to code cases unsupervised. The colleague, Yasemin Akbaba, has been involved in aspects of the RAS project and its coding for several years. Comparing backup codings to the primary codings is a standard method for assessing data reliability, known as intercoder reliability. The correlations between the primary and backup codings are presented in Table A.1.

All of the correlations are 0.973 and higher. Generally, a score of 0.800 is acceptable, and a score above 0.900 is preferable. These results clearly meet this standard.

---

[4] My assessment of the US State Department reports is based on a comparison with other sources, discussions with colleagues, and my experiences with referee reports that touch on the issue. For another perspective and a discussion of the genesis of the US State Department IRF reports as well as a review of the literature surrounding it, see Moore (2011).

TABLE A.1. *Intercoder Reliability Tests*

Year	Correlations between Primary and Backup Codings for:		
	Religious Discrimination	Religious Regulation	Religious Legislation
1990	.986	.989	.986
1991	.986	.977	.987
1992	.985	.973	.987
1993	.983	.973	.988
1994	.984	.973	.988
1995	.983	.973	.988
1996	.982	.973	.989
1997	.982	.973	.989
1998	.982	.974	.989
1999	.983	.975	.989
2000	.985	.975	.990
2001	.986	.982	.990
2002	.988	.983	.980
2003	.988	.983	.982
2004	.988	.984	.990
2005	.987	.984	.990
2006	.988	.980	.990
2007	.988	.980	.990
2008	.988	.976	.989

All correlations in the table have a significance of < .001.

For an extra reliability test, I correlated the RAS2 variables with relevant previous collections that had variables for most or all states in RAS2. First, I correlated the religious discrimination variable – in this case, only for 2005 rather than the average score for 1990 to 2008 – with the Grim and Finke variable for 2005, which is the most recent available for download.[5] They correlate at 0.806 for the 174 overlapping cases. This demonstrates that the variable is strongly related to another variable on the same topic but also sufficiently different to support the assertion that the RAS2 variables add value.

Second, I correlated the RAS2 variables for 2002 with the RAS1 variables for 2002. I selected 2002 because this is the most recent year available in RAS1. The correlations for religious discrimination, regulation, and legislation are 0.914, 0.788, and 0.855, respectively. While these correlations are high, they demonstrate that RAS1 and RAS2 are by no means identical. This is an optimal result because it demonstrates both that the RAS1 and RAS2 indexes

---

[5] Downloaded on May 27, 2011, from the Association of Religious Data Archives at www.thearda.com/Archive/Files/Descriptions/IRFAGG.asp.

Appendix

are measuring the same thing and that the RAS2 indexes are sufficiently different to suggest that adding more measures to an index increases its accuracy. That the correlations are lowest for the religious regulation index, which is the only one of the three indexes whose items more than doubled, supports this argument.

Building the Indexes

There are essentially three ways to create an index based on these component variables. The first is to simply add them, as is the methodology for both the RAS1 and RAS2 datasets. Most similar projects use the same methodology, so it is clear that additive indexes are currently the accepted standard in the field. The other methods involve weighting each component. The argument for weighting each component is to take into account that some items on the lists of component variables are simply more important or have a larger impact than others. How much impact they have can be determined by one of two methodologies, which constitute the second and third ways to create an index.

The second method uses factor analysis or some other statistical technique to weight the variables. For example, Grim and Finke (2006) used statistical methodology to build alternative versions of their indexes and found the results to be nearly identical to their additive indexes. The third method uses expert assessments; that is, experts on the issue are asked to use their expertise to weight each item in the index. In a previous discussion of the RAS1 indexes, I argued that this is impractical because

> there is no agreement as to which variables should be singled out in this manner. In other words when I present this data to colleagues, I usually get suggestions [to weight variables]... but the... variable I am asked to single out is rarely the same. Based on this I conclude that it is not feasible to achieve agreement over which of the RAS[1] variables should be weighted... and that giving all of them equal weight is likely the most transparent and least controversial option available. (Fox, 2008: 56)

If there is truly no agreement among experts, then to weight variables on this basis would be to weight them on the basis of personal bias. This would clearly be unacceptable.

Nevertheless, arguments in favor of both types of weighting are present in the literature to a small extent (e.g., Pinkus & Meyer, 2008; Spickard, 2010). Discussions with the creators of several other datasets revealed that such comments are also often raised by reviewers when manuscripts based on the datasets are submitted for publication. Accordingly, in this section, I compare two weighted versions of each index to indexes that were created by simply adding the component variables to form an index (the unweighted index). The first weighted index is based on expert assessment; the second is based on factor analysis.

All three indexes that were used for the analysis in this study are based on average scores for 1990–2008. Because the codings differed from year to year, this methodology allows for an assessment of averages for this entire period that arguably represents the true presence and impact of each component variable over time better than would data for any single year. This is especially important for the factor analysis because changes in the codings can result in changes in the weightings. The Cronbach's scores for the discrimination, regulation, and legislation unweighted indexes are 0.993, 0.881, and 0.903, respectively. Because a score above 0.700 is considered to demonstrate a substantial relationship between variables, this is sufficiently high that there is no methodological reason not to combine the variables included in the indexes.

The Expert Weighting Index

To create the expert weighting index, I asked approximately 40 colleagues to help me weight the variables, and I received full responses from 17. These colleagues are all political scientists or sociologists with expertise and a publishing record in religion. Each was asked to weight the components of each index on the basis of the following instructions:

A policy with a high importance/impact/severity/significance is defined as one which would meet one or both of the following criteria (a) the presence of such a policy demonstrates a stronger connection between the government and religion than do most of the other policies in the same category; (b) the policy with have a significantly greater influence on people's lives than most other policies in the same category.

The importance/impact/severity/significance of policies should be compared only to others in the same category of the three categories: restrictions on minorities, regulation of all religions or the majority religion, and religious legislation.

In each section I ask you to mark all policies which are clearly above average in importance/impact/severity/significance... and all those which are clearly below average in importance/impact/severity/significance.... I ask you to limit these codings to only the most clearly below and above average codings and in any case no more than 15% of any category as above average and 15% as below average. For the first two categories (restrictions on minorities and regulation of all groups or the majority group), 15% is 5 items, and for the last category (religious legislation) 15% is 8. It is perfectly acceptable to mark less than 15% as above or below average, the 15% is simply an upper limit.

I weighted the results as follows: Variables that were coded as above average were given a score of 1.5; variables that were coded as average were given a score of 1.0; and variables that were coded as below average were given a score of 0.5. I averaged all 17 scores to create a weighting based on the combined expertise of the experts who participated in the weighting process. The number of experts who coded each component as above or below average and the final expert weighting are presented in Tables A.2, A.3, and A.4.

Before the expert-weighted indexes are compared with the unweighted indexes, the results of the expert codings, in and of themselves, validate my argument that there is no agreement among experts (Fox, 2008: 56). All but 3 of the 30 components of the religious discrimination index were weighted by at least one expert, and all but five were weighted by two or more experts. In

TABLE A.2. *Factor and Expert Weightings for Religious Discrimination Components*

	Expert Weighting			Factor Weighting
Component Variable	Weight	Low	High	
Restrictions on public observance of religious services, festivals and/or holidays, including the Sabbath	1.118	0	4	.817
Restrictions on the private observance of religious services, festivals and/or holidays, including the Sabbath	1.294	0	9	.612
Restrictions on building, leasing, repairing, and/or maintaining places of worship	1.000	1	1	.726
Restrictions on access to existing places or worship	1.088	0	3	.580
Forced observance of religious laws of another group	1.382	0	13	.464
Restrictions on formal religious organizations	0.971	1	0	.558
Restrictions on the running of religious schools and/or religious education in general	0.912	2	5	.641
Restrictions on the ability to make and/or obtain materials necessary for religious rites, customs, and/or ceremonies	1.000	0	0	.529
Mandatory education in the majority religion	1.176	1	7	.524
Arrest/detention/official harassment of religious figures, officials, and/or members of religious parties for activities other than proselytizing	1.382	0	13	.749
State surveillance of minority religious activities not placed on the activities of the majority	1.000	0	0	.586
Restrictions on the ability to write, publish, or disseminate religious publications	1.118	0	2	.781
Restrictions on the ability to import religious publications	0.853	5	0	.782
Restrictions on access to religious publications for personal use	1.029	1	2	.600
Restrictions on the observance religious laws concerning personal status, including marriage, divorce, and burial	1.000	2	1	.556
Restrictions on wearing of religious symbols/clothing; includes presence/absence of facial hair but not weapons or face covering	0.941	3	1	.542

(*continued*)

TABLE A.2 (continued)

Component Variable	Expert Weighting				Factor Weighting
	Weight	Low	High		
Restrictions on the ordination of and/or access to clergy	0.941	2	0		.544
Restrictions on conversion to minority religions	1.000	1	1		.629
Forced renunciation of faith by recent converts to minority religions	1.118	0	3		.515
Forced conversions of people who were never members of the majority religion	1.176	0	6		.323
Efforts or campaigns to convert members of minority religions to the majority religion which fall short of using force	1.000	0	0		.609
Restrictions on proselytizing by permanent residents of state to members of the majority religion	1.000	2	2		.786
Restrictions on proselytizing by permanent residents of state to members of minority religions	1.000	1	1		.524
Restrictions on proselytizing by foreign clergy or missionaries.	0.824	5	0		.774
Requirement for minority religions (as opposed to all religions) to register in order to be legal or receive special tax status	0.971	4	2		.238
Custody of children granted to members of majority group solely or in part on the basis of religious affiliation or beliefs	1.029	0	1		.546
Restricted access of minority clergy to hospitals/jails/military bases/other places in comparison to chaplains of the majority religion	0.941	2	0		.459
There is a legal provision or policy of declaring some minority religions dangerous or extremist sects	1.029	1	2		.527
Anti-religious propaganda in official or semi-official government publications	1.059	0	2		.595
Restrictions on other types of observance of religious law; specify:	0.971	1	0		.695

TABLE A.3. *Factor and Expert Weightings for Religious Regulation Components*

Component Variable	Expert Weighting				Factor Weighting
	Weight	Low	High		
Restrictions on religious political parties	1.000	2	2		.299
Restrictions on trade associations or other civil associations being affiliated with a religion	0.941	2	0		.293
Restrictions on clergy holding political office	0.912	3	0		.355
Arrest, continued detention, or severe official harassment of religious figures, officials, and/or members of religious parties	1.324	0	11		.715
Government restricts/harasses members of majority religion who operate outside of the state sponsored/recognized ecclesiastical framework	1.118	0	4		.613
Restrictions on formal religious organizations other than political parties	1.000	1	1		.747
Restrictions on the public observance of religious practices, including religious holidays and the Sabbath	1.118	0	4		.661
Restrictions on religious activities outside of recognized religious facilities	1.000	0	0		.670
Restrictions on public religious speech	1.118	1	5		.781
Restrictions or monitoring of sermons by clergy	1.029	1	2		.660
Restrictions on in public political speech or propaganda or on political activity by clergy/religious organizations	0.971	1	0		.457
Restrictions on religious-based hate speech	0.882	4	0		-.045
Restrictions on access to places of worship	1.088	1	3		.718
Restrictions on the publication or dissemination of written religious material	1.000	1	1		.773
People are arrested for religious activities	1.294	0	10		.707
Restrictions on religious public gatherings that are not placed on other types of public gathering	1.059	0	2		.484

(*continued*)

TABLE A.3 (continued)

Component Variable	Expert Weighting			Factor Weighting
	Weight	Low	High	
Restrictions on the public display by private persons/organizations of religious symbols, including dress, presence/absence of facial hair, etc.	1.088	0	2	.615
Restrictions on or regulation of religious education in public schools (represents direct government control, not bans on religious education)	0.941	3	1	.410
Restrictions on or regulation of religious education outside of public schools or general government control of religious education	1.029	1	2	.702
Restrictions on or regulation of religious education at the university level	0.912	4	1	.619
Foreign religious organizations are required to have a local sponsor or affiliation	0.824	6	0	.227
Heads of religious organizations (e.g., bishops) must be citizens of the state	0.824	5	0	.313
All practicing clergy must be citizens of the state	0.853	5	0	.303
The government appoints, or must approve, clerical appointments or somehow takes part in the appointment process	1.147	0	5	.651
Other than appointments, the government legislates/officially influences internal workings/organization of religious institutions/organizations	1.088	0	3	.631
Laws governing the state religion are passed by the government or need the government's approval before being put into effect	0.971	3	1	.399
State ownership of some religious property or buildings	0.882	5	1	.416
Conscientious objectors to military service are not given other options for national service and are prosecuted	1.059	1	3	.271
Other religious restrictions; specify:	1.000	0	0	.376

TABLE A.4A. *Factor and Expert Weightings for Religious Legislation Components*

Component Variable	Expert Weighting				Factor Weighting
	Weight	Low	High		
Dietary laws (restrictions on the production, import, selling, or consumption of specific foods)	1.029	1	2		.690
Restrictions or prohibitions on the sale of alcoholic beverages	1.000	1	2		.854
Personal status defined by religion or clergy (i.e., marriage, divorce, and/or burial can only occur under religious auspices)	1.118	0	4		.729
Marriages performed by clergy of at least some religions are given automatic civil recognition, even in the absence of a state license	1.029	1	2		.224
Restrictions on interfaith marriages (includes when marriages are performed only by clergy which effectively restricts interfaith marriages)	1.176	0	6		.833
Laws of inheritance defined by religion	1.000	1	1		.789
Religious precepts used to define/set punishment for crimes (refers general criminal acts such as theft, rape, murder, etc.)	1.118	0	3		.702
The charging of interest is illegal or significantly restricted	1.029	0	1		.457
Women may not go out in public unescorted	1.294	0	9		.439
Restrictions on the public dress of women other than the common restrictions on public nudity (required dress, not banning of religious dress)	1.088	0	3		.623
General restrictions on public dress or appearance other than those included in the above category (this category is only for required behavior)	1.000	1	1		.507
Restrictions on intimate interactions between unmarried heterosexual couples	1.088	0	3		.706
Laws that specifically make it illegal to be a homosexual or engage in homosexual intimate interactions	1.206	0	7		.349
Restrictions on conversions away from the dominant religion	1.235	0	8		.758

(*continued*)

TABLE A.4A (continued)

Component Variable	Expert Weighting			Factor Weighting
	Weight	Low	High	
Blasphemy laws, or any other restriction on speech about majority religion or religious figures	1.029	1	2	.706
Blasphemy laws protecting minority religions or religious figures	0.941	3	1	.305
Censorship of press or other publications on grounds of being antireligious	1.088	0	3	.809
Significant restrictions on public music or dancing other than the usual zoning restrictions	0.971	1	0	.578
Mandatory closing of some or all businesses during religious holidays including the Sabbath or its equivalent	0.971	2	1	.361
Other restrictions on activities during religious holidays including the Sabbath or its equivalent ("blue laws"); specify	0.912	3	0	.493
Religious education is present in public schools	0.882	5	1	.340
Presence of official prayer sessions in public schools	1.029	0	1	.132
Government funding of religious primary or secondary schools or religious educational programs in nonpublic schools	0.941	2	0	.097
Government funding of seminary schools	0.971	1	0	.384
Government funding of religious education in colleges or universities	0.912	4	1	.368
Public schools are segregated by religion or separate public schools exist for members of some religions	1.029	0	1	.261
Government funding of religious charitable organizations including hospitals.	0.941	2	0	.174
Government collects taxes on behalf of religious organizations (religious taxes)	1.059	0	2	.290

TABLE A.4B. *Factor and Expert Weightings for Religious Legislation Components (Continued)*

	Expert Weighting			Factor Weighting
Component Variable	Weight	Low	High	
Official government positions, salaries or other funding for clergy other than salaries for teachers of religious courses	0.971	1	0	.336
Direct general grants to religious organizations (this does not include the religious taxes or religious charitable organization categories above)	1.000	1	1	.157
Funding for building, maintaining, or repairing religious sites	0.912	3	0	.335
Free air time on television or radio provided to religious organizations on government channels or by government decree	0.912	3	0	.176
Funding or other government support for religious pilgrimages such as the Hajj	1.000	0	0	.421
Funding for religious organizations or activities other than those listed above; specify:	1.000	0	0	-.014
Some religious leaders are given diplomatic status, diplomatic passports, or immunity from prosecution by virtue of their religious office	0.971	1	0	-.094
Presence of an official government ministry or department dealing with religious affairs	0.971	2	1	.361
Presence of a police force or other government agency that exists solely to enforce religious laws	1.176	0	6	.568
Certain government officials are also given an official position in the state church by virtue of their political office	1.000	0	0	.333
Certain religious officials become government officials by virtue of their religious position (i.e., as in Iran)	1.088	0	3	.292

(continued)

TABLE A.4B (continued)

Component Variable	Expert Weighting			Factor Weighting
	Weight	Low	High	
Some/all government officials must meet religious requirements to hold office (excludes religious positions such as head of state church)	1.118	0	4	.665
Presence of religious courts that have jurisdiction over matters of family law and inheritance	1.147	0	5	.651
Presence of religious courts that have jurisdiction over some matters of law other than family law and matters of inheritance	1.029	0	1	.595
Female testimony in government court is given less weight than male testimony	1.118	0	4	.803
Seats in legislative branch and/or cabinet are by law or custom granted, at least in part, along religious lines	1.000	0	0	.307
Prohibitive restrictions on abortion	1.088	2	5	.265
Restrictions on access to birth control	1.088	1	4	.235
The presence of religious symbols on the state's flag	0.941	2	0	.382
Religion listed on state identity cards or other government documents that most citizens must possess or fill out	1.000	1	1	.572
A registration process for religious organizations exists that is different from the registration process for other nonprofit organizations	0.971	1	0	-.301
Restrictions on women other than those listed above (i.e., restrictions on education or jobs that they can hold)	1.029	0	1	.705
Other religious prohibitions or practices that are mandatory; specify:	1.000	0	0	.400

TABLE A.5. *Correlations between Standard and Weighted Variables for Average Scores 1990* to 2008*

	Index		
Type of Index Correlated	Religious Discrimination	Religious Regulation	Religious Legislation
Equal and expert weighted	.999	.999	.999
Equal and factor weighted	.997	.986	.968
Expert and factor weighted	.997	.990	.976

* In cases in which the country was not coded for 1990, the first available year was used. All correlations in the table have a significance (p value) of less than .001.

addition, 11 components (36.7%) were coded as above average and as below average by different experts. The same is generally true for the other indexes. On the religious regulation index, all but 1 of 29 items were weighted by two or more experts, and 11 components (37.9%) were coded as above average and below average by different experts. Similarly, on the religious legislation index, all but 5 of 51 components were weighted by at least one expert, and all but 10 were weighted by at least two experts, 15 (29.4%) being weighted in both directions. So overall, nearly all of the components were weighted by at least one expert, and about one-third of them had experts weighting them in both directions.

This can be described as a relatively catastrophic failure of experts to agree. Accordingly, it is no surprise that the correlations between the unweighted indexes and the expert weighted indexes, presented in Table A.5, are very high, at 0.999 for all three indexes. The weighted indexes were calculated by multiplying the score for each component by the expert weighting for this component, and the results were added. Thus, despite the fact that there are significant differences in some of the weightings, the expert-weighted indexes are mathematically nearly identical to the unweighted indexes.

The Factor-Weighted Indexes

The factor-weighted indexes are presented in Tables A.2, A.3, and A.4. The correlations between these indexes and the unweighted indexes, shown in Table A.5, are high, although not as high as is the case with the expert-weighted index. Nevertheless, these correlations of 0.997, 0.986, and 0.968 for discrimination, regulation, and legislation, respectively, are more than sufficiently high to dispel the argument that mathematical weighting will create an index that is substantially different from the unweighted index. In fact, the difference between these two indexes is about the same as the agreement between coders in the intercoder reliability tests presented earlier.

In addition, the correlations between the expert-weighted and factor-weighted indexes are high. In fact, the three indexes – the unweighted, expert-weighted, and factor-weighted indexes – are so statistically similar as to be interchangeable. It would be unlikely that any statistical tests using these indexes as either independent or dependent variables would be substantially different depending on which weighting scheme was used. This supports my long-standing argument that the simpler and more transparent unweighted additive indexes are preferable (Fox, 2008: 56).

It is interesting to note that Grim and Finke (2006), when performing similar tests on their variables, obtained similar results. Despite using structural equation models and confirmatory factor analysis, they found little difference between the unweighted additive index and the indexes that were constructed by using statistically based weighting. This analysis is the only one of which I am aware, other than the one presented here, that compares statistical weighting schemes to additive indexes of religion. Their analysis, combined with the results from this study, seriously undermines the argument that indexes of religious factors should be weighted.

Conclusions

Overall, this evidence supports the validity of the data. Grim and Finke (2006: 15), in evaluating their own indexes, cite three methods for evaluating the data. The first is the characteristics of the judges. They argue that intercoder reliability of 0.9 or higher and the formal evaluation process of their codings meets this standard. The RAS2 coders meet and exceed this standard.

Grim and Finke's second method is evaluating the information available to the judges. The RAS2 project has invested between 10 and 70 hours collecting information for each of the 177 countries included in the dataset, for a total of approximately 8,000 hours of RA time as well as hundreds of hours of my time devoted to collecting and coding information. This time investment does not include the similar amount of time that was invested in the RAS1 reports, which were also used as a basis for the codings. As was described earlier, the RAS2 project cast a wide net in collecting information. Arguably, this is a significantly wider net than any other project coding data on state religion policy.

The final criterion in Grim and Finke's methods of evaluation is the characteristics of the scaling process. As was noted earlier, the scales include all government activities that are known to occur, and rescaling using expert assessments and mathematical techniques does not substantially change the indexes. Furthermore, the combination of the variables into scales is done according to a strict categorization of variables based on the type of government action and what religious groups it influences. Thus, the scaling process has high validity.

Bibliography

Abouharb, M. Rodwan, & David L. Cingranelli "The Human Rights Effect of World Bank Structural Adjustment, 1980–2001" *International Studies Quarterly*, 50 (2), 2006, 233–262.

Achterberg, Peter, Dick Houtman, Stef Aupers, Willem De Kister, Peter Mascini, & Jerome Van DerWaal "A Christian Cancellation of the Secularist Truce? Waning Christian Religiosity and Waxing Religious Deprivatization in the West" *Journal for the Scientific Study of Religion*, 48 (4), 2009, 687–701.

Almond, Gabriel, R. Scott Appleby, & Emmanuel Sivan *Strong Religion: The Rise of Fundamentalism around the World*, Chicago: University of Chicago Press, 2003.

Amore, Abdelfattah "Implementation of the Declaration on the Elimination of All Forms of Intolerance and of Discrimination Based on Religion or Belief" United Nations Economic and Social Council Commission on Human Rights, 1995.

Anderson, John *Religious Liberty in Transnational Societies: The Politics of Religions*, New York: Cambridge University Press, 2003.

Appleby, R. Scott *Religious Fundamentalisms and Global Conflict*, New York: Foreign Policy Association Headline Series #301, 1994.

Appleby, R. Scott *The Ambivalence of the Sacred: Religion, Violence, and Reconciliation*, New York: Rowman and Littlefield, 2000.

Bader, Veit "Religious Pluralism: Secularism or Priority for Democracy" *Political Theory*, 27 (5), 1999, 597–633.

Barret, D.B., G.T. Kurian, & T.M. Johnson *World Christian Encyclopedia*, 2nd ed. Oxford: Oxford University Press, 2001.

Barro, Robert J. & Rachel M. McCleary "Religion and Economic Growth Across Countries" *American Sociological Review*, 68 (5), 2003, 760–781.

Barro, Robert J. & Rachel M. McCleary "Which Countries Have State Religions?" *Quarterly Journal of Economics*, 120 (4), 2005, 1331–1370.

Beatty, David M. "The Forms and Limits of Constitutional Interpretation (National approaches to religious freedom)" *American Journal of Comparative Law*, 49 (1), Winter 2001, 79–120.

Beit-Hallahmi, Benjamin "The Return of Martyrdom: Honour, Death, and Immortality" *Totalitarian Movements and Political Religions*, 4 (3), 2003, 11–34.
Bennoune, Karima "Between Betrayal and Betrayal: Fundamentalism, Family Law and Feminist Struggle in Algeria," *Arab Studies Quarterly*, 17 (1–2), 1995.
Berger, Peter L. "Secularism in Retreat" *The National Interest*, Winter 1996/1997, 3–12.
Berger, Peter L. "Epistemological Modesty: An Interview with Peter Berger" *Christian Century*, 1145, 1997, 972–975.
Berger, Peter L. *The Desecularization of the World: Resurgent Religion in World Politics*, Grand Rapids, MI: Wm. B. Eerdmans, 1999.
Berger, Peter L. "Faith and Development" *Society*, 46 (1), 2009, 69–75.
Beyer, Peter "Secularization from the Perspective of Globalization: A Response to Dobbelaere" *Sociology of Religion*, 60 (3), 1999, 289–301.
Boyle, Kevin & Juliet Sheen, eds. *Freedom of Religion and Belief: A World Report*, London: Routledge, 1997.
Breakwell, Glynis *Coping with Threatened Identities*, London: Methuen 1986.
Bruce, Steve "Secularization and Politics" in Jeffrey Haynes, ed. *Routledge Handbook of Religion and Politics*, New York: Routledge, 2009, 145–158.
Bryan, Hehir H. "Expanding Military Intervention: Promise or Peril?" *Social Research*, 62 (1), 1995, 41–50.
Bugaric, Bojan "Poplism, Liberal Democracy, and the Rule of Law in Central and Eastern Europe" *Communist and Post-Communist Societies*, 41, 2008, 191–203.
Bush, Robin "Regional 'Sharia' Regulations in Indonesia: Anomaly or Symptom?" in Greg Fealy & Sally White, eds. *Expressing Islam: Religious Life and Politics in Indonesia*, Singapore: Institute of Southeast Asian Studies, 2008.
Buzan, Berry, Ole Waever, & Jaap de Wilde *Security: A New Framework for Analysis*, Boulder/London: Lynne Rienner, 1998.
Byrnes, Timothy & Peter Katzenstein, eds. *Religion in and Expanding Europe*, New York: Cambridge University Press, 2000.
Calhoun, Craig "Secularism, Citizenship and the Public Sphere" in Craig Calhoun, Mark Juergensmeyer, & Jonathan VanAntwerpen, eds. *Rethinking Secularism*, New York: Oxford University Press, 2012, 86–102.
Calhoun, Craig, Mark Juergensmeyer, & Jonathan VanAntwerpen, eds. *Rethinking Secularism*, New York: Oxford University Press, 2012.
Carlson, Eric "China's New Regulations on Religion: A Small Step, Not a Great Leap, Forward" *Brigham Young University Law Review*, 747, 2005, 747–797.
Casanova, Jose *Public Religions in the Modern World*, Chicago: University of Chicago Press, 1994.
Casanova, Jose "The Secular and Secularisms" *Social Research*, 76 (4), 2009, 1049–1066.
Casanova, Jose "The Secular, Secularization, and Secularisms" in Craig Calhoun, Mark Juergensmeyer, & Jonathan VanAntwerpen, eds. *Rethinking Secularism*, New York: Oxford University Press, 2012, 65–85.
Cesari, Jocelyne *When Islam and Democracy Meet: Muslims in Europe and in the United States*. New York: Palgrave Macmillan, 2004.
Chaves, Mark "Secularization as Declining Religious Authority" *Social Forces*, 72 (3), 1994, 749–774.

Chaves, Mark & David E. Cann "Religion, Pluralism and Religious Market Structure," *Rationality and Society*, 4 (3), 1992, 272–290.

Chaves, Mark, Peter J. Schraeder, & Mario Sprindys "State Regulation of Religion and Muslim Religious Vitality in the Industrialized West" *Journal of Politics*, 56 (4), 1994, 1087–1097.

Cosgel, Metin & Thomas J. Miceli "State and Religion" *Journal of Comparative Economics*, 37 (2), 2009, 402–416.

Crouch, Colin "The Quiet Continent: Religion and Politics in Europe" *The Political Quarterly*, 71 (Supplement 1), 2000, 90–103.

Crouch, Melissa "The Proselytization Case: Law, the Rise of Islamic Conservatism and Religious Discrimination in West Java" *Australian Journal of Asian Law*, 8 (3), 2006, 322–337.

Crouch, Melissa "Religious Regulations in Indonesia: Failing Vulnerable Groups" *Review of Indonesian and Malaysian Affairs*, 43 (2), 2009, 53–103.

Davenport, Christian "Constitutional Promises and Repressive Reality: A Cross-National Time-Series Investigation of Why Political and Civil Liberties Are Repressed" *Journal of Politics*, 58 (3), 1996, 627–654.

Davie, Grace *Religion in Modern Europe: A Memory Mutates*, Oxford: Oxford University Press, 2000.

Dawkins, Richard *The God Delusion*, New York: Mariner Books, 2008.

Day, Stephen "Updating Yemeni National Unity: Could Lingering Regional Divisions Bring Down the Regime?" *Middle East Journal*, 62 (3), 2008.

Demerath, N.J., III *Crossing the Gods: World Religions and Worldly Politics*, New Brunswick, NJ: Rutgers University Press, 2001.

Demerath, N.J., III & Karen S. Straight "Religion, Politics, and the State: Cross-Cultural Observations" *Cross Currents*, 47 (1), 1997, 43–58.

Dobbelaere, Karel "Secularization Theories and Sociological Paradigms: A Reformulation of the Private-Public Dichotomy and the Problem of Societal Integration" *Sociological Analysis*, 1985, 46 (4), 377–387.

Dobbelaere, Karel "Towards an Integrated Perspective of the Processes Related to the Descriptive Concept of Secularization" *Sociology of Religion*, 60 (3), 1999, 229–247.

Dolnik, Adam & Rohan Gunartna "On the Nature of Religious Terrorism" in Jeffrey Haynes, ed. *Routledge Handbook of Religion and Politics*, New York: Routledge, 2009, 343–350.

Driessen, Michael D.P. "Religion. State and Democracy: Analyzing Two Dimensions of Church-State Arrangements" *Politics and Religion*, 3 (1), 2010, 55–80.

Durham, W. Cole Jr. "Perspectives on Religious Liberty: A Comparative Framework" in John D. van der Vyver & John Witte Jr., eds. *Religious Human Rights in Global Perspective: Legal Perspectives*, Boston: Martinus Nijhoff, 1996, 1–44.

Du Plessis, Lourens M. "Religious Human Rights in South Africa" in John D. van der Vyver & John Witte Jr., eds. *Religious Human Rights in Global Perspective: Legal Perspectives*, Boston: Martinus Nijhoff Publishers, 1996, 441–464.

Ebaugh, Helen R. "Return of the Sacred: Reintegration Religion in the Social Sciences" *Journal for the Scientific Study of Religion*, 41 (3), 2002, 385–395.

Ellis, Anthony "What Is Special about Religion?" *Law and Philosophy*, 25 (2), 2006, 219–241.

Emerson, Michael O. & David Hartman "The Rise of Religious Fundamentalism" *Annual Review of Sociology*, 32, 2006, 127–144.

Esbeck, Carl H. "A Typology of Church-State Relations in American Thought" *Religion and Public Education*, 15 (1), 1988, 43–50.

Facchini, Francois "Religion, Law and Development: Islam and Christianity – Why Is It in Occident and Not in the Orient That Man Invented the Institutions of Religious Freedom?" *European Journal of Law and Economy*, 29 (1), 2010, 103–129.

Farr, Thomas F. "Diplomacy in an Age of Faith: Religious Freedom and National Security" *Foreign Affairs*, 87 (2), 2008.

Finke, Roger & Laurence R. Iannaccone "Supply-Side Explanations for Religious Change" *Annals of the American Association of Political and Social Sciences*, 527, May 1993, 27–39.

Finkel, Jodi "Judicial Reform in Argentina in the 1990s: How Electoral Incentives Shape Institutional Change" *Latin American Research Review*, 39 (3), 2004, 56–80.

Fombad, Charles M. "Challenges to Constitutionalism and Constitutional Rights in Africa and the Enabling Role of Political Parties: Lessons and Perspectives from Southern Africa" *American Journal of Comparative Law*, 55 (1), 2007, 1–46.

Fox, Jonathan *Ethnoreligious Conflict in the Late 20th Century: A General Theory*, Lanham, MD: Lexington Books, 2002.

Fox, Jonathan *Religion, Civilization and Civil War: 1945 Through the New Millennium*, Lanham, MD: Lexington Books, 2004.

Fox, Jonathan "Do Democracies Have Separation of Religion and State?" *Canadian Journal of Political Science*, 40 (01), 2007, 1–25.

Fox, Jonathan *A World Survey of Religion and the State*, New York: Cambridge University Press, 2008.

Fox, Jonathan "Separation of Religion and State and Secularism in Theory and in Practice" *Religion State & Society*, 39 (4), 2011a, 384–401.

Fox, Jonathan "Out of Sync: The Disconnect between Constitutional Clauses and State Legislation on Religion" *Canadian Journal of Political Science*, 44 (1), 2011b, 59–81.

Fox, Jonathan "Building Composite Measures of Religion and State" *Interdisciplinary Journal of Research on Religion*, 7 (8), 2011c, 1–39.

Fox, Jonathan *An Introduction to Religion and Politics: Theory and Practice*, London: Routledge, 2013.

Fox, Jonathan & Deborah Flores "Religions, Constitutions, and the State: A Cross-National Study" *Journal of Politics*, 71 (4), 2009, 1499–1513.

Fox, Jonathan & Shmuel Sandler *Bringing Religion into International Relations*, New York: Palgrave-Macmillan, 2004.

Fox, Jonathan & Ephraim Tabory "Contemporary Evidence Regarding the Impact of State Regulation of Religion on Religious Participation and Belief" *Sociology of Religion*, 69 (3), 2008, 245–271.

Fradkin, Hillel "Does Democracy Need Religion?" *Journal of Democracy* 11 (1), 2000, 87–94.

Friedland, Roger "Religious Nationalism and the Problem of Collective Representation" *Annual Review of Sociology*, 27, 2001, 125–152.

Froese, Paul "After Atheism: An Analysis of Religious Monopolies in the Post-Communist World" *Sociology of Religion*, 65 (1), 2004, 57–75.

Garlicki, Leszek Lech "Perspectives on Freedom of Conscience and Religion in the Jurisprudence of Constitutional Courts" *Brigham Young University Law Review*, 2001 (2), 467–510.
Gellner, Ernest *Postmodernism, Reason and Religion*, London: Routledge, 1992.
Gill, Anthony "Government Regulation, Social Anomie and Religious Pluralism in Latin America: A Cross-National Analysis" *Rationality and Society*, 11 (3), 1999, 287–316.
Gill, Anthony "Religion and Comparative Politics" *Annual Review of Political Science*, 4, 2001, 117–138.
Gill, Anthony "The Political Origins of Religious Liberty: A Theoretical Outline" *Interdisciplinary Journal of Research on Religion*, 1 (1), 2005, 1–35.
Gill, Anthony *The Political Origins of Religious Liberty*, New York: Cambridge University Press, 2008.
Ginsburg, Tom, Svitlana Chernykh, & Zachary Elkins "Commitment and Diffusion: How and Why national Constitutions Incorporate International Law" *University of Illinois Law Review*, 2008, 201–237.
Goldewijk, Berma K., ed. *Religion, International Relations, and Cooperation Development*, Wageningen, the Netherlands: Wageningen Academic Publishers, 2007.
Goodliffe, Jay & Darren G. Hawkins "Explaining Commitment: States and the Convention against Torture" *Journal of Politics*, 68 (2), 2006, 358–371.
Gorski, Phillip S. & Ates Altinordu "After Secularization" *Annual Review of Sociology*, 24, 2008, 55–85.
Greenawalt, Kent *Religious Convictions and Political Choice*, Oxford: Oxford University Press, 1988.
Grim, Brian J. & Roger Finke "International Religion Indexes: Government Regulation, Government Favoritism, and Social Regulation of Religion" *Interdisciplinary Journal of Research on Religion*, 2 (1), 2006, 1–40.
Grim, Brian J. & Roger Finke *The Price of Freedom Denied*, New York: Cambridge University Press, 2011.
Grim, Brian J. & Richard Wike "Cross-Validating Measures If Global Religious Intolerance: Comparing Coded State Department Reports with Survey Data and Expert Opinion" *Politics and Religion*, 3 (1), 2010, 102–129.
Gurr, Ted R. *Minorities at Risk*, Washington, DC: United States Institute of Peace, 1993.
Gurr, Ted R. *Peoples versus States: Minorities at Risk in the New Century*, Washington, DC: United States Institute of Peace Press, 2000.
Hadden, Jeffrey K. "Toward Desacralizing Secularization Theory" *Social Forces*, 65 (3), 1987, 587–611.
Hafner-Burton, Emilie & James Ron "Seeing Double: Human Rights Impact through Qualitative and Quantitative Eyes," *World Politics* 61 (2), 2009, 360–401.
Hallward, Maia Carter "Situation the 'Secular': Negotiating the Boundary between Religion and Politics" *International Political Sociology*, 2 (1), 2008, 1–16.
Hayes, Bernadette C. "The Impact of Religious Identification on Political Attitudes: An International Comparison" *Sociology of Religion*, 56 (2), 1995, 177–194.
Haynes, Jeff "Religion, Secularisation, and Politics: A Postmodern Conspectus" *Third World Quarterly*, 18 (4), 1997, 709–728.

Haynes, Jeff *Religion in Global Politics*, New York: Longman, 1998.
Haynes, Jeffrey "Religion and Foreign Policy" in Jeffrey Haynes, ed. *Routledge Handbook of Religion and Politics*, New York: Routledge, 2009, 293–307.
Hefner, Robert H. "Public Islam and the Problem of Democratization" *Sociology of Religion*, 62 (4), 2001, 491–514.
Henderson, Conway "Population Pressures and Political Repression" *Social Science Quarterly*, 74 (2), 1993, 322–333.
Hendon, David W. & Charles McDaniel "Notes on Church–State Affairs" *Journal of Church and State*, 48 (2), 2006, 717–726.
Hitchens, Christopher *God Is Not Great: How Religion Poisons Everything*, New York: Twelve, 2009.
Horowitz, Donald L. *Ethnic Groups in Conflict*, Berkeley: University. of California Press, 1985.
Huanzhong, Chen "A Brief Overview of Law and Religion in the People's Republic of China" *Brigham Young University Law Review*, 2, 2003, 465–473.
Huntington, Samuel P. "The Clash of Civilizations?" *Foreign Affairs*, 72 (3), 1993, 22–49.
Huntington, Samuel P. *The Clash of Civilizations and the Remaking of the World Order*, New York: Simon & Schuster, 1996.
Hurd, Elizabeth S. "The Political Authority of Secularism in International Relations" *European Journal of International Relations*, 10 (2), 2004a, 235–262.
Hurd, Elizabeth S. "The International Politics of Secularism: US Foreign Policy and the Islamic Republic of Iran" *Alternatives*, 29 (2), 2004b, 115–138.
Hurd, Elizabeth S. "Negotiating Europe: The Politics of Religion and the Prospects for Turkish Accession" *Review of International Studies*, 32, 2006, 401–418.
Iannaccone, Laurence R. "Voodoo Economics? Reviewing the Rational Choice Approach to Religion" *Journal for the Scientific Study of Religion*, 34 (1), 1995, 76–89.
Imran, Rahat "Legal Injustices: The Zina Hudood Ordinance of Pakistan and Its Implications for Women" *Journal of International Women's Studies*, 7 (2), 2005, http://vc.bridgew.edu/jiws/vol7/iss2/5.
Jaggers, Keith & Ted R. Gurr "Tracking Democracy's Third Wave with the Polity III Data" *Journal of Peace Research*, 32 (4), 1995, 469–482.
Jelen, Ted G. "The Constitutional Basis of Religious Pluralism in the United States: Causes and Consequences" *Annals of the American Association of Political and Social Sciences*, 612, 2007, 26–41.
Jervis, Robert "An Interim Assessment of September 11: What Has Changed and What Has Not?" *Political Science Quarterly*, 117 (1), 2002, 37–54.
Johnston, Hanh & Jozef Figa "The Church and Political Opposition," *Journal for the Scientific Study of Religion*, 1988, 27 (12), 32–47.
Juergensmeyer, Mark *The New Cold War?*, Berkeley: University of California Press, 1993.
Juergensmeyer, Mark "Terror Mandated by God" *Terrorism and Political Violence*, 9 (2), Summer 1997, 16–23.
Juergensmeyer, Mark *Global Rebellion: Religious Challenges to the Secular State, from Christian Militias to Al Qaeda*, Berkeley: University of California Press, 2008.

Juergensmeyer, Mark "Rethinking the Secular and Religious Aspects of Violence" in Craig Calhoun, Mark Juergensmeyer, & Jonathan VanAntwerpen, eds. *Rethinking Secularism*, New York: Oxford University Press, 2012, 195–253.

Karagiannis, Evangelos "Secularism in Context: The Relation between the Greek State and the Church of Greece in Crisis" *European Journal of Sociology*, 50 (1), 2009, 122–167.

Kaspersen, Kars B. & Johannes Lindvall "Why No Religious Politics? The Secularization of Poor Relief and Primary Education in Denmark and Sweden" *Archives of European Sociology*, 49 (1), 2008, 119–143.

Keane, John "Secularism?" *The Political Quarterly*, 71 (Supplement 1), 2000, 5–19.

Keith, Linda C. "Constitutional Provisions for Individual Human Rights (1977–1996): Are They More than Mere Window Dressing?" *Political Research Quarterly*, 55 (1), 2002, 111–143.

Kettell, Steven "Has Political Science Ignored Religion?" *PS: Political Science and Politics*, 45 (1), 2012, 93–100.

Kimball, Charles *When Religion Becomes Evil*, San Francisco: HarperCollins, 2002.

Kuhle, Lene "Concluding Remarks on Religion and State in the Nordic Countries" *Nordic Journal of Religion and Society*, 24 (2), 2011, 205–213.

Kuru, Ahmet T. *Secularism and State Policies toward Religion, The United States France and Turkey*, New York: Cambridge University Press, 2009.

Lai, Brian "An Empirical Examination of Religion and Conflict in the Middle East, 1950–1992" *Foreign Policy Analysis*, 2 (1), 2006, 21–36.

Lambert, Yves "Religion in Modernity as a New Axial Age: Secularization or New Religious Forms?" *Sociology of Religion*, 60 (3), 1999, 303–333.

Laustsen, Carsten B. & Ole Waever "In Defense of Religion: Sacred Referent Objects for Securitization" *Millennium*, 29 (3), 2000, 705–739.

Laycock, Douglass "The Underlying Unity of Separation and Neutrality" *Emory Law Journal*, 46, 1997, 43–75.

Lechner, Frank A. "The Case against Secularization: A Rebuttal" *Social Forces*, 69 (4), 1991, 1103–1119.

Ling-Chien Neo, Jaclyn "Malay Nationalism, Islamic Supremacy and the Constitutional Bargain in the Multi-ethnic Composition of Malaysia," *International Journal on Minority and Group Rights*, 13, 2006, 95–118.

Little, David "Belief, Ethnicity, and Nationalism" *Nationalism and Ethnic Politics*, 1995, 1, www.crvp.org/book/series01/i-7/chapter_i.htm

Luttwak, Edward "The Missing Dimension" in Douglas Johnston & Cynthia Sampson eds. *Religion, the Missing Dimension of Statecraft*, Oxford: Oxford University Press, 1994, 8–19.

Madeley, John T.S. "A Framework for the Comparative Analysis of Church–State Relations in Europe" *West European Politics*, 26 (1), 2003, 23–50.

Madeley, John T.S. and Enyedi, Z. (eds.) *Church and State in Contemporary Europe: The Chimera of Neutrality*, London: Frank Cass, 2003.

Mahmood, Tahir "Religion, Law and Judiciary in Modern India," *Brigham Young University Law Review*, 3, 2006, 755–776.

Marquand, D. & R.L. Nettler "Foreword" *The Political Quarterly*, 71 (Supplement 1), 2000, 1–4.

Marshall, Paul *A Religious Freedom in the World: A Global Report on Freedom and Persecution*, Nashville, TN: B & H, 2000.

Martin, David A. *A General Theory of Secularization*, Oxford: Blackwell, 1978.

Mazie, Steven V. "Rethinking Religious Establishment and Liberal Democracy: Lessons from Israel" *Brandywine Review of Faith and International Affairs*, 2 (2), 2004, 3–12.

McCleary, Rachel M. & Robert J. Barro "Religion and Economy" *Journal of Economic Perspectives*, 20 (2), 2006, 49–72.

McConnell, Michael W. "Religious Freedom at a Crossroads" *University of Chicago Law Review*, 59 (1), 1992, 115–194.

Miner, Christopher J. "Losing My Religion: Austria's New Religion Law in Light of International and European Standards of Religious Freedom" *Brigham Young University Law Review*, 2 (11), 1998, 607–647.

Minkenberg, Michael "Religion and Public Policy: Institutional, Cultural, and Political Impact on the Shaping of Abortion Policies in Western Democracies" *Comparative Political Studies*, 35 (2), 2002, 221–247.

Moore, Rick "The Genres of Religious Freedom: Creating Discourses on Religion at the State Department" in Barbara J. Denison, ed. *History, Time, Meaning, and Memory: Ideas for the Sociology of Religion*, Leiden: Brill, 2011, pp. 223–253.

Morgenstern, Mira "Religion and State: The View from the Enlightenment" *Journal of Law Religion and State*, 1 (2), 2012, 256–288.

Morigi, Andrea, Vittorio E. Vernole, & Chiara Verna "Report 2000 on Religious Freedom in the World," Aid to the Church in Need, Italian Secretariat, 2003.

Morrison, Trevor W. "Constitutional Avoidance in the Executive Branch" *Columbia Law Review*, 106 (6), 2006, 1189–1259.

Motilla, Augustín "Religious Pluralism in Spain: Striking the Balance between Religious Freedom and Constitutional Rights" *Brigham Young University Law Review*, 2004 (2), 575–606.

Norris, Pippa & Ronald Inglehart "Islamic Culture and Democracy: Testing the 'Clash of Civilizations' Thesis" *Comparative Sociology*, 1 (3–4), 2002, 235–263.

Norris, Pippa & Ronald Inglehart *Sacred and Secular: Religion and Politics Worldwide*, New York: Cambridge University Press, 2004.

North, Charles M. & Carl R. Gwin "Religious Freedom and the Unintended Consequences of State Religion" *Southern Economic Journal*, 71 (1), 2004, 103–117.

O'Brien, David M. *To Dream of Dreams: Religious Freedom and Constitutional Politics in Postwar* Japan, Honolulu: University of Hawaii Press, 1996.

Oldmixion, Elizabeth & William Hudson "When Church Teachings and Policy Commitments Collide: Perspectives on Catholics in the U.S. House of Representatives" *Politics and Religion*, 1 (1), 2008, 113–135.

Olowu, Dejo "Human Rights and the Avoidance of Domestic Implementation: The Phenomenon of Non-justiciable Constitutional Guarantees. (Comparative Constitutionalism and Rights: Global Perspectives)" *Saskatchewan Law Review*, 69 (1), 2006, 39–78.

Philpott, Daniel "The Challenge of September 11 to Secularism in International Relations" *World Politics*, 55 (1), 2002, 66–95.

Philpott, Daniel "Explaining the Political Ambivalence of Religion" *American Political Science Review*, 101 (3), 2007, 505–525.

Philpott, Daniel "Has the Study of Global Politics Found Religion?" *Annual Review of Political Science*, 12, 2009, 183–202.
Pinkus, Lauren E. & Katherine Meyer "Religious Noncoercive and Coercive Regulations: A New Typology for Cross-National Research" *International Journal of Sociology*, 38 (3), 2008, 82–107.
Poe, Steven C. & C. Neal Tate "Repression of Human Rights to Personal Integrity in the 1980s" *American Political Science Review*, 88 (4), 1994, 853–872.
Poe, Steven C., C. Neal Tate, & Linda Camp Keith "Repression of the Human Right to Personal Integrity Revisited: A Global Cross-National Study Covering the Years 1976–1993" *International Studies Quarterly*, 43 (2), 1999, 291–313.
Pollack, Detlef "Religious Change in Europe: Theoretical Considerations and Empirical Findings" *Social Compass*, 55 (2), 2008: 168–186.
Pollack, Detlef & Gett Pickel "Religious Individualization or Secularization? Testing Hypotheses of Religious Change in Eastern and Western Germany" *British Journal of Sociology*, 58 (1), 2007 603–632.
Potter, Pitman "Belief in Control: Regulation of Religion in China" *The China Quarterly*, 174, 2003, 317–337.
Poulter, Sebastian "Muslim Headscarves in School: Contrasting Legal Approaches in England and France," *Oxford Journal of Legal Studies*, 17 (1), 1997, 43–74.
Presser, Stanley & Mark Chaves "Is Religious Service Attendance Declining?" *Journal for the Scientific Study of Religion*, 46 (3), 2007, 417–423.
Rawls, A. *Theory of Justice*, Cambridge, MA: Belknap Press of Harvard University Press, 1971.
Rawls, John *Political Liberalism*, New York: Columbia University Press, 1993.
Raz, Joseph *The Morality of Freedom*, Oxford University Press, 1986.
Reddy, Rita "Marriage and Divorce Regulation and Recognition in Malaysia," *Family Law Quarterly*, 29 (3), 1995, 613–626.
Roberts, Christopher & Lee Poh Onn "Brunei Darussalam: Cautious on Political Reform, Comfortable in ASEAN, Pushing for Economic Diversification," *Southeast Asian Affairs*, 2009 (1), 2009, 61–82.
Roy, Oliver *Secularism Confronts Islam*, New York, Columbia University Press, 2007.
Sahliyeh, Emile, ed. *Religious Resurgence and Politics in the Contemporary World*, New York: State University of New York Press, 1990.
Sandal, Nukhet & Jonathan Fox *Religion in International Relations Theory: Interactions and Possibilities*, New York: Routledge, 2013.
Sarkissian, Ani "Religious Reestablishment in Post-Communist Polities" *Journal of Church and State*, 51 (3), 2010, 472–501.
Sarkissian, Ani "Religious Regulation and the Muslim Democracy Gap" *Politics & Religion*, 5 (3), 2012, 501–527.
Schanda, Balazs "Religious Freedom Issues in Hungry," *Brigham Young University Law Review*, 2002, 405–433.
Schedler, Andreas "The Nested Game of Democratization by Elections" *International Political Science Review*, 23 (1), 2002, 103–122.
Seul, Jefferey R. "'Ours Is the Way of God': Religion, Identity and Intergroup Conflict" *Journal of Peace Research*, 36 (3), 1999, 553–569.
Shah, Timothy S. "Making the Christian World Safe for Liberalism: From Grotius to Rawls" *The Political Quarterly*, 71 (s1), 2000, 121–139.

Shupe, Anson "The Stubborn Persistence of Religion in the Global Arena" in Emile Sahliyeh, ed. *Religious Resurgence and Politics in the Contemporary World*, New York: State University of New York Press, 1990, 17–26.

Smith, Anthony D. "Ethnic Election and National Destiny: Some Religious Origins of Nationalist Ideals" *Nations and Nationalism*, 5 (3), 1999, 331–355.

Smith, Anthony D. "The Sacred Dimension of Nationalism" *Millennium*, 29 (3), 2000, 791–814.

Solomon, Peter H. Jr. "Courts and Judges in Authoritarian Regimes" *World Politics*, 60, 2007, 122–145.

Sorek, Tamir & Alin M. Cebanu "Religiousity, National Identity and Legitimacy: Israel as an Extreme Case" *Sociology*, 43 (3), 2009, 477–496.

Spickard, James V. "Human Rights, Religious Conflict, and Globalization: Ultimate Values in a New World Order" *MOST, Journal on Multicultural Societies*, 1 (1), 1999, www.unesco.org./most/vl1n1ris.htm.

Spickard, James V. "Review: A World Survey of Religion and the State" *Journal of Contemporary Religion*, 25 (1), 2010, 137–138.

Spohn, Wilfried "Europeanization, Religion, and Collective Identities in Enlarging Europe: A Multiple Modernities Perspective" *European Journal of Social Theory*, 12 (3), 2009, 358–374.

Stark, Jan "Constructing an Islamic Model in Two Malaysian States: PAS Rule in Kelantan and Terengganu," *Sojourn*, 19 (1), 2004, 51–75.

Stark, Rodney "Secularization, R.I.P." *Sociology of Religion*, 60 (3), 1999, 249–273.

Stark, Rodney *One True God, Historical Consequences of Monotheism*, Princeton, NJ: Princeton University Press, 2001.

Stark, Rodney *For the Glory of God*, Princeton, NJ: Princeton University Press, 2003.

Stark, Rodney & William Bainbridge *The Future of Religion: Secularization, Revival and Cult Formation*, Berkeley: University of California Press, 1985.

Stark, Rodney & Roger Finke *Acts of Faith: Explaining the Human Side of Religion*, Berkeley: University of California Press, 2000.

Stark, Rodney & Lawrence R. Iannaccone "A Supply Side Reinterpretation of the 'Secularization' of Europe" *Journal for the Scientific Study of Religion*, 33 (3), 1994, 230–252.

Stepan, Alfred "Religion, Democracy, and the 'Twin Tolerations'" *Journal of Democracy*, 11 (4), 2000, 37–56.

Stepan, Alfred "The Multiple Secularisms of Modern Democratic and Non-Democratic Regimes" in Craig Calhoun, Mark Juergensmeyer, & Jonathan VanAntwerpen, eds. *Rethinking Secularism*, New York: Oxford University Press, 2012.

Stephens, Robert "Sites of Conflict in the Indian Secular State: Secularism, Caste and Religious Conversion" *Journal of Church and State*, 49 (2), 2007, 251–276.

Stern, Jessica *Terror in the Name of God: Why Religious Militants Kill*, New York: HarperCollins, 2003.

Subedi, Surya "Constitutional Accommodation of Ethnicity and National Identity in Nepal" *International Journal on Minority and Group Rights*, 6 (1–2), 122–147, 1999.

Swatos, William H. Jr. & Kevin J. Christiano "Secularization Theory: The Course of a Concept" *Sociology of Religion*, 60 (3), 1999, 209–228.

Talib, Naimah "A Resilient Monarch: The Sultanate of Brunei and Regime Legitimacy in an Era of Democratic Nation-States," *New Zealand Journal of Asian Studies*, 4 (2), 2002, 134–147.

Taylor, Charles *A Secular Age*, Cambridge, MA: Harvard University Press, 2007.

Tezcur, Gunes M., Taghi Azdarmaki, & Mehri Bahar "Religious Participation among Muslims: Iranian Exceptionalism" *Critique: Critical Middle Eastern Studies*, 15 (3), 2006, 217–232.

Thomas, George M. "Religions in Global Civil Society" *Sociology of Religion*, 62 (4), 2001, 515–533.

Thomas, Scott M. *The Global Resurgence of Religion and the Transformation of International Relations: The Struggle for the Soul of the Twenty-First Century*, New York: Palgrave Macmillan, 2005.

Thomas, Scott M. "Outwitting the Developed Countries? Existential Insecurity and the Global Resurgence of Religion" *Journal of International Affairs*, 61 (1), 2007, 21–45.

Tibi, Bassam "Post-Bipolar Disorder in Crisis: The Challenge of Politicized Islam" *Millennium*, 29 (4), 2000, 843–859.

Toft, Monica D., Daniel Philpott, & Timothy S. Shah *God's Century: Resurgent Religion and Global Politics*, New York: W. W. Norton, 2011.

Turner, Brian S. *Religion and Social Theory*, 2nd ed. London: Sage, 1991.

Uitz, Renata "Aiming for State Neutrality in Matters of Religion: The Hungarian Record" *University of Detroit Mercy Law Review*, 83 (5), 2006, 761–787.

Van Cott, Donna Lee "A Political Analysis of Legal Pluralism in Bolivia and Columbia" *Journal of Latin American Studies*, 32, 2000, 207–234.

van der Brug, Wouter, Sara B. Hobolt, & Claes H. de Vreese "Religion and Party Choice in Europe" *West European Politics*, 32 (6), 2009, 1266–1283.

Ver Beek, K. A. "Spirituality: A Development Taboo" in D. Eade, ed. *Development and Culture: Selected Essays from Development in Practice*, Oxford: Oxfam GB, 2002, 58–75.

Voicu, Malina "Religion and Gender across Europe" *Social Compass*, 56 (2), 2009, 144–162.

Voicu, Malina "Effect of Nationalism on Religiosity in 30 European Countries" *European Sociological Review*, 2011, doi:10.1093/esr/jcq-67.

Voye, Liliane "Secularization in a Context of Advanced Modernity" *Sociology of Religion*, 60 (3), 1999, 275–288.

Wach, Jochim "The Role of Religion in the Social Philosophy of Alex De Tocqueville" *Journal of the History of Ideas*, 7 (1) 1946, 74–90.

Wald, Kenneth D., Adam L. Silverman, & Kevin S. Friday "Making Sense of Religion in Political Life" *Annual Review of Political Science*, 8, 2005, 121–143.

Wald, Kenneth D. & Clyde Wilcox "Getting Religion: Has Political Science Discovered the Faith Factor?" *American Political Science Review*, 100 (4), 2006, 523–529.

Wallace, Anthony F.C. *Religion: An Anthropological View*, New York: Random House, 1966.

Warner, R. Stephen "Work in Progress toward a New Paradigm for the Sociological Study of Religion in the United States" *American Journal of Sociology*, 98 (5), 1993, 1044–1093.

Wilhelmsen, Julie "Islamism in Azerbaijan: How Potent?" *Studies in Conflict and Terrorism*, 32 (8), 2009, 726–742.

Wilson, Bryan R. *Religion in Sociological Perspective*. Oxford: Oxford University Press, 1982.
Witte, John Jr. "A Dickensian Era of Religious Rights: An Update on Religious Human Rights in Global Perspective" *William and Mary Law Review*, 42 (3), 2001, 707–770.
Witte, John Jr. "Facts and Fictions about the History of Separation of Church and State" *Journal of Church and State*, 48 (1), 2006, 15–45.
Witte, John R. & M. Christian Green "The American Constitutional Experiment in Religious Human Rights: The Perennial Search for Principles" in John D. van der Vyver & John R. Witte Jr. eds. *Religious Human Rights in Global Perspective: Legal Perspectives*, Boston: Martinus Nijhoff, 1996, 497–558.
Wuthnow, Robert & Steve Offutt "Transnational Religious Connections" in Dennis R. Hoover & Douglas M. Johnston, eds. *Religion and Foreign Affairs: Essential Readings*, Waco, TX: Baylor University Press, 2012, 337–352.
Yamane, David "Secularization on Trial: In Defense of a Neosecularization Paradigm" *Journal for the Scientific Study of Religion*, 36 (1), 1997, 109–122.
Yildirim, Seval "Expanding Secularism's Scope: An Indian Case Study" *American Journal of Comparative Law*, 52 (4), 2004, 901–908.
Yildiz, Ilhan "Minority Rights in Turkey" *Brigham Young Law Review*, 2007 (3), 2007, 791–812.
Zisser, Eyal "Syria, the Ba'th Regime and the Islamic Movement" *The Muslim World*, 95 (1), 2005, 43–65.
Zubadia, Sami "Trajectories of Political Islam: Egypt, Iran and Turkey" *Political Quarterly*, 71 (Supplement 1), 2000, 60–78.
Zumbeta, Evie "Religion, Modernity and Social Rights in European Education" *Intercultural Education*, 19 (4), 2008, 297–304.

Index

abortion, 6, 71, 72, 80, 162, 179–189, 199–200
Afghanistan, 12, 46, 61, 72, 75, 77, 83, 97, 99, 125, 142, 150, 160, 176, 198, 207, 233
Africa, sub-Saharan, 71, 108, 122, 130, 132, 149, 160, 161, 184
Albania, 80, 89, 99, 101, 122, 125
alcohol, ban on, 46, 54, 75, 79
Algeria, 74, 116, 126, 155, 193, 268
Andorra, 90, 101, 161, 184
Angola, 90
Appleby, R. Scott, 37
Arab spring, 8–9
Argentina, 6, 48, 61, 85, 89, 93, 132, 133, 204, 208, 211
Armenia, 12, 70, 155, 157
Asia, 46, 81, 99, 160, 184, 193, 216
Australia, 132, 145, 172, 174, 241
Austria, 52, 58, 88, 127, 144, 145, 149, 156, 174, 177, 183
Azerbaijan, 12, 80, 99, 112, 115, 123, 128, 233

Bahais, 145
Bahamas, the, 141, 183
Bahrain, 9, 96, 184, 207
Bangladesh, 83, 99, 125, 160, 183, 194
Barbados, 110, 141, 147, 189
Belarus, 12, 70, 112, 116, 141, 143, 147, 148, 157, 195, 233
Belgium, 53, 88, 89, 144, 155, 156, 157, 177, 183
Belize, 93, 152, 177, 189, 219

Benin, 133, 161, 214
Berger, Peter L., 18, 23, 24
Bhutan, 69, 70, 77, 84, 193
Bible, the, 55, 67, 120, 121, 143, 144, 200, 236
blasphemy, 48, 82–83, 84, 97
Bolivia, 6, 98, 110, 148, 175, 177, 204, 208, 211
Bosnia, 12, 81, 84, 97
Botswana, 132, 148
Brazil, 53, 172
Brunei, 46, 70, 74, 75, 83, 88, 92, 99, 101, 118, 126, 141, 153, 157, 160
Buddhism, 51, 53, 56, 60, 69, 77, 78, 80, 84, 87, 94, 96, 115, 121, 143, 145, 150, 156, 161, 175, 176, 193, 233, 242
Bulgaria, 49, 127, 144, 147, 149, 174, 207
burial, 67, 69, 142, 143, 145, 223
Burkina Faso, 80, 99, 133, 161, 214
Burundi, 92, 108, 161, 181
but Latin America, 132

Cambodia, 77, 150, 175, 189, 195
Cameroon, 71, 132, 161, 162, 183
Canada, 94, 161, 189
Cape Verde, 133, 198
capitalism, 20
Casanova, Jose, 28, 31
Catholic Church, the, 34, 40, 42, 48, 50, 52, 55, 56, 57, 58, 59, 61, 79, 84, 85, 87, 89, 90, 98, 115, 130, 173, 174, 175, 177, 180, 184, 188, 208, 234
censorship, 83, 143

Central African Republic, the, 108, 183
Chad, 71, 80, 189, 194
Chile, 70, 92, 133, 148, 149, 152, 177, 183, 189, 194
China, 52, 56, 66, 89, 111, 116, 117, 120, 121, 123, 128, 194, 195, 196
Comate, Agust, 18
Communism, 19, 31, 32, 34, 35, 56, 70, 106, 127, 147, 184, 188, 249
Comoros, 75, 79, 93, 141, 143, 183
competition perspective. See secular-religious competition perspective
Cong, Republic of, 108
Congo-Brazzaville, 128, 161, 183, 216
conversion, 77–78
Costa Rica, 6, 61, 89, 149, 152, 173, 177, 181, 194, 195
Croatia, 12, 79, 89, 174, 183, 189
Cuba, 55, 59, 111, 123, 125, 130, 147, 194
cults, 52, 138, 147, 156, 157
culture, 36, 42, 53, 62, 75, 138, 172, 185, 188, 192, 195, 244–245
Cyprus, 70, 80, 99, 101, 122, 143, 145, 169, 181, 189
Cyprus, Turkish, 210
Czech Republic, 58, 127, 174

Dawkins, Richard, 24
Democratic Republic of Congo, the. See Zaire
Denmark, 48, 61, 66, 88, 93, 145, 152, 173, 174, 189, 194, 195
divorce, 47, 48, 67–69, 70, 143, 150, 155
Djibouti, 98, 153, 194
Dominican Republic, 44, 133
Durkheim, Emile, 18

Ecuador, 125, 181, 189, 196, 216
Egypt, 9, 71, 74, 88, 101, 112, 117, 134, 148, 150, 155, 157
El Salvador, 101, 183, 189
Enlightenment, the, 19, 274
Ennahda party, 9
Equatorial Guinea, 59, 110, 128, 162, 174
Eretria, 194
Eritrea, 12, 108, 129, 143, 147, 161, 189, 194, 233
Estonia, 12, 116, 129, 161, 172, 216
Ethiopia, 83
European Court of Human Rights, 50, 235
European Union, the, 23, 103, 136, 149
exclusion of ideals, 31, 175, 213, 241

Fiji, 79, 142
Finke, Roger, 3, 4, 5, 13, 36, 65, 106, 107, 134, 137, 138, 203, 247, 256, 257, 268, 278
Finland, 66, 88, 129, 149, 153, 172, 174
France, 30, 32, 55, 121, 122, 127, 144, 149, 155, 156, 169, 208, 241
Freud, Sigmund, 18

Gabon, 74, 174
Gambia, 53, 80, 161
Georgia, 12, 70, 89, 92, 96, 116, 122, 147, 157
Germany, 6, 87, 88, 126, 127, 143, 144, 145, 156, 174
Ghana, 77, 142, 147, 183
Gill, Anthony, 3, 31, 36, 42, 62, 107, 135, 137, 192, 202, 239, 243, 245, 247
God's Century, 20, 31, 34–35, 66, 235–237
Greece, 69, 83, 96, 117, 122, 145, 147, 156, 173, 184, 193
Guatemala, 110, 183
Guinea, 80, 133, 152, 189, 210
Guinea Bissau, 89, 132, 161, 184
Guyana, 89, 133, 216

Haiti, 110, 177
Hare Krishnas, 52, 141
Hinduism, 53, 57, 69, 77, 80, 120, 142, 143, 150, 153, 193, 242
Hobbes, Thomas, 19
homosexuality, 65, 70–71, 80, 162, 236. See gay marriage
Honduras, 98, 116, 130
Hungary, 6, 52, 88, 132, 133, 156, 172, 245
Huntington, Samuel, 35, 36, 239, 242

Iceland, 61, 66, 88, 118, 129, 174
Imam, 45, 47, 48, 87, 88, 115, 116, 117, 125, 134, 147, 153, 195. See Mosque
India, 69, 77, 78, 83, 90, 101, 111, 120, 128, 136, 143, 150, 195, 210
Indonesia, 74, 75, 78, 79, 83, 88, 99, 101, 103, 112, 125, 153, 160, 174, 176, 234
Inglehart, Ronald. See Norris, Pippa
interest groups, 3
Iran, 46, 61, 70, 74, 75, 77, 83, 93, 121, 150, 157, 207
Iraq, 12, 58, 77, 81, 83, 89, 122, 125, 130, 133, 141, 142, 143, 145, 147, 152, 153, 158, 183, 193, 234

Ireland, 96, 161, 174, 177, 180, 184
Islamic Brotherhood, 9
Israel, 69, 70, 75, 84, 97, 110, 136, 157, 172, 194
Italy, 88, 97, 145, 153, 177, 208
Ivory Coast, 89, 90, 92, 148, 210

Jamaica, 53, 133, 172
Japan, 133, 156, 210, 216
Jehovah's Witnesses, 52, 81, 143, 147, 155, 156, 157, 189, 193
Jordan, 47, 74, 94, 117, 155, 173
Judaism, 46, 52, 58, 60, 69, 84, 87, 94, 96, 97, 121, 143, 156, 157, 174, 199, 223, 233, 245
Juergensmeyer, Mark, 35, 42

Kazakhstan, 12, 122, 128, 153, 194, 195, 210, 233
Kenya, 75, 83, 142
Koran, 67, 120, 144, 152, 173, 200
Kuwait, 46, 47, 70, 74, 83, 117, 127, 143, 153, 155, 157, 162
Kyrgyzstan, 12, 80, 99, 143, 194, 244

laicism, 32, 55, 212–213, 241
Laos, 97, 111, 112, 150, 184, 193
Latin America, 70, 130, 149, 160, 161, 166, 173, 177, 184
Latvia, 12, 96, 122, 245
Lebanon, 79, 110, 133
Lesotho, 74, 133, 145
Liberia, 79, 161, 183
Libya, 9, 74, 83
Liechtenstein, 40, 41, 101, 189
Lithuania, 6, 70, 81, 88, 92, 122, 152, 189, 194, 245
Lutheran Church, 48, 52, 66, 118
Luxembourg, 58, 117, 177

Macedonia, 12, 111, 118, 120, 122, 128, 147, 149
Madagascar, 93, 116, 210
Malawi, 133, 141, 147, 183
Malaysia, 46, 69, 70, 74, 78, 79, 83, 88, 97, 99, 101, 103, 125, 142, 150, 155, 160, 207, 234
Maldives, the, 45, 46, 70, 78, 93, 99, 112, 121, 141, 147, 155, 160
Mali, 92
Malta, 84, 132, 133, 149, 183, 184

marriage, 47, 48, 67–70, 90, 143, 148, 150
 gay, 66
Marx, Karl, 18, 19
Mauritania, 74, 77, 81, 116, 123, 173, 207
Mauritius, 128
Mexico, 89, 115, 116, 117, 127, 129, 130, 143, 234
Middle East, 8, 47, 53, 99, 103, 110, 121, 125, 130, 149, 158, 160, 161, 173, 174, 175, 176, 184
missionaries. *See* proselytizing
modernization. *See* secularization theory
Moldova, 12, 92, 145, 189
Mongolia, 60, 111, 145, 147, 210
Montenegro, 12, 133, 144, 147, 198, 251
Mormon Church, 222
Mormons, 156, 193, 194, 198
Morocco, 112, 145, 193, 207
Mosques, 45, 46, 47, 48, 51, 88, 92, 115, 116, 125, 126, 127, 134, 145, 244
Mozambique, 54, 108, 110, 145, 183
Myanmar, 71, 77, 96, 111, 112, 115, 128, 157, 175, 193

Namibia, 133, 161, 214
Nepal, 53, 57, 85, 183, 193
Netherlands, the, 87, 174
neutral political concern, 30, 175, 213, 241
New Zealand, 53, 132, 133, 161, 183
Nicaragua, 70, 208
Nietzsche, Friedrich, 18
Niger, 80, 99, 120, 161, 189
Nigeria, 6, 74, 75, 77, 81, 83, 84, 103, 120, 147, 152, 194, 195, 204, 233
Norri, Pippa, 3, 22, 24, 238
North Korea, 56, 115, 120, 121, 123, 162, 198
Norway, 61, 66, 93, 144, 145, 152, 189, 194, 207

Oman, 46, 83, 116, 121, 207
Orthodox Church, 88
 Belarusian, 141
 Bulgarian, 49
 Georgian, 89, 92
 Greek, 117
 Macedonian, 118
 Romanian, 51, 90, 142
 Russian, 58, 81, 87, 233

Pakistan, 46, 61, 70, 78, 79, 81, 88, 99, 101, 121, 125, 155, 157, 160, 183

Panama, 70, 92, 117, 152, 194
Papua New Guinea, 87, 133, 161, 183
Paraguay, 57, 93
Pentecostals, 155, 156
Peru, 50, 133, 149, 173, 174, 177
Philippines, the, 69, 83, 90, 161, 172, 183
Philpott, Daniel, 25, 27. *See* God's Century
Poland, 125, 147, 156, 184, 188
Portugal, 58, 88, 161, 177
prayer, 46, 116, 123, 128, 157
  bans on, 120
  in public schools, 94–96, 142, 152, 175, 236
proselytizing, 11, 47, 77, 115, 116, 117, 152, 189–198, 199

Qatar, 46, 74, 121, 157

Ramadan, 46, 47, 78, 79, 116
Rawls, John, 28, 108
registration, 55, 58
registration, religious, 52, 53, 54, 56, 97, 115, 121, 141, 143, 147, 148, 155, 174, 196, 223, 233
Religion and State Project, 6, 104, 106, 180–181, 246, 268
  methodology, 13
  variable summery and definitions, 4
religious courts, 60, 81, 83–84
religious economy, 3, 17
religious education, 40, 46, 47, 48, 50, 51, 52, 59, 65, 85–87, 94–96, 125–127, 153, 162, 169–179, 198–199, 235, 241
  in public schools, 126, 241
Religious Education, 94
religious freedom, 6
religious states
  definition, 43
Romania, 51, 70, 81, 85, 90, 96, 97, 142, 143, 147, 172
Rousseau, Jean-Jacques, 19
Russia, 60, 70, 81, 83, 85, 90, 122, 128, 143, 147, 148, 155, 210, 233
Rwanda, 121, 129, 153, 172, 181

Salafi, 9
Saudi Arabia, 38, 45, 61, 70, 72, 74, 75, 77, 78, 83, 88, 101, 141, 142, 145, 147, 150, 153, 155, 174
Scientology, 52, 143, 157
Scientoloists, 143, 147, 156
sects. *See* cults

secularism, 17, 26. *See* secularization theory; secular-religious competition perspective; secularization theory
secularism, political, 2. *See* secular-religious competition perspective
  definition, 28
secularization theory, 13, 14, 15, 25, 27, 103
secular-religious competition perspective, 2, 8, 14, 17, 35, 37, 39, 40, 42, 62, 64, 80, 103, 104, 135, 139, 165, 166–167, 168, 180, 188–189, 196, 199, 231, 232, 239–240, 242, 245, 247, 248–249
Senegal, 53, 54, 80, 161, 183
separation of religion and state, 6–7, 49, 79, 103, 108, 133, 161, 166, 177, 205, 207–216, 228, 230, 233, 238, 241, 243
  definitions, 28–31
  See secularism
separation of religion and state', 61
Serbia, 60, 87, 122, 143, 147. *See* Yugoslavia
Seventh Day Adventists, 155, 156
Sharia, 9, 45, 46, 47, 67, 69, 72, 74, 75, 77, 83, 84, 92, 204, 233. *See* Sharia courts
Sharia court, 97, 150
Sharia courts, 69, 70. *See* religious courts
Shaw, Timothy S. *See* God's Century
Sierra Leone, 108, 161
Sikhs, 121, 143, 144
Singapore, 69, 83, 143
Slovakia, 12, 58, 87
Slovenia, 12, 88, 132, 133, 145, 198
Solomon Islands, the, 133, 161, 183
Somalia, 60, 77
South Africa, 7, 101, 103, 105, 161, 162, 198, 212, 214, 233, 234, 243, 245, 270
South Korea, 161, 189, 195, 208, 216, 219
Soviet bloc, former, 12, 53, 56, 70, 90, 99, 132, 133, 147, 149, 160, 161, 173, 184, 188, 195, 249
Soviet Union, 8, 233
Spain, 69, 88, 89, 145, 149, 177, 208, 274
Sri Lanka, 69, 77, 133, 147, 184
Stark, Rodney, 3, 23, 24, 137, 138, 237
Sudan, 40, 41, 49, 58, 72, 75, 77, 81, 88, 97, 101, 145, 150, 176, 195
Suriname, 53, 161, 176
surveillance, 21, 53, 55, 155, 156
Swaziland, 71, 74
Sweden, 39, 41, 57, 66, 88, 117, 129, 142, 157, 174, 223, 234, 241

Index

Switzerland, 79, 88, 125, 129, 143, 144, 145, 147, 149, 152, 157, 194
Syria, 9, 74, 101, 120, 174, 278

Taiwan, 122, 161, 198, 214
Tajikistan, 12, 80, 99, 116, 125, 126, 127, 128, 189, 244
Tanzania, 69, 75, 183
Taylor, Charles, 23, 24, 33, 238
Thailand, 51, 52, 90, 94, 97, 101, 128, 176
Timor, 12, 128, 183, 251
Toennies, Ferdinand, 18
Toft, Monjca D. *See* God's Century
Togo, 53, 155, 210
Trinidad & Tobago, 53, 81, 153, 177
Tunisia, 9, 71, 123, 145, 162, 184
Turkey, 24, 80, 116, 123, 147, 161, 179, 208
Turkmenistan, 12, 80, 120, 121, 123, 126, 127, 143, 150, 233, 244

Uganda, 108, 155, 183, 208
Ukraine, 12, 59, 189, 194, 195
Unification Church, 52, 147, 156
United Arab Emirates, the, 70, 74, 84, 150, 153, 157, 193
United Kingdom, the, 92, 127, 174

United Nations, the, 136, 180, 235, 252
United States Supreme Court, 222
United States, the, 30, 54, 79, 87, 111, 136, 142, 148, 158, 168, 169, 198, 201, 208, 216, 219, 222, 241, 245, 272
Urbanization, 19
Uruguay, 127, 161, 189, 216
US Supreme Court, 136, 201
Uzbekistan, 12, 77, 116, 120, 121, 123, 126, 127, 147, 148, 157, 193, 233, 244

Venezuela, 125, 147, 194, 204
Vietnam, 59, 78, 112, 121, 122, 123, 128, 195, 196
Voltaire, 17, 18

Weber, Max, 18
Western democracies, 126, 129, 130, 145, 149, 152, 156, 160, 161, 166, 168, 169, 173, 177, 185, 214, 216, 238

Yemen, 9, 59, 77, 93, 126, 150
Yugoslavia, 60. *See* Serbia

Zaire, 59
Zambia, 59, 153, 173, 176, 208, 211
Zimbabwe, 120, 123, 179

Printed in Germany
by Amazon Distribution
GmbH, Leipzig